Roumania

GOTHIC RUINS IN ZAMBEK.   Frontispiece.

ROUMANIA:

THE

Border Land of the Christian and the Turk,

COMPRISING ADVENTURES OF TRAVEL IN

EASTERN EUROPE AND WESTERN ASIA.

BY

JAMES O. NOYES, M.D.,
SURGEON IN THE OTTOMAN ARMY.

NEW YORK:
RUDD & CARLETON, 310 BROADWAY.
M.DCCC.LVII.

R. CRAIGHEAD, PRINTER AND STEREOTYPER,
Caxton Building,
81, 83, and 85 Centre Street.

PREFACE.

In the second year of the late Russo-Turkish war, the author undertook the journey of which this volume is the result. His object has been to give a truthful picture of the everyday life of the people among whom he travelled, especially the poetical nations of the Lower Danube, whose names are scarcely known to American readers. What relates to humanity concerns us all, and to know the beliefs and sentiments of our fellow-beings, to learn with what songs, traditions and pastimes they amuse each other, interests us more than the dry details of governments, or the mere impressions of the passing traveller.

In the preparation of the work, he has derived much historical information from *L'Univers*, by M. Chopin and M. A. Ubicini; *La Hongrie Historique*, edited by Le Brun; and the admirable volumes of Robert and Vaillant.

J. O. N.

New York *September* 7, 1857.

CONTENTS.

LIST OF ILLUSTRATIONS.

ROUMANIA.

CHAPTER I.

HUNGARY.

"I stood among them, but not of them."

OFTEN, during a long residence in Vienna, I ascended a lofty mountain near the city, to dine in the room where Mozart caught his finest inspirations, and enjoy an evening prospect second to none in the world. Far beneath my feet rolled the turbid waters of the " Father of European rivers." Before me were walled cities, and battle-fields, and green islands smiling up from the broad Danubius, with all the works of men. To the westward towered the Austrian Alps, their glacier crowns tipped with opal and gold. How the tranquil rivers of light appeared to flow away to the gates of sunset! There, looking into the purple distance eastward of Agram, Essling and Sorano, I resolved to visit that mysterious Orient whose glowing portals seemed to open just beyond.

Months passed, and the time came for me to ex-

1

change the scalpel for the staff of the traveller. It was the loveliest morning that ever smiled upon the Danubian plain when we embarked on board the little steamer that was to convey us to the "Franz Joseph," moored in the main stream below. The ancient Romans were careful to found Vindobona, the germ of the present Vienna, upon an arm of the Danube, in order to secure it from the inundations caused by the sudden melting of the Alpine snows.

One does not forget the home of his youth, and as I was about to begin a journey to the distant Orient, I could not help turning a longing look toward my native land. Excepting the place of my birth, I never left a city with so much regret as Vienna. Among strangers who spoke a different language and possessed social and political ideas different from my own, I had made many friends whose memory shall endure. At parting they gave me a warm German embrace. Even the chief of the police, upon whose imagined persecutions American travellers have wasted reams of paper, shook my hand kindly, and wished me a happy journey and a safe return to my fatherland.

Gradually the lofty spire of St. Stephen's Cathedral sank in the distance. We soon passed the island of Lobau, where Napoleon's army was confined three months before the brilliant victory of Wagram in which he routed the Austrians under the Archduke Charles. At Simiring, a small town on the right bank, almost concealed by thick forests, Solyman the Magnificent pitched his tent during the Turkish invasion; and at Schwachat, Leopold of Austria met John Sobiesky, after the latter had routed the hosts of black Mustapha and saved the empire.

"How shall I receive Sobiesky?" asked the emperor of the Duke of Lorraine.

"With open arms," replied the duke.

"Am I not an emperor, and John merely a king elect?"

Leopold condescended to give his deliverer a cold embrace; the interview lasted but few moments. Austria afterwards manifested her gratitude by participating with Russia and Prussia in the division of Poland.

Before reaching the Hungarian frontier we passed Petronell, once destroyed by Attila but now containing a fine castle, near which may be seen the ruins of an ancient triumphal arch built by Augustus to commemorate the Conquest of Hungary.

As we advance beyond the broad plain fringing the Danube with dark forests and marsh-lands, the scenery grows in interest every moment. There are vineyards and plots of wavy grain, valleys opening among the hills afford, now and then, beautiful vistas of distant fields and villages, while crumbling castles and Romanesque ruins impart their historic charm.

An immense rock, rising from the bosom of the great river, is crowned at its summit with the ruins of an old chateau. This is Theben, situated at a point where the river is hemmed in between two mountain chains, and overlooking the noble Danube as it sweeps majestically into Hungary, just as the Iron Gate, between the Carpathians and the Balkans, guards its exit from the great plains of Central Europe.

In 1809 the French, under Napoleon, took possession of Theben, and left it a solitary pile of ruins. The castle is said to have been built in honor of a goddess, named Dewina, but in the language of the country is called "The Virgin's Tower." A young cavalier, enamored of a pretty nun in a neighboring convent, found means to escape with her. In order to protect his bride against the persecutions of the Church, enraged at this sacrilegious act, he took refuge with her in the ancient castle of Theben, resolved to defend himself to the last extremity. Unable to take the well-guarded fortress by assault, they determined to reduce it by famine. Then the cavalier and his bride, unable to escape, resolved to die together. Mounting to the summit of the tower, they threw themselves, in each other's arms, into the black and angry flood of the Danube far below.

We soon reached Presburg, formerly the capital of Hungary, where the kings were crowned and the Diet assembled once in three years to consult on national affairs. A bridge of boats connects the opposite banks of the river.

Before the revolution the most promising young as-
pirants of the kingdom were accustomed to go up to
Presburg to attend the sessions of the Diet, and from
mingling with the magnates and deputies, obtained a
kind of political education which contributed greatly
to that urbanity and elegance of manners so characteristic of the old Hungarian nobles. The proceedings of
the Diet, when in session, were very similar to those
of our two Houses, but such is the love of the Magyar
for music and the dance, that during the long vacations
the Director was accustomed to take the place of the
Palatine, and the walls to echo to Terpsichorean strains
instead of the fiery elocution of the Hungarian Deputies. The royal palace, in which Maria Theresa met
the Hungarian magnates to be delivered by them from
her enemies, is now little better than a pile of ruins.
The Hungarian kings were formerly crowned in this
edifice, after which ceremony they rode to an eminence
in the vicinity, and making the sign of the cross in the
four cardinal directions, swore to defend the kingdom
against all its enemies. Magnificent times, those coro-
nations, when the magnates of the land came up to attend the royal feasts, attired in their splendid national
costume, of which that of the Hussars is but a faint
imitation! Presburg contains fewer inhabitants than
it·did six years ago. Although in Hungary, it is too
near Vienna, too completely *Germanised* and alien-
ated from the affection of the Magyars, to become a

city of great importance for many years to come.
It exhibits neither life nor activity.

Beyond Presburg, the Danube, dividing into several
streams, flows across an immense plain, extending to
Gran. Fifty miles below is Comorn, the seat of a fortress never yet taken by an enemy. At the time of my
visit, it had by no means recovered from the injuries
suffered in 1849. Görgey defeated the Austrians at
Comorn, and having liberated the city, marched back
to Buda-Pesth, to give the enemy a severe blow before his treachery at Vilagos.

Gran is the residence of the Archbishop of Hungary, whose income was formerly more than $200,000
per annum. I remained there but a short time, yet
long enough to learn much concerning the Catholic
institutions of Hungary. The Cathedral is a modern
edifice, imposing, but far less interesting than those
grand old Gothic churches built in the middle ages.
At Zambek there is one of the noblest, now in ruins.

I am fond of lingering for hours in these old Catholic
churches, gorgeous with pictorial and statuesque treasures. In Vienna, it was my supreme delight, with
Faust or Alamontade in hand, to while away the sultry
hours in some sequestered corner of the grey-worn Cathedral of St. Stephen. There were soft paintings,
which had grown into things of beauty under the cunning hand toiling to realize the ideal; the marble
angels seemed poised for ascending or descending flight,

and the Madonnas looked so beautiful, that I ween the silent worshipper often forgets his prayer before those altars.

Though I love the simplicity of the Protestant faith, I do not envy that man's sensibility who can enter one of these old cathedrals without having his feelings subdued, and his heart affected. The long aisles and many-pillared arches; the stained windows, ornate with scriptural scenes and characters, the soft shadows of which an evening sun casts upon the pavement; the crucifixes and images of saints; the burning of incense, and the soft music and low responses of thousands of suppliant worshippers, may make the cold skeptic laugh, but with me they are solemn to look upon, and never to be forgotten.

A certain degree of equality is inculcated in the worship of the Catholic Church, to which, in my opinion, that institution owes not a little of its influence, and much of its perpetuity. In the cathedral, the peasant kneels by the side of the prince, and the poor apple-woman whispers her *pater noster* at the same shrine with velvet-robed beauty. The white-gloved officer puts off his haughty air when his sword rattles on the pavement of a holy place, and patrician pride is humbled when it crosses the threshold. This is one of the reasons why the Catholic Church maintains an absolute control over millions of subjects. Moreover, Rome illustrates the idea of the Church Universal.

She boasts of an intimate connection with that vast
spiritual brotherhood which has existed in all times
and in all lands. She has embalmed the memory of
the good and great of all ages, has enshrined the ancient chivalry of the faith, and realizes to her believing
children, in a literature of legends and prayers, lively
and beatified pictures of the saintliest virtues, combined with the most heroic deeds.*

Another reason, and one that I can fully comprehend in Austria, lies in the richness of their holy places
and their antiquity. The inhabitants of the Catholic
countries of Europe have not the migratory character
that belongs to the Anglo-Saxon race. The ancestors
of the thousands who attend mass at the Cathedral of
St. Stephen have worshipped there for centuries. They,
too, have so often knelt before those gilded shrines, and
so often put up their prayers to the life-like images,
that both have become to them doubly sacred.

With her solidarities of antiquity and her surroundings of pomp and show, the Church of Rome is revered
alike by the intelligent and the unlearned—alike by
the courted hero and the obscure orphan-girl,

> " For *de profundis* blessed her father's grave,
> That idol cross her dying mother gave."

In Austria I have frequently observed people going
almost directly from the church to the opera, or the

* Channing.

play. There is, after all, nothing unnatural in this, for there the cathedral and the theatre differ in reality but little from each other. The magnificent Gothic architecture, the gilded shrines, the profusion of images and pictures, the moving of solemn processions, the dress and genuflexions of the priests—are very like the ever-shifting scenes and changing characters that belong to the stage.

It is not a little amusing to examine the votive offerings suspended before Catholic shrines. Here are hung up miniature silver legs and arms, typical of human extremities relieved of luxations or fractures by celestial surgery, and models of ugly tumors removed without the aid of carnal instruments; there may be seen *tableaux* representing diseased spinal columns straightened by the interposition of a saint, and fevers, devils, and the like, exorcised by a simple sign of the cross—all modern miracles—cures witnessed by the eye of faith.

When Diagoras, the philosopher, visited the Samothracians, and saw the numerous pictures hung up in their temple as votive offerings for preservation from shipwreck, he naïvely inquired, "Where are the portraits of those who have been drowned?" I have in like manner sometimes asked for the models of legs and arms not cured, but was soon made to understand that I was venturing on forbidden ground.

Such is the exterior which the Church of Rome presents, but there is one great fact in her history which

1*

must not be lost sight of—which arises from the nature
of the institution itself.   So long as the Catholic Church
acts upon individuals alone, she gains strength and influence, but in her bosom rankles an insatiable ambition, an unconquerable love of power, that will no more
let her rest contented with her present acquirements
than the victim can rest quietly to whose flesh is applied the red-hot iron of torture.   Thus, leaguing herself with tyrants, she is goaded on to strivings after
power and deeds of open violence, when lo! the charm is
lost, and the structure raised up by years of patient labor
sinks to the ground in a moment.   There is no stronger
revolutionary element in Europe than the ambition of
the Jesuits, and lust and pride of power are hastening her fall faster even than Protestantism itself.
The Church of Rome can no longer dictate to princes
and kings—she can only keep her head above the waves
of revolution by clinging with the grasp of death to the
bayonets of temporal power.

In Hungary the Catholic clergy have immense power,
which is employed to persecute the Protestant sects,
rather than ameliorate the condition of the people.
Unfortunate is the person whose cause cannot be plead
before the Government by a priest.   This is the Nine-
teenth Century, and there are 2,000,000 Protestants in
Hungary!

The Orient is the land of pilgrimages.   It is there
that one best comprehends the charms of nomadic life.

It is there that man, regarding his existence as a transient halt, looks upon his house as a tent, and the world itself as a great caravanserai, from which all must soon journey to a spirit land.

The Magyars are of Asiatic origin, and exhibit many of the peculiarities of Eastern life on the soil of Europe. The two great ideas of the Orient—the idea of God and that of country—are strongly impressed upon their minds.

Love of pilgrimage is almost as characteristic of the Catholic Hungarians and Austrians as of the Greeks and Moslems farther East. The Emperor Ferdinand and his predecessor discouraged pilgrimages ; but as everything is now yielded up to the priests and soldiers, they are becoming more common every year. The rich and powerful, however, rarely take part in them, as they, the favored of men and gods, think to reach Heaven by the golden bridge of charity, or by the *essor* of ambition.

The pilgrims are peasants, and almost every day I saw large bands of them slowly winding their way to some consecrated spot. Aside from devotion, pilgrimages are to the peasantry what travelling and frequenting the great watering-places are to the nobility and rich burghers. They have also a double charm in countries like Austria and Hungary, abounding in wild and beautiful scenery. The shrines are often situated on mountain-tops, as if the feelings attending devotion

in such a place were a foretaste of those in the pure
Heaven above. In the months of summer, the traveller
frequently meets with bands of pilgrims among the
Austrian Alps. Dressed in the most primitive and
grotesque costumes and headed by priests carrying
banners or the cross, they wind their way slowly amid
the loneliest solitudes, chanting their hymns in a solemn
and earnest manner, and uniting, in the grand temple
of the God of Nature, their simple melody with the
sweet voices of the trees, the rocks, and the running
brooks.

The region below Gran becomes picturesque in the
extreme. The arms of the Danube unite in a single
stream, and the vine-clad hills rise into porphyry mountains, crowned here and there with noble ruins.

Visegrad, celebrated even in the time of the Romans, and once so magnificent that a Papal Envoy
termed it "a paradise on earth," now contains scarcely
an inhabitant. The castle by the river-side is in a
tolerable state of preservation, while that which crowned the mountain in the rear is in ruins. The latter is
said to have contained three hundred and fifty chambers, and the two were connected by a subterranean
passage. Charles Robert, after his marriage with the
Polish princess, Elizabeth, in 1317, chose for his royal
residence the fortress of Visegrad, which soon became
one of the most splendid courts in Europe. He expended upon it all the marvels which French art and

French taste could command, and the activity with which the magnificent enterprise was carried on was checked neither by the premature death of his two sons, nor by the constant efforts of the prince against the ambitious designs of Paul Subics, Count of Brebir, who claimed the title of Ban of Croatia and Servia. At Visegrad were assembled the wealth, the learning, and the fashion of Europe. There were held the splendid feasts and tournaments of the middle ages. How its old halls, now deserted and falling in ruins, must have rung with merriment, and its rocks and glades echoed the silvery laugh of brilliant dames and the shouts of mailed knights contending with lance and shield !

Cassimer of Poland, brother-in-law of Charles Robert, greatly disturbed the court of Hungary by an act which was followed by the most fearful results. Having visited Hungary, in 1330, in order to arrange the affairs of the German knights, under the mediation of Charles Robert, he became greatly enamored of one of the ladies attached to the service of the queen. Brilliant offers and warm protestations had no effect upon the mind of the virtuous Clarissa; but as violence comes to the aid of princes when persuasion fails, Cassimer, seconded by his sister, the queen, triumphed by brute force over helpless innocence.

The unfortunate Clarissa, in her shame and remorse, fled to her father, and related to him the act. Enraged at such an insult, Felicien Zacs, for that was the father's

name, swore to have revenge, even at the cost of royal
blood. But the ravisher had escaped immediately after
the commission of his crime, and his absence served
only to irritate the impatient spirit of the wretched
father. From moment to moment his fury became
more ungovernable, until at last he was no longer
master of his passion. Availing himself of the moment when the royal family were at table, Zacs rushed
into the room, and in default of the victim whom he
wished to immolate, turned to the queen, and with a
single blow of his sabre severed the four fingers from
her right hand. In vain the king sought to defend his
wife. Zacs wounded him also in the hand, and had
thrown himself upon the two sons of the prince, when
several noblemen rushed together upon the intruder,
and hewed him into pieces.

The violent death of Zacs did not satisfy the royal
vengeance. The attendants of the king seized the son
of the murdered man, and dragged him, attached to the
tail of a horse, through the streets of the city until he
was reduced to a hideous and lifeless mass.

The father's crime might have excused these frightful acts of vengeance committed in the first efferves-
cence of rage, but those which followed, more terrible
even than the former, could without doubt have been
prevented by Charles Robert. They cut off the nose,
the lips, and the fingers of the unfortunate Clarissa,
and in this mutilated condition compelled her to tra-

verse the streets of Visegrad, crying, "Behold how regicides are punished!" Vengeance was extended even to the third generation. The grandsons of Felicien Zacs were condemned to banishment, and all his relatives living at the time sacrificed with relentless cruelty.

Near Visegrad is an ancient cemetery in which I felt peculiar interest. I am equally fond of cities throbbing with life and these silent cities of the dead, and will not soon forget the hours I have spent in catholic burial-grounds. The Germans call them *Gottesäcker*, the Harvest-Fields of God, and how beautifully that name expresses the idea of resurrection, of God's gathering, as from a field, the fruits of redemption! I found the cemeteries everywhere in Germany surrounded with high walls. In stormier times people used to collect in them their families and goods for protection. In certain parts of Hungary, and on the border-lands of Christianity and barbarism, these walled burial-places still serve to protect the living and the dead from hands of violence. Within, owing to their antiquity, every inch of ground has been used, and doubtless used many times. All is laid out with the greatest regularity, and the dead sleep in lines as perfect as the ranks of living squadrons. Their monuments are neat and tasteful, but rarely so costly and gorgeous as many in Greenwood and Mount Auburn. In writing epitaphs for the departed, the Germans and Hungarians display far more taste and less vanity than ourselves. They do not all at once discover a person's good qualities as soon as he is dead, and place an epitaph over his head that would flatter his vanity if he were living. A simple word or sentence, as, "Asleep," "Not forgotten," "He will rise," tells the sad tale more effectively, and lodges a sweeter thought in the memory of the passer-by, than the most elaborate verse or far-fetched eulogy.

By way of episode I may say that, although the Catholics of Germany and Hungary plant more flowers over the graves of the dead than we are accustomed to in America, their estimate of the human dust and horror of the final dissolution, are by no means so great and so lively as our own. Post-mortem examinations, which are so dreaded in America, especially by the Catholic population, are there rather desired than otherwise. They wish to make sure that they are not burying a living friend, and the thought that "men turn in their graves" is to them far more awful than the sight of human blood and muscles. The law directs that burials shall not take place till after the lapse of a certain number of hours. Persons watching with the dead usually sit in the same room with the corpse; when that is not the case they place a bell-cord in its hand so as to be summoned by any movement that may occur.

Should the traveller tarrying in Vienna wish to be-

THEBEN.

p. 4

hold a sight that he will never forget, let him repair to the "Court of Death," attached to the great hospital whose inmates are numbered by thousands. The breathless sleepers are arranged in long rows, each grasping the tiny cord, the frailest thread to which hope can cling—for of the multitude who have taken up a temporary abode in that gloomy mansion, but one has buffeted the Lethean waters and returned to the shore of life. Once, indeed, the little bell tinkled, breaking the long silence of years, and a seeming corpse arose, and, clad in the severe habiliments of death, stalked forth among the living.

I have spent much of my life among the dying and the dead, but there is one spot near Vienna by which I never loved to pass. It is where the poor of Vienna are buried. Deep pits are dug in the ground, each for a particular day. During the dark and silent hours of the night, the *dead wagon* rattles over the stony streets of the imperial city, collecting the victims that have here and there been cut down in their abodes of misery. When all have been thus gathered for a single night, the *Todtenwagen*, followed by neither chanting priest nor weeping relative, is driven to the Potter's field, where the naked bodies, coffinless and shroudless, are plunged into their dark home, embracing each other in the accidental movements of death.

Touchingly beautiful, however, are many of the Catholic customs relating to the departed. When I

awoke and went to my window one November morning, I saw the walks lined with persons passing out of
the city through the *Schotten Thor*, one of the twelve
gates of Vienna, towards the large cemetery in Währ-
ing. Almost without exception they were carrying
wreaths and bouquets of flowers, and many of them
also large globe lamps of colored glass, in which wax
tapers were burning. At first I could hardly understand so novel a spectacle, having never heard of but
one sensible person carrying a lighted lantern in the
streets by day—Diogenes in search of an honest man.
But, remembering that it was All-Saints' day, I knew
that the festoons and wreaths of sweet-smelling flowers
were intended to hang over the tombstones of the dead,
and the lamps to be placed over their graves many
hours, in order that, according to their childish belief,
the dim taper might light the unbound soul to its heaven home. Having but little to do, I dressed myself
and fell in with the crowds that were passing towards
the cemetery.

Though so late in-the season it was made to blossom
with roses, and the dewy tears on the cold marble sat
like gems among the flowers. All the avenues were
filled with people walking here and there, or busied in
decorating the graves. The festoons and wreaths were
hung over the monuments which, both large and small,
were generally of the shape of a cross. The soil over
the little mounds, which with us few love to disturb, is

there from year to year made into a small flower-bed, which is never so carefully arranged as on All-Saints' day. Tapers were lighted over them all, and the good mothers and sisters were kneeling on the cold ground beside them, repeating the prayer which is prescribed for releasing the souls of their friends from the plagues of purgatory. I noticed, however, but few manifestations of grief; for disturbing the earth over those they had once loved did not seem greatly to harrow up bitter thoughts in the hearts of the living.

I saw many poor women, very poor women, kneeling by the side of monuments far too costly for them or theirs, and asked why they did so in the cold morning air. *"Wir beten für die Seelen der Todten"* (we are praying for the souls of the dead), said one of them; "and if you will give us a *kreutzer* we will pray for you also." Wherever there is human life, something can be learned of human nature. These poor women, such as we see only in the streets of European cities, are so accustomed to look up to the rich and powerful when alive that they go and whisper their *pater-nosters* by their graves when dead.

I spent an hour in wandering among the graves and reading the epitaphs. Among the monuments were those of dukes, counts, and great generals who had rendered their names memorable in Austrian history. By chance I came before the tomb of Beethoven, over which is an obelisk, ornamented with a lyre and sur-

rounded with acacias. It is almost worth a pilgrimage
across the Atlantic to stand by the grave of that great
genius. Who would not like to go there yearly, when
All-Saints' day returns, and say a *pater-noster ?* He
must have a heart of stone who will not give the poor
old woman who often kneels there, a few *kreutzers* for
her pious prayers.

That evening I attended worship at the cathedral
of St. Stephen, when all the saints of the calendar were
invoked. After music began the great prayer, which
was responded to by thousands. The invocation was
approximating to the length of a Calvinistic sermon.
I grew impatient, and could not help whispering to a
young lady by my side :

"Allow me, how many saints are there ? "

"More than three hundred and fifty," she replied,
smiling.

That was enough. Not to appear irreverent I
bowed to the Madonna, and passed out through the
Gothic archway into the world that was beating and
throbbing on the great square of St. Stephen.

Below Visegrad the Danube rivals in beauty the
Hudson and the Rhine. Towards evening the lofty
fortress of Buda came in view, and Pesth, on the opposite bank of the river, rose like a Sphynx from its
waves. Shooting under the massive suspension bridge,
more than one thousand feet in length, we landed in a
few moments on the busy quay.

The Magyar, like the American, has a genuine love for spacious hotels, magnificent steamers, and long railways; in fact, for grand undertakings of every kind. There was something so un-European about Pesth, I saw so many engravings of Washington in the shop windows, that I could have thought myself in New York had it not been for the mosaic of nationalities in the streets. I happened to be there during one of the quarterly fairs. Wild-looking Slovacks, Hungarians with broad-brimmed hats, differing in no respect from the companions of Arpad, and long-haired Wallacks dressed in sheepskins with the wool-side out, contrasted strangely with the Magyars attired in their splendid national costume. Two ages seemed to be brought together, and the roughnesses of barbarism to be patched upon the silken robe of civilization.

The Museum is one of the finest structures in Pesth, and owes its origin to the enterprise of Count Szecheny. His son projected the finest bridge in Europe, shattered the chains of the Hungarian serfs, and broke through the Iron Gate of the Danube. Alas, that such a man should experience such a fate! Disappointment and sorrow for the fall of Hungarian liberty so wrought upon his mind that he became a furious maniac, and as such is now confined in Bohemia.

I have visited most of the great galleries of Europe and studied their pictures and statues, but I must confess, with feelings of pain mingled with the pleasure

that celebrated works of art bestow. I ask myself,
How came these here? How is it that this or that
sovereign—for these great collections belong to kings
and princes—has been able to pay so many thousand
dollars for an old painting or a piece of statuary? The
answer is simple: they are rather the exponents of
wrong and oppression; kings exhibit and enjoy them,
but the people have had to pay for them—at the cost
of how much suffering, how many tears! The longer
I lived in Europe the prouder did I become of my native country and its institutions. There one finds more
splendid specimens of art, men more profound in certain branches of science, and individual instances of
greater wealth; but the glory of our Republic is that
every man is a sovereign, that want is limited, that
education is diffused, and that even in the lower classes
there is a great amount of intelligence and virtue. Art,
however, is not of necessity confined to the hot-bed of
European despotism; happier accidents will yet be discovered for her development. Under the fostering
smile of Liberty nobler ideals will arise and loftier
conceptions be realized. If not, may that art which
adorns the palaces of kings perish for ever.

These thoughts were suggested by a visit to the gallery of paintings in the museum at Pesth. The pieces,
relating for the most part to important events in Hungarian history, were not numerous, but like our own
productions, strictly national, original in conception,

and bold in execution. Like ourselves the Hungarians have been too busily engaged in developing their political system to bestow much time and study upon art. It was with them, before they lost all liberty, as with the ancient Athenians; the man who did not engage in political life was regarded not only as a harmless, but also as a useless person.

When the National Academy was founded for the purpose of developing the resources of the Magyar tongue, Count Zeleki gave it his library of more than 80,000 volumes, and Count Szecheny his income for a year, amounting to $30,000. During the building of the Hungarian theatre, a poor journeyman came forward and asked the privilege of contributing fifteen days' labor, as he could not give from his purse. Such was the national enthusiasm which resulted in the insurrection of 1848! Renewed efforts are now being made to develop Hungarian literature. They have a noble galaxy of poets and historians.

I cannot sufficiently admire the force, flexibility, and beauty of the Hungarian language. Soft, rich, vigorous, concise, filled with proverbs and strange marriages of thoughts, it is, like all Oriental idioms, euphonic, and essentially poetical. The misfortunes of the nation seem to have saddened its very language. The Magyar is proud of the land conquered by his ancestors. No one can boast of a nobler history, but with his patriarchal simplicity of manners, he loves best to describe

the beauties of nature and the joys of pastoral life.
When scenes of terror and blood are presented, he
kindly draws a veil of tender sympathy over the
melancholy picture. With its soft inflections and melodious accentuations, the language of the Magyars is
equally fitted to portray the shock of armies, the impetuosity of the mountain torrent, and the finest conceptions of Oriental thought. Sonorous and energetic,
without being harsh or barbaric, it adapts itself with
the same facility to poetry and the eloquence of the
tribune as to the sciences and the arts. It has no
patois, and is always the same, whether spoken by
nobles, peasants, or shepherds whether it breathes
the plaints of an enamored heart, murmurs the sweet
accents of the idyl, soars among the heights of philosophy, or echoes, in more than Bacchic fury, the tumult of war. One must hear a Magyar lady speak, to
get an idea of the sweetness and the fascination of her
language. When, on the contrary, an orator over-
whelms his adversaries at the stormy forum, or a chief
calls his warriors to the combat, you cannot conceive
of anything more forcible or majestic. "A man must
pray in Hungarian if he would be heard in heaven," is
a maxim of the country.

The Magyar race was cradled on the confines of the
Chinese empire. Its language resembles the Finnish,
and bears a still closer affinity to the Turkish, showing
thereby identity of origin. Strange how kindred peo-

ples, wandering from central Asia, that prolific mother of nations, here warring with each other and there unmindful of each other's existence, have preserved in their language the proofs of their brotherhood! More enduring than pyramids or coliseums, or the noblest thoughts embalmed in literature, are the spoken words of those old barbaric nations.

The Hungarians are passionately fond of music and song. On sunny afternoons the Magyar chivalry repair to the sylvan retreats along the Danube, to engage in conversation with the stately Hungarian dames, or wind with them the labyrinths of the dance. The evening breeze creeps softly up the river. A band of gipsy musicians mounts the rostrum. Rude in appearance are they, possessing all the physical characteristics of their uncultivated race. But up to these dusky children of Asia the Magyars look, as the conservers of the primitive music and song of their nation. They render the *csárdás*, the famous national airs of Hungary, in all their varied expression, now sad and energetic, now wild and grandiose, as the moving periods of the drama. Piece after piece is given, whose intonations, changing and impassioned, quicken the Magyar pulse and touch his breast with fire. The war march of Rákoczi, the *Marseillaise* of Hungary, is at last given with a warmth and originality that wake a storm of tumultuous excitement. A thousand plaudits ring upon the air a thousand voices accompany the wild concord

of the instruments, and those haughty Magyars yield to
the swelling tide of song as the oaks of many winters
yield to the stroke of the tempest.

Next to the mothers and daughters of America I admire the Hungarian ladies. They are also passionate
admirers of American institutions. " We revere your
Washington as a demi-god," said one of them to me,
one day. " You Americans ought to build a monument to his memory that would kiss the very sky.
You should then say your prayers at its base, and I
should like to repeat mine there for my bleeding country." I replied that I would be but too happy to accompany her on an expedition of that nature. " No,"
said she, " we Hungarian women have resolved never to
leave our country. We wept over her fall, we share
her humiliation, and will remain here hopeful and ever
confident that we shall one day enjoy her triumph."

In patriotism, the Hungarian women do not fall behind their lords. Nor, perhaps, is it an excess of hero-
worship, that they name half of their male offspring
Louis Kossuth. Though unfortunate in war, and exiled,
the great Hungarian leader is first in the hearts of his
people. The Austrians assert that as Kossuth's birth-
place was by the side of Attila's grave, the ashes of the
Scourge of God were infiltrated into the veins of him
who sought to liberate his country. Times change.
He who was the " Scourge of God " in one age, may
become the scourge of tyrants in another.

Crimes never grow old, are never forgotten in the lives of nations; and it is the crime of tyranny that the despotic powers of Europe must expiate with seas of blood.

> " Were all the streams which wind
>   Their mazy progress to the main,
> To cleanse these odious stains in one combined,
>   The streams combined would flow in vain."

Those who have been brought up around the despotic thrones of Europe talk pompously of absolutism and the sword as the only panaceas for all social and political evils; but it is by no means easy to account for the apathy of the great mass of Europeans. Survey the vast military establishments on the Continent; behold millions of men arrayed in the severe habiliments of war; look upon their fields of infantry and torrents of cavalry! What are all these worth for the cause of liberty? By the enchantment of kingly power, not only the armed millions of Europe stand silent and motionless, like splendid petrifactions, but her wealth, her commerce, and learning are all made the slaves of despotism.

The Frenchman looks upon Liberty as a capricious mistress; the German,

> " Fuddled by the profound philosophy of beer,"

regards her much as he does the great-grandmother

whom he never saw ; but the Hungarian, like the American, loves liberty as he loves his wife.

While England was striving to whiten the sea with ships and clothe the world in cotton, while all the uncertain schemes floating in the limbo of French politics had for their ultimate object the glory and aggrandizement of kingly power, while the sovereigns of Austria and Prussia were struggling for the crown of Germany, lost amid the surges of revolution, the Hungarians were quietly developing their free institutions.

Of the Bund—that clumsy organization of German States—the Swedish Chancellor Oxensteirn long ago remarked that it was "a state of confusion existing only by the grace of God," and the estimation in which Teutonic servility is held by the Russians is aptly set forth in their proverb, "Heaven has sufficiently punished a man in permitting him to be born a German." Had the house of Hapsburg been true to its mission, there would be some meaning in that political axiom, " S'il n'y avait pas une Autriche, il faudrait la créer." Instead of producing a nationality strong, earnest, and growing out of the wishes of a great people, the court of Austria has preferred one concentrating in, and radiating from, the body of Francis Joseph, a tyrant at once hated and obeyed by twenty nations.

" Carthage must be destroyed." Carthage was destroyed, but from her ashes rose an avenging genius, which, by awakening strife between Sylla and Marius, caused the fall of Rome herself. So it may be with Austria. Panslavism, the evil genius that threatens her, is of Hungarian growth, though of Bohemian origin. The principles of Panslavism—or the fusion of all the Slave tribes—were first thoroughly eliminated in a book styled, " The History of the Slave Language and Literature," published in 1826, by Schāfarik, a native of Upper Hungary.

This novel idea of bringing into one organization the *membra disjecta* of a great family was eagerly caught up the following year by the Hungarian Kollar, also of Slave origin, who, with all the zeal of the most earnest agitator, baptized it in burning song. The enthusiasm of Kollar carried him, as was believed, far into the regions of extravagance, if not of delirium, and no greater proof of the liberality of the Hungarians can be given than that these first adepts of Panslavism were permitted quietly to develop principles among them which were to result in the overthrow of their country. Kollar, hurling defiance alike at Magyars, Germans, and Mussulmans, ventured even to declare in his heroic poem, Slavy Dcèia, that the costume, the customs, and songs of his people would one day prevail on the banks of the Elbe and Seine. This may be an ebullition of poetical frenzy, but its fulfilment would not be more strange than that clouds of Cossack cavalry should have already watered their horses on the banks of those noble rivers.

The Magyars, like the Liberals in other parts of Europe, do not forget how Russia has enslaved her patient millions, how, during the forty years of peace which preceded the Eastern war, all the conservative hands of Europe were engaged in building up the Northern Colossus, and how England and France have, in reality, assisted that Power in the futile task of enslaving the European world. Though checked in a career which promised so much for themselves and for Europe, and for the present crushed to the earth, they are not without hope: they remember that " It is not fleets and armies; it is not wealth and great possessions that constitute the strength of States; but it is watchfulness."

An avenging power is, however, slowly springing up in Continental Europe—I mean Public Opinion in favor of liberty. Already the prestige of kings, the traditions of absolutism, and respect for dynasties are beginning to fade away before it. Tyranny has not yet spoken her last word, but the day will come when men who think like Brutus will act like Brutus.

From one great annoyance to travellers in Hungary, I was gratefully relieved. The *Chef de Police* at Vienna had kindly given me permission to travel anywhere in the Austrian dominions, and my passport bore the signature of the American *Chargé d'Affaires*. But on my arrival at Pesth the police, not being familiar with English, applied the above title to myself. The mistake was entirely their own, and during my stay in Hungary, I did not care to undeceive them. The Koszta affair was then fresh in the memory of the Austrians. My title acted like enchantment. Not an impediment was thrown in the way, and the Austrian officials, generally so stiff and unyielding, stood ready to gratify my every wish.

Pesth contains 20,000 inhabitants less than in 1848. Were a man to go there from the uttermost parts of the earth, without knowing anything of the history of the Magyars for the last eight years, he would find it all written in the looks and bearing of that noble race.

Buda, so named from a brother of Attila, occupies a commanding position on the opposite side of the river. The Turks occupied the fortress while they were in possession of Hungary, and constructed many of the buildings yet standing inside the walls. The immense cellars excavated in the solid rock, served for places of refuge during the bombardments in 1849. When Görgey besieged the city, at that time in the hands of the Austrians, his wife persuaded him to direct his heaviest fire upon the castle, in order, that if taken, it might never be occupied by Madame Kossuth, whom she regarded as a rival.

While at Buda I visited Alt-Ofen, the Aquineum of the ancients, three or four miles above. Though now a wretched Jewish village, it once contained a Roman population of one hundred thousand souls. In the

vicinity may be seen the remains of an aqueduct,
sanctified by holy pictures in later times. Other ruins
are pointed out, but I was unable to discover any traces
of the ancient amphitheatre, said to have been sufficiently large to accommodate 8000 spectators. The
Roman.baths in the vicinity of the village are much frequented. Near by is a Turkish mosque, to which a
pious pilgrim occasionally wanders from distant Mecca.

After a short sojourn in Buda-Pesth I embarked on
board the steamer one pleasant morning for Semlin.
As we steamed down the magnificent Danube, I felt
myself no longer in Europe : I seemed to touch the soil
of Asia. This illusion was strengthened by the Oriental costume and bearing of the people. The Magyar
hates the mountains. Preferring the pastoral life to the
tumult of cities, he has a Bedouin passion for the free
air and horizon of the plains upon which he tends his
flocks. A child of the Orient, his horse is his insepa-
rable companion. He wears loose flowing garments,
and has an Eastern love of display in dress and equestrian trappings.

The cities along the Danube and in the interior, are
for the most part immense villages whose very appearance indicates that they belong to a once nomadic people. The low wooden houses, small, white-washed, and
many feet apart, look in the distance like long rows
of tents. The towns were formerly encampments, in
which the cottage has taken the place of the pavilion,

and the church risen up where once stood the tent of the chief. Thither the peasants repair at nightfall to repose, as their ancestors, in earlier times, rested during their migrations and battles.

Hungary embraces two immense plains, surrounded by boulevards of lofty mountains. Parts of these, rivalling in fertility the prairies of the West, are dotted with villages and ocean-like fields of grain. Here and there also are wide pampas, grown up with luxuriant grass, upon which a solitary horseman is occasionally to be seen. Bordering the Danube are immense marshy tracts, submerged in the spring, and grazed during the months of summer by herds of dun-colored cattle. None but the most hardy venture into this region of gloom, and solitude, and fatal miasmas.

Farther back, especially between the Danube and the Theiss, is a vast plain, forming a veritable desert. It is Africa in Europe. For weary, weary leagues the horizon is unbroken by a tree or a human habitation. Shrubs and tufts of coarse wiry grass take root wherever moisture can be found for their support. Above is a fervid and brassy sky, below a parched and arid soil. By day the sun hangs over the inhospitable waste like a burning meteor; by night chilly exhalations creep over it from the marsh lands, poisoning the air, and misguiding the lonely traveller with their flickering *ignes fatui*. The winds that sweep over the *pusztas*, for by that name the Hungarians designate these plains, fill the heated air, and redden the horizon with clouds of shifting sand. The few shepherds and travellers roaming over this inhospitable region are tormented by the illusory appearances of the *mirage*, which unlike the reflections of cities and forest-embosomed lakes that gladden the eye on the deserts of Africa, have the appearance of seas, now wild and gloomy, then placid and dreamy, or of flowery prairies with shepherd huts and peaceful folds.

Stretching from the Danube towards Transylvania are the remains of a wall and canal, which, as was usual with the Romans, marked the boundary of their empire in this direction. Both Hungarians and Austrians used these ancient works for intrenchments in 1849. But the unlettered Magyar shepherds, ignorant alike of the Romans and their achievements, connect, by a beautiful legend, the origin of these old Roman defences with the illusions of the mirage.

Csörsz, as the shepherds tell when they assemble in their tents by night, was the gallant son of the king of the Transylvanian Alps, whose treasures of gold and salt were greater than those of all the kings and princes in the world. Csörsz heard of the celestial beauty of Deli Bab, the daughter of the king of the Southern Sea (Adriatic), and his heart was inflamed with love for her. He therefore sent heralds from his Alps, down to the borders of the Adriatic, with loads of the most costly gifts of salt and gold, and sued for the hand of the lovely

Deli Bab. But the proud King of the Sea despising the kings of the Earth, said that he would never grant the daughter of the Sea to the son of the Alps until he came with a fleet down from his mountains to convey his bride by water to his palace, as her feet were too delicate to be exposed to the rough stones of the Earth. But the heralds, convinced of the power of their king, threw the bridal ring and the presents of gold and salt into the sea, which from this time became rich in salt; and having thus sealed the betrothal, returned to their prince. In despair about the desire of the King of the Sea, and knowing not how to comply with his condition, Csörsz called on the devil and entreated his aid. The arch fiend, without delay, put two buffaloes to his glowing plough, and in a single night dug the canal from Transylvania to the Danube, and thence down to the sea. Csörsz speedily had a fleet constructed, and joyfully steered down to the Adriatic to take away his bride. Her princely father gave up his daughter with deep regret: however, he was bound by his word, as the new diplomacy was not yet invented; and the pledges of monarchs were still considered sacred.

But the beautiful bride was sorry to leave her cool palace of crystal, her innumerable toys of shells and pearls, and even the monsters of the sea, who had served her with unbounded devotion. She promised not to forget their home, and often to visit her father and sisters in summer, when the hot sunbeams might prove

too intense for her on the dry earth. Csörsz, with festive songs and merry sounds, conveyed his beloved up
the canal. Deli Bab was delighted with the mountains,
woods, fields, and meadows, which swiftly passed her:
she was highly amused with the objects wholly new to
her sight. But when by chance she looked backward,
she beheld with terror, that behind the fleet the waters
dried up in the canal, and that thus the return to her
father's realm became impossible. She never could feel
at home in the gold and salt vaults of the Transylvania
mountains; the heavy masses of the Alps depressed her
soul; the wintry snow chilled her thoughts; the burning beams of the summer sun melted her into tears.
She never laughed, and always dreamed of her transparent abode in the sea. The love of the princely son of
the Alps remained sterile. Deli Bab was childless.
She melted away with longing, and was transformed
into the Mirage, or Fata Morgana, a dreamy appearance
of the sea which vanishes away as soon as you approach,
and which in Hungary yet bears the name of the fair
Deli Bab. The remains of the canal are still called
Csörsz ärka, the Canal of Csörsz.*

The immense plain between the Danube and the
Theiss is the classic land of the Magyars. Filled with
the souvenirs of ancient migrations and recent combats, it bears the name of Jazygia, from a wandering
tribe supposed to have settled there before the Roman

* Memoirs of Hungary.

conquest. The descendants of the Jazyges preserve, as a precious relic, the ivory drinking horn of Lehel, a son of one of the warriors of Arpad. When a guest is welcomed in their chief town, or the right of citizenship is conferred, the horn of Lehel is filled with wine, and must be emptied at a single breath.

In this region Attila held his court, here settled the companions of Arpad, and here still roam shepherds and herdsmen scarcely differing from their nomadic ancestors. The Magyars, leaving Asia by the gate of the Ural and the Altaï, took up their stately march across the plains of Russia, and reached Central Europe by the passes of the Carpathians, bringing with them the germs of their future institutions. During their migration westward, they assembled more than once to select those who should lead them to conquest, to distribute the burdens of war or the spoils of victory.

The appearance of the host was such as to excite terror even in those barbaric times. On horseback, always on horseback, the wild chivalry of Asia marched before a confused multitude of women and children. Then followed immense herds of cattle and rude wagons, some of which were already filled with booty, while others awaited the fruits of future victories. The terror-stricken nations of Europe recognised in the grim-visaged strangers the bands of Gog and Magog, spoken of in the Apocalypse, whose advent was immediately to precede the destruction of the world. Ad-

mitting in their faith the dualism of the Persians, the
eternal conflict between the spirits of good and of evil,
the Magyars worshipped the elements, especially fire,
which was personified in the sun.   To the Supreme
God, embracing in himself all other divinities, to
Magyarok-Istene, the god of the Magyars, they never
sacrificed human beings, but immolated upon his altars
milk-white horses.   They addressed hymns to the Earth,
whence come the harvest and the flowers, the useful
iron and the sparkling diamond.   As many enemies as
the valiant Magyar had slain in battle, so many servants would he have in the future world.

Our first day's journey below Pesth was weary
and monotonous.   Now and then we stopped for passengers at some lonely village, near which were moored
a number of clacking gristmills, propelled by the force
of the current.   The horizon, much of the way, was
bounded only by the great plain of Central Hungary.
Troops of horses and of long-horned cattle, stood in
the shallow margin of the river, enjoying, with droop-
ing heads, the shade of the overhanging trees.   Flocks
of wild fowl, scarcely frightened by our approach,
rose hesitatingly from the surface of the river, and
winged their way to other haunts.   Vividly the lines
of Campbell came to mind—

> "Unknown, unploughed, untrodden shore,
> Where scarce the peasant finds a road,
> And scarce the fisher plies an oar."

VISEGRAD.

p. 13

Towards evening we passed Mohacz, where, in 1526, perished Louis II. of Hungary in the war with Solyman, that fatal day of the Magyars, which gave their country to the Turks, and afterwards to the Austrians. Christian Europe, however, avenged the deed a century and a half later, on the same bloody field, by the splendid victories of the Duke of Lorraine, an achievement speedily followed by the expulsion of the Moslems from Hungary.

We passed the night at the mouth of the Drave, which flows into the Danube from Croatia and Slavonia. Near by us, on the shore, was an encampment of boatmen, their coarse brawny figures strongly set forth by the glowing fire, around which they were partaking of their evening meal. A rude tent had been spread for shelter, and the horses turned loose on the adjacent plain. A rough and perilous life is theirs. The huge barges in which they convey the productions of Lower Hungary to Pesth and Vienna, are drawn up stream by horses, sometimes thirty in number, each of which is mounted by an experienced rider; and the whole cavalcade directed by a guide. Often they are obliged to swim from shore to shore, or to make long détours in order to avoid the sand-banks and morasses skirting the river. To see them reposing under the silent stars, relating the vicissitudes of the day around their camp fires, calls to mind the tented life of the desert.

Early the following day we passed the fortress

of Peterwardein, made illustrious by one of the victories of Prince Eugene, and Carlovitz, where in the
peace of 1699, the Turks agreed to abandon their conquests in Hungary and Slavonia. At Carlovitz, also,
resides the head of the Greek Church in Austria.

The Danube, after receiving the waters of the
Theiss, a noble river stretching away to the north,
makes two great bends before reaching the confluence
of the Save, at Belgrade. Approaching Servia, the
prospect becomes really magnificent. The Danube
flows on grandly between the richest plains of Europe
on the one hand, and the vine-clad hills of Slavonia on
the other. The Temesvar Banat is the granary of Central Europe.

Towards evening, Mount Awala rose in the distance, with Belgrade at its base. The lofty position of
the fortress, and the white minarets of the Turkish
mosques, with a bewitching region in the background,
made one of the most beautiful pictures I ever beheld.
As the steamer swept round a sharp curve, the whole
of Semlin came suddenly into view, and in a few
minutes we were landed at the last Austrian town on
the right bank of the Danube.

I asked for the best hotel, and was directed to the
Golden Lion. The houses, churches, and mud hovels
thatched with straw, appeared to have dropped from
the sky and sunk deep in the earth. The streets were
destitute of sidewalks. Now and then a deep slough

appeared to offer an impassable barrier to further progress, while, as the central parts were lowest, pools of liquid filth had settled midway between the houses, in these nasty, stony lanes.

A servant conducted me to my chamber through a dark alley paved with bricks. The walls were ornamented with dirty pictures of the Madonna and Greek saints; and, as if for burlesque, over the entrance to my miserable lodgings stood the sentence, " Welcome, my guests."

During my short stay at Semlin I ascended Gipsy Mountain, where may be seen the remains of an old castle, in which John Hunyad died, in 1456, worn out in the long wars with the Turks. These hills, the plains beyond the Danube, and the mountains and valleys across the Save, planted with corn or the vine, and so marvellously beautiful in the distance, have been again and again deluged with Christian and Moslem blood. The cemetery on the slope of the mountain was thrown open to the swine and dogs. I continued my walk through the suburbs of the city. The wide streets, the low whitewashed houses—the end towards the road serving as a residence for the family, the other for the cattle—the green trees and ricks of wheat, groups of peasants attired in their national costume, and maidens carrying water from the Danube in shining vessels, all these did not fail to interest and delight.

CHAPTER II.

> "Lingering
> O'er the white walls of the fortress Belgrade,
> Gazing there on strange events and wonders."

At Belgrade, the capital of Servia, I first felt myself in the East. One has but to cross the Danube from Hungarian Semlin, to see crowds of well-bearded and well-turbaned Moslems, to hear the prayer-invoking cry of the muezzin in concert with vesper-bells, and witness, indeed, the strangest blending of Oriental and Occidental life.

During my stay at Belgrade, I visited the old Turkish fortress, the object of so many conflicts between the Moslems and Christians. From a commanding position it overlooks the city, but the two hundred soldiers within its decaying walls are prisoners, instead of being, as in former times, masters of the Servians. I had hoped to smoke a friendly pipe with old Izzet Pacha, but he was too ill to receive company. Servia nominally acknowledges the sovereignty of the Porte, but is practically independent. A few Turks are merely tolerated in the principality.

Infinitely amusing was my first walk in the Turkish quarter of Belgrade. The wretched cabins seemed just ready to fall in ruins. The little shops and stalls were all open towards the street. The grave Mussulmans regarded me as a stranger, and the few veiled women in the narrow lanes avoided me as if I had been the bearer of the plague.

At the only German hotel in the city, built several years ago by Prince Milosh, I had the good fortune to meet an old college associate in Vienna who had become a surgeon in the Servian army. While he was expatiating upon the cheapness of everything in Servia, I mentioned to him that I had paid roundly for my purchases.

"Ah!" said he; "you will understand the Servians better in a few days. Like the Spartans, they deem it right to rob any one but a blind man."

To give me a better acquaintance with the people, he proposed an excursion of a few days in the interior. We procured horses and set off the same afternoon for Karanovaz sixteen miles distant, whither Prince Alexander had in part transferred the government to avoid the officious interference of foreign powers at Belgrade. On horseback is the usual mode of travelling in Servia, there being in fact but two wagon roads in the whole principality.

The way led among hills clothed with magnificent forests. There was a delicious sensation of freedom, all the more agreeable after the restraint one has to endure in despotic Austria. The people dared to look each other in the face, and think and act as freemen, while even the streams that flowed down from the mountains seemed to murmur songs of liberty.

At Karanovaz we were hospitably entertained by a family with whom my companion happened to be acquainted. The Slaves are everywhere distinguished for their hospitality. When a stranger enters a Servian village, the families dispute with each other the honor of entertaining him. He is received as a guest sent by Providence. The venerable patriarch of the household causes the stranger to be seated at his side. The mistress of the cottage hastens to serve him. The youngest daughter will sometimes ask to wash his feet.

The Servians have a legend, which gives a terrible picture of this national virtue.

" Day departs, and the moon shines upon the white fields of snow. A stranger enters the dwelling of poor Lazar.

" ' Welcome !' says Lazar; and, turning to his wife—

" ' Lubitza, light the fire, and prepare the evening meal.'

" ' The forest is large,' responds Lubitza. ' The fire sparkles and blazes upon the hearth, but how provide the evening meal ? Have we not fasted for two days ?'

" Shame and confusion seize upon poor Lazar.

" 'Art thou a Servian ?" inquires the stranger; ' and hast nothing to offer thy guest ?'

" Poor Lazar searches everywhere, but finds nothing; not a crumb of bread, not a piece of fruit. Shame and confusion seize upon him.

" 'Here is food,' says the stranger, placing his hand upon the head of Yanko, a child of golden locks. Lubitza shrieks as she beholds him, and falls upon the earth.

"'Never! never!' cries Lazar, 'shall it be said that a Servian hath failed in the duty of hospitality;' and, seizing a hatchet, he slays Yanko as if he were a lamb.

" Oh! who shall describe the stranger's meal ?

" Lazar sleeps. At midnight he hears the stranger calling him—

" 'Arise, Lazar! I am the Lord thy God. Servian hospitality hath remained inviolate. Thy son is raised from the dead, and abundance is in thy house.' "

Perhaps the most remarkable institution of the Servians is "The Brotherhood," a usage descended from primitive times. Such is their affection for each other, that, when a young man has lost a natural brother, he seeks in the neighborhood a brother by adoption, and confers upon him all the rights appertaining to the deceased. The two unite with each other in the name of God and St. John for mutual fidelity and assistance during the remainder of their lives. Persons thus allied call themselves "brothers in God." The union concerns those only by whom it has been formed. The benediction of the church is not requisite to form such an alliance. In certain parts of Servia it is customary for the youths, and maidens also, to enter into this relation on the second Monday after Easter, whilst kissing each other through garlands which are afterwards exchanged. The first bond, however, is merely initiatory. At the expiration of a year they either confirm the original choice or make a new selection. A similar relation often exists between the two sexes; a man may call a woman his "mother or sister in God." A maiden may elect an old man her "father in God," or a youth her "brother in God." This alliance between the sexes is usual in cases of distress; and when persons whose assistance is thus invoked accept the appellation, they are bound to protect and care for the unfortunates placing themselves in their hands. A violation of so solemn a contract is supposed to incur severe punishment in heaven. Enemies as well as friends enter into this singular relation. It not unfrequently exists between Turks and Servians during their bloodiest feuds.

The adoption of an orphan into a family is attended with a touching ceremony. The adopting parent places his hand upon the child's head as a sign of protection, saying at the same time: "I adopt thee; for my heart hath named thee my child. This house is thy house;

all that belongs to me is thine, and death alone shall break this bond."

Fraternity in arms also exists among Slaves, as among the ancient Greeks. The contracting parties repair to a church with a few friends for witnesses. They cross their weapons on the ground and swear to live and die for each other. They then exchange weapons. Brothers in arms share each other's pleasures and combats, and when one of them dies, the fraternal weapons belong to the survivor.

The haughty Servians preserve this institution with jealous care. They relate that two brothers-in-arms, enamored of a beautiful Turkish captive, put her to death rather than violate the sacred relation between them. In consequence of these friendly alliances, a stranger, when accompanied by a native of the country, is perfectly safe, being received everywhere as the friend of a brother. A Montenegrin, having murdered his guest, was at once slain by his brother for having dishonored both his family and country by so base an act. By this means, the Turks and Servians, in their border wars, not unfrequently traverse the enemy's country, and even visit the camps of the contending tribes.

I have found the higher class in Europe, and especially the nobility, to be everywhere much the same, excepting in language and religion. For striking national traits, for traditions and time-honored usages, in fact,

for almost everything that can interest the thinking
traveller, we most look to the humble classes. This I
did from the first. Shortly after landing at Liverpool,
and while standing in front of St. George's Hall, ad-
miring the allegorical sculpture which adorns the tym-
panum of its portico, I was beset by half-a-dozen professional peripatetic bootblacks. They urged their
claims as if a night's lodging had depended on their success, and in a knowing and cunning manner that must
have been borrowed from the gowned and powdered
barristers who frequent the Courts of St. George's Hall.
One fellow evidently saw that I was fresh from the
New World, and for a penny begged to give my boots
" the real Yankee shine," but he was quickly underbid
by a black little urchin, who with a more artistic air,
" his eye with a fine frenzy rolling," wished to put on
" the Exhibition touch."

Evening overtakes the traveller at a *celo*—a Servian
village hid away among the recesses of the Balkans.
The peasants, male and female, are singing merrily
while they lead their flocks down the mountains, or
return in groups from their little fields. As the sun
goes down,

" Far sinking into splendor without end,"

the youths and maidens of the village meet under the
great forest trees to celebrate the dances of their peo-

ple, each one of which is a history, wherein pantomime takes the place of words, and action and sentiment beautifully blend the poetical present with the legendary past. Near by, the elders of the *celo*, seated on the grass around the village bard, like a group in the pastoral age of Agamemnon, listen while he recites the heroic deeds of their ancestors, or, as if to call back their spring-time of life, improvises the tender agitations of youthful hearts.

The young men select partners, and a ring is formed alternately of males and females. Then to the song, accompanied by the monotonous notes of the *guzla*, begins the dance of the circle. The fairest maiden of the village,

> " White her cheeks, but tinged with rosy blushes
> As if morning's beam had shone upon them,"

leads her companions in the mazy evolutions. Now the dancers move slowly, separating and uniting in graceful figures, and then wind in labyrinthine folds so quickly as almost to elude sight.

In the groups before us are only unlettered peasants, ignorant of all the world beyond their native forests, the names of whose ancient kings are scarcely preserved in the national ballads, and whose only archives are the traditions and songs that resound among their mountains. But the Kolo, which they celebrate, is

3

the *Romaika* of Greece, the Dædalian dance of the early Greeks—so ancient, indeed, as to have been traced upon Achilles' shield, and described by Homer precisely as it is now performed.

> "A figured dance succeeds—
> A comely band
> Of youths and maidens bounding hand in hand,
> The maids in soft cymars of linen drest.
> * * * * * * *
> Now all at once they rise, at once descend,
> With well-taught feet now slope in oblique ways,
> Confus'dly regular the moving maze;
> Now forth at once, too swift for sight they spring,
> And undistinguished blend the flying ring;
> So whirls a wheel in giddy circles tost,
> And rapid as it runs, the single spokes are lost."

Pass out from Athens on the evening of the 1st of April, along the Piræus road, until you reach the temple of Theseus, at no great distance from the ascent to the Acropolis. Near at hand is the Hill of Mars, and the gently rising ground upon which is built the oldest temple of hero-worship, stretches up to the Pnyx. The open space between, the agora of the ancient Athenians, is now converted into a field of wheat. I have often visited the spot when the silence was unbroken and no human being was near, save the guardian of the temple and an Albanian shepherd, watching his flock on the Hill of Mars.

But on this occasion crowds of Athenians assemble there long before the sun gilds with his departing rays the Parthenon and Erectheum, perched proudly on that magnificent pedestal, the Acropolis. All Athens repairs to this fabulous spot, as her citizens did centuries ago, to listen to the harangues of her great orator.

You see before you a curious mosaic of all the tribes and nationalities of Greece, but none of the garlands and processions of ancient times. There are the fine forms, the classic features of Greek women, beautiful enough to have served as models for the Cariatides, and the splendid outlines of the Hellenic face, united with a bearing which no one but a Greek can assume. The aged Athenians repose on the marble seats ranged on the southern side of the temple of Theseus—the seats said to have once been occupied by the judges of the Areopagus. The young men are threading the mazes of a dance, which is at once unique, national, and historical. Ask one of them why they came there on that occasion, and they can only tell you that it is in obedience to an ancient custom. They only know that their fathers did so before them. But that is the ancient Pyrrhic dance you look upon, and the *fête* around the columns of the temple of Theseus shows how the usages of a people can traverse centuries.

Let us change the scene from Athens to a city beyond the Danube, to Bukarest, the gay and luxurious

capital of Wallachia. It is evening, and there are also
merry groups assembled on the banks of the Dumbovitza. They, too, are dancing, but it is the *hora roumanesca* to gipsy music. There are female figures of
bewitching grace and beauty, but the splendid forms
and dignified bearing of their companions remind us
strongly of the Latins. They also speak a language
that would have been understood by the rustic multitudes who thronged

      " To see great Pompey walk the streets of Rome."

The Haemus, old Danubius, and the distance of many
hundred miles intervene between fair Italy and this ancient Dacian province. Seventeen centuries have elap-
sed since the tide of Roman conquest was swept back
by the waves of barbaric invasion, and yet the simple
dance of these Wallachian peasants brings before us
the most celebrated chorographic entertainment of the
ancient Romans. Maidens and youths join hands and
form a large ring, in the centre of which are gipsy
musicians, called *Lautari* in the *limba roumanesca.*
One of the circle sings during the dance, and the
songs on these occasions, termed *horas,* as among the
Latins, are of singular force and beauty. The ring of
dancers undulates from right to left and left to right;
and when it breaks up in a feigned *melée,* the young
men seize by the waist, and bear away, the blushing

and struggling maidens, as their Roman ancestors once did the Sabine women.

Is it not strange that the simple customs of a people should in this manner be made to endure for ages? That which is most labored and heralded forth with most pomp is not always remembered longest. In the quarries of Pentelicus I deciphered names carelessly scratched upon the marble walls by workmen more than two thousand years ago. The slave who hewed from the quarry the rough block has left us at least the legacy of his name—far more, in many instances, than he who chiselled it to a form of beauty, and almost imparted life to the pulseless stone.

The student of history may not despise the song, the dance, and the legend, embalming, as they frequently do, the usages and sentiments of ancient times. In them we usually catch the truest reflection of the history and social condition of a people. The literature of ballads and legends, neither taught in schools nor crowned by academies, how modestly it has come down to us from the ages, delighting with its music, like a familiar bird, the household where it takes its rest! Its materials, as rich and varied as those of the tissues displayed in the bazaars of the Orient, have been collected and woven by unknown hands, it may have been under a Bedouin tent—it may have been in the smoky cabin of the Northman.

No envious poet claims as his own these sweet inspi-

rations that have leaped forth from the heart of the
people, as the water leaped from the rock under the
rod of Moses. Belonging to all who will listen to
them, to all who love the tender and the beautiful, they
vibrate in the air like the songs of birds. Full of naïf
conceptions and marvellous inventions they delight the
poor man at his humble hearth, make the aged smile,
awaken sentiments of love and virtue, and strengthen
patriotism by the souvenirs of glorious deeds.

The Servians are passionately fond of the song and
the dance. Their history is preserved in ballads and traditions, and the ordinary events of life are *improvised* as
was once the case among the Greeks. We would in fact
take them for descendants of the latter, were it not for
the proofs of Slavic origin in their language and history.

As one travels among the pastor tribes groups rise
before him resembling *tableaux* from the age and
country of Agamemnon. Their princes rule in the
manner of Homer's princes; their heroes sup in the
manner of Homer's heroes; their chiefs assemble round
their hospodars like the kings of the Iliad round the
" king of men;" their youth exercise themselves in the
sports and games of the Grecian youth.

Among the mountains of Servia I have seen many a
worthy successor of the blind old bard of Ios, and where
a Slavic woman " is," says Shaffarik, " there is also song.
House and yard, mountain and valley, meadow and

forest, she fills them all with the sounds of her voice."

" The poetry of the Servians is most admirably interwoven with their daily life. It is the picture of their thoughts, feelings, actions, and sufferings; it is the mental reproduction of the respective conditions of the mass of individuals who compose the nation. The hall where the women sit spinning around the fireside, the mountains on which the boys pasture their flocks, the square where the village youth assemble to dance the *kolo*, the plains where the harvest is reaped, the forest through which the lonely traveller journeys, all resound with song. Song accompanies all kinds of business, and frequently relates to it. The Servian *lives* his poetry."*

Among the Servians, the institution of " the family" retains its primitive character, every household being in itself an entire community. In the villages, picturesquely situated on the borders of the streams, or for greater security concealed in the fastnesses of the mountains, the low rude dwellings are at a distance from each other, and of such a size, that one not unfrequently forms an entire street. Around the main room, which contains a hearth in the centre, are chambers for the younger married people. Iron is scarcely used in the erection of Servian dwellings, chimneys and windows are rare, the well-trodden earth serves for a

* Talvi.

floor, while the loam walls and bark roof are blackened
with soot and smoke. The father is the patriarch of
the family. When he dies, one of the sons appointed
by his brethren, becomes master of the house. All the
members of the family work and eat together, sharing
each other's joys, and alike independent of the world
for support. Individual interest is merged in that of
the family. Paternal and filial affection are strong :
the brother is the chosen protector of the sister, of
whom he is the joy and the pride.

Marriage is arranged by the fathers of the two
families. At her new abode the young bride dresses
an infant, touches the walls with a distaff, and spreads
a table with food, wine, and water. Her mouth is
sealed by a piece of sugar, indicating that she should
utter only what is good. For a whole year she is
termed the "betrothed." In the presence of others
she scarcely converses with her husband.

Every family has a patron saint, and the whole
year is a round of festivals and sacred rites. They pray
three times a day ; and at table no person ventures to
accept the place of honor without being able to improvise an appropriate expression of thanks.

Endowed with an active imagination, the Servians
believe in the existence of a multitude of supernatural
beings, of hideous vampires fond of devouring human
hearts, and of beautiful, though malignant *vilas*, mingling their sweet voices with the murmurs of torrents,

flitting with magic wings through the depths of the
forests, or leading their nocturnal dances on the banks
of the mountain streams.

Ravens are regarded as the messengers of unhappy
news.

> " Flying came a pair of coal black ravens,
> Far away from the broad field of Mishar;
> Far from Shabatz, from the high white fortress;
> Bloody were their beaks unto the eyelids,
> Bloody were their talons to the ankles."

CHAPTER III.

LA PORTE DE FER.

"We build with what we deem eternal rock,
A future age asks where the structure stood."

I WOULD gladly have remained long in Servia, to enjoy its magnificent mountain scenery, and study the naïf customs of its people, but the battle fields and pyramids of the Orient called me away. Though very hospitable, many of the Servians with whom I came in contact, especially at Belgrade, regarded my inquisitive curiosity with a certain degree of suspicion.

The rigorous quarantine formerly maintained between Austria and Servia is no longer kept up. The custom-house at Belgrade reminded me of a description of a similar institution in Constantinople by a friend, familiar with the East.

" The floor of the governmental edifice was nowhere visible. Avalanches of assorted goods occupied every point, but with the most sublime irregularity. Large and ponderous boxes crushed small and weaker ones, heavy and cumbrous bales damaged fragile parcels, barrels chafed against sacks, chests misused trunks, and everything seemed bent on doing as great an injury as possible to everything else."*

It was a beautiful August evening when we embarked on the steamer at Semlin for Orsova, about ninety miles below. After the confluence of the Save the Danube expands to a great width, embosoming a number of woody islands. My eyes clung to Belgrade, that old city of combats and sieges, until in the hazy distance her minarets and ramparts sank beneath the placid surface of the river. There were views on the Servian bank worthy of picturesque Arva in Northern Hungary.

We remained over night at a German settlement on the Austrian side. Whole districts in Lower Hungary and Transylvania have been settled by emigrants from the German States, welcomed thither by the Magyars, and permitted to retain their language and institutions, a circumstance which has been adroitly turned to account by the house of Hapsburg. Generosity has ever been the fault of the Hungarians, and their history a perpetual martyrdom! On the broad plains surrounded by boulevards of lofty mountains,

"Where struggled Arpad's gallant crew,"

they were content in developing their free institutions, never ambitious of foreign conquest, and unmindful of the maxim of Corneille,

* R. C. McCormick, Jr.

Below Semlin, on the Hungarian side of the river, I
noticed at short intervals the stations of the border
guard, sentinelled at all times and at night indicated
by gleaming fires. This military guard, extending along
the whole Turkish frontier of Hungary, is capable of
furnishing, in case of emergency, two hundred thousand
men. The territory is under military rule. Every
male is destined to be a soldier, and the land is cultivated by families of many persons, under the direction of a patriarch.

Groups of passengers, exhibiting a remarkable
diversity of costumes and languages, assembled on
deck to enjoy the beautiful evening. I made the
acquaintance of a gay young Wallachian, named Aristias, just returning from his medical studies in Paris, a
French officer on his way to the East, and Reschid
Effendi, secretary of Sami Pacha, from Widdin. A
Hungarian poet says that his unfortunate country contains people of every European race ; and in the great
hall of the University of Vienna, I have often counted
the representatives of twenty-five different nations.

As we steamed down the Danube the following
morning, the scenery became beautiful, then surpass-
ingly grand. The well-wooded hills on either side, the
forerunners of the Balkans and Carpathians, rose into
rugged mountains, between which the narrowed Danube rushed and surged into the great Wallachian plain,

ANCIENT JAZYGES.

p. 36

far away toward the Euxine. Below the island of
Moldova, a huge black rock projects from the bosom
of the river, upon which a jealous Turk is said to have
left his suspected bride, saying to her, "*Babakai!
babakai!*" (repent! repent!) a name which has been
applied to the rock itself. Near by, is the cavern of
Golumbatz where St. George is believed to have slain
the dragon from whose body, still decaying, proceed
swarms of noxious flies.

High on the rocks above are the picturesque ruins
of Golumbatz, whose crumbling towers seem just ready
to fall into the abyss below.

And now the steamer rushes into the most magnificent gorge in Europe, if not in the world. Here, as
if in anger, the grizzly mountains seem to shake their
hoary heads at each other across the foaming torrent,
and there, smile at each other in embosomed lakes,
from which can be seen no point of ingress or egress.
In one place the eye is greeted with soft vistas and
idyllic retreats, in another it looks upon the semblance
of battlements and cathedral towers. How grandly
the echoes die away among these glorious mountains!
Now we dart down the narrow foam-crested rapids, and
then float away calmly between retreating heights.

This kind of scenery continues for a distance of
seventy miles. Near the lofty peak of Sterbetz, front-
ing the Danube with a wall of rock three thousand
five hundred feet high, is the Cave of Veterani, cele

brated in the wars of the Christians and Turks. On the Austrian side of the river is the new road, built at a great expense by the Austrians; and on the opposite side, I noticed in many places the remains of Trajan's Way. A tablet hewn into the solid rock bears a Latin inscription commemorative of this stupendous work. Rude fishermen now build their fires on the spot. At Orsova we took a small barge to pass the Iron Gate, the most dangerous rapids in the Lower Danube, the river falling thirteen feet in three quarters of a mile. Just below the Austrian frontier was pointed out to me the place where Kossuth concealed the Hungarian crown in 1849.

Towards sunset we reached Turnul Severin, on the left bank of the river, nearly opposite the Servian village of Fetti-Islam. There we found the Austrian steamer which was to convey us down to Rustchuk. Some of my company strolled up to the village, consisting of a few wretched Wallachian huts perched upon the neighboring hill. Alone, I wandered down the river bank to the ruins of Trajan's Bridge.

A few minutes' walk brought me to the ruins. Here the conqueror of Dacia executed one of those gigantic projects with which all similar efforts of modern enterprise in this part of the world can scarcely be compared. The lowest stone bridge over the Danube is at Ratisbon, where the river is but a few yards in width, but Trajan spanned the noble stream at Turnul Severin nearly a thousand miles nearer its mouth, with the longest structure of the kind ever erected, it being, according to the measurement of Marsigli, almost three thousand feet from shore to shore.

Trajan's Bridge was built during the Emperor's second campaign to the lower Danube, when, after many reverses to the legions and a recent revolt of the Dacians, he resolved effectually to subdue those stubborn enemies of Rome. Apollodorus, of Damascus, was the architect. Dion Cassius has left a description of this remarkable structure, parts of which have withstood the floods and ice of seventeen centuries. Twenty piers sixty feet wide, one hundred and fifty feet high, and nearly one hundred feet apart, sustained the enormous weight. Some authors maintain that the upper portions of the bridge were of wood. The current, at this point, is slow and regular. The level spaces at both ends of the bridge were well adapted to the marshalling of the legions. The massive towers erected there, served to protect it from the attacks of the barbarians. A few of the truncated piers and abutments of solid masonry are still to be traced by the curious traveller. In 1844, a number of arms and rare utensils were found in the vicinity, which shed no little light upon the camp life of the Romans. Trajan's Bridge, like Trajan's Way, was constructed for military purposes, and stood only so long as the Romans maintained their sway on the left shore of the Danube. Hadrian, the successor of Trajan, destroyed the splendid monument of his predecessor but a few years after it had been built.

Near at hand were the scattered ruins of the citadel of Theodorus, erected by Justinian, and of great importance in the wars of the Romans and barbarians. But more imposing are the ruins of the crumbling tower of Severinus, half a mile from the site of Trajan's Bridge. This structure, famous in earlier times, was built by Severinus, governor of Mœsia, about 240 A. D. All that remains, after the ravages of time and the barbarians, is a lofty and tottering portion of the ancient wall, situated on an artificial elevation and partly surrounded by a *fosse* whose two extremities unite with the Danube. The moat is grown up with small trees and underbrush, and the tower itself partially concealed from sight by the thick foliage. At its base is a large marble sarcophagus. I clambered up the ruin as far as possible, just as the sun was flinging his last golden glances over the grizzly crests of the Carpathians. How full of glory was his departure, fringing with sapphire edges the dark clouds that floated so tranquilly in the western sky, and bathing the mountain tops in seas of moist mellow light!

The twinkling stars found me seated on the tower of Severinus, reflecting upon the magnitude of that ancient power the sites of whose camps and cities I have traced along the Rhine and the Rhone, the Nile and the Jordan. Rome imparted somewhat of her own greatness to the most distant provinces conquered by her arms. Surely it was a glorious thing to build up, in those barbaric ages, an empire whose laws and systems still survive for the government of mankind, and whose public works, stupendous in their ruins, serve, in our feebler efforts, as models of strength and beauty! Honor enough was it even for the conquered nations, to share the glory of the Roman name.

In the gathering mists of the evening, I conjured up before me the scenes and events of former times. I peopled the valley of old Danubius once more as in the days of Trajan. I restored the fallen arches which spanned the river, and rebuilt, in imagination, the ancient towers. The sound of rushing waters floating down from the Iron Gate seemed like the distant tramp of legions, and the voices of evening were not unlike the softened din of camps and villages. But when the moon rose above the Wallachian hills, filling the world with pearly light, the fair vision disappeared, and again I saw but ruins and fragments of ruins.

Turnul Severin being too poor to furnish an inn, I returned to sleep on board the steamer. She was built after an American model and furnished in the American style, with the exception of our ample berths and state rooms. There were but four of the latter, and those on the main deck. How gratifying to see the genius and enterprise of my countrymen acknowledged

in these remote regions. " Nothing is impossible with
an American," has become an axiom in Eastern Europe.
We dined at the *table d'hôte* in the French style,
or *à la carte* upon German dishes. Conversation
was carried on in French, German, Hungarian, Illyrian,
Turkish, and Wallachian. The last has a great simi-
larity to the Italian in the sounds of the letters, and
especially in the smooth open flow of the vowels. The
Hungarians, whose language is cognate with the Turkish, are excellent linguists. This results from the fact
that they are accustomed from childhood to speak German in addition to their vernacular. Proficiency in
acquiring languages is dependent less upon memory
or a peculiar talent, than upon the habit of express-
ing the same thoughts in different idioms. The edu-
cated Russians are, however, the best linguists in the
world. A nobleman, who rarely speaks the native
Russ, will converse fluently in the polished tongues of
Western Europe. The language of the Russians is said
to contain not only all the sounds of the latter, but also
many of those peculiar to the speech of the Orientals.

Late in the evening, the cabin of the Albrecht
underwent a marvellous " sea-change," the divans, set-
tees, and even the tables being magically converted
into comfortable beds.

It was amusing to see Turks in twisted turbans,
Germans in night-caps, white-coated Austrians, and
well-booted Magyars, Servians and Wallachs, Jews and

Gentiles, lying down quietly together, as if the millennium had dawned in the close, dimly lighted saloon of the Albrecht. But more amusing was it to listen to the cacophonia of fifty noses of all sizes, nationalities, shades of color and varieties of tone. Snoring seemed contagious; I could only liken the saloon to a vast æolian harp, or to an orchestra of dead men, playing funeral dirges upon the harshest wind instruments. I fancied that I could trace in their monotonous discords the influence of wine, and love and sorrow, of nightmare visions from distended stomachs, and of beautiful dreams weaving their golden threads in the gossamer tissues of the brain. It was in vain that I covered my head and stopped my ears. More than once during the long watches, I left the hot and mephitic cabin to enjoy on deck the sweet influences of night and of the stars. The aversion of the Germans to fresh air is incomprehensible. .

I became not a little interested in a heavy sleeper in the other end of the saloon, whom I remembered to have seen in Vienna. He was of the sable people who rank cooking among the liberal arts—

> " A creature of one mighty sense,
> Concentrated impudence."

Brought from the region of the Upper Nile when a child, he had been sold by a dealer in eunuchs to an Egyptian of rank, and on the death of the latter, by some caprice of fortune, was exposed for sale in the slave market of Constantinople. The Nubian became the property of a pacha who was then commanding on the Servian frontier. After a time they were surprised by the Servians at night and made prisoners. The eunuch was retained as a part of the spoils, and having made a favorable impression upon Prince Milosch, became his attendant, and afterwards his physician. The Nubian's acquaintance with charms and spells and the secret arts of the Turkish hakeems, was entirely satisfactory to old Prince Milosch, who could neither read nor write, having been a swine-herd in his youth. Here the sable disciple of Esculapius enjoyed many smiles of fortune, until the expulsion of the prince from Servia, when he took refuge with his patron in Wallachia.

CHAPTER IV.

" Sons of inanity,
Smoke and vanity."

I WAS on deck at an early hour the next morning to
see the sun rise above the Wallachian hills. At my
right were the Balkans. Towering with clear sharp
outlines against the southern sky, they bend away
from the Iron Gate toward the distant Euxine, a continuous chain of forest-capped giants. In like manner,
at the north, sweep away the Carpathians, surpassing, if possible, their southern rivals in hoary magnificence. The two chains, inclosing Bulgaria and Wallachia, form a grand amphitheatre, where successive
hordes of barbarians first appeared on the stage of
Europe to open the ever-changing scenes of her history. It was on the plains of the lower Danube that
the legions of Cyrus melted away like snow beneath
the arrows of the Scythians—there Alexander the
Great fought the barbarians of the north—there millions of men perished in the early wars of the Christians and the Turks; and on that *terrain*, in the oracu-
lar language of Napoleon, " the destiny of Europe is yet

to be determined." The Danube having received the great rivers of Hungary, and lashed with its myriad streams the Tyrolean and Norican Alps, rests below the Iron Gate like a tired giant, and falls away to the Euxine, "a broad, silent, magnificent river."

The morning air was of Italian softness. Filmy clouds of vapor hung over the lazy river in places shadowed by the mountains, like flocks of white-breasted swans, or timid spirits that flee from light to the realms of darkness. How daintily they danced away over the moving waters, as if the mists loved the crystal drops from which the sun had set them free. The wavy cornfields on the Servian hills had already a golden hue, indicating the climate to be more friendly than on the slope of the Carpathians. On the Servian bank opened fine vistas of villages half concealed in a sea of verdure, and hills blushing with purple vineyards. How beautifully the great river took upon her bosom the shadows of the forests and mountains, and tremblingly pictured them there with all their finery of green and gold!

A few well bearded Turks, smoking their chibouques in Pythagorean silence, and myself, were the only persons on deck to enjoy the changing landscape as the steamer glided between the sunken piles of Trajan's Bridge. As we advanced, the mountains receded from the river, and the Wallachian shore became low and sterile. The Danube makes a great bend below Turnul

Severin, and for some time we were steaming westward
toward the lofty Sterbetz, the silent spectator of so
many contests between the Occident and the Orient.
A few wretched villages were passed, and the steamer
touched at Rakovitza, where the river Timrok, forming
the boundary between Servia and Bulgaria, flows into
the Danube.

Three hours more, and Reschid Effendi pointed out
to me a succession of sandhills on the Wallachian side
of the Danube, dotted here and there with trees and
spots of verdure. Those who have coasted along Cape
Cod have seen precisely the counterpart of the desolate
region around Cetate, the place where the Turks under
Achmet Pacha gave the Russians a terrible blow during
the campaign of Kalafat, neither party asking or giving
quarter. The wretched village, destined hereafter to
have a name in history, is situated at the base of
the sandhills, a mile and a half from the river, and
consists of a dozen or more mud hovels and subterranean cabins. Reschid Effendi assured me that the field
of slaughter was still covered with the garments and
skeletons of the unburied dead, upon whom swine and
vultures had feasted for weeks. The officers had been
plundered of their watches, and finery of apparel; and
hands and fingers were still found strewn about, brutally
cut off for the diamond rings which other soft fingers
had put upon them with tender wishes in happier days!

Cetate is hardly passed before, turning to the south,

the minarets and fortifications of Widdin come fully
into view. The Danube here makes a sudden bend
southward so as to form a kind of semicircle, and the
high sand banks on the Wallachian shore shut out for
a few minutes the distant view.

At their base I noticed the blackened walls of an
establishment—where a few months previous swine had
been slaughtered for exportation to England—of which
the pious bashi-bazouks had left scarcely one stone
upon another. The passengers assembled on the deck
to view what, during the previous winter months, had
attracted more attention than any other spot on the
globe. A moment more, and the world-renowned fortifications of Kalafat rose before our eyes. The works
on the highest point of land first made their appearance,
and then a long, black line, running from hillock to
hillock, and here and there changing its direction, became visible on the horizon. The line of fortifications,
six thousand paces in length, swept round to the north-
west, so as again to meet the Danube. I cannot say
whether I was more struck with the extent of these
celebrated works, crowning the hills and terminating
in two strong forts, the one above and the other far
below Widdin, or by the loneliness which everywhere
prevailed. Three months before my visit Kalafat had
been occupied by 50,000 men, and its long lines of
entrenchments bristled with hundreds of heavy cannon:
then it was as naked as the desert of Sahara. It was

frightful from very solitude to wander among the deserted works. Not a soldier, not even a bashi-bazouk was to be seen. The skeletons of many of those who had died in camp or fallen in the frequent skirmishes with the enemy were strewn upon the uneven ground, the same as at Cetate.

When man loses the best characteristics of his nature and assumes those of a savage, the very brutes seem to become humanized as if to shame him of his folly. Among the deserted works of Kalafat, so desolate that scarcely any one ventured to approach them, I found a number of lean and famished dogs which had followed their masters thither, it may have been from the wilds of Asia; and neither hunger nor solitude could force the faithful creatures to leave the spot where they had lain themselves down to die. It is a terrible commentary on the miseries of the camp that fifteen thousand Turkish soldiers died from disease and wounds within the walls of Kalafat. Patient Mussulmans—and who so patient as they?—became raving maniacs from very suffering. A surgeon who was stationed there has described to me scenes of privation, which far surpass anything related of the Ten Thousand who retreated from Asia.

The Turk is a fatalist in view of sufferings, wounds, and death, otherwise the fifty thousand soldiers at Kalafat would not have endured the terrible campaign of 1853-4.

4

The Mussulman will not submit to surgical operations, and consequently but one amputation took
place during the entire siege, when judicious medical treatment might have saved thousands of lives.
Of the three hundred wounded sent over to Widdin
after the battle of Cetate, but five ever recrossed the
river.

Widdin, the head of a Pachalik and the residence of
a Greek Bishop, was a place of considerable importance
in the time of the Romans.   It is a genuine Turkish
city, with a population of 25,000 souls. Although
picturesque in the distance, its magnificence, like that
of everything in the Orient, disappeared as we approached. The walls of an immense fortress line the
river's edge for a considerable distance.   Scarcely a
sentinel could be seen, but the long lines of Turkish
cannon showed that Sami Pacha had not been idle
during the campaign.   A few Turkish vessels, rivalling
Chinese junks in awkwardness of appearance, lay along
the beach.   Beside the fortress were pitched the tents
of a horde of gipsies.   The shore was lined with a
ragged, fez-capped multitude, composed chiefly of fero-
cious-looking Arnouts and bashi-bazouks, some of
them mounted on sorry horses and others a-foot, or
seated cross-legged in the mud and sand.   Their
tents were even more despicable than those of the
gipsies.

Should a dozen steamers land their passengers

together at one of the piers of New York, the confusion would hardly exceed that which took place when the Albrecht stopped at Widdin. The Turk is usually silent, but on occasion can make more noise than a score of unbelievers. As soon as the guard was opened a crowd of barbarians rushed upon deck, carrying boxes, sacks, and all the cumbrous appliances of a Turk's travelling equipage.

The few soldiers stationed on the narrow wooden pier for the purpose of keeping order serve only to increase the confusion. The ragged multitude shout, jabber, and quarrel in a dozen different languages, and those in authority wield their batons lustily over the backs of the scrambling wretches.

While this was going on I took a short ramble in Widdin with Reschid Effendi. There were the mosques, the cemeteries with broken columns and the funereal cypress, the rows of huts, the muddy lanes, the dogs, and the listless idleness which characterize every Turkish city. I drank a friendly *salaam* with Reschid in a dingy cahvé, regretting that I could not avail myself of his invitation to visit Sami Pacha.

Several Beys and high Turkish officers, with servants and pipe-bearers, came on board to join the troops below. Turkish servants usually receive from their masters no more than their food and clothing, a circumstance which explains the number of attendants generally seen about Ottomans of rank. The din began to cease, and after an hour's delay, the Albrecht proceeded on her voyage.

Steaming down the ancient Ister, every hour carried me further within the portals of the sultry Orient. Below Widdin, the Danube varies from half a mile to two miles in width, and rolls away to the Euxine, as calm and sluggish as the pale rivers of the North. The long reaches of the Amazon could scarcely have been more monotonous, as hour after hour we held on our winding course. Multitudes of cranes and pelicans, frightened from their grotesque positions by the splash of the steamer, took refuge in the Wallachian swamps, while an occasional eagle from the Carpathians wheeled above us in airy circles, undisturbed by the presence of man.

Here and there the northern shore is fringed with immense morasses, the home of wolves, and bears, and poisonous miasmas. Beyond, stretches away the low Wallachian plain, a magnificent field for the moving of armies; and in the far distance the eye sometimes catches sight of the gentle undulations which swell into the Carpathians. The vast level tracts of Daco-Romania are connected with the Steppes of Bessarabia, and are open to the winds that sweep across the plains of Southern Russia.

Rising, in several instances, to the height of six thousand feet, the Carpathians form an almost uninterrupted chain to the eastward, until they are broken through by the Aluta. This river, flowing down from the elevated valley of Transylvania, rushes through the pass of the Red Tower, and in its course to the Danube divides Little from Great Wallachia. Midway from the Aluta to the Pruth, the Carpathians deflect suddenly northward, and form the boundary between Moldavia and the land of the Secklers. Great Wallachia, as well as Moldavia, is crossed by several rivers, as the Argisch and Sereth. Among the head waters of the Bistritza, some of the mountain peaks, as Pion and Tschakleo, reach above the limits of the oak and pine into the region of snow, and ice, and Alpine plants.

Several spurs from the principal chain extend down into Wallachia, among which are many beautiful lakes united by crystal streams with the Danube. When the swarms of Goths and Huns pitched their rude encampments along the Ister, the Daco-Romans were frequently obliged to take refuge in the fastnesses of the Carpathians. Thither they carried their language and their institutions, prepared to return again to the fertile plains, where the conflicting waves of civilization and barbarism often meet each other, as the ocean current meets the ocean storm. Strange Nemesis that controlled the destiny of those early nomadic races! Wonderful, indeed, the fluctuations and changes of their history, rising and fading away in the dim past like dissolving views.

Far different is the scenery on the Bulgarian side.
Widdin is situated on a small plain, but the barren
hills in its rear soon sweep round, as if they loved the
Danube, and form a splendid natural defence to a considerable distance below Silistria, where the river suddenly bends northward, and the Dobrudscha becomes as
low and swampy as the Wallachian shore. This continuous bluff, three hundred miles in length, and varying from thirty to one hundred and fifty feet in height,
rests upon a calcareous base. In some places the
Danube is flanked for miles with a perpendicular wall
of limestone, while in others the bluff retires from the
shore a short distance, giving place to delightful little
eyots grown up with tall grass, in which droves of
tame buffaloes or white Bulgarian oxen were occasionally to be seen, as we swept along.

The action of water, assisted, perhaps, by other
natural causes, has worn the Bulgarian hills into curious and fantastic shapes, having, in many instances,
the exact resemblance of military works. High walls
of earth stretch along the river or crown the rocky
eminences as evenly and regularly as if they were
artificial, while here and there natural forts, and
parapets, and towers look as if the giants had been
at work in piling up immense fortresses to defend
Old Danubius. I can now appreciate the tremendous efforts which the Turks have repeatedly made
to protect the Bulgarian shore against the Russians

in preference to falling back upon the line of the Balkans.

Peculiarly favored and unfortunate have been the regions along the Rhine and the Danube. The former of these rivers, rising among the Alps, and flowing many hundreds of miles to the sea through the noblest portion of Europe, the German, in his admiration, calls the "Father of Rivers." Yet no traveller can wander among the walled towns and cities which line its banks, without seeing how vastly inferior the Rheingau is to the central parts of France and Germany in everything but natural advantages. Those battered walls and crumbling towers have a wild story of their own. History tells of scenes of violence and deeds of war that have occurred there ever since the Ubii and Sicambii lived on opposite sides of the river, and Roman camps and colonies were planted among the rude nations of Germania. The position of the Rhine provinces between belligerent powers has counterbalanced many of their natural advantages. At short intervals of peace their prosperity has been almost unparalleled. No part of Europe was so flourishing during the Hanseatic league; no part of Europe has suffered so much, and so often, from the incursions of foreign armies.

Owing to the diseases which at certain seasons prevail along the lower Danube, but more than all else to the calamities of war, that magnificent river

. has thus far been the enemy rather than the friend of the nations inhabiting its banks. The numerous islands which, in a country like our own, would have long ago become great commercial marts, are, almost without an exception, uninhabited wastes; while in places where the traveller expects to see smiling towns and cities, he finds nothing but silence and solitude. The fever, plague, and the mutual fear of Turks and Christians, have, for the most part, kept in desolation one shore and the other. Immense regions along the lower Danube, once the busy theatre of Roman life and industry, are now inhabited by a few Servian fishermen and Wallachian shepherds.

In the crowd of Mussulmans who took passage on the steamer, I soon learned to distinguish the Europeanized from the genuine Asiatic. The latter, the Moslems of the old school, retain the magnificent white turban folded in the ancient Moslem style, the broad girdle serving as a receptacle for weapons, piastres, or other personal effects, and those wonderful pantaloons, so ample below the waist, and so narrow above the ankle, as if purposely designed to give the wearer an inexpressibly awkward appearance. The tailors' shears indicate how far the ideas of the West have gained acceptance among the faithful. The turbans become reduced to the close-fitting fez, the baggy parts contract in size, the girdle disappears, the French coat takes the place of the cumbrous gown, and infidel boots supplant the shuffling

yellow slippers, so easy to be cast off when the Mussulman squats upon his crooked legs, or rubs his forehead
upon the ground in prayer. I was delighted with the
opportunity to study the characteristics of those well
bearded Orientals who still maintained the letter and
the spirit of the Koran. It was a great pleasure to
look upon their noble countenances, so honest, so dignified, so unmoved by all that was passing around them.

Cross-legged on little mats spread upon the deck,
they smoked their long *chibouques* in silence, or collected
in groups, without leaving their national posture, conversed in low and earnest tones of voice, but with a
gravity unknown to the politicians of the West, however trivial the subject. There is something genuine
in the politeness of these Orientals. They never tread
upon each other's toes, or interrupt each other's conversation. Haste, they say, comes of Satan, and patience is the key of reason. How different the conduct
of the Europeanized Moslems! They lounged in the
saloon, dined at the public table upon dishes declared
by the Koran to be unclean, and drank as freely of the
purple juice of the grape, as if the Prophet had never in-
terdicted its use. " Wine, tobacco, coffee and opium,"
say the Oriental poets, " are the four cushions of the
sofa of pleasure, and the chief elements of the world
of enjoyment," whilst the strict interpreters of the law
declare them to be "the ministers of Satan, and the
four pillars of the temple of licentiousness." Still more

4*

interesting to me was a bevy of Turkish females.
They came on board at Nicopolis. Who they were
or whither they were going I did not venture to inquire of the Mussulman, who looked jealous enough to
be the husband of the entire company. They spread a
carpet in an unfrequented corner of the deck, and
while some took care of the children, crowned with the
Turkish fez, although too young to lisp the name of
the Prophet, others laughed and chatted with each
other, lowly of course when Giaour ears were listening, but loud enough to show that woman is woman
the wide world over. I was not a little surprised to
see some of the elderly females smoking quite as dili-
gently as their lords, and it was curious to observe them
handling their slender, amber-tipped chibouques, so
as not to show their faces. With most of them but
little was lost by the use of the all-obscuring veil.
The eye is the window of the soul, but by no means
the index of beauty or deformity, and hence I wonder
that the Turkish veil has not been introduced into
other lands, where persons wish to appear more beautiful than Nature intended them to be. If it is the
intention of sweet-eyed Zuleika to convert an ugly
into a handsome face, does she not show much better
sense in using for that purpose a preparation of silk
or cotton, than our cousin Amanda who uniformly employs a preparation of chalk? One or two of the
Turkish females were really beautiful, a fact which

LEHEL AND HIS HORN.   p. 37

they naturally did not wish to conceal, for the curiosity and vanity of woman are beyond restraint. I made free to cultivate the acquaintance of a young Mussulman but a few months old, to the great horror of his Nubian nurse, whose pouting lips showered a stream of imprecations upon my beardless chin : but the mother, who appeared to be a person of family, seemed delighted to have me pull the cheeks, and tickle the ribs of the laughing boy. If you would gain the mother's heart speak kindly to her child. I have observed that Turkish parents treat their children with peculiar tenderness. The mothers usually nourish their own offspring, but when from necessity that duty devolves upon a female slave, the latter is entitled to her freedom. One is witness of many strange things among the Moslems, but I have yet to see a Turkish mother airing an ugly dog in her arms, her cherub of an infant at the same time given over to a nurse trudging along behind.

Notwithstanding the many patriarchal institutions of the Turks, that of the family can hardly be said to exist among them. There is no such thing as collecting around the family fireside, the table, or the altar. The husband eats by himself, and is waited upon by his wives, who make their meal upon what remains. The household is merely an *aggregation* of persons.

The birth of an infant, however, is an important event in a Turkish household, especially if it be a male. Then the doors are thrown open, friends come in to

congratulate the father and mother, the parents can
hardly find words for their joy, and there is no end to
the rejoicings and festivities. Is it a female? the father
hangs his head, the mother is grieved, the friends keep
away; all regard it as a sore infliction of Providence,
and the less that is said about the unfortunate affair the
better. One of the first duties to be performed on the
birth of a child is to whisper into its right ear, " There
is but one God, and Mohammed is his prophet." The
father names the sons, the mother the daughters. The
Moslem law prohibits the mother from weaning her
child before the age of two years without the consent
of the father, which, however, is usually given a few
months earlier.

After circumcision the father instructs his son in
the manner of making the ablutions and prayers. The
Prophet enjoins that male children be taught to pray at
the age of seven years, and recommends the use of the
rod if they are not proficient at the age of ten. Very
few, however, pray before reaching maturity, and then,
I am afraid, their prayers rarely ascend higher than
their heads.

We tarried a short time at Lom Palanka, and also
at Nicopolis. The cities built by the Slaves along the
lower Danube, on the sites of the old Roman camps,
consisted originally of three distinct parts, the *grad* or
fortress, occupying the most elevated position ; the
barosch, or lower city, the quarter of the merchants

and artisans, generally surrounded by a fortified wall, with gates closed at night; and lastly the *palanke*, or suburbs outside the *barosch*, which formed the residence of the poorer classes, and were surrounded simply by palisades. This plan, however, has been greatly modified by the Turks, who have destroyed without rebuilding. Though Bulgaria is filled with Jews, Armenians, and Greek Christians, the Danubian cities are of the genuine Turkish character. They are alike unaffected by the proximity of Hungary, and the French and English ideas, which are constantly gaining ground at Stamboul. The numerous mosques, the crooked rows of cabins, the stony lanes, need be seen but once never to be forgotten.

Agriculture has been banished from the vicinity of the towns, while the hills and valleys of this once fertile region are given up to flocks and herds watched by Bulgarian shepherds. Large tracts have been laid waste for the coursings of the Turkish horsemen. No wonder that the Mussulman squatting in perennial filth should always be dreaming of a beautiful heaven! "In the shade of the crossing of cimiters is paradise," said the old Moslems, but their descendants dream of its fruition in the midst of poverty and wretchedness.

Of all the Turkish towns below Widdin, Nicopolis was the only one allowed to retain its fortifications after the Russian campaign of 1829. Nicopolis is also celebrated for the victory gained there in 1396 by Bajazet

over Sigismond, King of Hungary. It is said that 60,000
Turks, a number far superior to the entire Christian
army, remained dead on the field, a circumstance which
so enraged the Sultan Bajazet, that he ordered all the
prisoners to be put to the sword. Ten thousand men
were thus massacred in cold blood—the work of death
continuing from sunrise to late in the afternoon, when
some of the great dignitaries of the Empire fell at the
feet of the Sultan and besought him to permit the
remaining prisoners to be led into slavery. This request
was granted, and the few Christian warriors who survived the foolhardy attempt of King Sigismond were
afterward ransomed at the price of 200,000 pieces of
gold. Before the French cavaliers departed for their
native country, Bajazet, who was fond of the chase,
invited them to a magnificent hunt, in which 7,000 fal-
cons and 6,000 hounds were employed. Instead of
commanding them never again to bear arms against
the Turks, the Sultan was magnanimous enough to
request the Duke of Nevers to unite and lead against
the Ottomans the powers of Christendom.

Near Nicopolis are shown the remains of the bridge
erected by Constantine during his campaign against the
Goths and Sarmatians, rivalling that of Trajan at
Turnul Severin. It was evening when we left the city,
and dropped down to the mouth of the Aluta, a short
distance below, where the Captain determined to remain until morning. Islas and Turnul stand on oppo-

site sides of the river. We gathered on deck in groups to enjoy the soft, starry, Asiatic night. How still and beautiful it was as our steamer lay moored to the bank. Up the broad Danube I could see no horizon. There were stars above and below; the river seemed so unlike Old Danubius floating down from his Alpine source. Two Turkish officers, Italians by birth, brought their guitars on deck. They began with some common Turkish airs, but the strains of music soon led their thoughts back to the sunny hills of their fatherland, and hour after hour, in the sweet surroundings of night, we listened to the plaintive songs of the sons of Italy.

The scenery below Nicopolis continued dreary and monotonous. Here and there I noticed on the Wallachian shore the quarantine posts which had been deserted since the retreat of the Russians.

At ten o'clock we reached Sistova, a city of 20,000 inhabitants, and of some commercial importance. The high bluff upon which it is built is traversed by a deep ravine. The hills beyond the city were clothed, in part, by vineyards. It was more cheerful than anything I had yet seen in Turkey. Omer Pacha had left 3000 men to garrison the city.

At Sistova came on board a company of bashi-bazouks to join the army below. Among them were fierce Arnauts from the mountains of Albania, and turbaned warriors from the distant East—

"The sun, the desert, stamped in each dark haughty face."

The great peculiarity of the Russo-Turkish struggle, which, from a war of monarchs, came so near merging into a war of races, consisted in the variety of the forces engaged. It levied upon three continents, drawing together the representatives of more nations, languages, and religions, than were ever before assembled in any conflict. Bands of fanatic Moslems from the wild tribes of Central Asia—from regions so remote that a year's journey would scarcely suffice to reach the banks of the Danube—wandered hither, taking Mecca in their way, to meet in combat the half-starved recruits from the Asiatic provinces of Russia, belonging, perhaps, to their own race and speaking their own dialect. In the Orient men follow the faith of their kings, and in fighting for them vainly believe that they are battling in the cause of God.

Different, however, will it be in the struggle between freedom and despotism, which must come alike in the East and the West, bringing

"War with a thousand battles and shaking a hundred thrones."

The picturesque costumes of the bashi-bazouks were worn and ragged. Serving as volunteers, they received little or no support from the government, and compelled to subsist by plunder, often proved more troublesome to their friends than to their foes. To me, however, their dress, their arms, and Eastern customs were highly interesting, reminding me of the rough warriors of Asia, with whom the first Sultans achieved their conquests. Among them was a Scheik from beyond the Lebanon, whose beard had attained the utmost limit of capillary licentiousness. He seemed perfectly at home in the saloon, and through an interpreter I learned many curious things concerning his people.

Near us stood a Greek merchant from Galatz, a young man of finished education and manners, with whom I had become well acquainted. I cannot convey the contempt with which he looked upon these wild children of Asia, descendants of the rude warriors who enslaved his ancestors four centuries ago. "*Ce sont des brigands, Monsieur,*" said my friend as we promenaded the deck. "*Ce sont des brigands! des barbares!*" and again he twirled his elegant moustache, and cast upon the enemies of his race a look of unutterable scorn.

At two o'clock a bend in the river brought into view the city of Rustchuk, and shortly after the steamer was moored under one of the forts upon the high bluff. In consequence of a moderate wind blowing down the Danube, Said Pacha refused to open the bridge of boats thrown across the river a few days previous for the passage of Omer Pacha's army. I was astonished at the number of cannon bristling on the heights above. The Turks were celebrating the festival of the Courban Beiram after the manner of our Inde-

pendence Day, and as the thunders of their heavy
ordnance rolled away among the Bulgarian hills, I witnessed, in imagination, one of the recent cannonades
across the Danube.   On the opposite side of the river
was the little village of Slobosia, occupied a few days
previous by the Russians.   I amused myself during the
afternoon with watching a company of bashi-bazouks
who were racing on the narrow strand of Rustchuk.
The little horses, upon which they had ridden from
their distant homes in Asia, looked poor and sorry, but
were nimble-footed and trained in the rapid irregular
charges peculiar to Turcoman warfare.   It was an ex-
citing spectacle to see a troop of these wild horsemen,
with picturesque garments streaming in the wind, dart
away through clouds of sand and dust, and brandish
their glittering weapons in the air.

The sound of evening bells floating across the lazy
rivers from Slobosia and Giurgevo, fell gratefully upon
the ear, and contrasted strangely with the chants of the
muezzins upon the Turkish mosques.

The following day there being no prospect of
reaching Giurgevo, I rambled through Rustchuk with
Aristias and my Greek friend. Excepting Widdin,
Rustchuk is the most important place on the lower
Danube, having numerous silk and morocco factories,
and being the rendezvous of the caravans from Sophia
and the cities of Roumelia.   As the navigation from
the Black Sea is very liable to interruption, many of

the rich fabrics and products of the East reach the Danubian cities through the passes of the Balkans, to be sold at the great quarterly fairs in Bulgaria, or to supply the markets of Wallachia and Hungary. A railway from Rustchuk to the Archipelago, with a branch to Constantinople, is now in contemplation. The project has met the approval of the Porte, always lavish in promises, and even a hundred million piastres have been subscribed, but some time will intervene before the wild solitudes of Bulgaria are startled by the shrill neighings of the iron steed. Eastern Europe, however, must ultimately become the great highway between the Occident and the Orient, and we may hope that her dormant races will be galvanized into activity by contact with the forces of civilization, as the passes of the mesmeriser rouse the motionless subject.

We visited the Pacha and the Cadi's Court. Until then I had believed, with many others, that there was some virtue in Turkish reforms. The firman equalizing the Christian and the Turk in the eye of the law, had been recently promulgated at Constantinople with the usual surroundings of parade and bombast, but was little heeded at Rustchuk. Let the Sultan, who is a humane though a weak man, devise one method to improve the condition of his Christian subjects, the cunning and bigoted Ulemas will devise ten, by elastic interpretations of the Koran or otherwise, to keep

them in an enslaved condition. What will it avail to
make the testimony of a Christian valid, while the Turks
remain the judges and executors of the law? How
shall I describe the Cadi's court at Rutschuk? The
low damp room, the holes in the floor and the walls,
the imbecile ignorance of the judge and the arrogance
of the attendants, men trembling and weeping over
the misfortunes brought upon them by unrighteous
judgment—the sight of all this produced a most painful impression upon my mind.

"God first created reason," say the Mussulmans,
but they rarely employ the faculty divine in the practical affairs of life. The best feature of the Turkish
Courts is, that the person who gains a suit must pay
the expenses. Should a witness be so far off his guard
as to answer, "I don't know," to any question, however
absurd, his testimony may at once be set aside. Ingenious, though irrelevant questions are often asked in
order to dispose of disagreeable testimony, as for instance, "Who married Adam and Eve?" to which the
witness usually replies, "I didn't go to the wedding."
Elsewhere, *bilmem* (I don't know) is ever upon the lips
of the faithful. Perjury is astonishingly prevalent
among the Turks. It is quite common to bring forward
a forged note with the two witnesses indispensable to
prove its validity. This the opponent does not deny,
but produces in turn a forged receipt for the sum in
dispute, with testimony to prove that the debt has been

paid. Red tape and pleadings are unknown to Turkish lawyers, and when the witnesses are absent, the defendant himself is sworn.

From the uneven plateau upon which Rustchuk is situated, we descended to the bridge of boats a short distance below the city. In the vicinity was a large Turkish camp from which troops were moving over to the opposite bank of the Danube to join Omer Pacha's army at Bukarest. The utmost activity prevailed. As in the narrow lanes of Rustchuk, I could only wonder at the great variety of races and costumes. Jews, Greeks, and Armenians mingled freely with Turks in flowing robes, and Bulgarians in sheepskin caps and barbarous garments. Here a company of the awkward Nizam preceded files of Egyptians, and there the dusky squadrons of the Bey of Tunis followed bands of Arnauts and mountaineers from Asia. Now the eye rested upon an Arab sheik with a group of dark warriors and dervishes, their faces full of fire and Asia, and then upon a Circassian chief as wild and untamed as the eagles upon his native rocks. French, English, Hungarian and Polish officers served to diversify the curious picture of nationalities.

The banks of the Danube have exhibited a strange array of life and customs from the east and the west, from the frozen north and the sultry south. The swarthy sons of the desert have here met the children of the frigid zone, and warriors from the Nile and the Niger,

from the banks of the Oxus and the Jaxartes, have seen
in the smoke of battle the Cossacks of the Volga and
the forced recruits from the Dniester and the Dwina.
When, oh when, shall the nations forget the dreadful art
of war, and the fair bosom of the earth no longer be stained with rivers of blood?

After a delay of two days, we left Rustchuk for
Giurgevo, on the opposite side of the Danube about
three miles below. We fell down the river some distance,
and then returned by the narrow channel between the
Wallachian shore and the islands of Mokan and Smurda.
On the latter, which were nearly covered with reeds
and thick undertrees, I noticed the remains of the fortifications abandoned by the Russians in July. Near them
fell Burke and Arnold in the insane attempt of the
Pacha to dislodge the Cossacks. Burke's servant, who
gave me an account of the battle, bore away the body
of his master, pierced with thirty-five wounds. The
brave fellow afterward received a decoration from
Omer Pacha. We landed near the old Genoese castle
of Giurgevo, and after breakfasting at a casino kept by
an Italian, I called upon the Commandant of the city.
He was a Hungarian officer, and treated me with great
politeness.

CHAPTER V.

LOW LIFE AMONG THE DACO-ROMANS.

"Now I believe in the Troglodytes of old
  Whereof Herodotus and Strabo told,
Since everywhere about these parts, in holes
Cunicular men I find, and human moles."

At 10 o'clock, we were all ready to set out for Bukarest, the capital of Wallachia, distant from Giurgevo five posts, or forty miles. The Khan-keeper who
had bargained for our conveyance conducted us to a
heavy, lumbering vehicle, to which were harnessed,
or rather tied with long ropes, ten small Bulgarian
horses. The French and Austrian Captains, a French
Colonel just from Varna, the Count, Aristias, and myself took seats in the rickety coach which must have
been imported from Vienna a quarter of a century
before. We were told that it was infinitely better
than the native Wallach conveyances, but I questioned
the possibility of reaching Bukarest in such a vehicle.
Three long-haired Wallachs, of the color of Choctaw
Indians, with slouched hats, and sheepskin *jubas* thrown
over their shoulders, mounted as many of the horses,
shouted at the top of their voices, and away we dashed

through the wide streets of Giurgevo. The latter are unpaved and radiate from an open space, in the centre of which stands the town hall, resembling a church rather than a public edifice.

On the outskirts of the town we rapidly approached what at first appeared like a well-pole, but turned out to be a kind of gateway at the outer barrier.

The *surrujus*, our horsemen, shouted again and brought us to a sudden halt. A man emerged from a hole in the ground and asked for our passports.

I was astonished.

Looking around I observed two or three small conical elevations resembling magnified ant-hills with a large hole by the side of each.

"What are these little mounds?" I inquired of Aristias.

"They are Wallach houses," he replied. "The peasants call them *Kolibes*. You will see them everywhere in the Danubian principalities."

"*Eh bien!* I understand: fuel is scarce on the Wallachian prairies and the Daco-Romans burrow into the bosom of mother Earth in order to enjoy her warmth!"

"*Oui, Monsieur!*"

The examination of the passports promised to be tedious, but was speedily cut short by dropping a couple of piastres into the hand of the pole-tender. The *surrujus* swung their long whips and the caval-

cade sped across the smooth plain as if a squadron of
Cossacks had been in close pursuit. The black, rich
soil was grown up with tall weeds and coarse prairie-
grass. During the first post we passed by only one
small field of Indian corn. An estate belonging to
Prince Milosh of Serbia, was pointed out to me in the
distance. The horses were kept upon a run, and in
a short time the *surrujus* reined up at a collection
of miserable huts named Frataschi, where the Russians
had made a stand the previous winter. Ten fresh
horses, caught from a large number that were feeding
upon the adjacent plain, were harnessed in. As we
advanced, the face of the country became more uneven.
Large tracts were grown up with brushwood, and here
and there we passed by small fields of wheat and
Indian corn. I noticed several places where the Russians had halted, the ashes of their camp fires and their
temporary huts of bushes still remaining. Now and.
then the *surrujus* apparently forgot themselves, thinking, perhaps, of the charms of a few dark-haired Wallachian maidens, whom we saw at the relays. The
horses would then fall into an easy gait, but the recol-
lection of the promised backsheesh soon dispelled these
rosy imaginings from the minds of our rustic horsemen,
when their wild shouts and gestures again sent us
wheeling over the prairie as before. We met a large
number of arabás, drawn by buffaloes, on their way
to Giurgevo. They were returning under Turkish

5

colors from the camp of Omer Pacha, whither they
had conveyed his baggage and military stores. It
was before them that the *surrujus* took occasion to
display, to our sore discomfort, their peculiar feats
of horsemanship. The Bulgarian drivers stopped their
arabás and looked with mute astonishment upon our
fleet little horses pawing the earth to escape the lashes
of the indomitable Wallachs.

The large Greek crosses set up along the road had
alone escaped mutilation by the Russians. One of
these rude monuments marked the place where Michael
the Brave, a Wallachian prince, once gained a great
victory over the Turks.

We halted an hour at the village of Kalougareni
for dinner. The khan was crowded with Wallachs in
Phrygian caps of sheepskin, and ragged gipsies. We
called for the best that the place could afford, but my
dinner consisted of a tough omelet and a crust of black
bread, washed down by a vile fluid that would pass for
vinegar in any other part of the world, but was paid
for as Wallachian wine.

Directly in front of the khan a gipsy was engaged
in slaughtering kids. Having cut the throat of one of
the animals and permitted it to bleed sufficiently, he
drew a cord tightly around its neck below the incision.
Then puncturing the skin on one of the fore legs and
placing his mouth over the opening, with a succession
of efforts he forced the air under the integument, and

to my surprise, inflated the kid to twice or three times its former size. This done, and the air confined by a string tied round the leg, he began to beat the animal vigorously with a rod. I did not understand the object of all this, but was informed by the butcher that the beating would make the kid's flesh more tender and delicate.

Many lands, many customs!

While the rest of the company loitered around the khan, Aristias and myself took a stroll through the village. Passing near the humble church I looked in for a moment. A kind of trial by jury was going on, under the direction of the *papa*, or village priest, assisted by three other persons appointed annually for that purpose.

A few of the peasants invited us to enter their rude cabins. The furniture was scanty, but I noticed in all a large wooden trough, used ordinarily as a cradle for the children, for a wash-tub on washing day, a kneading trough on baking day, and as an occasional receptacle for provisions.

The people were enjoying themselves with dancing and music, it being the holiday in honor of one of the Greek saints. These simple-hearted people are very kind to each other, as, indeed, the lowly are everywhere. There has existed from time immemorial in Moldo-Wallachia a charitable custom of aiding the poor, the newly married, the priests, or any family not possessed of cattle or horses. On the holidays the youths and

maidens, men, women, and children, assemble with their
teams to labor for such as cannot work themselves.
This pious labor is called *claca*. By this means the
family is supported, although they may be unable to
plough and sow. In too many instances, however, the
priests have availed themselves of the *claca* to impose
upon the benevolence of their parishioners, while this
pious and touching usage aided the Boyards in fastening
upon the peasants a cruel and odious servitude.

Bands of Wallachian *lautari* wander from village
to village, like the guzlars of Servia, or the old minstrels
of Western Europe, repeating the national traditions
which the people so much love, and accompanying their
recitals with simple and touching melodies—now as
wild as the battle songs of the mountain hyduks, and
now as soft and fresh as the idyls of the Wallach shepherds.

The Daco-Romans, though for the most part an
unlettered people, exhibit a remarkable appreciation of
nature and beauty, seeming, indeed, to dispel the
memory of their misfortunes by fairy thoughts and ideal
conceptions that astonish us, coming from so humble a
source. The Wallachs call the earth mother. A beautiful female is a fragment of the sun. The avalanche is
God's voice, the echoing mountains talk, and the milky
way is the path of slaves. "As good as the bosom of
a mother," is with them a frequent comparison, and
"silence is the devil's eye."

"When I chant," says Vidra, the heroine of a Wallach *doïna*, "when I chant my sweet song of woman, the waters move, the fir trees incline their heads, the hills tremble, and I awake in its retreat the terrible genius of the mountains."

"Miho," says another *doïna*, or popular song, "Miho plays upon his flute an air so passionate and tender that the mountains answer, the eagles pause in their flight to listen, the torrents suspend their course, and the glad stars shoot forth their brightest twinklings."

Here is the little doïna of "The Rose and the Sun:"—

"Daylight is breaking in the east. A young princess goes down from her garden to bathe in the silvery waves of the sea. The whiteness of her limbs shines through the light veil thrown over them, and gleams in the azure waves like the morning star in the blue heavens.

"She glides softly into the crystal flood.

"The sun stands still to look at her: he regards her with love, and forgets his duty. Once, twice, three times, night advances to extend her sceptre over the world. Three times she finds the sun standing still in his course. The Master of the universe hath transformed the princess into a rose. Behold why the rose hangs her head and blushes when the sun looks upon her."

In a filthy khan, where a number of gipsy children

were distorting their tawny limbs to "the wiry tinkling of a tamborine," we paused a few minutes to hear a peasant sing the famous ballad of *Miorita*, the substance of which I obtained from Aristias.

"Down the mountain side as beautiful as the entrance to Paradise, descend toward the valley three flocks of lambs, led by three young shepherds: one of them is an inhabitant of the plains of Moldavia, another is a Hungarian, and the third a mountaineer of Vrantchia.

"The Hungarian and the Vrantchian counsel together and resolve to slay their companion at the setting of the sun, for the reason that he is the richest; that he possesses a greater number of sheep with beautiful horns, horses better trained, and more vigorous dogs.

"For three days a little ewe lamb of white and silky wool, tastes not of the mountain grass. Its plaintive voice ceases not to be heard.

"'Gentle lamb, round and gentle, why, for three days, hath not thy voice ceased to be heard? Doth not the grass of the mountain please thee, or art thou ill? tell me, gentle pet.

"'Oh my beloved shepherd, lead thy flock down the mountain side. There, there, is grass for us and shelter for thee. Master, call without delay the bravest and strongest of thy dogs, for the Hungarian and the Mountaineer have resolved to slay at the setting of the sun.'

"'Pet of my flock, if I must perish, tell the Hungarian and the Mountaineer to bury me within the sheepfold, that I may always be with my cherished lambs, or near it, that I may always hear the voice of my faithful dogs.

"'Tell them this, and after I am buried, place thou at the head of my grave a small lute of beach wood for accents of love, a small lute of horn for sounds of harmony, a small lute of elder for notes of passion; and when the wind shall breathe through their tubes they will give forth dulcet and plaintive sounds, and suddenly my lambs will gather round my tomb and weep for me. But speak not to them of murder,—tell them only that I have married a beautiful queen, the bride of the world (death): Say to them that at the moment of our union a star disappeared, that the sun and the moon placed the crown upon my head, that I had for witnesses the pines and plane trees of the forests, for priests the high mountains, for an orchestra the birds, the myriad birds, and for torches the stars of the firmament.

"'And if thou shouldst ever meet a poor old mother with a woollen girdle, traversing the fields and the prairies, and with tearful eyes inquiring of every one, "Hast thou seen a young and beautiful shepherd of tall and graceful form? his face is white as the foam of milk; his locks of hair are like the plumage of the raven, and his eyes resemble the mulberry in the field:"

then, my pet, take pity upon her sorrow and tell her
simply that I have married the daughter of a king in a
country beautiful as the entrance to Paradise.

"'But be careful to say that at my nuptials a star
went out, that I had for witnesses the pines and the
plane trees of the forests, for priests the high mountains,
for an orchestra myriads of birds, and for torches the
stars of night.'"

We met a group of peasants armed with clubs and
rusty yataghans, and headed by a Wallach blowing
vigorously on a bagpipe. They were going to a betrothal, and my companion proposed that we should
follow. Among the Daco-Romans, asking in marriage,
betrothal, and the marriage ceremony itself, form curious dramas, intermingled with warlike contests, and
terminating, as among the ancient Romans, with the
semblance of forcibly carrying away the bride. Immediately after she has received the proposal of marriage the young man sends a number of messengers on
the errand of betrothal, like the company to which I
have alluded.

Arrived in front of the cottage of the parents,
the musician dropped his bagpipe, and addressed to
them, looking out of the door, the following senten-
tious speech:

"Our grandfathers, and the ancestors of our fathers,
going to the chase, and hunting in the woods, discovered the land which we inhabit, and which gives us

the enjoyment of its milk and honey. The honorable youth, Barbo Michael, following their example, also went forth to the chase among the forests and mountains, and discovered a doe, which timidly fled from his presence, and hid itself away. But the rest of us, following its tracks, have been led to this house. Give into our hands what we seek, or show us where is concealed the doe which we have pursued with so many fatigues and difficulties."

"It has not entered into this house," respond the parents.

The musician again employs all the resources of his eloquence, ornamenting his discourse with metaphors and allegories peculiar to the East.

The other messengers join in with him.

The parents bring the great-grandmother of the girl to the door, and ask—

"Is it she whom you seek?"

"No!"

The grandmother comes.

"Perhaps it is she?"

"No!"

The mother presents herself in turn.

The same response.

"Well, then, here she is!" say they, and at the same time bring forward an ugly old hag, in tatters.

"No! no! Our doe has golden hair, and the eyes of the sparrow-hawk; her teeth are rows of pearls, her ruby lips look like cherries, her bosom is firm and round, and her neck has the whiteness of the swan; more delicate than wax are her fingers, and the sun and the moon are not so radiant as her face."

At last, when violence is threatened, the parents lead out the young girl, dressed as richly as they can afford, in the costume of the country. The betrothal then takes place, and the maiden returns to her chamber, not to leave it again until her wedding-day.

When the happy time arrives, the young man, if he live in another village, sends in advance a number of men on horseback to announce his coming. These the parents and friends of the affianced waylay on the road, and carry home as prisoners. When questioned, they respond that they were the heralds sent to declare war, and that the army is coming up to storm the fortress. The parents then go forth with their prisoners to meet the betrothed, who presents himself with a suite more or less numerous. When the two parties are at no great distance from the dwelling of the maiden, they suddenly put spurs to their horses, and the first arrived receives an embroidered veil from the hands of the affianced.

Among the Wallachs, in Transylvania, the bride is closely veiled on her wedding-day, as well as the day previous. Whoever unveils her is entitled to a kiss, and, if she desire it, is obliged to make her a present.

These ceremonies finished, they all repair to the

village church. The bridegroom and the bride stand upon a carpet, over which pieces of money have been thrown, to show how little they make of riches in comparison with domestic happiness. As the *papa* (Greek priest) places the nuptial crown upon their foreheads, an assistant scatters walnuts and hazelnuts right and left, indicating thereby that the married ones have renounced for ever the amusements of childhood for objects of a more serious nature.

On their return home all sit down to dinner, the newly-married couple at the head of the table, and the father-in-law and witnesses on their right and left. Then one of the brothers, or, in his absence, one of the nearest relatives of the bridegroom, rises and addresses the latter in these terms:

"O, brother! you are arrived at the age of marriage and of joy. Our father grants you a place at his table, and unites you to-day happily with another family. But always cherish the memory of those to whom you owe the light, and ever retain your love for your brothers. Continue submissive in heart to the wishes of your parents, that you may obtain their benediction: honor your father, and always think how much your mother has suffered for you; for they have given you life. May the benediction of the Lord ever keep you in joy."

After the rustic repast, when the young man is on the point of retiring with his wife, the *votachel*, a person who carries a staff ornamented with flowers and ribbons behind the bride, rises, and, in the name of the latter, entreats pardon of her parents in the following words:

"When we ask ourselves, beloved parents, what constitutes the true happiness of life, we find that it consists in raising good families. This is conformable to nature and the Scriptures. The wife should be a fertile and abundant vine, and children surround the table like young olive plants. Behold your daughter arrived at the happy age of marriage, and about to quit your house to live in another, which God has chosen for her! She cannot find sighs and tears enough wherewith to beg your pardon; she has not sweet words of gratitude enough for all your tender, parental cares."

This address finished, the newly-married pair make their *adieux*, and kiss the hands of the bride's parents.

The latter respond, their eyes bathed in tears:

"Young man, in giving you our cherished daughter, we only submit to the decrees of Divine Providence. Love thy wife. And thou, dear child, whom we have raised in our arms, whom we have surrounded with our love, nourished with the milk of our tenderness, and fortified with our instruction, in permitting thee to be thus torn from our arms, we perform an agreeable, but at the same time a sorrowful duty. You have our blessings; go in peace."

The young bride then throws herself into the trembling arms of her parents.

At last the husband is about to depart with his wife, when her brothers place themselves in the doorway, with axes or daggers in their hands, and will not permit him to pass until he has bought their sister with a large present. After this she gets into a wagon, which carries the dower, having her mother-in-law on one side of her and a sister-in-law on the other. The husband follows on horseback, his companions shouting loudly on the way, and constantly firing their guns, for much joy.

But the husband has not yet reached the end of his tribulations. Scarcely has he arrived home when the bride's parents lay hold of their daughter, and confine her in a chamber. The friends of the young man demand her, with loud cries, and, no answer being given, burst through the door. The happy husband then snatches his wife from the arms of her parents. On the point of crossing the threshold, in commemoration of the seizure of the Sabine virgins, he takes her up in his arms, and carries her to the nuptial-chamber. This is the marriage ceremony among the Wallachs, as related by Voinesco. The Daco-Roman peasant never marries out of his own people. " When you take a wife," says he, " know her stock and origin."

There are also curious local customs pertaining to the marriage ceremony, many of which, however, have nearly lost their force. In some districts the nuptials are prolonged through eight days. In others, the church sextons are privileged to close the door against the bridal procession until they have received a present. The ring is exchanged three times. An iron crown is placed upon their heads to remind them of the possible hardships of matrimony. They pour wine into the same glass and throw pieces of bread behind their backs. In other localities one of the guests at the nuptial feast crows in imitation of a cock, to announce the coming of day. Cantemir speaks of a custom which is no longer in vogue in the Principalities. The jealous husband formerly made use of the same means to determine the virginity of his bride that are now employed among the Egyptians. The parents of the female visited their son-in-law on the third day. If she had been found virtuous they were received with great honor, and the proof of virginity joyously exhibited at the feast which ensued. If the husband had been disappointed, he at once summoned his relatives and took counsel. The parents, on their arrival, were harnessed to the meanest cart that could be found, and, under the jeers and lusty blows of the offended ones, were compelled to draw home their unfortunate daughter. No person dared to interfere. The husband retained the dower and received complete indemnity for all the expenses of the wedding.

At the little village of Padika, where the *surrujus*

halted a moment to pull the ears of his horses and give them water, groups of peasants were singing lustily in front of the khans. Aristias informed me that they were jubilant over the retreat of the Russians, and that their principal song was the "Chant of the Pruth," known to every Daco-Roman from the Carpathians to the Euxine.

"O Pruth! accursed river!
Mayest thou swell,
Like the deluge of troubled waters,
So that bank may not see bank,
Nor voice hear voice,
Nor eye meet eye,
Across thy vast extent.
When the clouds of locusts pass thee,
By that bank let them perish;
When the plague and pestilence pass thee,
In mid stream let them perish;
When our enemies pass thee,
By this bank let them perish.
And thou, O Pruth! proud of thy rushing flood,
Bear them, bear them all,
Down to the Danube, down to the sea,
Down to the gates of Hell!"

To the Daco-Roman the Pruth is the black-watered Cocytus separating flowery Roumania from a land of terrors. In their six different occupations of the Principalities, the Russians have usually seized upon the public chests, compelled the people to provision their

armies, and in more than one instance taxed them
heavily for the so-called "protection" of the Czar.
Famine and pestilence have generally followed these
invasions, and the Wallach peasants affirm that the
Russians have invariably brought with them hard
winters, inundations, swarms of locusts, the murrain,
and evils innumerable.

"How many remain of the 36,000 cattle which you
have drawn from the Principalities?" asked the Grand
Duke Michael of the Russian Commissariat-General,
during the occupation of 1828..

"Not a beef-steak for your Highness!" responded
the latter.

Thirty-six thousand more were ordered; they disappeared in the same manner, for enough was wasted and
peculated to feed ten armies.

In the terrible campaign of 1829 the Wallach
peasants were forced into the Russian service like
beasts of burden. Cossacks were to be seen driving
with the *knout* men and women loaded with provisions
and timber for the construction of bridges, or yoked to
wagons in place of horses and oxen.

At last they came to inform General Zoltonchin
that the supply of peasants had failed.

"Very well; then harness in the boyards," was the
reply.

Everywhere I saw the evidences of cruel war. We
were obliged to ford the river, as the Russians, in their

hasty retreat, had destroyed the bridges. Deserted villages and dwellings burned to the earth, cornfields and vineyards trampled to the ground, whole districts uninhabited save by wolfish dogs and flocks of carnivorous birds still feasting upon the carcasses of horses and of men exhumed from their shallow graves—these were among the blessings left by the Cossack hordes of the Czar to a land that otherwise would have smiled with peace and plenty.

Now oppressed by the Turks and the Russians, and then given over to the Phanariots, or to the still more tyrannical rule of the native Hospodars, the Moldo-Wallachs have been the worst governed people in the world. Alexander Sepuchano was the Nero of Moldavia. During his reign, in the sixteenth century, nothing but blood, tears, despair, and anathemas was seen and heard in the Principality. The highways were strewn with corpses of parents and children with hands and ears cut off, and unfortunates, whose eyes had been plucked out, wandered through the land. At last the Voïvode came to his deathbed.

"Pardon me," said he—having called to his side the great boyards, bishops, and the Archbishop Theophanus, "and take pity on my son! If I do not die, I make a vow to take the gown and go to Slatina in order to ask pardon of God for the past. Priests! when you see that death is approaching, cut off my hair, put on the black cap, and make a monk of me!"

A few hours afterward he was obeyed. His locks were cut off, and the monk's cap drawn upon his head. A candle burned at his feet, the image of the Virgin leaned upon his pillow, and over his body were extended the hair cloth and the priestly gown.

But he revived, and opening his haggard eyes, murmured in a blunt and savage tone—

"What signifies all this?"

"How dost thou feel, brother Paisir?" asked one of the monks present. At these words Alexander raised his head, and letting it fall again, cried with an accent of rage that seemed to defy death—

"Ah! if I recover, I shall make monks!"

The archbishop besought him to think of his approaching end.

"Hold thy tongue, impostor!" interrupted the Voïvode, his teeth chattering with the chills of death. Then, his eyes happening to fall upon his wife, he continued—

"I'll quarter her with her son! No, I am not a monk! I am dying of thirst! Water! water!"

At that moment Stroïca and Spancioc, two nobles who had escaped his fury, entered the door. The former handed the princess a cup into which the other turned a powder.

"Poison! poison!" cried Roxandra.

"Poison!" responded both.

"Choose between thy husband and thy son!"

Overwhelmed by this fatal alternative, Roxandra turned imploringly to the Archbishop.

"God pardon thee," said Theophanus; and the princess with a trembling hand offered the cup to the dying man.

The latter would not drink: his teeth were firmly set. Roxandra was about to let fall the cup when Spancioc snatched it from her hand.

Stroica drew his poniard.

"Go, princess!" said both; and while one, with his blade, pried open the jaws of the Voïvode, the other poured down the poison, saying—"Drink! drink! and thank Stroica and Spancioc!"

Alexander heard nothing more, but opening his eyes for the last time, he recognised the boyards. He died, as seemed proper, in rage and despair, "after having been all his life," says Thou, "an object of horror to his own subjects."

Basil, the Wolf, ruled over Moldavia near the middle of the 17th century. Some of the regulations in his celebrated code form a striking contrast to the laws of the Voïvode, whose death I have just described.

1. Whoever shall discover a treasure by means of sorcery, has no right to touch it: the whole belongs to the Voïvode.

2. The husband who will not call a physician when his wife is ill, or refuses to buy proper medicines for

her, shall lose, in case the wife dies, the income derived from her domains.

3. If a doctor shall declare that a wound is dangerous when it is not, he is to be believed in preference to a barber or a sorcerer.

4. Love, which resembles drunkenness and folly, mitigates guilt.

5. He who commits a fault under the influence of love shall not be punished according to the full measure of the law.

6. He who meets a female in the road, and prompted by love embraces her, shall not be punished.

7. Nobility also lessens the degree of guilt. Boyards shall neither be hung, empaled, nor condemned to the galleys or mines, but may be decapitated or banished from the country.

We crossed the Argisch at Kapatschini, and forded several other unimportant rivers that flow down from the Carpathians. The country became more fertile as we advanced. The plain was dotted with immense flocks of sheep, and the dusty road almost filled with droves of dun-colored cattle, in care of Turkish and Arab soldiers—bleating and horned holocausts for the 50,000 Ottomans encamped near Bucharest.

Towards sunset I saw in the distance the green tents of the Arabs, ten thousand of whom, in the light, half Oriental uniform of the Egyptian troops, had been sent from the banks of the Nile, to fight the battles of

the great padishah along the Danube. Their picturesque tents extended in long lines over the plain.
The dusky soldiers bore a brave and martial appearance. The cornfields adjoining the camp were un-
touched, showing in this respect a remarkable contrast
to the ravages of the Cossacks.

The sun was just sinking behind the distant Carpathians, as we passed under the shadow of an old Greek
monastery, near the barrier of Bukarest.   It was one
of those gloomy Byzantine castles scattered thickly
over Roumelia and the low Danubian countries, in
which Greek learning took refuge after the destruction
of the Eastern Empire, and where the works of the great
Attic writers were conned and preserved by pious old
monks, when even the existence of Athens was unknown to the western world. The day of their utility
has long since passed, and they are now the abodes of
ignorance, indolence, and impiety. As I rode by the
sombre piles, ivy-clad and crumbling in ruins, I often
thought that if their mysterious walls could be made to
speak, they would tell strange stories of crime, of romance, and of genuine piety.

Unmarried ladies of an uncertain age, I am informed, are scarcely to be found in the Danubian principalities. Wives are there taken in consideration of the
dower. The sons of wealthy families are sent out into
the world with scarcely a piastre, so as to give the
daughters fine establishments. It is considered highly

disgraceful to have the latter remain with their parents
beyond a certain age; and if all means fail to open the
way to matrimony, the unfortunate creature, who would
fain marry an earthly lord, is reluctantly compelled to
become the bride of heaven, and thenceforth remain
the inmate of a convent. Should there be several
daughters in a family, or at least more than can be
handsomely settled, one of them is condemned to
cloister life, even in childhood, since by this means a
comfortable subsistence is secured for life. Voluntarily
taking the veil is rare. The nuns belonging to Greek
convents by no means lead secluded lives. They inter-
change visits, make journeys, and, in fine, do almost as
they please: only church hours must be nominally observed, and on fast days no conversation be held with
males. As the Wallachs are the most dissolute people
in the world, many Magdalenes doubtless find their
way into these institutions.

Our passports were taken from us at the well-pole
gate, and after rattling for nearly half an hour over
corduroy roads and rough pavements, the *surrujus* set
us down at the Hôtel d'Europe. The furniture, cuisine,
language, dress—everything, was French. Having traversed Europe, I could have believed myself lodged
again in Paris.

Pietron, my servant, was an old Russian, whose
never-failing theme of conversation was Napoleon I.
Notwithstanding his Muscovite birth, he had spent

many years in the service of *Le Grand Empereur.* There were but few points of interest in Europe, or in the East, which Pietron had not visited; and his stories about the great generals and the great events of the last generation, as well as his racy anecdotes and personal adventures, I shall not soon forget.

CHAPTER VI.

CITY PLAGUES AND LAND PLAGUES.

"Dumbovitza, apa dulce,
   Quien? O, fea nu de mai duci."

"C'était le temple où les femmes Moldaves
   Servaient d'exemple aux hommes les plus braves."

WHILE descending the Danube, a fellow traveller informed me that Bukarest was a city of immense distances, boasting of more luxury than Paris or London. The jealous, slaveholding nobles do not allow an accurate census to be taken, but multiplying the number of houses in Bukarest by five, we have a population of 100,000 souls. Bukarest became the capital of Wallachia in the 17th century. The city covers almost as much ground as Paris. It is situated on the Dumbovitza, a little river that flows down from the Carpathians, and unites with the Argish a short distance below the city. According to a popular saying, embodied in the distich at the head of the chapter, they who have drunk of the sweet waters of the Dumbovitza, would fain linger along its banks. This may account for the frequent appearance of the Russians in Bukarest, but as the muddy and putrid stream is the very "mother of dead dogs," I avoided it as much as possible.

The only buildings in Bukarest worthy of particular mention, are the Khan of Manouk Bey, the Hospice of Brancovan, and the Hospital of Coltsa with its curious tower built in 1715 by the soldiers of Charles XII., but now falling in ruins. The "City of Peace," as the name Bukarest implies, is composed of palaces and hovels. It is merely an aggregation of large villages. Here are beautiful gardens tastefully laid out with walks and flowers, and there morasses submerged every spring, where frogs and lizards hold their uninterrupted concerts. The wretched streets paved with stones, or with logs placed crosswise, are deeply covered with mud in winter, and dust in summer.

In Bukarest legs are a luxury, and carriages, on the contrary, a necessity. Everybody who can afford it, rides; your servant takes a carriage when he goes on an errand. The carriage is, in fact, a mark of respectability, for to go on foot in Bukarest, is the same as going barefoot elsewhere. The streets are always full of vehicles, dashing through the mud or dust at a furious rate. Such is the mania for establishments of this kind, that you will often see a Boyard riding out in a gaudy carriage imported from Vienna, drawn by the poorest racks of Wallach blood, and mounted with gipsy postillions in rags. Here peasants clothed in sheepskins drive their cart-loads of wood and hay, and

6

there roll by magnificent equipages with superb horses
and gold-laced footmen in the picturesque Hungarian
or Albanian costume. Now we approach the palace
of a Boyard, which turns out to be a rickety, white-
washed pile, just ready to fall in ruins, and then cross
vast open spaces where half naked gipsies pitch their
tents, or leaning a few boards against a wall live under
them in the most abject misery. Never have I seen
luxury and want, beauty and deformity, pride and
poverty, brought into such glaring contrast. They exhibit a perfect carnival of civilization, just as freedom
and slavery always do, when existing side by side.
The Boyards are eager to possess constitutional liberty,
but their houses are filled with slaves. Intrigue takes
the place of politics: parties the place of nationality.
Bukarest resounds with an incessant concert of fêtes,
of sports, of the neighing of horses, the howlings of
dogs, and the weepings of slaves.* One sees here the
strangest blending of Asiatic costumes and European
manners. Many of the old Boyards dress in the rich
Turkish costume, excepting the tall, pear-shaped *cal-
pak*, which has taken the place of the graceful turban.
The ladies attire themselves in the latest modes of
Paris, while the servants who attend them sport the
flowing robes and brilliant colors of the Albanians.

Many of the Boyards have the well marked Greek
physiognomy. Their Phanariot education has rendered

* Vaillant.

them vain, suspicious, prodigal of words, bold in prosperity, and feeble in adversity. They are remarkably precocious, being men at fifteen and politicians at twenty. Though ambitious to improve themselves, and to develop their nationality, the Bukarestians are destitute of true devotion to principle, are without patriotism, without gratitude for services rendered, without union, and excessively proud of a nobility, which in most instances can boast of neither wealth, talent, nor parchment. They travel much in foreign lands, and hospitality is their chief virtue.

The Wallach ladies of Bukarest have the soft, light complexions and delicate features peculiar to Eastern beauty. "They are," says Vaillant, "sweet, spirituelle creatures, less passionate than Spaniards, less romanesque than the Germans, and less stiff than the English." The Daco-Roman women of rank think it well, perhaps, to be faithful to their husbands, but very improper, indeed, not to be faithful to their lovers. Marriage is greatly abused in Bukarest, and divorces are frequently granted for the most trivial cause. "Have you seen them dance the Mazourka ?" inquired a Wallach Boyard of the French traveller S. Mark Girardin.

"Yes !" replied the latter.

"Very well ! Marriages with us resemble not a little the Mazourka, in which our ladies take a turn with one cavalier and then with another." Many of them have at least as much judgment as their husbands, and are even more capable than they of great things.

In Bukarest there are also many Hungarian and Armenian families.

"What strikes one most in this town," says a Russian traveller,[*] "is the variety of costumes and countenances—a fresh type occurring every moment amidst this large population. The people here go about the town in a much more brisk and busy way than would be expected in the lower orders who have retained their oriental character. The artisans, porters, and working men of Bukarest do not seem to be afraid of work; but that which gives peculiar animation to this place is the immense number of Jews who inhabit it; active, insinuating, and never discouraged; they disseminate life and movement about them, for they spare neither trouble nor fatigue in the hope of obtaining the smallest recompense. Thus, the moment you perceive the broad brimmed hat and black rusty gown of a Jew, you may reckon upon commanding, if you please, the services of a clever, intelligent, indefatigable servant, ready to submit to everything— contempt or anger.

"You may, without fear, ask anything of this man: he will answer you in German, in Italian, perhaps in as many as four languages; and for a few piastres, putting aside all other business—his identity, his ingenuity, his

* Demidoff.

silence, his patience, his eloquence, his virtues, his vices, his soul, and his body—are all yours. And if for a momentary service on some slight occasion you have once employed an Israelite, do not imagine it an easy thing to get rid of him: he is henceforth yours, or rather you are his, he will never leave you; he will follow you at twenty paces' distance in the street, and at the distance of twenty paces divine what you want. He will take his seat upon the threshold of the house you have just entered, and on coming out you will meet his wily respectful glance, soliciting some command. He sleeps on your staircase, under your carriage, becomes the servant of your people, greets your dog in the streets, and is never absent from you an instant; though you may have repelled him with roughness twenty times, he still persists and perseveres in his attentions.

" After thus rebuffing him, you may find yourself at some particular moment, for some passing whim, in want of a Jew. Scarcely have you formed the wish than he appears, as though starting up from the earth, bending with his accustomed humility in that peculiar attitude of the Jews, which is neither erect nor bowed down, with submissive air and attentive ears. This moment is the triumph of the Jew. He has purchased it at the cost of forty-eight hours of incessant watching, fatigue, and humiliation. Scarcely have you spoken when your wishes are obeyed—obeyed with punctuality, acuteness, and respect; and when, after all this trouble

and self-denial, the poor bearded and tattered sprite
fingers his cherished recompense—that coin which he
has dogged, which he has invoked, whose humble valet
he has been for two days—you see by his grateful
expression that he commends you to the gracious protection of Abraham and Isaac, and that he is ready to
undergo the same trouble and fatigue for a smaller
reward."

The Jews in the Principalities number more than
100,000 souls. At the time of the destruction of Jerusalem by Titus, large numbers of them fled from Palestine and took refuge among the Dacians. It is supposed that Decebalus gave them Thalmun, not far from
the pass of the Red Tower, for a dwelling-place.

Certainly, the vilest specimens of the race of
Anubis ever encountered in my life, I have met with
in Wallachia. The shepherds, however, have excellent
dogs; "but the valuable qualities of these animals,"
says the same piquant writer, " scarcely counterbalance
the inconveniences which the unlimited propagation of
the canine race produces in the cities. Without men-
tioning the martyrdom of hearing at the approach of
night the doleful howlings and angry growlings of the
pack of dogs which invade the streets perfectly unmo-
lested, there is real danger in finding one's self alone
and without the defence of a good cudgel, exposed to
become the object of a chase, from which, even with
the nimbleness of a stag, it would be impossible to

escape in safety. The safest plan, if you are armed with a cudgel, is on the first demonstration of hostile intentions, to deal a good sounding blow on the nearest orator of the band. The remainder continue barking, but they do not approach near enough to bite."

A few years ago there are said to have been more than 30,000 dogs in Bukarest alone. Starved and infuriated by their long fasts, the scarred and haggard skeletons, with ears torn, and foaming at the mouth, fell without mercy upon the cur who had been so fortunate as to steal a bone, tripped up pedestrians in the streets, and sometimes tore each other to pieces in their ferocious onslaughts. At last the gipsies were called into requisition to rid the city of these four-footed plagues. Stimulated by the few paras offered for the carcase of every unmuzzled dog, they waged a war of extermination against the unfortunate quadrupeds, and dragged the victims in triumph through the streets.

The greatest plagues of the Moldo-Wallachs, especially those inhabiting the plains, are the clouds of locusts which at times make their appearance from the *steppes* of Southern Russia. They occasioned great ravages in the year 1825, but in 1828–9 visited the Principalities in such multitudes as to intercept for hours the light of the sun, destroying the crops, and in some localities, leaving not a trace of vegetation behind. A few hours sufficed to transform an oasis into a desert, for " every locust," says a Russian proverb, "bites like a horse, eats as voraciously as a wolf, and digests what it devours more easily and quickly than any other animal." The inhabitants believed that the day of judgment had come. The most superstitious of them would not assist in chasing the locusts into the rivers, or help drive them away, believing that they were sent by Providence, and therefore not to be disturbed. In other places as soon as a cloud of locusts made its appearance on the horizon, the people, men and women, young and old, ran together, and with hand-bells, guns, drums, and tin pans, set up such a din as not unfrequently to frighten away the winged scourges.

Smoke was found to be still more effective. When the locusts showed themselves in the air, immense bonfires of straw and prairie grass were kindled, which sometimes caused the locusts to change their direction, but occasionally brought about the very evil they were intended to prevent. The last ranks, neither seeing nor being sensible of the smoke, pushed those before them into the flames; the heaps of victims extinguished the fire, and the entire host then settled down upon the earth, and began their ravages.

It was calculated that one of these clouds of locusts, many square acres in extent and so thick as to shade the earth like a pavilion, contained at least one billion of insects. They turned from their course on either side to devastate the gardens in the cities and villages; and were so numerous as to cover the earth to the depth of several inches. At times they rested only for a moment, and then flew away to give place to myriads of others. They could be heard at a great distance, such was the noise made by their wings. The people were seized with terror upon their approach. The locusts fell upon the ground with the force of large hailstones; and it was necessary to close the doors, the windows, and even the chimneys against them. In some instances the inhabitants were successful in driving the swarms of insects into a lake, or into the sea. The advance guard would fall into the water and form small floating islands, upon which myriads upon myriads then settled down in solid living masses three feet in depth. If the wind blew from the shore they all perished: otherwise they sometimes managed to get back, and after drying their wings resumed their flight.

When the sun shines the locusts generally fly about two hundred feet above the earth, but in dark, cloudy weather so low that a man who is encountered by the locusts is obliged to turn his back upon them and stand firmly until they have passed. The young locusts show themselves in the first days of spring, and attain their full size, about two inches in length, in three or four weeks. The females deposit fifty to sixty eggs in the earth in the month of August, after which both males and females perish.

The gipsy population of the Danubian Principalities numbers about three hundred thousand souls, and pre-

sents the marked physical and mental characteristics
of the wandering Bohemians of Central Europe and
the *Gitanos* of Spain.

The ubiquity of the tsigan or gipsy race is one of
the most astonishing of ethnographical phenomena.
They pitch their tents on the southern slope of the
Himalayas, and along the Indus and the Tigris. I met
them under the shady palm-trees of the Nile, among
the mountains of Palestine and Syria, and in the shadow of the Acropolis of Athens. They are to be seen
in the streets of Jerusalem and Damascus; there is a
considerable colony of them near one of the gates of
Constantinople; and I found them scattered thickly
over eastern Europe, among the hills of Bulgaria, and
along the auriferous streams of Transylvania. They
dwell among the swarthy tribes of Nubia, Abyssinia,
and Soudan, as well as in the Barbary states. Families
of them have been seen in Siberia. They mingle with
the Turkomans of Independent Tartary, with the Les-
ghians of the Caucasus, and with the Ilihans of Persia.
Save China, Siam, and Japan, there is no part of Asia
in which the race of Roma cannot be found. In Russia they are scarcely less numerous than in Hungary,
which, after the Danubian Principalities, appears to be
the chosen land of the gipsies. In Italy, in Bohemia,
in the rural districts of France and England, and especially in the southern provinces of Spain, the traveller
can hardly avoid coming in contact with numerous

representatives of this singular people. In all of these lands, from the heaths of "merrie England" to the distant shores of the Ganges, we behold an exhibition of the same rustic life, and meet the tawny children of a race scattered over the earth, as fallen leaves are scattered by the winds of autumn.

That the gipsies should be so widely dispersed is marvellous, but by no means so singular as that they should have preserved, in so marked a manner, their distinguishing characteristics. In the Occident and in the Orient, exposed to the chilly winds of the north or basking in the sunny skies of the south, the gipsies wear the same dress, speak the same language, and pursue in the main the same nomadic and precarious life; and this, when the representatives of the race, now known under many different names, have been separated from each other by centuries, oceans, and continents.

Neither climate, time, nor example has exercised its usual influence upon them. They do not become darker under the burning sun of Africa, nor whiter among the pale-faced children of the North. The gipsies of to-day are essentially the same as their ancestors whose nomadic bands appeared centuries ago on the confines of Europe. They learn nothing from those among whom they live, and exist an unsocial and promiscuous multitude floating among the fixed dwellings of civilization. Not one of the waves of immigration,

which have, from time to time, swept into Europe from
Asia, resembles that of the gipsies.   Their history is
unique.   Conquered provinces and cities have imposed
their customs upon the conquerors; but the gipsies,
coming as simple pilgrims, have imposed nothing upon,
have borrowed nothing from, the nations among whom
they have encamped.

Dispersed more widely over the world than even the
tattered remnants of Israel, they are, ethnographically,
wandering vagabonds—politically, democrats of the
open air and good adventure—religiously, outward conformists to the faith of those among whom they move
and have a temporary being, but cherishing at the
same time a mysterious belief of their own.   Holding
themselves usually for Christians or Mohammedans,
they are without Christian or Mohammedan worship;
belonging to the great world, they are without worldly
possessions; and, making a pretence to patriarchal
customs, they lead a vagrant life, and exhibit the characteristics of carnivorous animals.

Scattered as they are, and recognising the temporal
and religious authority of those whose lands they inhabit, it is believed by persons who have studied them
and their institutions that they have a secret but extended political organization—nay, that there is a king
of the gipsies; but where he lives, where the court
of this monarch whose domains are wider than those
ruled over by spiritual Rome, is a question still open.

The impression prevails throughout the East of Europe that the gipsies are one of the lost tribes of Israel; that they are descendants of the Israelites who caused our Saviour to be crucified, and for that offence have been scattered over the earth, and condemned to personate the Wandering Jew.

The gipsies declare themselves to be of Egyptian origin, and are, in fact, termed Egyptians in many parts of Europe; hence also the name gipsy. Their features cannot be mistaken. They are of ordinary stature, robust, nervous, and manifest a Bedouin partiality for tent life, the open air, and the beautiful stars. The bronze complexion of the gipsies, their black hair, burning eyes, teeth of ivory whiteness, long chests and projecting shoulders suggest an Ethiopian origin. Their nakedness, relieved by a few scattering rags, a haughty and almost warlike gait, and the expressive gestures which characterize their conversation, also give them a striking resemblance to wandering Hottentots or Kaffirs. Theirs, however, is not an African origin. The language of the gipsies is a *melange* of the Sanscrit, with terminations and words borrowed from the people among whom they live. In Turkey, for instance, they employ the Sanscrit root, with the Turkish terminations. The many traces of patriarchal life which they exhibit —each nomadic band having its chief—their oriental language, and many things about them suggest eastern life, eastern origin, eastern institutions.

Though their manner of life, *sans feu et lieu*, is highly unfavorable for the retention of beauty, I have often seen females among them whose forms Phidias would have chosen for models. He has a conception of gipsy beauty, without beholding it, who has seen the fair damsels of Cyprus, where once stood the hundred Paphian altars burning incense to Venus; or watched, on the islands of the Ægean, or in the shady villages of Asia Minor, the timid daughters of Grecian blood collected round some gushing fountain, or bearing away its crystal wealth in graceful vases, as in the days of old.

In lower Hungary I heard a gipsy song, which is said to be a great favorite with the wandering children of Roma. The son of a nobleman became enamored of a beautiful gipsy girl, and married her. But she pined away in the castle of her lord. One day a band of gipsies encamped near by, and as she sat by the window, her ears caught the weird accents of her race. I give the words from Marmier.

> "The wind whistles over the heath,
> The moon dances upon the waves,
> The Gipsy lights his fire in the shade of the forest,
> Yuchza, Yuchza.
>
> Free is the eagle in the air,
> Free the salmon in the river,
> Free the deer in the forest—
> Freer the Gipsy where'er he wanders,
> Yuchza, Yuchza.

Maiden, wilt thou live in my dwelling?
I'll give thee garments of zibeline,
And necklaces of golden ducats.

The untamed horse leaves not the green prairie for a glittering harness,
The eagle leaves not the rocks of the mountain for a gilded cage,
The child of Roma leaves not the liberty of the fields for garments of
    zibeline and necklaces of golden ducats.

Maiden, wilt thou go with me?
I'll give thee pearls and diamonds,
I'll give thee a couch of purple,
I'll give thee a royal palace.

My pearls are my white teeth,
My diamonds are my black eyes that shine like the lightning,
My couch is the green Earth,
My palace the world,
Yuchza, Yuchza.

Free is the eagle in the air,
Free the salmon in the river,
Free the deer in the forest,
Freer the Gipsy where'er he wanders,
Yuchza, Yuchza."

When the nobleman returned he found his castle desolate. The gipsy bride had flown, to return to the romantic life of her people.

Gipsy bands first appeared in Moldavia in the year 1417, and in a short time the race became widely disseminated over Europe. In the Danubian Principalities they are speedily reduced to the condition of slavery, not as prisoners of war, nor as the debtors of the wealthy

Boyards, but by the right of the stronger; and the few
efforts made to ameliorate their pitiable condition have
thus far been attended with but little success.

The possession of the 250,000 gipsy slaves now held
in Moldavia and Wallachia is about equally divided
between the governments of the respective Principalities and private individuals. The Crown Gipsies are
subdivided into four classes. Some of them are employed in washing the river sands for gold. Others
labor as smiths, make wooden spoons, or wander from
village to village with bears which they have taught
to dance; and others still pay a small tribute, and lead
the lives of vagabonds.

The gipsies held as private property belong either
to the monasteries or to private individuals.

In 1844 a law was passed, manumitting the slaves
which belonged to the government and the monasteries,
but has not been carried into execution.

The gipsies belonging to private individuals have
fixed dwellings, their position corresponding nearly to
that of the slaves in our own country. They are, for
the most part, the house and field servants of the
wealthy Boyard families. From being constantly
brought in contact with their masters, they have lost
many of the distinctive characteristics of the gipsy
race. So completely have the *vatrassi* forgotten the
language and peculiar customs of their nomadic brethren, that it is difficult to distinguish them from the

Wallachian peasantry. Some of them live in villages, engaged in agriculture, or serving as masons, tailors, and shoemakers; but the greater part do service in the city palaces of the Boyards. The influence of this hateful institution upon both the master and the slave must be everywhere essentially the same. Families are broken up, virtue disregarded, marriage dishonored, humanity insulted and wronged in Wallachia and Moldavia, the same as in other slave-holding countries. The bastinado upon the soles of the feet, the latter elevated, so that merely the head and shoulders of the sufferer rested on the ground, was formerly the ordinary mode of punishment for the slaves. The lash, spiked collar, and close confinement are now employed. In Bukarest it is a common thing to hear that this or that Boyard has murdered one or more slaves. Gipsy blood flows in the veins of the best Boyard families. Able-bodied males can be purchased for less than $100. Females, however, are usually much more expensive, their value depending upon their youth and natural charms. No thought or attention is paid to the education of the slaves; and so complete is the authority of the Boyards over these human chattels, that the government officers are not allowed to enumerate them in the census. This unlimited authority of ownership, the entire absence of instruction, and the cheapness of the article, are evidently improvements upon the system as it exists in the Southern States. But in

Eastern Europe there are no bloodhounds—no fugitive Slave Laws. Even Austria, with all her political sins, unbinds the chains of the slave, and makes of the serf a freeman. Before the occupation of the Danubian Principalities, thousands of Wallachian gipsies were under the protection of the Austrian Consulate at Bukarest, and since that event they have not failed to protect the unfortunate slaves from the cruelty and rapacity of their Boyard masters. A movement is now on foot to emancipate the gipsy slaves in Moldavia, but, owing to the disordered condition of the Principalities, little good is to be expected from that quarter.

CHAPTER VII.

THE DACO-ROMANS.

"Thracians who howl around an infant's birth,
And give their funeral hours to songs and mirth."

" Mare-milking Scythians living in wagons."

IN the *orbis terrarum* of the ancients, all that immense region which lies between the Volga and the Danube, was regarded as a part of Scythia, whose rude tribes first became known after the campaign of Darius Hystaspes. The Dacæ and the Getæ, who were usually termed Scythians, and whose laws, language, and customs were the same, belonged to the great Sarmatian family inhabiting the region of the Oxus and Jaxartes. Impelled to nomadic life by a love of adventure, and closely pursued by the Alans, they migrated into Europe in the fourth century before the Christian era, and gave the name of Sarmatia to the vast region which they there inhabited. After settling in Europe, the Sarmatians appear to have made some progress in civilization. Antiquity boasts of the simplicity of their customs, their attachment to pastoral life, and hatred of foreign domination. Zamolxis, a disciple of Pythagoras, became their lawgiver, and after his death their god.

Alexander, in pushing his conquests northward, met with a most obstinate resistance from the Dacian king, Sarmis. They were ultimately subdued, however, by the conqueror of the world, and after his death, Dacia, with Thrace, fell to the share of Lysimachus. To the latter the Dacæ were unwilling to submit, and in attempting to bring them under his authority, Lysima-chus himself was drawn into an ambush on the Scythian plains; and his entire army, when on the point of perish-ing with thirst, fell into the hands of the enemy. They relate that Lysimachus was set at liberty, and from a feeling of gratitude married the daughter of the barbaric king. It is more probable, however, that he was ran-somed with gold.

From this time the history of the Dacæ is quite obscure, until 50 B. C., when they chose Barabestes for their leader, and under him carried their conquests to the sources of the Drave. The successes of the Dacian chieftain rendering it necessary to check his career, Octavianus Augustus marched against him, but having been wounded in Dalmatia, intrusted the legions to Statilius Taurus. Barabestes promised to co-operate with Anthony, but was slain by his own people, so jealous were they of the Roman power. When Crassus was sent against the Dacians they chose Cotyson for their king, who fell in battle, after having proved so dangerous an enemy to the Emperor Augustus, that the latter wished to make an ally of the barbarian by receiving his daughter in marriage.

In the long interval to the reign of Domitian we hear but little of the Dacæ, except that both Tiberius and Titius Cato made unsuccessful expeditions against them. During the reign of Domitian, Durus, the Dacian king, led his army across the Danube, and overcame the Romans in a pitched battle, in which Appius Sabinus lost his life. After waging a long and terrible war against the Romans, Durus resigned his power in favor of Decebalus, who, in connexion with the king of the Parthians and the Sarmatians, carried his arms so far into the Roman empire that Domitian was compelled to purchase peace by the payment of an annual tribute.

The Dacian kings were chosen from among the people, but when elected, their power was absolute. Decebalus owed his elevation to his valor and his intense hatred of the Romans. Ambitious of glory and jealous of the fame of Durus, he resolved to continue the war which the latter had begun. All, however, appeared to be lost at Talpa. Defeated and closely pursued by Julianus, the lieutenant of Domitian, he caused an immense number of trees to be cut down, and the tall stumps to be clothed so as to give them the appearance of Dacian soldiers. The stratagem succeeded, and the Romans gave over the pursuit. Decebalus speedily revenged himself upon his enemies, and in addition to

the tribute imposed upon Domitian, obliged him to
send the most skilful artisans in Rome to instruct his
people and fortify his cities.

Trajan mounted the imperial throne in the year 98,
and assumed the reins of government with a degree of
energy unknown to his immediate predecessors. In less
than two years he was at the head of the legions attempting to recover what Rome had already lost, and
if possible to free her for ever from the barbarians of the
North.

When the messengers of the Dacian king presented
themselves for the usual tribute—"Go," said he, "to
your master, and tell him that I give not money, but
arms." Both sides prepared for the struggle. The
Dacæ were the first great swarm from the northern
hive, and the imperial eagles had, thus far in their
course of conquest, encountered no enemies so fierce
and formidable. They preferred death to subjugation,
and believed that Rome, already tributary, would soon
hear within her walls the tramp of their barbaric
legions.

Danger as well as ambition induced Trajan to direct
the campaign in person. His march lay through Hungary, the ancient Pannonia, across the Theiss, and along
the valley of the Maros to Sarmisegethusa, the stronghold of Decebalus. With some difficulty the Emperor
brought the barbarians to a pitched battle near Thorda,
in Transylvania. The Dacæ were entirely routed.

They retreated to their capital, and to this day the Wallachian peasant points to the cross fields of Thorda as the "prat de Trajan," or Trajan's field.

According to the Moldavian traditions, Decebalus first encountered the Romans in Mœsia, and after a signal defeat, was forced to recross the Danube. The following year Trajan carried the war into Dacia, and with such sanguinary vigor that on one occasion he was obliged to use the greater part of his wardrobe in supplying bandages for the wounded. Decebalus, humiliated by successive defeats, repaired at last to the Roman camp, and sued for peace. This was granted on condition of surrendering all his fortified posts and instruments of war into the hands of the Romans.

The campaign having thus terminated, Trajan left a strong garrison in Sarmisegethusa, and returned to Rome. The haughty spirit of Decebalus could not long endure subjection. Regardless of his oath to the Emperor, he secretly reorganized the Dacæ, put the Roman garrisons to the sword, constructed new fortifications and implements of war, and attacked the Jazyges, the allies of the Romans. Trajan again placed himself at the head of the legions in order to reduce the stubborn Dacæ to a complete state of subjection, or exterminate them altogether. The Emperor was accompanied by his nephew Hadrian. Having reached the Danube by a shorter route than in the previous campaign, he wintered in Mœsia, and spent the following summer in erecting the bridge below the Iron Gate to which I have already alluded.

These stupendous preparations struck terror into the hearts of the barbarians. Decebalus offered and even sued for peace, but his proposals were rejected. He then attempted to enlist the kindred nations against the Romans. Amazed at the splendid achievements of Trajan, none would consent to engage in a cause which promised so little to the Dacian king.

The courage and genius of Decebalus rose in proportion to the emergency. While the Emperor was spanning the Danube he fortified his camp near the Iron Gate with a triple wall, which, however, crumbled before the massive engines of the Romans.

It soon became evident to both parties that they were engaged in a war of extermination. No quarter was asked, and none was given. The Romans who fell into the hands of the barbarians were subjected to the most inhuman tortures, the women and children even urging the rough soldiers to greater cruelty, and staining their own white arms with the blood of their enemies.

What Decebalus could not attain by force he attempted to accomplish by stratagem. Secret emissaries were sent to assassinate Trajan, but failed in the bloody purpose. Messengers from Decebalus at last announced his determination to surrender, and requested that Longinus, the friend of the Emperor, might be sent to his camp to impose the terms of peace.

No sooner was this complied with than the treacherous king murdered him in cold blood. Trajan swore by the twelve gods of Rome that he would avenge her son, and exterminate the Dacæ for ever. He had shared the dangers of the common soldiery, and even given his linen to bandage their wounds; now he would yield up his life for Longinus and the glory of Rome. Ambition and revenge incited the Romans to blood and carnage: patriotism and despair, the most powerful motives to action, urged the barbarians to the unequal conflict.

Slowly Decebalus retreated towards his capital, disputing every inch of soil with determined vigor. The Dacæ, as if wishing to hasten their own destruction by exasperating their enemies, suspended the body of Longinus from the walls of Sarmisegethusa in full view of the Roman cohorts. The siege of the ill-fated city was one of the most remarkable in ancient times. We can only regret that no Sallust or Livy has given us the particulars of a defence as heroic as that of Carthage, and more dreadful in its results than the fall of Saragossa. Barbarian courage and stratagem could not successfully withstand the well organized operations of the besieging army. The walls of Sarmisegethusa trembled and fell before the terrible engines of destruction brought to bear upon them.

7

After a long and bloody assault the Romans entered
the city to find it inhabited mainly by the dead.
Neither war, nor famine, nor pestilence had broken
the spirit of the besieged. Women had emulated men
in combat and in heroic endurance. The Roman soldiers beheld with amazement the dreadful spectacle
exhibited within the city walls. The few survivors
were put to the sword, or escaped to the mountains.
The fate of Longinus was reserved for Decebalus, but,
rather than fall into the hands of the victors, he plunged
a dagger into his breast, and died as he had lived an
implacable enemy of Rome. Many of his brave companions also chose to die by their own hands rather
than be led in triumph down the Sacred Way. Vicilis,
the secretary of Decebalus, saved his life by discover-
ing to Trajan the immense treasures which his master
had concealed in the bed of a river.

The city was razed to the dust. As Scipio had
destroyed Carthage, Licinius Corinth, and Titus Jerusalem, so did Trajan Sarmisegethusa. The other Dacian cities experienced the fate of the capital. The
Romans pursued the work of destruction even beyond
the banks of the Dniester. Trajan had sworn to exterminate the Dacæ, and at the close of the war, 106
A.D., all that remained of the haughty nation were a
few refugees in the wilds of the Carpathians. In his
oration to the Senate he declared, "I alone have dared
to attack the inhabitants of the Danube; I have anni-

hilated the nation of the Dacæ, and that in less than five years."

Next to Hannibal, Decebalus was the most dangerous enemy of Rome; and had there been no Trajan on the throne of the Cæsars, the standards of the Dacian king might have floated above the walls of the Eternal City.

Few of her enemies, indeed, so little deserved the name of barbarian as Decebalus. S. Mark Girardin says of him, that he invited to his kingdom artists and savans from every part of the civilized world. Caninius selected the conquest of Dacia as the subject of a heroic poem, and Pliny the Younger, in a congratulatory letter to his friend upon the excellence of his choice, wrote :—

"No subject is more appropriate or more poetical. You will have to describe long canals dug in unknown countries, immense bridges constructed for the first time over wide rivers and impetuous torrents, camps pitched among mountains never before trod by civilized men, and a king who was forced to flee, to die—but who died the death of a hero."

All of the immense region between the Theiss and the Euxine, the Dniester and the Danube, was converted into a Roman province, and Moldavia and Wallachia became known on the chart of the empire as Dacia Transalpina.

While Apollodorus of Damascus was wreathing

the conquest of Dacia upon the slender column which Trajan erected between the Capitol and the Quirinal Hill, so that the visitor of to-day may trace upon its well sculptured tablets the fortresses, arms, and costumes of the fallen people, the emperor conceived the idea of making Dacia the defence of Italy, and the garden of Europe. Rome was at that time at the very zenith of her power; and though there was little to invite the march of the legions farther north, it was hoped that Dacia would prove an effective bulwark against the Huns, whose countless hordes were then approaching, and the fame of whose deeds had already reached the imperial city.

The mineral wealth of Dacia, rendering her, indeed, the *El dorado* of the East, and the astonishing richness of the soil, attracted thither thousands of colonists from the Roman world. Eutropius says that Trajan sent thither countless multitudes of men for the purpose of cultivating the land, and building and inhabiting cities.

Another and a more important cause also occasioned a vast emigration from Italy.

Already, within the first half-dozen years of the Christian era, great scarcity had begun to be experienced at Rome. More than two hundred thousand paupers were fed from the public magazines, and, according to Suetonius, the Emperor Augustus compelled eighty thousand persons to leave the city, and seek a livelihood in the country or in the distant provinces.

Rome and all Italy became dependent upon the importation of corn from abroad, especially from Africa.

The price of provisions greatly advanced after the destruction of the city by Nero, so that peacocks, which were in common use on the tables of the patricians, were sold in the market-place for two hundred and fifty denarii,* while a pair of the meanest plebeian shoes cost no less than two-fifths of the same sum. A pound of meat brought eight denarii, and for less than two the barber put not his razor to the Roman chin. Great public festivals were as characteristic of Roman life as were the *Jul* feasts among the nations of ancient Germany, and were continued down to a late period of the empire. Two hundred thousand citizens were frequently invited at once, and while, in the time of Augustus, the entertainment of each guest cost the state but ten denarii, the same cost, in the time of Commodus, nearly seventy times as much.

But the provinces of Italy, though vieing with the most favored parts of Europe in fertility and natural wealth, were totally unable to sustain the efflux of population from Rome. The cause of this lay in the wretched system of agriculture pursued by the Romans in consequence of a vital defect in their social system. Already, in the year 92, Domitian had ordered that no more vineyards should be planted, and that half of those

* The denarius was worth about sixteen cents.

then grown should be destroyed, in order to make way
for the fields of corn.

Abundant experience had proved that, to develop
the agricultural resources of a state to the utmost extent,
the land must be divided into small estates, the cultivators of which have a greater or less interest in the
soil upon which they labor. Troops of slaves, pining
for the liberty which they or their ancestors had enjoyed
in the provinces overrun by the Roman legions, and
worked by cruel masters of plebeian blood, naturally
took but little care in cultivating the estates along the
Tiber and the Po, whose patrician owners were acting
as questors or proconsuls in distant parts of the empire,
or lounged away the long Italian summers in country
villas, to return with more zest during the months of
winter to the excitements of the forum and the gladia-
torial exhibitions, where were wont to assemble the
pride and wealth of the Eternal City.

This social evil increased to a remarkable extent.
It was decreed that any person might cultivate unoc-
cupied land, but notwithstanding this wise regulation,
vast tracts remained unsown almost in sight of the walls
of Rome. Wealth accumulated in the imperial city,
and, while Rome grew more opulent, Italy became im-
poverished. Many of the artisans and free citizens
emigrated, but some of those who remained acquired
by speculation enormous wealth. Shoemakers rivalled
patricians in display, and Martial mentions a barber,

Cyrenias, who possessed consular estates. It was in vain that Cæsar ordered that half of the shepherds should ·be freemen. In the Senate S. Severus moved that the slaves should be designated by their dress, but his motion was lost on the ground that they far outnumbered the freemen, and that, by wearing a badge, they would become conscious of their strength. Pliny also complained that the land was for the most part inhabited by beggars and slaves. Hence, when the rich plains of Dacia were thrown open to the starving millions of Italy, paupers were not only attracted thither by thousands, but even patricians of proconsular rank, whose slaves were numbered by hundreds, and in many cases by thousands, were seen moving along Trajan's Way.

Fair Italy seemed to have been transported to the region of the Ister. Sarmisegethusa rose from her ruins and received the name of Ulpia Trajana. Forests disappeared, and the vast prairies and marshes of Dacia were soon covered with cultivated fields and growing hamlets. Vineyards purpled the Dacian hills; and sumptuous villas, modelled after those of Italy, became the seats of culture and opulence. Roman "ways," such as no other people ever built, and whose remains still attest their ancient magnificence. furrowed the land, serving as arteries of commerce, and military roads for the legions. Cities, deemed worthy of receiving prefects and magistrates from home, sprung up as if by enchantment along the

lower Danube. The gods of the Eternal City, usurp-
ing the seats of the Sarmatian divinities, took up their
residence in splendid temples. Beautiful statues, the
creations of Grecian and Roman art, replaced the
shapeless simulacra of the Dacian deities, and the
polytheism of the unlettered pagan readily gave way
to the pantheism of his more civilized conqueror.
After all, there was but a slight difference between
Phoran and Jupiter, Mithra and Mars, Belen and
Apollo. Men everywhere resemble each other, and
men represent their gods in themselves.

Where the Romans conquered there they lived,
there reproduced Italy and Rome. Such was the
result of their victories, " bearing the sword in one hand
and the torch of civilization in the other."

The fall of Dacia, however, marked the culminating
point of Roman dominion, as well as of Roman greatness. . It was in that distant province that the tide of
empire first turned, and flowed back toward the imperial city. There, stubborn Terminus for the first time
yielded and retired. Wave after wave of barbarism
came rushing down from the north, each extending
further than the last, until Rome herself was submerged.

Hadrian, jealous of the fame of Trajan, and envious
of the architect who had immortalized the triumphs of·
his master in marble, destroyed the bridge across the
Danube only eighteen years after its erection. The

Romans, however, held possession of Dacia many years afterwards. Under Antoninus Philosophus alone numerous representatives of sixteen nations are said to have settled in their midst. Down to the year 212 the colonists in Dacia were acknowledged as Roman citizens. In 257 A.D., the Goths overran the country, and thirteen years later the Emperor Aurelian entirely withdrew the legions from the left bank of the Danube. Many thousands of the colonists settled in Mœsia, while others took refuge among the Carpathians. The power of the Sarmatian tribes was broken by the irruption of the Goths, the Vandals, and other Teutonic races. They in turn disappeared before the Huns, while the latter were succeeded by the Gepidæ and the Lombards. The Slavic races first made their appearance on the lower Danube in the fifth century of our era. In 812, the Bulgarians, under Crumus, planted their standards before the walls of Byzantium.

As early as the beginning of the ninth century the Magyars appeared west of the Ural mountains and the Volga. The Ukraine fell into their hands, and the Slaves were obliged to give way before the two hundred thousand Asiatic warriors, who formed the van of the conquering host. Arpad became the founder of a dynasty, and before the close of the ninth century clouds of Magyar cavalry watered their horses on the banks of the Sereth and the Danube. They soon made themselves masters of Dacia and Pannonia. Transyl-

7*

vania was placed under the government of a Palatine, and compelled to defend the eastern boundary of the kingdom, while the adventurous Magyars were intent upon carrying their conquests further to the west.

I have thus merely given the names of some of the barbarous tribes which swarmed in Eastern Europe, and cannot proceed without referring to a few of their peculiarities. Until the time of Sarmis, the Scythians do not appear to have been acquainted with the art of building houses, even in the simplest form. Besides their wagons, the sound of whose wheels rolling on the frozen Danube, Ovid enumerated among his afflictions, they dwelt in the recesses of the forests and the caves of the mountains. Scorning to touch the plough, they knew nothing of agriculture, and subsisted chiefly upon the milk and flesh of their herds. Some of the Scythian tribes cut off the thumbs of their prisoners. The Avars yoked their women to the wagons in which their nomadic bands were accustomed to wander from plain to plain. The Huns mutilated the faces of their new-born infants, in order that they might become acquainted with iron sooner than with the maternal milk.

Among the Huns and the Magyars the chiefs took the lead in the battles and migrations, but were in no other respect elevated above their companions. Any warrior might bring them before the ancients of the people for judgment. The latter were selected on account of their deeds in war and skill in council.

The Alans lived in wagons. In these rude structures, with covers woven from the twigs of trees, they traversed the steppes of Asia and Europe. There, their children were born and nourished, and in them the women pursued their peaceful occupations. Wherever they wandered, there was their home, their country. When they halted, the wagons were disposed in an immense circle, within which they guarded the flocks and herds.

From youth the Alans were accustomed to equestrian exercise. It was disgraceful to go on foot. So fond of their horses were they, that the rider and the steed often partook of the same repast. When the pastures and forages were exhausted in one locality, the rolling city moved to another.

With the Alans war was equally a pleasure and a pursuit. To die of old age, or from accident, was the greatest of misfortunes. The survivors envied the fate of such as fell in combat. There was something wild and fearful in the appearance of the light-haired squadrons, as, armed with rude shields and spears, they rushed into the conflict, the earth quaking beneath the hoofs of their horses. Skilled in stratagem, the plan of their attack was as secret as the onset was terrible. For trophies, they covered their steeds with skins of the enemies they had slain in battle.

Slavery was not permitted among them, and after a time the prisoners were set free. Hospitality was a sacred duty. The stranger passed from family to family, each one accountable to the last for the safety of the guest, until he reached his destination. They had neither temples nor altars, but in imitation of the neighboring nations set up a spear in the earth, and worshipped it as the emblem of the god of war. Among some of the barbarians, wives were obliged to slay themselves upon the graves of their husbands.

The time had come for the Daco-Romans to play a more conspicuous part in the history of eastern Europe. In 1290 Rudolph the Black, or *Radu Negru*, as he is called in the Roumanian dialect, with a large band of faithful adherents, departed for the last time from the Carpathians, and descending towards the Danube, took possession of Tergovist and the adjacent plain. He afterwards chose Argisch for his residence, and adopted the Roman eagle and the cross as the escutcheon of the Principality. Rudolph styled himself, by the grace of God, Prince of all Roumania and Duke of Amlosh. He divided the land among his favorite chiefs, and formed a senate, consisting of twelve persons, to assist in its government. The boundaries of the Principality were soon extended from the Carpathians to the Danube.

Another band of Daco-Romans had found a secure retreat among the head waters of the Theiss. But, in 1359, about seventy years after the foundation of Wallachia, and one year before Murad made Adrianople the capital of the Ottoman empire in Europe, Bogden Dragosch, with a large band of his countrymen, left his adopted home, and recrossed the Carpathians. They descended among the Tartar tribes, and founded a new Principality, which was first named after their chief, but afterwards became known as Moldavia, from one of its principal rivers. From the circumstance of the chief having found a buffalo's skull in the river Theiss, he adopted that as the escutcheon of the new state. The government of the Principality differed but little in form from that of Wallachia. In both, the nobles, from whom the present Boyards are descended, soon became feudal lords. Originally the peasants were allowed to possess land, and the prisoners of war became slaves. Both of these classes, however, were reduced to the same level in the course of one or two generations.

The Principality founded by Dragosch soon acquired more than its present extent of territory. Its princes, like those of Wallachia, were elective.

From the 13th to the 16th century was by far the most brilliant period in the history of the Principalities. Many useful institutions were founded, and the land was enriched by trade and industry.

The Boyards formed, in time, an aristocratic republic, the same as in republican Poland, with the difference only that in the Principalities they did not possess the right of life and death over the peasants. Rarely faithful to the Princes, or faithful to each other, they were perpetually engaged in factions which enervated the strength of the governments, and even threatened their existence. Third parties were frequently called in as mediators, and the Turks did not fail to make use of the opportunity thus afforded to extend their power north of the Danube.*

Compared with the European States, Moldavia is almost as large as the kingdom of Greece, and contains a greater number of inhabitants, while Wallachia is considerably larger than Holland and Belgium together. Bukarest has the same latitude as the capital of Maine, and Yassy, the chief city of Moldavia, is further north than Quebec.

The people may be divided into two great classes—first, taxable persons, and, second, such as are exempt from taxation. To the latter belong the Boyards, numbering about two thousand, who alone enjoy political rights, the clergy, privileged families, and servants. The artisans, licensed traders, and peasants alone bear the heavy burdens of the state. The condition of the peasants is but little removed from that of slaves.

Though among the most thinly settled portions of Europe, the Danubian Principalities have a population of 4,000,000 souls, of whom 2,500,000 belong to Wal-

---

* Vide Historical Sketch of the Danubian Principalities under the Phanariots and in later times.—Zallony.

lachia, and the remainder to Moldavia. The Roumani, however, are not confined to the Principalities, but are scattered through Transylvania, Bessarabia, and the Bukovania numbering in all · more than 7,000,000 people. They have preserved in an eminent degree the physical type and the customs of their ancestors, the Roman colonists who settled in Dacia and absorbed the remnant of the haughty nation conquered by Trajan.

The Daco-Romans call their land *Zara Roumanesca*, the Roman country, and their language *Limba Roumanesca*, the Roman tongue. Trajan is the Romulus of Dacia. There are souvenirs of him everywhere, in the traditions as well as in the superstitions of the people. The Milky Way is "Trajan's Way," the mountain peak is his watch-tower. The elevated forehead, the aquiline nose, the full, dark, melancholy eye, the southern tinge, all tell of the old Roman, though the peasant be clothed in sheepskins, and knows not the names of the heroes from whom he may have descended.

Ask the simplest peasant who he is, and he will answer, "*Eo sum Rouman.*" The common saying, *La un Rouman dece Sassi*, one Rouman is worth ten Saxons, shows the estimation in which these ignorant people hold themselves in comparison with their neighbors.

The *Limba Romanesca* is the eldest daughter of the

Latin tongue, and differs not essentially from the vulgar Latin, the *lingua rustica*, of the time of Trajan.   The Daco-Romans have adopted many Slavic and Turkish words, yet their dialect so nearly resembles the Italian that I could make myself understood among them. One of the Austrian regiments stationed in Bukarest during my visit was from Italy, and these mutual descendants of the ancient Romans—though separated from each other more than seventeen centuries—conversed together without difficulty, and as far as permitted, fraternized with each other.   But how changed! Their ancestors were the conquering Romans; the Italians bend the knee to an Austrian tyrant who bears the name of Cæsar without any of his virtues; the Daco-Romans are the ready slaves of any despot who may wish to extend over them the iron arm of his power.   The latter dream of Pan-Romanism, or a union of all the Roumanian race, but their nationality, their soul, their virtues, have been crushed out.

That the Daco-Romans are proud of their origin may be learned from the following verse from a Moldavian poet:—

> " Nemul t'éri Moldavi de unde derad'à
> Din t'era Italii tot omul sé cred'à.
> Flacŭ antéiu, apoi Traian au adus pe aice
> Pre stremos'i questor t'eri de nemu cu ferice;
> Resàdit au t'erilor hotarele tote
> Pre semne que statĭ in veci a se vedĕ pote.

Iei cŭ vit'a questûi nem, t'era romanesca
Implut aŭ Ardialul s'i Moldovenesca,
Semnele staŭ de se vid de densul făcute
Turul Severinului se custa'n vremi multe."*

The most cultivated of the Daco-Romans are to be
found in Wallachia and Moldavia. The following is an
account of the Wallachs in Transylvania and Lower
Hungary, in the description of which I have employed
some of the quaint forms of expressions used by an old
German author.

Their manner of living is extremely rough and
savage; they are destitute of religion, arts, and sciences.
From their infancy the children are washed every day
in warm water, and then swathed in coarse linen or
woollen cloth. The seasons and the weather make
herein no difference. From the fifth to the twelfth or
fourteenth year of their age they are left to attend the
herds and flocks, the girls being taught in the meantime
washing, baking, spinning, needle-work, and weaving.
The dress of the boys and girls is the same.

The houses of the Wallachs usually consist of but
one small room, in which old and young, men and

* " The Moldavian race—whence proceeded it? From Italy, as every
one believes. Flaccus first, and then Trajan, brought thither the ancestors
of the happy inhabitants of this land. They fixed its limits, which are still
to be seen in the vestiges that remain. Trajan, from this stock, filled the
Roumanian land, Ardalia and Moldavia. The proofs of this are everywhere. Long has stood the Tower of Severinus."

women are indiscriminately mixed : pigs and fowls also
frequently come in for their share of the accommoda-
tion.   Before the door is generally a semi-fluid puddle,
where the swine and children indulge in their siesta.
The house is constructed of the unhewn branches of
trees, lined inside with mud, and covered with a high
straw roof held in its place by branches of trees hung
across it.   The light is usually admitted through a piece
of bladder.

Their mode of dress is various.   The men wear white
trousers of coarse cloth, very large, and descending to
the ankles.   In summer these are made of linen instead
of woollen; over this is worn a coarse shirt, with wide
open sleeves, reaching partly over the thighs, and hang-
ing outside of the breeches; hence, by way of contempt,
the Hungarians call the Wallachs "people who let
their shirts hang out."   A leather girdle is worn around
the waist, in which they carry a knife, flint, steel, and a
tobacco pipe.   They wrap rags round the feet, and
bind over them sandals of raw leather, with coarse
thongs.

The fashion varies in almost every village, and is
even more tyrannical than in Paris.   When the peasant
goes to purchase an article of dress, she mentions the
name of her village to the merchant, who then produces
the article fashionable in that locality.

The males never cover the head while in mourning,
let the weather be what it may.   The common people

suffer the beard to grow after the age of forty, when they are called *grandfathers;* although the Wallachian, marrying at the age of fifteen, is frequently a grandfather at the age of thirty.

The girls go bareheaded; their ornaments consist of earrings of brass, colored glass beads, and pieces of money fastened to a string, and tied round the head or neck. The latter give a ringing noise, so that the well dressed Wallachian girl "makes a fine music wherever she goes," and may very often be heard sooner than seen. She carries her entire dower upon her person. In order to appear more beautiful, the women paint their cheeks red, and color their eyebrows black.

They wear a long chemise, reaching down almost to the ankles. From a small girdle are suspended two aprons, one before and the other behind. The embroidery upon these fringed and many-colored garments is esteemed an important part of ornamental attire. The women also wear, under the chemise, in winter, wide drawers of coarse woollen cloth, and like the males, put on the *juba*, or sheep-skin cloak, with the wool inside. The front of the chemise is always open, and serves as a receptacle for cabbages, meat, and perhaps a dozen other articles, thus forming, altogether, a most astonishing protuberance. Nothing can be more ridiculous than the appearance of a Wallachian woman returning from the market with her bosom bulged out with the purchases of the day.

No woman is seen going about without some work in hand, or is ever by any chance idle. The peasant's wife goes to market with a basket of goods balanced on her head, an infant on her back, and twirling her distaff at the same time, as dexterously as one of the princesses of Homer. She spins, weaves, and makes the dresses of her family, helps her lazy husband cut the corn in harvest time, and trudges along in the mud while he rides on horseback. If you ask a peasant for what he wants a wife, he usually answers, "To comb me, and keep me clean." Yet, so far as cleanliness goes, she is, in Transylvania, a bad housewife. Neither does her labor produce so much as might be imagined. Among the German settlers it is a proverb "to be as busy as a Wallach woman, and do as little."

The men are indolent and cowardly, except when it comes to smuggling, plundering, horse-stealing, or attacking a bear. A long succession of ill-treatment has made them timid and suspicious. An old countess in Transylvania regretted to Paget that "times were sadly changed; peasants were no longer so respectful as they used to be;" she could remember walking to church on the backs of the peasants, who knelt down in the mud to allow her to pass over them without soiling her shoes. From sheer indolence they bask in the sun in summer and starve in winter.

The Wallachs do not attend much to the cultivation of grain, but devote themselves especially to the breeding and tending of cattle, wintering their herds in Moldavia and Wallachia at a trifling expense, and conducting them home again in the spring. *Kukurutz*, or maize, from which is prepared a thick porridge, called *Mamaglia*, resembling the *polenta* of the Italians, is chiefly cultivated by them.

I have good reason to believe that the native male peasants of Wallachia are the laziest people in the world. For the acres which they cultivate they have to render annually twenty-eight days' labor to the Boyard proprietor, and pay a moderate tax to the government. In addition to this, a month's labor per year will support their families in the humble style in which they live. The chief concern of the men seems to be how they may best squander away their time.

In the beginning of May, the proper month for planting, they devote an entire week to unmitigated idleness, making it almost an object of worship, under the supposition that their fruits will thereby be protected from the late frosts. The laggard husbands frighten their industrious wives into greater diligence, by pretending that a fairy visits every house early on the morning of Holy Thursday, and will punish them with barrenness, or some other dreadful affliction, if all be not found in order. They impose, indeed, upon these patient and tender creatures the hardships often visited upon themselves by their Boyard masters.

The food of the Wallachian peasants is as simple as

their dress. Meal cakes are baked in the ashes, and they also use milk, cheese, fat, garlic, and beans. But little animal food is eaten, on account of the fasts which are rigorously observed, although every other law be broken. Meat, eggs, and milk are then forbidden, and their scanty food is prepared with salt and water; great debility is caused thereby, and sometimes even death.

At their feasts the Wallachs drink all the wine and brandy they can get. Raki then flows in rivulets, and the peasant not unfrequently runs in debt to treat his friends with a sheep roasted whole. If the Wallach is so fortunate as to find a pipe or violin, in addition to a full pitcher, he seldom ceases from revelry until he is quite drunk, and is carried home senseless. These feasts are kept up like Irish wakes.

In certain parts of Transylvania the Wallachs have a curious custom. A party of idle young fellows sell themselves, as they say, to the devil, for a term of three, five, or seven years—the number must be odd, or the devil will not hold to the bargain—engaging to dance the whole of that time, except when they sleep: in consideration of which they expect their infernal purchaser will supply them with food and wine liberally, and render them irresistible among the rustic belles. Accordingly, dressed in their gayest attire, these merry vagabonds start out from their native village, and literally dance through the country. Every-

where they are received with open arms; the men glad
of an excuse for jollity, the women anxious, perhaps, to
prove their power, all unite to feed and fête the "devil's
dancers;" so that it is scarcely wonderful that there
should be willing slaves to so merry a servitude. When
their time is up they return home, and become quiet
peasants for the rest of their lives.[*]

The religious rites and ceremonies of the Transylvanian Wallachs favor Paganism and Judaism, rather
than the religion which they profess. For example,
no woman will attempt to kill an animal, whatever it
may be. They make no scruple of employing the most
shocking oaths on every trifling occasion, and carefully
avoid going into Catholic churches, but if there by
accident, purify themselves afterwards by ablutions.
To be sprinkled in a Catholic church, or to undergo
any ceremonies with consecrated water, is a matter of
the greatest horror to them, for the reason that the
water is sprinkled about with an instrument made of
pork-bristles. This, in their own opinion, renders them
highly impure. The dresses contaminated by such an
accident cannot be worn again without being washed.
Their *papas* (Greek priests) distribute the consecrated
water by means of a branch, or a nosegay of hyssop,
as is directed in the Psalm. Stealing and adultery are
looked upon as trifling crimes. Their *papas* cannot
grant absolution for murder, that being left to God

* Paget.

alone; but murders, as well as robberies, are very common. The Wallachs regard their priests with superstitious reverence, and attach still higher importance to the sacraments of the Church. An attempt was made not many years ago, to *catholicize* the Greek Church in Transylvania. Conformists were allowed to participate in the government of the country. Many of the priests apostatized, for solid reasons, and some brought over their flocks with them. In other cases, however, the people refused to change their religion. In certain villages, where Greek priests were not allowed to officiate, no Christian ceremony or sacrament was performed for thirty years. Men were born, married, and died unchristened, unblessed, and unshriven.

When the Wallachs engage themselves in an indissoluble friendship *in life and death*, they put a cross in the vessel, or the cup from which they eat or drink, swearing thereby everlasting fidelity. This ceremony is never to be slighted. It is generally a preliminary rite to robberies. The same ceremony is resorted to as the most efficacious bond; for example, if robbers release a man by whom they fear being apprehended, they condemn him to silence with an oath by the cross, the salt, and the bread, which they call *giurar pe cruce, pe pite, pe fare.*

Their funerals are singular. With dismal shrieks the corpse is brought to the tomb, in which it is sunk down as soon as the *papa* has finished the ritual.

At this moment the friends and relatives of the deceased raise horrid cries; they remind the dead of his friends, parents, cattle, house, and household, and ask for what reason he left them. As no answer ensues, the grave is filled up, and a wooden cross with a large stone placed at the head, so that the deceased may not become a *vampyre*, or strolling, nocturnal bloodsucker. Wine is thrown upon the grave, and frankincense burned around it, to drive away witches and evil spirits. This done, they go home, bake bread of wheat flour, which they eat to the expiation of the deceased, plentifully drinking to be the more comforted themselves. The solemn shrieks, libations of wine, and fumigations about the tomb, continue during some days, nay, even for weeks. The funeral of a bridegroom is still more solemn. A pole several fathoms long is raised over his tomb, and the bride hangs on it a garland, a quill, and a white handkerchief. The Wallachs of Transylvania plant a plum-tree at the head, and another at the foot of every grave, from the fruit of which they make their brandy: a very literal illustration, says Paget, "of seeking consolation from the tomb."

The Wallachs are ignorant beyond comparison. Ask an old man his age, and he will answer: "At the conclusion of the peace," or when that prince died, or that metropolitan was elected, "I attended the swine," or the sheep, or went into the field, married; and so on; and then you may compute his age.

Any phenomenon, or effect of unknown causes, is regarded by them as a miracle. They look upon a solar eclipse as a fray between the infernal dragon and the sun: for that reason, during the eclipse, a great firing is heard throughout the land, to frighten away the dragon which otherwise might devour the sun, and plunge the world into eternal darkness. A Wallach will never cut a spit of beech wood whereon to roast his meat. The reason is this: in the spring the beech yieds a red sap, and according to the profound observations of the Wallachs, the tree weeps these bloody tears because the Turkish bloodhounds used to roast Christians upon spits made of beech wood.

No capital punishment is in greater abhorrence among the Wallachs than that by the rope. The wheel and pale are greatly preferable: a rope "ties the neck, and forces the soul out downward." This they call a most disgusting defilement; and " their singular nicety on this point," says an old German writer, "is true psychological materialism."

The Daco-Romans are remarkably superstitious. They believe in fairies, monsters, both horrid and picturesque, strolling vampires, sorceries, and the blighting charms of the evil eye. A Wallach hardly dares go out after sundown on Tuesday or Friday for fear of being whisked away by witches in the shape of vindictive old women, who are perfectly harmless during the daytime. Woe to the Daco-Roman who has any day neglected to set aside food and drink for the hideous vampyres which suck out men's blood by night, or for the malevolent spirits dwelling among ruins in solitary places, and waging implacable warfare upon the human race. No neighborhood is so dreadful as theirs.

Unless the peasant has worn for three weeks a talismanic paper dipped in consecrated oil by his priest, folded in a mysterious manner, and tied to his forehead by seven hairs, he is momentarily in fear of being gulped down by a dragon of such enormous proportions that one of his jaws touches the heavens while the other rests upon the earth. These fabulous monsters are for ever intercepting adventurous travellers and ballad-sung heroes, and getting themselves cut into a thousand pieces, but the dismembered parts are so endowed with vitality that they speedily grow together, if the sun do but happen to shine upon them.

Has the Wallach tasted a drop of milk during Lent, or forgotten to make the sign of the cross from right to left in the presence of his priest? Until the sin is absolved he is in constant apprehension of being picked up by winged monsters of supernatural size, that live in impenetrable forests, where they conceal their treasures, as well as the princesses of royal blood whom they have carried away.

Usually in affairs of the heart

> "The village maid
> Seeks the dark gipsy's fearful aid."

By night, when only the peeping stars can behold her
naked loveliness, she steals, timidly and blushingly, to
the neighboring stream or fountain, thinking to see
therein her future husband. Their little love ditties,
full of tenderness and rosy thoughts of matrimony,
remind one of the evening prayer of the German peasant girl:—

> "Schemmel, Ich tritt dich,
> St. Andreas Ich bitt dich,
> Gieb mir in dem Traum ein
> Welcher wird mein Mann sein."

But the stork, the swallow, and even the serpent
take shelter under the hospitable roof of the Daco-
Roman.   He regards the little field-snake with a
degree of respect little short of idolatry, sees in it a
protecting household god, welcomes it, permits it to
nestle on his warm hearth in winter, and feeds the
sacred guest with milk every morning and evening.
M. Michelet relates that having called at the hut of a
Wallach peasant in Transylvania, he found the wife in
tears. She had just lost her little boy three years of
age. "We had noticed," said she to the traveller,
"that every day our child ate no food at breakfast, and
shortly after absented himself for a full hour. One

day I followed him into the thicket, and saw an immense serpent glide up and take from the child's hand a piece of bread which he had brought. The following day my husband went with me. Frightened at the sight of this undomesticated and perhaps noxious serpent, he killed it with a blow of his axe. The child came a few moments afterwards and found his friend dead. In despair he returned home, weeping and crying, *pouiu!* (my dear little bird). Nothing would console him, and after five days' weeping he died, crying to the last, *pouiu, pouiu!*"

The Daco-Roman, like his Italian ancestors, believes that the destiny of every man is mysteriously united with a star which, in the far-off heavens, reflects the plans and accidents of his life. Thus when a misfortune befalls him his star becomes darkened; when he dies it disappears in space. When the sky is red, he imagines that there is war in heaven, and in the fiery planets reads dire catastrophes to earth. The poor gods and goddesses of heathen Rome, when chased out of Italy, seem to have taken a last refuge among the Daco-Romans, more, however, in the character of strolling theatrical performers than the divinities of high Olympus. The infant literature of the country chants their praises, and the peasant girl of Daco-Roumania never fills her vase-like pitcher without first breathing upon the water and pouring some of the fluid upon the ground as a libation to the nymph of the fountain. I have already alluded to the custom of putting a coin in the hand or the mouth of the deceased for Charon, the boatman of the Styx.

In the opinion of the Wallach precious stones are made of the saliva of serpents, and the poor peasant, mush fed and clothed in sheepskins, is ever dreaming of finding some viper's den or noxious bird's nest filled with incalculable riches. The eating of an infant's heart, he believes, will render his body bullet-proof, and this horrible repast is not unfrequently prepared.

One day in a village near Bukarest, I fell in with a curious burial procession, composed of Wallach peasants. The rude bier was supported by half-a-dozen villagers. The face of the deceased, a young man, was exposed to the burning sun, as is the custom in the East, in order to detect any indications of human life— a usage that originated in times of the plague. It was an excessively hot day, and a swarm of black, ugly flies hovered around the pale face of the corpse, and were doing their busy work while it was borne along. Before the bier walked a person with a basket of un-leavened cakes, to be eaten in honor of the *manes* of the dead. He also carried a little May-pole, orna-mented with tresses, like those with which the peasant bride in Wallachia decks herself on her marriage day. Following the bier were a couple of the village priests, the parents, and friends, all carrying little torches, and then a number of wailing women, haggard and wan, hired for the occasion. The latter, like the *præficæ* in ancient Roman funerals, tore their hair and shrieked as if the peace of the dead had depended upon their efforts.

I followed the procession, which halted several times before reaching the village church. The bier-carriers rested their burden upon the ground. The nearest relatives and the wailing women crowded round the coffin, addressed the tenderest expressions to the dead, embraced it, and begged forgiveness for all the little vexations they had caused it during life, testifying their sorrow at the same time by mournful chants of praise and regrets, by groans, and rending their garments in a frightful manner. These singular manifestations disturbed the beautiful thoughts which we are accustomed to associate with the last offices to the departed and the peaceful rest of the grave.

On leaving the church the corpse was carried to a shallow grave in the courtyard, called the " Garden of the Dead." After the priests had recited the last prayer, the dead and the living were sprinkled with consecrated water. The following beautiful verses were then chanted in a doleful manner :—" Come, brethren, let us give the last embrace to the deceased, thanking God. What woe, what wailing in the present change ! He is consigned to the grave; his abode is with the dead. Now are we separated. Now all the evil and vain festivity of life are dissolved. The clay hath become black ; the vessel is broken, speechless, dead.

Truly, like a flower, and as vapor, and as morning dew, is our life., Come, then, let us look down narrowly into the grave. Where is the comeliness of the body, and where is youth? Where are the eyes and the beauty of the flesh? All his comeliness is cast away,—dissolved in the grave—food for worms—in darkness, covered with earth." The coffin was lowered into the grave, and a rude wooden cross left to mark the resting-place of the Wallachian youth. Aside from the few symbols of Christianity, I could have believed myself at the burial of a man in the time of ancient Rome.

When a Wallach is about to draw his last breath, the weeping attendants put a lighted candle in his hand, and a priest recites prayers in a voice more or less loud and agonizing, according to the number of piastres he expects for his services. Soon after death the corpse is washed, shaved, shrouded for the tomb as expensively as the family can afford, the feet turned towards the door, and frequently a piece of money slipped into the hand or mouth to pay for the passage of the dead into the other world. In the Boyard families much display is made at funerals, and many of the superstitious observances to which I have alluded dispensed with.

The Wallachs, like the ancient Romans, piously revere the *manes*, or shades of the departed. This, as among the Turks, is an abundant source of alms. On the anniversary of the deceased, the family, if able, give money and clothing to the poor, together with unleavened cakes made of meal, sugar, honey, nuts, and cheese. Vessels filled with water, and sometimes provisions, are placed along the road for the use of the traveller.

Like the Turks, the Wallachs have their lucky and unlucky days. Every day has, in fact, its peculiar work which should be done upon no other. The Wallach women wash on Wednesday and spin on Saturday. Tuesday is the most unlucky of all. Upon that day the women scarcely wash and comb themselves: no journey is then begun or any work of importance undertaken.

During certain days of the year they abstain from cutting anything with shears, as at the Roman festival of the Lupercalia, in order that the wolves may not injure their sheep. Tailors, I believe, exempt themselves from this observance. No peasant woman will take a neddle in her fingers on Tuesday, for fear that the Saviour would feel every stitch, and thus be crucified anew. They imagine that the plague may be averted by burning a shirt which has been spun, woven, and made up in less than twenty-four hours. When it begins to thunder and lighten, the superstitious Wallach makes the sign of the cross and falls upon the ground.

Idiots are everywhere welcome. During " Fool's week " lunatics are permitted to run through the streets somewhat like the Thugs of India, beating whomsoever they may meet, and doing no little harm besides.

8*

The sports and the dances of the Wallachs bear a striking resemblance to those of the Roman peasantry in the time of Trajan. The Daco-Romans have two national dances, the *hora* and the *colusari*. The latter, according to Gerando, is probably the ancient dance of the Salii, who had a temple upon the Quirinal hill of Rome, and performed on the ides of April, under the direction of a leader, chanting, at the same time, unintelligible rhapsodies. The Wallach dancers, when executing the *colusari*, wear leather straps across the shoulders ornamented with copper buttons, and brandish long clubs in their hands, while vaulting and leaping with the Bacchic frenzy of whirling dervishes.

The *hora* recalled to my mind the Roman chorus precisely as we see it figured on ancient bas-reliefs. The dancers, both men and women, taking hold of each other's hands, formed a large circle, in the centre of which were the *lautari*, or gipsy musicians. One of the latter sang while the ring whirled round and round with arms and feet moving in harmony, the performers now advancing and then retreating, so as to diminish or enlarge the circle.

There was something in these slow and monotonous evolutions, as well as in the mournful chants of the *lautari*, in perfect keeping with the melancholy genius of the Daco-Romans. Besides the *hora* and the *colusari*, I saw the dance of the girdle. The couples placed the left hand upon each other's girdles, and rested the right on the shoulder. Though exceedingly slow at first, their movements soon became astonishingly rapid.

Bear in mind, O reader, that I am describing the holiday sports of Daco-Roman peasants, and not those of the Europeanized dwellers in Bukarest, who, forgetting their nationality, have adopted both the pleasures and manners of the West—who perform the graceful minuet, tread the labyrinth of the French quadrille, and wind the whirling mazes of the mazourka.

The Daco-Romans celebrate a great number of festivals. That in honor of Flora occurs the first Sunday in May.

Beautiful is the harvest festival of the Wallachs. "Dragaika" they call the fair one whom the village damsels select from their midst, and crown with a wreath of leaves and heads of grain. Then under the lead of their Ceres, they go singing through the fields and villages, like joyous birds, delighting the eyes and hearts of all who look upon them. The wreath of the Dragaika is much sought for by the maidens, although the burden of her song is that she will not be married in three years.

In summer, when the fields are scorched with drought, the peasants dress a little girl under ten years of age in a garment of leaves. All the other children of the same age follow her through the village, dancing and singing—

"Papulunga!
Go up to Heaven,
Open its windows
And let the rain down,
That the corn and the wheat
May grow well and ripen."

The religious festivities are equally interesting. On Christmas-day is celebrated a masquerade, the object of which is to represent the birth of our Saviour. A boy leads the procession, bearing for a banner a paper star of immense size and gaudily painted. Then follow the Magi in Eastern costume, and an escort of Roman soldiers with lances in the right hand. Each one is supplied with a lantern. They also represent the manger in which the Saviour is supposed to be born at midnight. The procession goes from door to door reciting pious anthems called *Balinda*.

The New Year is opened in Bukarest with a great baptismal ceremony. The Dumbovitza is blessed by the Metropolitan, just as he blesses the horses of the Prince when they are turned out to pasture in the beginning of May. Or, to obviate the difficulty which arises from the constant flow of the river, a priest is sent to bless it at or near the source. Infants of tender age are immersed in the icy stream, and bottles of the sacred water kept for many days.

The Easter festival is the most brilliant during the year, and lasts eight days. Great preparations are made in the towns and villages. The houses are newly garnished : every one parades his best garments, visits are exchanged, and all hearts leap with joy. In the street they salute each other with the sacramental phrase *a inviât Kristu, Kristu a inviât!* (Christ hath risen, Christ hath indeed risen.)

CHAPTER VIII.

THE GREEK CHURCH.

"Wretchedest age since the world began,
That cannot even bury a man."

THE Daco-Romans follow the Greek rite and the doctrines of the Council of Nice, which, it is asserted,
assure them the Catholicity of time, while the Church
of Rome can only boast of the Catholicity of places.
Like all Orthodox Greek Christians, they deny that the
Church of Rome is the true Catholic Church, and on
Holy Thursday excommunicate the Pope and Latin
prelates, praying that all who offer up unleavened
bread may be covered with confusion.

The Greeks, though manifesting far less veneration
for the Eucharist than the Latins, have adopted the
seven sacraments, commune according to the rules of
St. Basil and Chrysostom, observe four great fasts, and
abstain from meat on Wednesdays and Fridays. They
maintain that the Holy Ghost proceeds from the Father
alone, and believe not in the immediate admission of the
saints and martyrs to the beatific vision. The Greeks
baptize by immersion, use leavened bread, and contend for the bodily presence.

The Orthodox Greek Church has not, like the church of Rome, made herself "drunk with the blood of martyrs." The Greeks profess a certain degree of toleration, but it is by no means certain that they would not have displayed the same sanguinary spirit as the Latins, had similar inducements to persecution been presented.

They do not extend the name of Christians to any sect out of the pale of their own church. Neither in Russia nor in any of the provinces of European Turkey where the influence of the Czar has made itself felt, are Catholics or Protestants permitted to win, or to attempt to win, souls from the orthodox faith. Such is the bigotry of this remarkable church, and the character of its self-assumed head at St. Petersburgh, that a Chinese wall is built around the institution to protect it from all foreign influence, as if it were too perfect to learn anything from, too sacred to come into contact with, the rest of the Christian world. Neither light nor knowledge nor example is admitted from other sources.

Rigid and unchanging in character, the Greek church is the instrument of tyranny alike in Constantinople, St. Petersburgh, and Belgrade. The Czar of Russia, the Patriarch of Stamboul, and the petty princes who subsist upon their bounty, in making the faith the tool of ambition and avarice, are only doing on a grand scale what is common to every bishop and priest.

The enmity between the rival Christian sects is bitter and abiding. Not many years ago, the son of a wealthy Greek of Constantinople became a convert to Islamism. The *papa*, or Greek priest, was called in to console the bereaved father. "You are indeed afflicted," said he, "but let us be thankful that the case is by no means so bad as it might have been. Your son has only become a Mussulman; think what would have been your grief had he been converted into a hateful Catholic!"

Though practising auricular confession, the Greeks deny that the rite is a divine precept, regarding it merely as an injunction of the church. They insist that it is lawful to deceive an enemy, also that it is no sin to injure and oppress him. The majority are of the opinion that to be saved it is not necessary to make restitution of goods stolen or fraudulently obtained.

Many of the Eastern Christians, especially those who speak the language of Plato, leave the Eighth Commandment entirely out of their Creed, and practise largely upon the conjugation and declension of the Greek verb *kleptein* in all of its moods and tenses.

They entertain an extreme horror of excommunication, which, with them, " excludes the guilty one from the pale of the church, from the communion of the Trinity, the saints, and the three hundred and eighteen Fathers before the fourth Council of Nice, consigns him over to the Devil and the traitor Judas, and, unless he humbly repents, condemns his body to remain after death as hard as stone."

As a church, the Greek Christians make no claim to infallibility or temporal sovereignty. Even in Russia, where the orthodox church has attained a colossal development, where the oracles of an ancient faith have lent wings for the *essor* of ambition, and absolutism has impiously engrafted upon itself the principle of theocracy, even there the aureola of the church pales in the effulgent blaze of temporal authority. The Holy Synod, once ancient and independent, is now under the spiritual direction of a commander of the cavalry.

Politically speaking, the influence of the Latin church has been disorganizing, while that of the eastern church has been conservative. It was the latter which held together the *membra disjecta* of the Russian empire during the Tartar irruption, and it was through the active co-operation of the Greek Christians of the Ottoman empire that the Czar Nicholas hoped to replace the cross on St. Sophia.

The organization of the Greek church varies but slightly in different parts of Eastern Europe. Its clergy are divided into regular and secular. The former are all monks, and can alone be advanced to the first dignities of the church. The lower orders of the regular clergy, *i.e.* below the metropolitans, archbishops, and bishops, are termed, in Russia, the black clergy. The bishops and those above them in rank are regarded as smoking holocausts upon the altar of the church. They must practise celibacy, and abstain from the flesh of animals, but the black clergy, so called from the color of their caps and robes, are permitted to marry before entering the order, yet not afterwards. They are exempt from taxes, conscription, and corporeal chastisement,—the last mentioned exemption being also extended to their wives.

The secular priests, or white clergy, are far more numerous than the above, and perform the greater part of the ecclesiastical functions of the Church. Marriage is an indispensable pre-requisite for every candidate for ordination into this class, but if, being a priest, he loses his wife, his sacerdotal powers expire at once, and can only be revived by marrying again. This is the case in certain parts of Russia. In the Danubian Principalities the priest can be the husband of but one wife, upon the preservation of whose life his prosperity in a great measure depends.

Literally, however, the Greek priest marries three times; when he is admitted as a deacon, when ordained to the priestly office, and lastly, when he takes an earthly bride.

Thus, in the Orthodox Church, marriage forms the basis of the priestly order, and the benefices of the sacred ministry are in fact a premium awarded to the husband whose conjugal solicitude succeeds best in prolonging the days of his wife. Hence also the Russian proverb, "As happy as a priest's wife."

The secular priests, having no settled and competent livings, are obliged to subsist by simoniacal practices, to dispense with religion rather than to dispense its hopes and consolations. They are in fact. driven to sell the divine mysteries intrusted to their charge. No one can procure absolution, be admitted to confession, have his children baptized or his relatives buried, get married or divorced, or have an enemy excommunicated, without paying the priest in advance; and the price put on his spiritual commodities depends upon the ability and devotion of the parishioner.

A situation so deplorable reacts fatally upon the morals of the orthodox priesthood. As their houses furnish but a scanty subsistence, they seek every occasion to sit at the tables of others, where they are too apt to abandon themselves without restraint to the gratifications of an insatiable appetite and inextinguishable thirst. "Am I a priest, that I should eat and drink twice as much as another person?" is a Christian proverb in the East. Intemperance leads to all vices.

According to the Report of the Holy Synod of Russia, during the year 1836, 208 ecclesiastics were degraded for infamous crimes, and 1,995 for minor offences. In that year the total Russian clergy numbered 102,456 individuals, giving two out of every hundred condemned by the tribunals. In the year 1839 the proportion of

priests condemned was one to twenty, and taking three
years together we find that one-sixth of the Russian
clergy were disgraced for crimes and misdemeanors.
Yet the Russian Church styles herself Orthodox, and
Románoff and serf boast of the spiritual mission of Holy
Russia.   Nor in view of these statistics can we wonder
at the startling remark of St. Chrysostom when speaking of the Greek Clergy, " I do not think there are
many priests who will be saved, but that the greater
part of them will perish."

The superior clergy, forming the *élite* of the Church,
are not entirely without virtue and intelligence, but
they are not brought into immediate contact with the
people, and consequently exercise but little influence
over them.

The secular clergy, owing to their ignorance and
degraded position, are scarcely respected even during
the performance of the sacred offices, while at other
times they are treated with a familiarity bordering on
contempt.   There are proverbs and particular sarcasms
relative to the priesthood not surpassed in point by
anything in Greek epigram or French madrigal.
Throughout the East the secular clergy can scarcely be
distinguished from the peasantry, and are as ignorant
as the people over whom they have charge.   When
wandering among the ruins of the temple of Ceres at
Eleusis, I remember to have seen a Greek priest curry-
ing his horse, while his savage wife with her daughters,

in the Grotto of the Nymphs hard by, looked like a harpy surrounded by furies.

The monks are of the order of St. Basil. The monasteries, some of which are free and others consecrated to the sees of Alexandria, Antioch, and Jerusalem, possess more than one third of the landed estate in the Principalities. Those dependent upon Mt. Athos are especially wealthy. The old monastery of Niamzo formerly contributed to the intellectual advancement of the country, but is at present nothing more than a hospital.

In Wallachia there is a church to every six hundred inhabitants, and, including the families of the priests, every forty-sixth person belongs to the clerical profession.

There are two seminaries in Wallachia and one in Moldavia for their education, but the degree of cultivation which the students receive cannot be compared with that imparted in a district school of New York. Almost any one can become a Greek priest in Wallachia by paying $75, the fee for initiation into the clerical order. The applicant for orders is not expected to be able to write. Ability to read the Liturgy of the Orthodox Church is ostensibly required, but even this accomplishment is often wanting; in which case the priest repeats the service from memory, as Homer repeated his songs. In the towns and cities, the secular clergy, though ignorant and depraved, often have a respectable appearance.

It is only in the Wallachian villages, of whose
wretchedness no one can obtain an idea without actual
inspection, that the genuine type of the character can
be seen. Living upon a patch of land given by the
Boyard who owns the village, and distinguishable from
the meanest peasant only by his long beard, tchako,
and boots, he works and goes to market just like the
ignorant parishioners whose sins, past, present, and fu-
turo, he is empowered to absolve. The piastres derived
from the sale of the sacraments and holy water are of
but little benefit to his family, for most of them must
be given over to the bishop as an annual present for
the privilege of retaining his situation. What wonder,
then, that he should grant an indulgence for a few
paras, and heartily forgive the person who shares with
him a stolen sheep or sack of corn.

The almost innumerable holidays of the Greek
Church—during which the peasant is strictly forbidden to labor for his worldly profit, "the priest
adroitly avails himself of, by assuring him that he may
labor in God's service, which being literally interpreted, means his priest's,—and so the lazy and superstitious Wallach, who will scarcely move a limb for his
own support, willingly wastes the sweat of his brow
in tilling the *papa's* glebe on fast days, and thus earns
his soul's salvation."

To make the sign of the cross from right to left
when about to pray or when it thunders, to repeat the

sign of the cross when meeting a priest, passing before a
church, or attempting to drive away the devil, to make
prostrations *à la Turque*, being careful to avoid the
kneeling posture of Catholic heretics, to revere *pápas*
and curse the Pope and the Mussulmans, to keep one
hundred and fifty holidays in the year, and fast one
hundred and ten—this is the instruction afforded by the
orthodox Greek church to the millions of her votaries.
The abstinence enjoined on fast days is so severe that
you cannot buy even a cup of milk with gold. The
Russian or the Wallachian peasant could not be induced to sweeten his tea with sugar purified with the
blood of oxen. Basil, the celebrated Daco-Roman robber, having murdered an entire family and pillaged
their dwelling on Friday, was shocked to see one of
his band lick with his tongue a dish that had contained
butter. "Heathen!" cried he, giving the fast-breaker
a savage blow, "hast thou then no fear of God?"

The wealthy grandee and the sly monk, however,
rest satisfied with observing merely the first and last
days of the long fasts. The poor say that the wealthy
can propitiate the will of Heaven by other means, as
acts of charity, but that for them remains but one way.
The lowly thus add the mortification of the flesh to
their poverty, while the rich think to obtain more easily
the favor of God, and reach heaven by the golden
bridge of charity.

To burn greasy red candles to a patron saint, to

adore hideous images partially in relief, to cry out unceasingly, *Gospodi pomelici!* (Lord, have mercy upon us!) to have the name of God much upon the lips, with but little of his love in the heart—this is worship in the Orthodox Greek church!

The Greek Christians maintain the perpetual virginity of the Virgin. In their adoration, in fact, she usurps the place of the Redeemer. Maryites would be their most appropriate name. They also pray to the cross as an intercessor.

Greek churches are built uniformly in the Byzantine style of architecture. Many of the old edifices, of rude and curious construction, are now crumbling into ruins. The modern structures, usually built with sums derived from the rich Greek monasteries, appear at a distance not unlike Methodist chapels. The court-yards of the old Greek churches are surrounded by high walls, and still used as resting-places for the dead. Their slumber, however, beneath so much filth and rubbish, is usually short; for these unholy places are mostly given over to the dogs and swine, and are literally filled with dead men's bones and all manner of uncleanness. As one passes by them at night in the Wallachian capital, it is no uncommon sight to see

> "The lean dogs beneath the wall
> Hold o'er the dead their carnival,
> Gorging and growling o'er carcass and limbs."

ON THE STEPPE.   p. 97

POSTING IN WALLACHIA.   p. 95

Should the dead, however, be buried too deep for these nocturnal resurrectionists, their remains are disinterred after the lapse of three, or at least seven years. The Wallachs believe that although the soul is unable to leave the corpse until the latter is entirely decayed, it goes out of the tomb at night in order to visit the living. The people are greatly concerned when the earth moves over the grave of a relative, as it is sometimes made to do by a cunning device of the priest.

The exhumation usually takes place on the death of a friend. If the body be not completely decomposed, it is a sign of excommunication. As a test, in doubtful cases, the putrid corpse is set up against the wall. If it fall to pieces all is supposed to be well, and the remains, after having been washed with wine, and liberally prayed for by the priest, are again consigned to the earth, to share with a fresh body the same uncertain tenement. But if the corpse remain erect, the attending relatives and spectators set up a cry of despair. The case is too serious for a common priest. A bishop is called, and at least a third of the property left by the unfortunate subject must be promised for the support of the clergy and the poor, before the friends are assured of his release from excommunication, and of the future happiness of his soul.

The Greek Christians believe in a many-mansioned heaven, but reject from their creed the half-way-house purgatory of the Latins. The superstitious ideas to

9

which I have just alluded were doubtless derived from
the ancient inhabitants of the country, to whom a disciple of Pythagoras taught the doctrine of the transmi-
gration of souls.

The severe iconoclastic dogmas of the Greek Christians condemn the use of statuary in their places of
worship; but by way of compensation, they cover the
walls internally and externally with daubs of red-lipped
Greek saints with broad halos around their heads, so
wretchedly executed that I can hardly charge the ador-
ing worshippers with idolatry, and so numerous, that
the run of the calendar must be nearly exhausted in
the celestial ornamentation of a single edifice. I have
never seen anything like these cloud-treading saints in
the heavens above, on the earth, or in the waters under
the earth. There are also rude inscriptions on the church
walls in the old Slave language.

"I have often been much amused," says Paget,
"with these pictures in the Wallach churches; for
though too gross for description, they contain so much
of that racy, often sarcastic wit, proper to Rabelais or
Chaucer, wrought out with a minuteness of diabolical
detail and fertility of imagination worthy of a Breughel,
that it recalls to one's mind the labored illuminations of
our old missals. Notwithstanding its sins against pure
taste, there is often much that is good in the church
humor; nor, despite the reverence due to the holy
character of the subject, is it possible to repress a smile

at the malice of the monkish illuminator, when he decks
out the Pharisee in the robes and jewels of some neighboring bishop, or at the prurient imagination of the
cloister, when it breaks forth in warm delineations of
all the charms and temptations by which sin can lead
poor man astray."

During the palmy days of Russian influence, holy
pictures, relics, and church ornaments were sent regularly to the pious Wallachs to keep them in the best
opinion of the Czar, whom many of them look upon as
the great head of the Greek church, although they are
dependent upon the Patriarch of Constantinople.

Church bells have been allowed in the Principalities only since they came under the protection of Russia. As the Turks were never partial to the sound of
bells, the Christians were formerly called to the house
of worship by the *tocca*, a wooden hammer rattled upon
a board. This usage is still kept up in many of the
churches of Bukarest, and I was every morning waked
from my slumbers by a horrid tune of the above kind,
rapped off in the dome-like cupola of an adjoining
church.

In Greek churches the main body of the edifice,
where the auditors *stand* instead of being seated, is
separated from the orchestra and altar by the *Iconas-
tese*, a lofty screen behind which the priests chant and
go through the multitude of manipulations and semi-
prostrations that characterize the service of the Eastern

church. Now and then a veil is removed, allowing a
glance into the secret *penetralia*, or a little door is
opened through which the priest emerges bearing the
host, at the sight of which the audience falls upon the
pavement, each one repeating the sign of the cross time
after time.

I attended worship one day at the Metropolitan
church, one of the most interesting buildings in the
Wallachian capital, from the fact that it contains the
ashes of St. Demetrius, and was in former times the
seat of the General Assembly of the Principality.

On the way, at the early hour of eight, the streets
were filled with wagons from the country. From in-
quiry I learned that the principal market of the week
was held on Sabbath morning, in order that the peasants might sell their vegetables, and purchase forgiveness of their sins from the priest on the same occasion,
without loss of time. I was not a little surprised to see
such an exhibition of practical talent on the part of
the miserable Wallachs, but the custom doubtless descended from the ancient Greeks, who sacrificed to the
gods at the great games and other important gatherings.

On entering the Metropolitan church I found the
immense inclosure packed with a miscellaneous audience of Boyards, citizens and peasants. The males
and females occupied different parts of the house. A
more uninteresting assemblage I never beheld. The
want of intelligence, the bigoted and fanatical look,

the soulless expression of that mass of men and women, was surpassed only by the careless, ignorant, and sensual appearance of the crowd of priests who assisted their bishop in going through what seemed a shocking mockery of divine service. There was not a thought of solemnity in the whole affair. I am in no danger of forgetting those priestly petrifactions in brimless hats and long black robes, whose consecrated locks and beards had apparently never been desecrated by unholy shears and razors. They yawned, laughed, and sent their roving eyes over the audience, and occasionally I saw indignant glances falling upon myself for not choosing to fall down at the sight of a gewgaw, and refusing to kiss a bad picture of the *Panghia*, or All-holy Virgin, defiled already by hundreds of nasty lips.

The love of the Oriental Christians for relics known to be forged is something remarkable. They do not admit images, but employ both in their dwellings and churches raised pictures which must be worked by a person lying flat upon the floor, and not be sold for money. The latter restriction, however, is sometimes adroitly avoided. The manner in which even well-dressed persons kiss the hands and garments of priests more ignorant than themselves is enough to disgust the spectator. Sermons are unknown amongst them. Almost the entire service is made up of prayers and readings in the ancient Slavonic lan-

guage, chanted through the nose in a way that would
do honor to a Jewish synagogue, and furnishing a magnificent exaggeration of the old Puritan twang. The
nasal organ seems to be almost the only part of the
vocal apparatus brought into requisition in the apparent
attempt

> "To crack the voice of melody,
> And break the legs of time."

Yet this kind of music, continued for two hours, with
scarcely a moment's interval,

> "To heal the blows of sound,"

is regarded as superlatively beautiful. The inclosed air
became mephitic from the clouds of burning incense
and the smoke of scores of tallow candles. I was glad
to leave the edifice as well as the four-and-twenty
pitiable beggars whom I counted at the door.

CHAPTER IX.

" Fast, fast with wild speed spurning,
The dark grey charger fled."

AFTER a six weeks' residence I determined to leave
Bukarest. I had lived long enough among its Boyards
and slaves, its palaces and hovels, its gardens and
morasses; had seen enough of its Parisian luxury and
Parian poverty!

The Daco-Romans have a capital substitute for a
fast American railway. Nothing can be more primitive than their *carutzas*, or post-wagons, the origin of
which must date back to the time when the Scythians
wandered over the Wallachian plains. Not a particle
of iron is used in the construction of the four diminutive
wooden wheels upon which is fastened a wicker basket,
resembling a crate for crockery ware, and just large
enough to hold a single person of flexible extremities
and moderate horizontal dimensions.

To this vehicle, but little larger than a wheel-
barrow, and uniting in itself all possible inconveniences, are attached by meshes of ropes from four

to eight Wallachian horses, or mares, perhaps, with
as many colts, frisking around them. The traveller
imbeds himself in the fermented hay, which is to be
his only cushion, and is sufficiently supplied with
thorns to keep up a cutaneous as well as mental irrita-
tion. The *surruju*, a swarthy long-haired Wallach,
wearing a slouched hat and ample breeches secured at
the waist by a broad leather girdle, mounts one of
the hind horses, and at his shrill cry the fleet little
steeds lay back their ears, and start off at a speed that
sets ordinary locomotion at defiance. Should any of
the wild-looking horses give out, they are abandoned by
the *surruju*, to be picked up on his return.

In the streets of Bukarest I was asphyxiated with
dust, and twice, before leaving the city, the wooden
linch-pins flew out, leading me to fear a total breaking
up of my strange vehicle.

Soon after passing the outer barrier a drizzling rain
came on, driven by a fierce south-east wind, directly
into my face. Instead of flying through a cloud of
dust, I thenceforth experienced a continuous shower of
liquid mud.

Kalarasche is seven Wallachian posts from Bukarest, a distance of about seventy English miles. The
road extends over the broad prairies, or rather the
successive *plateaux*, elevated a few feet above each
other, in the direction of the Carpathians. Scarcely a
tree or shrub was to be seen. More than once I

imagined myself on the familiar prairies of Illinois.
The crops had been gathered in the vicinity of Bukarest, and, as I advanced, the country bore fewer evidences of cultivation. In the times of Turkish authority
the peasants constructed their rude huts as far as possible from the travelled routes, so as to avoid the oppres-
sive visitations of their masters; and the recent incursions of the Cossacks have not tended to encourage
familiarity on the part of the poor Wallachs.

The road is in a state of nature, but the indomitable
surruju, to use a Germanism, soon lays behind the
distance of a single post. His prolonged shout indicates
that the solitary buildings on the plain before us are
the relay station. We have arrived. The *surruju* dis-
mounts in front of a low cabin with paper windows.
Here is the master of the station in slippers; his neck
and bosom exposed, a pipe in hand, and the sheepskin
juba thrown carelessly over his shoulders.

"The horses, Director!"

"They will be here presently."

"Where are they?" I continue.

"Feeding yonder upon the plain. Patience! patience!" he replies; and sure enough, instead of standing ready in the stable, the horses were quietly grazing
nearly a mile away. The *arândus* (hostler) mounts one
of the last relay, brings up the drove at a furious
gallop, and selects four fresh horses at hazard. The
tschaousch (assistant) slips the collars over their heads,

9*

shortens one of the rope traces and lengthens another, ties a few loose knots, and all is ready. The new *surruju* mounts. My way-bill has been visée, and in the meantime I have enjoyed for a few minutes the pipe of contentment. The *surruju* of the last post holds out his hat for the customary *backsheesh*. "Here is a zwanziger!" and I throw twenty paras to the *tschaousch*.

We dash forward with headlong speed, and fly through two or three Wallachian villages, proximity to which is indicated by a collection of conical elevations above the level of the plain. The shouts of the postillion bring out the rude denizens of these subterraneous abodes, the same as when the traveller approaches the villages of the prairie dog in the West.

Nothing in the way of description can give an idea of a Wallachian village inhabited by the poorer class of peasants and the gipsies. There, animals and human beings enjoy the shelter, food, breath, and social pleasures of each other,—man and nature being on most familiar terms. Never before, not even in the by-lanes of London, where stinging poverty and corruption slink away from the eye of charity, have I seen such cutting want, such abject, intense misery. Happy, thrice happy in comparison are the poor families of New York, crowded into subterranean chambers, filthy, diminutive, and even chalked off by lines into still smaller compartments. The roofs of these miserable underground huts do not even conceal from sight the filthy beings within, who live in an atmosphere in immediate *rapport* with the burning or freezing sky above. " O master," said a wretched Wallachian woman to a traveller, " you see these two mats, all soiled and trodden in the mud. I have a goat and two sheep, and in the winter I sleep with them to keep me and my little one warm." Near the first relay station I noticed a peasant crouched in the corner of his cabin, to keep dry. " Why don't you repair the roof of your hut ?" I inquired.

" It rains too fast, master," was the answer.

" But why not repair it when the weather is good ?"

" Oh, it's of no use then."

These wretched beings have the secret of dissolving their sorrows in liquors of the vilest quality, and when a wandering band of gipsies appears among them the dirt-besmeared and ragged creatures will dance and caper about as nimbly as the rocks and trees to the strains of Orpheus.

We push onward. The fourth station is at last reached. It has already been dark three hours, and such darkness !—black enough to

> "——— be bottled up
> And sold for Tyrian dye."

Sixteen horses and four postillions had been exhausted.

Though wet, hungry, and well nigh shaken to pieces, I determined to push forward. The *surruju* shouted as he reined up before the low post-house, and the master soon appeared with a paper lantern. They shuddered when untackling the panting horses, and motioned me to enter the hut. But I kept my seat, pointed to the thatched stable around which the wind was whistling in fitful gusts, and then towards Kalarasche, still three posts distant.

From my Turkish uniform they doubtless took me for an officer of Omar Pacha's staff hastening to Stamboul with despatches. They were accustomed to obey, and on producing my passport reluctantly complied. The swarthy Wallach mounts, the long *peitsche* swings and cracks, and into the thick night we plunge, regardless of darkness and the storm. How shall I forget that inky sky, that driving sleet piercing coldly to the very bones, that foolish adventure worthy of one of the heroes of Ossian.

The *surruju* had selected the fleetest horses at the station. I had promised liberal *backsheesh*, and such was the speed with which we flew across the plain, without any attempt to follow the road, that the little *carutza* seemed hardly to touch the earth. Suddenly the wind changed and blew upon my back. An unexpected flash of lightning, followed by the muttering of distant thunder, relieved for a moment the intense darkness.

A thunderstorm, cradled among the Carpathians and

hurried furiously onward, was about to burst upon us.
The surruju *orienting* himself by a dim light that
glimmered several miles from us on the prairie, urged
his horses to the top of their speed. Escape was impossible. It was one of those fearful tempests which
often break unexpectedly upon the lonely traveller on
the Wallachian plains—more fearful than the storms
that sweep over our prairie seas. Vivid flashes of
lightning, such as blind the eyes and almost wither
the soul, now and then revealed the storm-clouds piled
above each other—the revolving squadrons of heaven's
artillery whose reverberations became more terrific
every moment.

Our fleet little horses strove in vain to distance the
fiery chariot wheels of the tempest. The *surruju*,
inclining forward and vigorously applying the *peitsche*,
his long loose sleeves and locks of hair floating in the
wind, looked to me like one of the warlike Centaurs in
pursuit of the Lapithæ; nor could I dispel from my
mind the classic illusion. I was apprehensive of danger. The storm bust upon us in all its fury. The
jolting of the *carutza*, which I feared every moment
would fly in pieces, became unendurable. I thought
of all the hideous instruments formerly used to torture
criminals, and more than once imagined myself to be
Mazeppa bound upon a wild steed of the Ukraine.

"Halt! halt!" I shouted to the *surruju*.

" *Hie! Morg! hie! Bàlan!* " was the only answer

amid the roaring of the wind and the crashes of thunder. Just then we happened to leave the velvety track
of the prairie and strike a section of the road that had
been badly cut up by the Russian artillery wagons.
A crash ensued; one of the leaders stumbled and fell,
and I was thrown, fortunately without injury, upon the
grass. The glimmering light had disappeared several
minutes before. The *surruju*, guided by the sense of
feeling, collected the wreck of the *carutza*, but with all
his rude skill could not put it together.   We determined to abandon it.   My carpet bags were lashed upon
one of the horses, and I had mounted another to grope
our way over the plain, when a brilliant and prolonged
flash of lightning, opening as it seemed a panoramic
view into another world, revealed the isolated station
scarcely a quarter of a mile distant. We reached
it without great difficulty, and gained admittance.

The post-house was of the better sort of Wallachian
tenements. Travelling in those low Danubian countries, however, makes one acquainted with strange
bedfellows. In true Daco-Roman style, parents, children, and guest lodged in the same diminutive chamber,
Overcome with fatigue and the excitement of the last
post, I threw myself, hungry and drenched as I was,
upon the rude divan, and using an urchin for a pillow,
sank immediately into a refreshing sleep, which, however, was not of long duration. Amid the howlings
of the storm I dreamed that I was at sea. I thought I

had climbed aloft one glorious evening, as was my wont, to see the sun dip his golden tresses in the ocean. A tempest burst upon us almost instantaneously. For some reason I could not descend from the dizzy height, and hour after hour, as the ship plunged, and bathed her yard-arms in the yeasty crests of the waves, I clung to the slender mast with a deathlike grasp. What agony! That dream will never cease to haunt my sleeping hours.

When I awoke the sun had not yet risen above the Wallachian plain. The storm had swept past. The golden and vermilion tint of the eastern sky, and a sweet and balmy freshness of the air, promised a magnificent day. The humble blades of grass had bedecked themselves with queenly pearl-drops, and Nature smiled the more sweetly after the fierce strife of her elements.

After partaking of a cup of Turkish coffee, with black bread, I seated myself in a new *carutza*, and was soon rolling over the soft prairie, almost as swiftly and gently as a car moves upon the even rail. While enjoying a landscape that would have delighted Paul Veronese, I did not omit the long chibouque, loaded with the fragrant tobacco of the Orient. An hour carried us to the next station. My waybill was nowhere to be found. I had left it where I remained over night. It being impossible to proceed without the document, the *tschaousch* was mounted on a fleet horse, and sent

back with the promise of liberal *backsheesh*, in case of
a speedy return.

As the house of the director promised more than
usual comfort, I ordered the best they could prepare
for breakfast. The host was a noble Wallach, with a
strong Roman cast of countenance, who fortunately
spoke German; his wife, a charming little woman, as
blooming and natural as the fresh daisies scattered over
the prairie. Save her own maternal *limba roumanesca*,
she spoke only the language of bright eyes, sweet looks,
and winning smiles.

Their house furnished a good specimen of Wallachian
dwellings in the country. These, whether subterraneous or not, are usually oblong, and divided into
three apartments, the middle one of which opens into
the two others. From the central compartment a large
clay furnace, or rather an immense oven, usually white-
washed on the outside, projects into the room occupied
by the family, and furnishes an agreeable warmth.
For a floor, the inmates use a piece of the soil which
God gave to be lived upon, while a raised divan or a
simple bank of earth extending around three sides of
the room, is so covered with mats and blankets as to
serve for seats by day and a couch by night.

I was often surprised at the order and neatness
prevailing in these unique dwellings, which are so unpromising externally. The men are as idle as the
lazzaroni of Italy, but the women are active, and

exhibit considerable taste in ornamenting the interior
of their rude cabins with sundry figures and frescoes
unknown to the plastic art elsewhere, and produced
from the variously colored clays found in the neighborhood. Unless there be great pretensions to respectability, the apartment in the other end of the *kolibe* is
given over to the animal creation, which there enjoys a
degree of familiarity with its masters that must astonish
shepherd-loving poets, and all sentimentalists of that
school.

The little table, spread *à la Turque*, with the additional luxury of knives and forks, was soon brought in,
and we squatted around it upon the divan. I had for
some weeks enjoyed the magnificent dinners of Muza
Pacha, commandant of Bukarest, where, at the expense
of the Government, the treasures of the French and
Wallachian *cuisine* were daily exhausted in spreading
a luxurious feast. Pachas and post directors, however,
live in a different style. Before me were no sweet rolls
and *café au lait* of Bukarest, no caviar of Giurgevo, no
game from the Bastarnic Alps, nor trout from the icy
torrents of Mount Pion, no confiture of Yassy, with sweet
doultchas, no generous wine of Butzeo or Cotnar, and
no luscious grapes from the blushing hills of Campina,
to be eaten to the soft music of the *lautari*. In place
of these luxuries we had eggs, salted fish from the
Danube, and plastic *mamaglia*, made of corn-meal and
water.

Yet, in respect to intelligence and family comforts, my host, Jian Bibesco, was of the better class of Wallachs. After our meal—more suitable, it must be confessed, for a fastidious vegetarian than a hungry traveller—his smiling little wife brought in pipes and coffee. In the use of these Oriental luxuries—and where, O reader, can they be enjoyed as in the East?—the Wallachs have adopted the manner of the Turks. The moments passed by insensibly, as, reclining upon the rude divan, we related our various adventures.

" Are there no robbers, no Wallach *hyduks* among the Carpathians, like Basil and Bujor and the polished Jian of the last generation?" I inquired.

"Few since the breaking out of the Greek revolution," he replied, "they thrive better among the Balkans. But I can relate an adventure with one who for years was the terror of the Principalities—who was more famous than either of the names you have mentioned."

" Let me hear the story."

" Many years ago," began Bibesco, " I was travelling among the Plaiul Hotilor (the home of the Goths) in the northern part of Wallachia. There were two of us. While threading a deep mountain gorge, all at once we heard near us the sharp report of a gun, which in laconic Pandour style means, halt! We stopped. Seven men emerged from the dark thicket near at hand, and ran up to us. They were armed to the teeth, richly clothed in Albanian costumes, and with faces so con-

cealed by the folds of full silk turbans that their eyes
only could be seen.

" 'Halt there! *techokoi* (dogs),' cried the chief, who
alone was uncovered, ' whither do you journey ?'

" 'To Campina.'

" 'Have you any arms or powder ?' and, without
waiting for an answer, he ordered us to dismount.

" My companion drew a pistol, but he had hardly
touched the ground when the chief leaped upon him
like a tiger, wrested the weapon from his hand, and
brought him to the ground with a blow of the breech.
I thought him dead.

" 'Here is the powder.'

" He snatched it from my hand, and then in a more
familiar tone asked, ' How much money have you in
specie ?'

" 'Thirty ducats.'

" 'We will divide.'

" I gave him the purse. You will see that our mountain klepht was more generous than Basil, who let his
victim pass by in order to attack him from behind, and
make himself drunk with blood,—braver and nobler
than that superstitious fanatic, Bujor, who used to
pray in a church on Sunday and pillage it on Monday, who would not eat meat on Tuesday for an empire,
but would have assassinated you the day following for a
pipe of tobacco.

" 'There are nine of us,' said the chief : ' four times

seven make twenty-eight;' and opening the purse he took from it two ducats, and handed them to me, saying, 'That is enough for two such *coconasi* (timid females) to reach Campina. Remount and go in peace! you have nothing to fear—I am Kirjali!'"

"Did that happen in the open day?" I inquired.

"In the open day—in the very face of the sun. Kirjali was as brave as his yataghan, and would have blushed to use the night."

"He reminds me," said I, "of the mountain brigands of Anatolia, who, notwithstanding their nefarious profession, practise the motto that 'honesty is the best policy.' They secrete themselves in the fastnesses of the mountains, and watching an opportunity, make prisoners of persons who can command a heavy ransom. Not long ago, in the very street of a city, they seized upon the son of a wealthy merchant and hurried him away with impunity. Word was sent to the father that his child would be delivered up in a certain place for 20,000 piastres, but if not ransomed at a given date, they might have his head. The distressed parent, hoping that something would intervene, delayed sending the money until a few hours after the stipulated time. It was too late. The bandits were true to their word. The bloody head was sent back together with the bags of piastres."

"But the story of Kirjali—let me hear the story of his life," and we charged our long chibouques once

more with fragrant latakiah, once more married it with
the aromatic nectar of Mocha.

"Kirjali was an Albanian," resumed my companion.
"His real name is unknown; the Turks call him Kirjali,
which signifies the *brave*, and you will see how well he
merited the appellation. He is the Mandrin and Jack
Sheppard of the Moldo-Wallachs. There is not a
Roumanian maiden but sings his gallant deeds; not
a peasant on the plains or among the mountains who
does not recite his daring exploits by the winter fire.
The Russian poets and painters have celebrated the
curious episodes of his history, and both Pousckhine
and Vaillant have given to the world many of the circumstances which I am about to relate.

"Kirjali was five-and-twenty years of age when a
strange adventure threw him this side the Danube.
The kékaya of the village violated his wife. That is a
crime which the injured man nowhere pardons, and
least of all, in Turkey. Kirjali resolves to be revenged.
At the news of his dishonor, he relates it to his assembled associates, and, while he moves them to pity, leads
them to fear the repetition of his wrongs upon themselves. With him they repair to the dwelling of the
kékaya. At the noise of the crowd collected in the
courtyard the latter steps out upon the balcony, but
quick as lightning, before he has time to ask the cause
of their presence, Kirjali stands before him with menacing
gestures, foaming mouth, and eyes burning with rage.

"'Wretch!' cries the injured man, 'ask pardon of this multitude.'

"The kékaya, with true Mussulman hauteur, responds only with a smile of contempt.

"'Demand pardon!' again cries the infuriated Kirjali.

"'Away, Giaour!' rejoins the kékaya, gnashing his teeth in rage, and bringing his hand to the hilt of his handjar.

"'Giaour!' reiterates Kirjali with fury. 'Giaour! Yes, Oghlan Ali, thou base slave!' and he throws himself upon the kékaya. 'Pardon, Oghlan Ali! ask pardon of this multitude, by Christ! by Allah! Thou wilt not? Yet once—no? accursed be thou!' Inclining over the balcony he cried to the multitude below—'Christians! make place for this brute.' The crowd draws back. He exerts all his strength. 'Beware of the stone!' shouts he, and a hoarse groan is heard below. The blood flows, the kékaya expires, and the crowd disperses, saying coldly, 'The dog of a Moslem is dead.' Kirjali has taken flight, carrying with him only his implacable enmity to the Turks.

"Arrived in Wallachia he enters the service of the Boyard Dudesco, and makes the acquaintance of Svedko, the Servian, and also of Mikalaké. The tall stature of Svedko, the robust and trained body of the Moldavian, and the audacious bravery of both, mark them as proper men for Kirjali. He gains their friendship, and inspires them with his own hatred of the Moslems. When he thinks them weaned from the domestic life which is so repugnant to himself, and comes to regard them as men after his own heart, he communicates his projects, organizes a band of robbers, and makes the two brigands his aids.

"At that time the Phanariot Greeks were in possession of most of the resources of the Principalities which were farmed out to them by the Turks. The latter regarded themselves as masters of the soil. Mussulmans with well-filled girdles were to be met everywhere, in the khans of the cities, in the caravanserais, and upon the grand routes, even to the defiles of the Carpathians. The Wallachs were but little removed from slaves, and Kirjali found thousands of opportunities to satisfy his vengeance upon their cruel Turkish masters. For three years he enriched himself with their plunder alone. Many a wealthy merchant, who had journeyed into Moldavia to purchase its famous wax, and honey, and *tassao*, never revisited his kindred; many a wife and daughter wept in the Turkish harems in vain for a wished return. The name of Kirjali became terrible on both banks of the Danube.

"Among other exploits he crossed over into Bulgaria, and assisted by Mikalaké alone, attacked a large village. Kirjali entered many of the houses, and set them on fire, cutting down without pity whosoever resisted, while his lieutenant was occupied in collecting and guarding the booty. They retired without molestation. Nor did Kirjali always spare the Christians. Thus with a band of three hundred Pandours he went from one Principality to the other, levying contributions upon villages, pillaging the mansions of wealthy Boyards, and scattering fire and carnage until 1821, when Alexander Ypsilanti incited a general insurrection in Wallachia and Moldavia. Influenced on the one hand by the *hetarie*, that vast association organized for the liberation of Greece, and on the other by the eloquent appeals of Theodore Vladimiresco to the Daco-Romans, he resolved from a *hyduk* to become a hero in the cause of the Greeks—from a brigand to become an Albanian prince. Assembling his companions, he addresses them in these words :—

" ' Brothers! for four years we have shared the same dangers and the same joys. If you are satisfied with your brother he is satisfied with you. But the moment is come when I must leave you, if you prefer not to follow me, for the hour of independence has sounded for the Christians of Turkey. Ypsilanti is at Burlata : he is marching upon Foschana. Theodore Vladimiresco is at Crajova, and will soon attack Bukarest. Choose for yourselves : you are free. He who loves me will be with me.'

" At these words Mikalaké and three-fourths of the band ranged themselves around their chief; the remainder placed themselves behind Svedko.

" 'Adieu, comrade,' said Kirjali to the latter, 'but let us always be brothers.'

"The next morning beheld our new Scanderbeg on a Persian carpet, smoking and sipping coffee, à la Turque, in the tent of Ypsilanti.

"Kirjali was to the last a faithful partisan of the Hetarists.

"But neither he, nor the chiefs under whom he fought, had a just comprehension of the movement in which they were engaged. Their forces were insufficient. Material resources were wanting, while the Turks were well organized and prepared for the emergency. The neighboring powers also looked upon this premature uprising of the Hellenists and Hetarists with apathy and indifference. Ypsilanti found himself unequal to the crisis. Having quickly become master of the greater part of the country, and even of Bukarest, he lost precious time in irresolution and vain parades, and when, at last, forced to engage with the Turks in earnest, the flower of his army perished, while the chief himself fled to Austria. Kirjali fought like a lion at Dragaschan. Ten Osmanlis, they say, fell under his yataghan. With Mikalaké and a few others, he escaped the massacre of the sacred battalion. The cause of the Hetarists was lost in Wallachia, and the insurrection completely suppressed.

"The remnant of the revolutionists, who had escaped into Moldavia, seven hundred in all, made a last stand

10

on the Pruth, opposite the small Russian town of
Skoulianzy. Their leader Cantacuzène ran away as soon
as the Turkish army of 12,000 men made its appearance. Kirjali, Contoguni, Safionos, and the other brave
men who composed this little army had, however, no
need of a chief in order to do their duty. While the
first kept the enemy at bay by means of two small field-
pieces, carried from Jassy, Contoguni by a skilful
manœuvre attacked them in the rear. Overwhelmed
by numbers the leader perished and three hundred of his
brave followers with him. Kirjali and his band soon
exhausted their supply of shot, but loading with broken
arms, sword points, and spear heads, still kept up a fire
upon the Turks.

"The latter were well supplied with artillery, but
abstained almost entirely from using it for fear that
their projectiles would fly across the Pruth, and implant
themselves in Russian soil. A few balls, however, did
whistle near the ears of the Commandant of Skoulianzy,
when, greatly enraged, he addressed a violent expos-
tulation to the Turkish pacha, who turned pale at this
violation of Russian territory, and was careful not to
commit a second offence. Kirjali's band, having fired
away their silver ornaments, their short daggers, and
even the few pieces of money in their pockets, were
forced to give way. Nothing remained to them but their
pistols and yataghans.

"'Let him save himself who can,' cried Kirjali,

when the survivors plunged into the river, and twenty
of them succeeded in reaching the opposite bank. There
they embraced each other like brothers, and fled to the
Russian town of Kissénief. Kirjali and Mikalaké were
among the survivors."

"Shall we depart, seignors?" said the *aràndus*, looking in at the door, uncovered.

The *tschaousch* had returned with my waybill and a
fresh relay of horses stood before the *carutza*. Jian Bibesco determined to accompany me to the next station,
and filling the little box with fragrant hay we managed
to make a comfortable seat for both upon the top.

"Haidee! haidee!" (hasten! away!) and we were
soon whirling over the soft green prairie,

. "As fast as fast could be."

"But, Kirjali?" said I, when my companion had
finished his chibouque: "what became of the brave
hyduk?"

"I will tell you. After his escape from the Turks
on the Pruth, he lived for some time *incognito* at Kissénief. He and his companions spent their days in the
coffee-houses, smoking long pipes and entertaining each
other with long stories of adventure. They wore their
old Albanian costume with girdles glittering with
pistols and yataghans, and though apparently poor, bore
themselves as proudly as in the days of their prosperity.
It came to be whispered that Kirjali was among them.

"The party assembled one evening at a coffee-house, and were disputing with warmth about the flight of Ypsilanti and the death of Vladimiresco, when Kirjali rose and bringing his hand to his yataghan, exclaimed, ' Accursed be the assassin of Theodore Vladimiresco !' An hour after he was arrested by a dozen Cossacks, and carried before the governor of the town. He knew not what awaited him, but thinking that he had merited well of Russia, supposed that the reputation of his bravery had reached the ears of the Emperor, and that he was now about to be presented with a decoration or a sword of honor."

" Fortunate man !" I interrupted.

" Wait a moment !" replied my companion.

"Kirjali was brought into the presence of the governor.

" 'You are a brigand !' said the latter, sternly eyeing the prisoner. The chief was stupified, and for an instant lost all courage, but recovering himself, replied, ' I fought after the flight of Ypsilanti, and emptied my pockets to pay the Turks in the battle on the Pruth.'

" 'Then you are Kirjali ?' continued the governor.

" 'Himself !' answered the chief. ' God knows I am Kirjali.'

" 'Enough,—the pacha of Yassy claims you. According to the conventions between the Turks and ourselves you must be given up.'

" Kirjali threw himself at the feet of the governor.

The lion-hearted man trembled, and wept like a woman. 'Mercy! mercy!' cried he. 'In Turkey it is true I was a brigand, but my hand fell only upon the Turks and the Boyards. God is my witness, that while I have been a refugee in your midst, I have harmed no one. I gave my last pieces of silver to charge our cannon in the affair of the Pruth. Since then I have not had a para. I, Kirjali, have lived upon alms! What have I done that Russia should sell me to my enemies?'

" In vain that he sought to touch the stony heart of the governor.

" 'You must explain with the pacha,' said the latter, and an order was immediately issued for the extradition of Kirjali to Yassy. Loaded with chains and thrown upon a *kibitka*, he was escorted to the frontier, and there handed over to the Turks. Mikalaké was near him.

" Brought before the pacha, Kirjali expected nothing but death. 'Save my wife and child,' said he, 'for myself, I have nothing to ask.'

" He was condemned to be impaled, but it being then the fast of the Ramazan, his execution was deferred a few days. A guard of seven Turks conducted him to prison, still loaded with chains, with orders to watch him closely, even in his cell. All resistance was impossible. A brave chief, Kirjali was also a strategist of consummate skill. He was humble—so mild and compliant that the pride of his guardians was flattered.

He understood their weakness, and acted his part so skilfully that the very first day they looked upon him with a degree of compassion unusual to their ferocious natures. The second day they spoke with him, and the exploits of the bandit inspired in them an involuntary respect. The third day, with the naïf curiosity peculiar to the Orientals, they listened eagerly to the recital of his numerous adventures. The fourth, an intimacy sprang up between them. The fifth, they were his friends: and the sixth day, without intending it, they were——"

" His liberators ?" I eagerly demanded.

" You shall see," replied my companion.

" Seated in a circle round him on the evening of the sixth day, they listened as he spoke to them of his approaching death. His voice flattered, his eyes caressed them. He saw that they were moved.

" 'The will of God be done!' said he. 'No one can escape his destiny. My hour is near; but before I die I would like to give you some testimonial of my regard.'

" The Turks opened their eyes with attention.

" 'When about three years ago I was briganding with Mikalaké (may God give peace to his soul!) I buried my money here and there : at Scaunu-hotilor, in Wallachia, in Moldavia——'

" 'Where ? where in Moldavia ?' eagerly demanded Aslan, the chief of the Mussulman guard.

"'At Vulcanu.'

"'Far away?'

"'Among the mountains.'

"'In which direction?'

"'At the foot of Cicliu.'

"'*Pekee! ben pekee!*' (good! very good!) rejoined the Turks.

"'But here,' continued Kirjali, 'near by, only a league from Yassy, behind the monastery of Cetatue, in an open place, twenty paces from a rock which resembles a mastiff that has lain down to guard the pistols of his master——'

"'*Ev-Allah!*' exclaimed the Turks.

"'There, twenty paces from that rock we buried a jar full of gold ducats. It is fated that I shall not enjoy them. Find them; they are yours.'

"At these words the Mussulmans could hardly moderate their expressions of delight. Aslan alone was suspicious.

"'Is Kirjali a traitor or a brave man?' asked he.

"'Brave! brave!' responded his companions; 'brave is Kirjali!'

"'If he should conduct us to the place?' said Aslan.

"'Why not?' replied the six others.

"'That would compromise you,' interrupted Kirjali; 'I have given you the locality; you can easily find the treasure.'

"'Why compromise us?' they all inquired. 'There

is no danger. The night favors us. You shall be our
guide; and if you are not a brave man, there are seven
of us.'

" At midnight they took off his chains, tied his hands
firmly behind his back, and placing him in their midst,
left the prison without being perceived.

" Now Kirjali leads them. He traverses the city;
descends by Tàtàras; passes before the convent of
Formosa, ascends the woody escarpment of the monastery of Cetatue, and stops a moment to take breath and
orient himself. He is in excellent spirits—overflowing
with that modest joy that accompanies a good action,
and speaks not, except to testify his pleasure at being
useful to his companions.

" 'Shall we soon be there?' demands Aslan.

" 'Soon,' replies Kirjali, ' a hundred paces further
and—if I do not enter the paradise of the Christians,
pray Mohammed to open for me his own.'

" They advance : a slight rustling is heard, and a
dark shadow glides stealthily through the underwood.
Kirjali, with the ear of a rat and the eyes of a lynx, has
seen, heard, and understood. But when Aslan, turning
towards him, asks—

" 'Hast thou seen anything?'

" 'Why then,' responds he—'Only a hare or a par-
tridge startled by our approach;' and to turn away all
suspicion adds, 'To the right a little : let us leave the
woods.'

"Advancing a few rods further among the scattered mounds, he stops short by a rock rising about two feet above the ground, looks around for a moment, and then says to his guardians—

"'Measure twenty paces in this direction, and dig.'

"Five of the Turks draw their yataghans and begin to remove the earth with them, while the two others guard the prisoner seated on the stone. They dig some time in silence, and, to work with more ease, take off their turbans, detach their girdles, and lay their pistols on the ground. Kirjali watches them. 'Not yet? Not yet come to it?' cries he, after they have worked away fifteen minutes. 'Not yet. Allah help us!' respond the Ottomans, the perspiration dropping from their faces.

"'Courage, you will soon reach the gold,' and to the two others he said playfully, in a low voice, 'Let them work; they will think all the more of me for it. But I am afraid they have not selected the precise spot.'

"'Comrades!' cries one of the guards, 'dig more to the right. You will never find it—let Kirjali assist you.'

"'Let him assist us,' responds Aslan, wiping the perspiration from his brow.

"Kirjali is brought to the spot. Aslan unbinds him, and places a yataghan in his hand. The two guards also lay aside their pistols, and all fall eagerly to work. Kirjali digs with all his might, now and then ceasing for a moment to stimulate the avidity of the Mussul-

10*

mans with a word of encouragement.   At his example
the latter take courage: the thirst of gold renews their
strength: they dig—dig with eager impatience.

"'I have it!' at last cries Kirjali, 'here it is! here
it is!'

"At these words the Turks throw aside their yataghans and fall to work with their hands in impatient
haste to uncover the treasure.

"Kirjali rises up with a groan of fatigue, and quicker
than lightning plunges his yataghan into one of the
prostrate Turks.   Leaving the steel in the wound, he
snatches up two of the pistols, shouts in a voice of
thunder, 'Slaves! here is my gold!' and buries their
contents in two of his guards.

"'Kirjali!' speaks a voice near by.

"'Mikalaké!' responds Kirjali—and the four remaining Turks save themselves by flight.

"Masters of the field, Kirjali and Mikalaké embrace
each other as brothers.

"'My wife and my son?' asked Kirjali.

"'They are saved, and in a secure retreat.'

"'*Mashallah!* I have wept for them: God is merciful!'

"Thus reunited, and having nothing to hope for from
the Turks, Kirjali and Mikalaké continued for a long
time their depredations in the vicinity of Yassy.   They
even pushed their audacity so far as to threaten to burn
the city unless the Hospodar, Jian Stourd'a, should

remit the sum of 50,000 piastres within a week. The money was paid. But fortune ceased to favor Kirjali. Betrayed by one of his own men, and surprised while asleep, he sold his life as dearly as possible in defending himself and Mikalaké."

"Generous and heroic man, he deserved a better life and a better fate, yet doubtless esteemed it fortunate to die with his arms in his hands rather than to be strangled or gibbeted.

"On the 20th of September, 1824," said Bibesco, "two bodies, covered with wounds, swung from the gallows of the Meïdan of Capo. They were those of Kirjali and Mikalaké, but the former was hung many hours after life had departed. You have the story of Kirjali."

Towards noon we halted a few minutes at the hut of a shepherd with whom the *surruju* was acquainted. His lonely home was the only dwelling in sight on the broad prairie, where, with his faithful dogs, in pastor costume and crook in hand, he watched the bleating flocks and lowing herds of his Wallachian lord. Rude and scanty was the furniture of his hut, but the shepherd did his best in the way of hospitality. His was a life of ease, if not of contentment. In a legend of the country it is related that a shepherd, having been suddenly transported into the celestial regions, was not in the least dazzled by its golden splendor, but simply prayed God for a bagpipe.

After all, shepherds and shepherdesses are not the delightful creatures represented by poets. Their manner of life, though sighed for by the inexperienced and the sentimental, is not enviable. It has been my experience to find them frequently the idlest of the idle, the vilest of the vile, while their cottages, so poetical in description, are generally the abodes of squalid filth and corroding poverty.

"Tout poète est menteur et son metier l'excuse;"

yet if we may venture to believe a Daco-Roman legend, my shepherd host on the plain of Wallachia may have been a happy man. Here it is.

"Listen to me, O Emperor, in all patience. I am come to answer concerning the heavy task imposed upon me. For the purpose of restoring thee to health, O Emperor, thou hast ordered me to buy the shirt of a happy man. Anxious to serve thee and find a remedy for thine affliction, I have traversed the whole earth searching with care for the desired garment. But this world is a chaos of sorrows. There is no person without troubles: no one is happy. I found a young man, handsome, rich, and of noble birth, but the companion of his heart was faithless; and he was miserable. Here a father wept over a lost son, there one lamented that he had none over whom to weep: neither of them was happy. With all the beauty, all the poetry, all the wealth, all the health, all the satisfied desires of this world, still no person is happy. I saw that my companions even were penetrated with grief to find that there was not a single happy man in the whole world.

"I despaired of thy recovery, when from the bottom of a valley I heard one day the soft music of a lute. We listened to the delightful notes: we ran to the place whence they proceeded. O heaven, what beauty! A lovely brook murmured through the valley, slowly and softly. A little flock was lying down with the flowers and grazing among the trees. The shepherd sang: what happiness! 'Shepherd!' said I to him, 'thou livest in misery. Thy flock is too small. Come with me to my Emperor, who wishes that the poor and the lowly may, hereafter, have him for a father, in order that he may be happy.'

"Long live the Emperor! but I have need of nothing. I am rich with my flocks, content with my cottage. I love God, my dog loves me: this brook assuages my thirst: this flock nourishes me—I am happy."

"Quick, quick! his shirt; let me put it on; hasten, O my benefactor!" cried the Emperor.

"Alas! sire, how great is my sorrow to tell you that this happy man had not even a shirt to his back."

Within a few miles of the Danube the country became somewhat broken and uneven. From a low ridge I caught sight of the river. With what joy did I salute the noble stream gleaming there in the sunshine and ever hurrying its broad and ceaseless flood towards the Euxine! Achmet Pacha's army was stationed near Kalarasche. From the immense number of cattle and sheep slaughtered to feed 30,000 soldiers, and the filthiness of the Ottomans in everything but person and dress, my olfactory organs announced the proximity of the camp before the green tents of the Nizam became visible. Soon, however, I saw the latter stretching away in long picturesque lines, and beyond them the town of Kalarasche, the wide morass skirting the left bank of the Danube, and the hills of Bulgaria looming up in the soft grey distance.

The road ran directly through the Ottoman camp. I wore the uniform of the Nizam, but fearing delay and the possibility of being taken for a Russian spy, directed the *surruju* to cross the lines with all possible speed. Two sentinels, however, ran up to the road, and threatened to fire unless we came to a halt. The frightened *surruju* checked his horses so suddenly that he almost brought them upon their haunches. My passport was carefully examined, but as it had been *visé* by the commandant at Bukarest, I was allowed to proceed. Some of the troops were being reviewed, others slaughtering animals, or engaged around the camp fires, while others still, seated in groups on the grass, were smoking long pipes and alleviating the fatigues of war with the naïf recitals of the Orientals. Many

of them were from sunny Tunis and the shady villages
along the Nile.   And they, O reader, with their worn
weapons and soiled standards, were no holiday troops,
but soldiers of many a hard-fought contest—men who
had shared the triumphs of Oltenitza and Oetate, and
shivered the Cossack ranks before the redoubts of
Kalafat and Silistria.

Just within the barrier of Kalarasche—a filthy
Wallachian town of some 5000 inhabitants—I noticed
the long subterranean houses, or rather covered trenches,
in which the Russian troops had been quartered the
previous winter.   The *surruju* set me down in the open
street.   Leaving my baggage at the shop of a Jew
who fortunately spoke German, I sallied out to have
my passport put in order for Silistria, whither I hoped
to proceed before nightfall.   Precious hours, however,
were consumed in running from the military Commandant
to the police and from the latter to the quarantine.
The Chief of the last mentioned institution, without
whose signature it was impossible to cross the Danube,
I could not find at home, and having obtained a description of his person, began to search for him in the
streets.

While wandering about the town I came near
plunging headlong into an unguarded hole in the earth
which I at first supposed to be a well, but found to be
the entrance to an immense subterranean chamber used
as a depository for grain.   Granaries like this are com-

mon in Wallachia, and indeed throughout the East. It is of such that the rich man said, "I will tear down my barns and build greater."

I also visited the grave of General Schilders, who was altogether the most capable man in the Russian army in the Principalities, and sacrificed himself in the failure before the outworks of Silistria. He sleeps by the side of a small Greek church. Two or three Wallachian soldiers dressed *à la Russe*, were standing guard near by.

With much trouble I ultimately found the quarantine officer quietly enjoying his chibouque in front of a Turkish khan, as unconcerned as if the plague and cholera had never been heard of. He was a fair sample of government officials in the East.

At sunset I strolled to the pavilion of Achmet Pacha which had been erected on the low bluff bounding the morasses of the Danube. On the latter, which are dry in the months of summer and autumn, a large Russian force had operated during the siege of Silistria. The sea of verdure was dotted here and there with herds of cattle for the Nizam. Beyond the Danube, and partially obscured by the golden shadows of the Bulgarian hills, were the tall minarets of Silistria.

A military band, composed of Italians, played in front of the pacha's tent. Softly their martial notes floated away on the evening air, and after that oriental sunset, all was so still and calm and beautiful that I

could hardly realize how recently its quiet had been
broken by the rude clamor of Mars. Terribly magnificent, from this point, must have appeared the night
bombardments of Silistria! Through streets crowded
with loitering officers and soldiers from the neighboring camp, I repaired to a Wallachian Khan. They
could furnish me with supper but not with lodgings.
The same apartment served for a kitchen and eating-room.
Paint is a luxury unknown in Kalarasche. In place
of tables and chairs rude benches were ranged along
a couple of forms not unlike those from which I remember to have received my first mental pabulum in
the old country school-house. Instead of consulting a
bill of fare, I had only to look into a row of flat copper
kettles seething over a charcoal fire, and choose from
which to make a meal. Different kinds of meat and
vegetables were compounded and seasoned so as to
furnish the variety desirable to Wallachian palates.
Red pepper alone appeared to be a common ingredi-
ent. The cook, who was also host, scullion, and dispen-
ser of raki, judging from his overgrown form and careless, sensual expression, would have regarded death
itself as merely

> "* * * A card of invitation
> To sup with all the saints on high."

I ordered a bowl to be filled from one of the kettles;
and its contents, a doubtful compromise between solidi-

ty and fluidity, with a piece of Spartan bread, composed
my evening meal. The luxury of a bed I did not an-
ticipate for weeks to come, and had despaired of finding
a room or shelter of any kind, when a Greek merchant
from Galatz generously offered to share his chamber
with me. We visited a neighboring khan, where pipes
and coffee were served *à la Turque*. A number of Wallachs of the better class had called in to talk over the
events of the day. From the recent affairs of Kalafat
and Silistria the conversation turned to the earlier wars
of the Christians and the Turks. The Wallachs do not
regard themselves as a conquered people, and of late
circumstances have tended greatly to mitigate their
ancient hatred of the Turks. The cruel burdens imposed upon them by the Russians, the treacherous
character of the Austrians, and the remoteness of the
Gallic and Italian races, with which the Daco-Romans
would naturally sympathize, have drawn them nearer
to the Osmanlis. They prefer remaining subjects of
the Padishah to obeying a Hapsburg or a Romanoff,
especially as their subjection to the former is nominal,
imposing upon them merely the payment of a small
annual tribute. My friend kindly interpreted for me.
We listened long to thrilling incidents and heroic adventures pertaining to the border land of the Christian and
the Turk. Their earnest recitals, embracing the truth
of history and fresh with patriotism and local interest,
were now and then interspersed with *doïnas*, or popular

songs. The latter were fragrant with the aroma of poetry that springs from the heart, and possessed the enthusiastic vigor and untamed force which characterize the infant productions of a liberty-loving people. Both songs and recitals related principally to famous Wallach chiefs of earlier times and the bold hyduks of the mountains, who often taught the Moslems manners by nailing their turbans fast to their heads. The law treats the hyduks as brigands, but the people forgive, and often glorify them. Why not? have they not always attacked the enemies of the common country? Though they murdered the Turk and the Tartar and robbed the insolent Boyard, they were none the less faithful Christians, in the estimation of the people, and were always mindful of the poor.

One of the mountain bandits having been arrested and brought before the Cadi, the latter said to him, "Tell me where thy treasures are concealed, and thy life shall be spared."

"I have concealed them," replied the robber, disdainfully, "in such a manner that neither thou nor thine will ever enjoy them. I have hid them in the hollows of trees, where the poor only will find them."

Another hyduk was taken before a pacha of Constantinople. When asked how many Christians he had slain, he answered boldly:

"I? I have never in my life caused the death of a single Christian; but I have shed the blood of many an infidel. When I fell in with a rich Christian I asked him only to divide with me. If he had two horses I kept one and left him the other. If he had twenty piastres I gave him back ten ; but when I met a Turk, I took his head and left his body."

The Daco-Romans are proud of having preserved their Christian faith. Neither the threats nor the promises of the Turks have induced them to apostatize. In their long conflict with Islamism, however, the humiliation of defeat has not unfrequently been followed by the palm of martyrdom. One of the princes, Constantine Brancovano, submitted to the most cruel agonies rather than renounce his faith. A popular *doïna* relates his heroic conduct ; and Daco-Romans, young and old, love to hear the story of his death.

" After a bloody conflict, Brancovano was taken prisoner, with his three sons. They were embarked on board of a ship, and transported to a fortress on the banks of the Bosphorus.

" 'Constantine Brancovano,' said the pacha before whom he was brought, 'if thou would'st save the lives of thy children, become a Mussulman.'

" 'Infidel !' responded the prince, with disdain ; ' thou canst murder my children, but I shall never renounce the faith of my fathers. Do as thou wilt.'

" The furious pacha sent for two black executioners. They took the eldest of the sons of Constantine, a sweet and delicate child, seated him upon a stool, and cut off his head.

"The father, unable to suppress a sigh of anguish from his wounded heart, cried, 'O Lord, thy will be done.' The second child was brought forward, his full eyes bathed with tears, and long auburn locks floating round his neck. The executioner severed his head from his body.

"Brancovano sighed a second time, and from his pale lips escaped the same words of resignation. The pacha was moved by such constancy. A sentiment of pity was wakened in his heart.

"'Brancovano,' said the latter to him, 'thou hadst three sons, thou hast now but one; wilt thou save him?'

"'God is great!' responded the wretched father. 'I was born a Rouman and a Christian; I wish to die a Christian.' Then turning to the only child which remained to him, he said:

"'Do not weep, my dear boy; do not deprive me of my remaining strength. Die with thy faith, and heaven shall be thy heritage.'

"The pacha gave the fatal signal, and the child's head dropped from his shoulders.

"'Lord, thy will be done,' murmured Brancovano.

"His vision darkened; his heart was ready to break; then he exclaimed—

"'May my curse, O Turks, fall for ever upon your heads! May you be swept from the earth like the clouds that are dissipated by the winds! May you die without a child near to close your eyes, and rot upon the soil without sepulture!'

"He spoke, and his head fell under the same sword that had slain his three sons."

At a late hour we returned to the chamber of my Hellenic friend. He professed himself highly delighted to extend hospitality to a citizen of the great Republic, proposed toasts innumerable to the memory of Washington, and exhausted his French lexicon in praise of our institutions; but when I set out the following day for Silistria, he scarcely objected to my paying roundly for his ostentatious hospitality. That is the way with the Greeks.

O Mendax Græcia!

Finding it impossible to obtain a *carutza* to convey me to the Danube, I bargained for a ride with a Jew who was going down to the landing with a load of Kalerasche apples. He promised to be ready at ten o'clock, and was careful to demand his piastres in advance. But hour after hour rolled away, and the Jew fretted and quarrelled, and piled apples upon his miserable cart, until there was no place left for a seat. I had determined to set out on foot and leave my baggage with the Israelite, when Colonel Bent drove up from Bukarest. I had often met him in Bukarest. He was *en route* for Constantinople, with dispatches from Omer Pacha, and offered me a seat in his covered wagon. A new relay of horses was obtained at the post-house, and an hour later we stood on the left bank of the Danube. A division of Turkish troops was engaged in erecting a *tête du pont* opposite Silistria, and awkward barges filled with the Nizam were crossing to reinforce the army of Achmet Pacha.

CHAPTER X.

SILISTRIA.

"Unfading their fame,
As their sacrifice great,
Who leave a good trade
To take care of the state."

AN old Turkish boatman, the very picture of Charon, ferried me across the Danube for a few paras, and set me down on the narrow strand of Silistria. A half-dozen houses were scattered along the sandy shore, but the city appeared to be sunk below the level of its wall, a few tall minarets alone being visible. Colonel Bent hastened on in the first arabá that could be obtained. His dragoman informed me that Silistria contained neither a hotel nor lodgings of any kind kept by a Christian. At the promise of a couple of piastres, a greasy *cawas* shouldered my carpet-bags, and led the way to a Turkish khan. A few Ottoman soldiers were leaning idly on their muskets at the gate through which we passed. It seemed as if the genius of death reigned within those solitary walls. Nothing save the desert, the wilderness, and the calm ocean, is so silent as a Turkish city. There is no rattling of carriages or tramp of hurried feet; there are no brawling voices; men, silent men, in the grave costume of the Orientals, and women veiled from the sight of the most inquisitive eye, glide along the narrow streets and stony lanes, more like ghosts than human beings.

The khan, where a board was promised me for a couch, contained but a single square room, with mats for squatting Turks, racks for chibouques, and shelves for nargilehs and the diminutive cups in which coffee was served by a bustling little *cahvidji*. For a guide I employed a sleek, good-natured Mussulman, who, in the comprehensive language of the Orientals, "knew everything." Mustapha was shaven as to his head, wore his beard after the manner of the Osmanlis, and gloried in a girdle glittering with bright weapons. He slept at my feet on the hard boards, drank black coffee, and ate fiery dishes of *paprika* at my expense, having no objection to my piastres, however much he may have hated me in his heart as a Christian.

Silistria, the chief city of the *Sandjac* of Silistria, has a population of about twenty thousand souls. It is surrounded by a wall and *fosse*, the former varying from fifteen to twenty feet in height, and mounted, at proper intervals, with saucy cannon. There is no "distressing regularity" of streets. In the open places winged and four-footed carnivora may often be seen dismembering an unfortunate donkey, or other animal that has died by the way. In Turkish cities filth, and mud-and-dust,

her twin sister, "most do congregate." There is not a
painted house in Silistria, and, with the exception of
the mosques, but two structures more than a single
story in height. One of these is the residence of the
pacha; the other the half-finished Greek Church, the
erection of which the Russians began while in possession
of the city, from 1829 to 1833. In the end towards the
Arab Tabia I counted where twenty cannon-balls had
struck and done good execution. The Russians were
compelled to batter down the work of their own hands.
That is typical of Russian—of European policy. Ab-
solutists are blinded: they plan and work merely for
to-day, and build not upon strong and permanent bases.
The tyrants of our generation are doomed to roll the
stone of Sisyphus: would that they had also to grasp
after the delusive cup of Tantalus!

The low cabins of Silistria are surrounded by little
court-yards; and walking through the streets is passing
between two continuous, windowless walls. These
wicker-walls—for such is their construction in the Danubian cities—are so well plastered, internally and
externally, as to defy the eye of the curious howadji on
the *qui vive* for the veiled beauties within. The one
great object for which Mussulmans appear to live, is
to conceal their women from the inquiring eyes of
men.

The manner of building these low Bulgarian houses
is unique. Four posts are driven into the earth,

and joined by means of cross-pieces, between which are interwoven the pliant twigs of the willow. The framework is done by the awkward native carpenters after the posts are driven into the earth, and not while they are lying on the ground. The low roof is tiled. A coating of clay, mixed with animal manure, is applied outside, and on the inside a plastic material affords a hard wall which can be whitewashed or ornamented with the wretched daubs in which the artists of the gentler sex sometimes indulge. For the floor they employ a piece of the soil given by Allah to be inhabited by his children.

Acres of such habitations may be swept away in a few minutes by fire; and hence the immense conflagrations which so often occur in the large Turkish cities. They are, however, the best structures to withstand a siege. I did not see a house that had not been perforated by one or more cannon-balls; but they had merely passed through the wicker-walls, leaving small round holes, the same as when bullets are fired through a glass window. It was only where a bomb-shell had burst, that great injury had been done. The Russians appear to have aimed particularly at the five mosques of Silistria, whose tall minarets were excellent targets. Shot and shell had made curious work with those barn-like edifices.

It is astonishing that seventy thousand balls and bomb-shells should have been fired into a city like

Silistria without producing more damage than a few
Bulgarian masons could repair in a short time. There
was also but a small loss of life in the garrison
and among the inhabitants. The general rule that it
requires nearly ten thousand discharges to put one of
the enemy *hors du combat* was more than true of the
Russians, and less than true of the Turkish and Arab
troops who defended Silistria during an eventful siege
of thirty-nine days. In vain did Paskiewitch attempt
to unlock the gates of Silistria with a golden key.

By the side of one of the ruined mosques lies Mussa
Pacha, who fell during the siege when about to engage
in the morning-prayer. His successor was an arrant
coward, and took refuge in one of the subterranean
chambers, where most of the inhabitants repaired for
safety. In the course of a few days his hair became
snow-white through fear and mental anguish. Butler,
who also fell during the siege, was buried in the court-
yard of a Greek church. The Bishop of Silistria would
not at first permit the desecration of what the orthodox
Greeks call holy ground, by the dust of an Englishman, but was obliged to yield to the order of the
pacha.

Let justice be done to the true defenders of Silistria.
The English claim that the exertions of Butler and Naysmith alone saved the city from falling into the hands
of the Russians. Such was not the case. The first
place of honor belongs to Grach, a brave Prussian, who

unfortunately died at Rustchuk one month after the repulse of the Russians before the outworks of Silistria. Butler and Naysmith were Indian officers, good in hand-to-hand conflict, but nothing more. Neither of them made any pretensions to skill in engineering, and both were unpopular with the inhabitants of Silistria, as also among the defenders of the Arab Tabia. Grach was an excellent engineer; to him was given the charge of repairing the breaches effected by the Russians, and to him, more than any one else, were the Turks indebted for the preservation of Silistria.

A strong garrison was still stationed in the city, and there was great fear that the dreaded *Moskos*, as they called the Russians, would return.

I had seen everything worthy of attention in dingy, battered Silistria. Anxious to study the rural life of the Turks, and still more anxious to experience the Oriental life of Stamboul and Grand Cairo, I resolved to avail myself of the first opportunity to depart. Terzin Bashí, a little Hungarian tailor with whom I had become acquainted through Mustapha, conducted me to Ibrahim Pacha, the governor of Silistria. His Excellency was reclining in the *selamlik*, or male apartment, making, with a company of grave Mussulmans, the delicious *kief*. Our entrance scarcely interrupted their placid intoxication. Terzin meekly slipped off his shoes in the presence of the pacha, who, in his province, is the representative of the august Abdul

Medjid, or, as the faithful delight to call the Sultan,
" The Unmuzzled Lion, and Proud Tamer of Infidels."
The pachas of the different provinces and cities are appointed by the Padishah, and to him alone are they
answerable.   In Turkey, posts of honor and profit, like
the governorships, are given to those who offer most
piastres for them, and are usually continued on the
annual payment of a stipulated sum, although the principal occupation of the pachas is " to suck the very
vitals of their provinces."   They control the revenue,
command the military force, and exercise criminal
jurisdiction in their respective governments, but notwithstanding these powers are called " statues of glass"
by the Turks, and can be deposed and punished at the
will of the Sultan.

I judged Ibrahim Pacha to be a man of the most
profound incapacity.   In a country where hereditary
aristocracy has no existence, and where slaves become
Grand Viziers, the highest offices are often administered
by persons taken from the very dregs of society.   The
traveller occasionally has the opportunity of enjoying
the hospitality of these officials, who, however, cannot
be esteemed, and must be looked upon with that feeling
of mingled regard and pity which is excited by the
simplicity and goodness of very benevolent but at the
same time very illiterate old women.

Ibrahim Pacha gave one twitch of his superior
ocular muscles, regarded me for a moment, and then

directed that I should be seated. It was not my first interview with a pacha, and I did not stop to enjoy the proffered pipe and coffee.

"What does the howadji desire?" inquired the pacha.

"The howadji, O Ibrahim Pacha! desires permission from your Excellency to travel through Bulgaria on his way to Stamboul," replied Terzin Bashi. The governor gave another twitch of his ocular muscles, and waved his hand towards the police-office, where I was to procure the *teskery*, or Turkish passport.

The office of the police bore a close resemblance to a tailor's shop, the officers and scribes all seated cross-legged upon mats and low divans.

My original purpose had been to proceed from Silistria to Schumla, cross the range of the Balkans and reach Stamboul by Adrianople, the second city of European Turkey. But there was no Turkish post between Silistria and Schumla, and I could find neither horses nor a Tartar to act as guide. Terzin Bashá said that I might possibly procure an arabá, or Turkish carriage, at a khan in the city, and we started off to see what could be done. The keeper of the khan, a dark, thin-visaged Turk, with deep-sunken eyes, informed us that he could furnish the desired conveyance to Varna, but in consideration of the length of the route, the escort necessary to keep off the vagrant klephts and bashi-bazouks, and innumerable perils by the way, he de-

manded three hundred piastres. I finally brought him
down to two hundred and twenty-five piastres, about
ten dollars of our money. We were to start the next
morning; the escort was to be strong, the horses superb,
and the arabá the best of the kind.

Our bargaining had been carried on in a group of
silent smoke-consumers.

A collection of the pipes of all nations would give
the best possible idea of national characteristics. The
calumet of the American Indians, ornamented with
feathers and porcupine quills, and made to be smoked
by a whole tribe, indicates a certain advance of the
social state, but gives no idea of individuality. The
universal pipe of the Yankee nation, short, cheap, and
thoroughly practical, is a decided indication of progress.
The American must smoke as he runs and reads, else
he would not get time to smoke at all—earnestness and
activity being chief elements of his character. The
sharp, money-getting American physiognomy seems, in
fact, hardly complete without the accompaniment of a
pipe or a cigar directed towards one of the wandering
planets.

The more cumbrous article used by the English
denotes a spirit that does not like to be small in smoke,
literal or symbolical. The *pipe en boue* of the French,
with its *penchant* forward, like the French military cap,
gives us an idea of the future, but is most liable to be
ruinée by the force of opposing obstacles, as is the case

with all schemes floating in the undefined limbo of French politics. The German *Meerschaum*, a cross between the Teian lute and a polypus, has a smack of the Oriental mingled with Occidental habits and usages.

One lingers before the windows of a Viennese *Fabrik* as he would in a gallery of antiques, for on those huge *Meerschaum* bowls the cunning hands of artists have toiled to reproduce what was most wonderful in the smoky myths of the Greeks, from the funeral games round the tomb of Patroclus to the lesser glories delineated on Achilles' shield. Still the smoking Dutchman is a working Dutchman. He suspends his pipe so as not to interfere with locomotion or manipulation. Without tobacco-smoke we should not have the metaphysical ravings and the ontological vagaries of the Teutonics.

The pipes become longer and more cumbrous as one penetrates further in the east of Europe. It was in the family of a Hungarian Count that I first learned to appreciate the Turkish chibouque charged with fragrant latakieh. French civilization has done something in the way of reducing the folds of the Ottoman turban, in diminishing the ampler parts of the baggy pantaloons in which the true Mussulman delights, and in displacing the cumbrous, all-concealing veil by the "woven air" that reveals the flushing tints and rich outlines of Circassian beauty, but the Turks will never become a pro-

gressive people until their pipes are reduced from the
dimensions of feet to those of inches.

Smoking is *par excellence* the peculiar institution of
the Ottomans. The influence of the latakieh seems to
have penetrated their very souls, and lends a hazy,
dreamy outline to all the manifestations of their outward
life. The genuine Turk, dressed like a fillibuster, enjoys
his long chibouque or snaky nargileh from morn to eve,
with the gravity of an alderman, and the glowing visions
of the great-eyed Orient appear ever to float before his
mental vision as hé yields himself up to their perennial
charm.

I was, indeed, greatly amused to see how the Turks,
on their own soil, and uncorrupted by foreign tastes,
persevere in the use of tobacco. At college, my·room-
mate persisted in going to sleep every night with an
ignited cigar between his teeth. The Dutch pilot who
took us into Rotterdam, after

"A two weeks' tipsy time on cold salt water merely,"

must have descended from the Wouter Van Twiller who
smoked away the embarrassments attending the early
settlement of New York, although at the time, his pisca-
torial face, the fishy expression about his eyes, and two
short arms, moving precisely as a dolphin moves its
pectoral fins, led me more than once to cast my eyes
under his long-tailed coat in search of a like caudal
appendage, and suggested that he might have had an

existence in that remote age when, according to Vathek,
Holland was all water, and the ancestors of the present
inhabitants all fish. Not everywhere, as in the canals
of Rotterdam, can one behold sailors mounting the rig-
ging of lofty ships, and handling the sails with pipes in
their mouths. When, at the inn of the Three Lions in
Semlin, I saw my Hungarian neighbor complacently
shaving himself, with a huge Meerschaum suspended
from his teeth, I verily thought the Mont-Blanc of
fumitory achievements attained; but stranger experiences were in store for me among the Orientals. The
chiboukdji, or pipe-bearer, takes the first rank among
the servants of every Turkish grandee. Pipe-cleaners
perambulate the streets of Turkish cities, and announce
their craft after the manner of charcoal-men with us.
Turkish troops often go into action with their long pipes
lashed upon their knapsacks, and at the close of the
daily fasts of the Ramazan, the chibouque takes the pre-
cedence of food and water.

It was on a mild autumnal evening that I rode out
in company with an Italian surgeon in the Turkish service, to visit the celebrated outpost of Arab Tabia. I
had spent the day with my friend in attending the invalids at the different hospitals, crowded to excess with
the sick and wounded. As we passed through the
land-gate of the city I noticed, in a nook of the wall
near by, a company of Turkish troops piously engaged
in the evening prayer. They had carefully gone

through the requisite ablutions, and having spread mats and garments on the earth in the direction of Mecca, performed the impressive devotions which characterize the followers of Mohammed. There was the absorption peculiar to the Ottoman worship of to-day, and not the fervor of the Janissaries kneeling in solid squadrons, shouting *Allah hou !* as they rushed into the combat, and with an enthusiasm unknown to the less devout Nizam, overrunning province after province, with the sword in one hand and the Koran in the other. An officer appeared to lead, and they performed their prostrations and semi-prostrations as if they had been accustomed to press shoulder to shoulder into the conflict.

A ride of a few minutes brought us to the base of the hill on the crest of which the Arab Tabia is situated. The bluffy bank of the Danube is here interrupted for a distance of several miles, the hills, or hrater the line of elevated ridges, which disappear in a *plateau* at the southward and westward, sweeping around Silistria in the form of an amphitheatre. What would otherwise be a continuous but elevated plain, is broken into several ridges by defiles that radiate back into the country a distance of many miles. On the crests of the ridges, thus thrown into a semi-circle, are situated the five out-posts of Silistria, the two nearest the river, namely, the one above and the other below Silistria, being of less importance than the three others, the Arab Tabia at the south-east, the Medjidie, nearly south from the city, and a smaller fortification between them. The Medjidie appeared to be the only one of the out-works worthy the name of a fort.

The hill-side, formerly covered with fields and vine-yards, had been ploughed by cannon balls, and was thickly strown with the fragments of exploded bombs. The Russians approached Silistria from the south-east, and so puny was the obstacle in their way, that an ora-tor in the House of Commons was entirely correct in saying: "The first wave of that remarkable invasion was scattered into foam before the out-works of a fifth-rate fortress."

I shall never be able to comprehend the Russian defeat at Silistria. The Arab Tabia, a mere out-work, simply an earth fortification, was defended by no more than six guns. Never was there offered a better posi-tion for bombarding a city than from the *plateau* which stretches away from the Tabia, and affords a command-ing point of rare advantage, an indispensable acquisi-tion in the successful carrying on of a siege. Yet Paskiewitch was foiled, and lost the flower of his offi-cers, with fifteen thousand men, before beating a retreat.

I examined every inch of ground with the greatest care. There were the mines laid by Schilders, and sprung precisely at the moment to create dreadful havoc among his own troops; there were the long

trenches by which the enemy thought to approach near
the Tabia, but were so often foiled by the watchful
Arabs within; there were the hard-trodden spots of
hand-to-hand conflicts in which the fierce Arnauts had
cut to pieces whole squadrons with their terrible yataghans; and there, O horrid sight! were the pits
into which the thousands slain had been promiscu-
ously thrown. A div'sion of Turkish troops, which
had been engaged in extending and repairing the fortification, slowly descended from the Tabia, and with
beating drum and glittering bayonet, marched up the
declivity of the Medjidie.

The extended view from the Arab Tabia is not
uninteresting. At the southward and eastward, beyond the plain on which the Russians operated, are
the forest-clad hills of Bulgaria. At the northward
flows old Danubius as proudly as in the days when
Roman legions were encamped along his banks; while
beyond stretches away, farther than the eye can reach,
the low plain of Wallachia, once the highway of nomadic nations pressing towards the Occident, but in later
times the battle-ground of empires struggling for the
mastery of the world.

After our return to Silistria I dined *à la Turque* with
my Italian friend in an old Turkish house assigned
for his quarters by the Pacha. The meal consisted of
numerous dishes prepared in genuine Turkish style by
a soldier-servant, the names of which are unimportant,

the ingredients of which I never knew, save those of
the rice *pillaff*, the crowning glory of every Turkish
feast. We were joined by another Italian surgeon,
also in the service of the Sultan. After dinner pipes
and coffee were brought in, but more pleasing to me
than the dainty morsels of the Turkish *cuisine*, the fragrant latakieh, or the aromatic Mocha, were the racy
anecdotes of Turkish life, and the imbroglios of adventure with which, reclining upon the divan, we beguiled
the long hours. My companions were political exiles.
They spoke feelingly, almost tearfully, of their loved
Italy, of her fair hills and poet-sung skies, and seemed
to bemoan the cruel fate which had exiled them from
their home on the yellow Tiber to the inhospitable
banks of the Danube.

At a late hour they sallied out to accompany me to
the lodgings of Terzin Bashi. Gas was never dreamed
of in a Turkish city; the streets are without names;
the houses without numbers. Every person who ventures out after dark must carry a paper lantern, or incur
the risk of being arrested by the police and kept in
custody until morning. An English ambassador at
Constantinople, not Stratford de Redcliffe, occasionally
ventured abroad incognito in the dark. In one of his
nocturnal sallies without the customary light, he fell
into the hands of the police; and, as they could not
distinguish an English lord from an ordinary Frank
traveller, was, in spite of all his protestations, put in the

lock-up to sleep with rogues and vagabonds. The
following morning the authorities were shocked at
having caged a British lion. With the usual tact of the
Ottomans in getting out of difficulties, they hastily summoned the largest Turkish band in Pera, formed a hollow
square for his Excellency, and persisted in marching
him down to his Palace through crowds of wondering
Turks, and amid the frenzied dissonance which a Turkish
band alone can produce.

It was a night of Bulgaro-Egyptian darkness. Now
and then a sleepy watchman whose girdle glistened with
weapons would stop us for a moment, and the wolfish
dogs over which we stumbled in the street followed us
with their flashing eyes and ceaseless barking.

We were soon lost in the interminable labyrinth of
Silistria, and wandered about a long time without being
able to find Terzin Bashi, or even the house from which
we had started. Some one at last conducted us to the
lodgings of the little tailor. My friend bade me *buena
notte*. Terzin lived in an Armenian family, who, with
characteristic inhospitality, insisted that I should not
spend the night under their roof, as in their peculiar
godliness, they would not sleep with a heretic believing
in the divinity of CHRIST and the eternal punishment
of sins.

The Bashi—may the blessing of Allah rest upon him
and all honest tailors!—then conducted me to his little
business sanctum in another part of the city. On his

platform as a couch, and his goose for a pillow, I soon
fell asleep, dreaming of klephts, fleas, and especially
of the luxurious arabá in which I was to be suspended between heaven and earth on the following
day.

At this point of my narrative it is proper to allude
more fully to the Turkish service and to my own connection with the Ottoman army. On my arrival at
Bukarest, the last of August, I immediately called upon
the English Consul General to place myself under his
protection, there being no American Agent in the
Principalities. At his house I met Muza Pacha, an
English officer who had greatly distinguished himself
in Southern Africa, and held the rank of a general in
Omer Pacha's Staff. He desired me to accept of the
position of a surgeon in the Turkish Army, physicians
being at that time in great demand. A few days afterwards we called upon Omer Pacha, who also requested
that I should remain. An order was given me to join
a regiment in the camp outside the city barrier, but my
attention, during a stay of six weeks, was confined
almost entirely to the inmates of the hospitals and a
few Russian prisoners. The enemy had retreated, so
that there was no opportunity for active field service
short of the Crimea. For a time the cholera raged
fearfully in the army. A number of the Boyard
palaces were converted into hospitals, but in spite of all
our efforts, 4000 men were swept away by the frightful

disease. Ice applied externally and internally was generally found to be the most efficacious remedy.

I have a high opinion of the bravery and the patient endurance of the Turkish troops. Like the Russians they need only to be well officered to make most efficient soldiers. A narrow spot was pointed out to me in the Arab Tabia where it was necessary that a single person should be constantly exposed to the fire of the enemy. The position was as fatal as death, but no sooner had one occupant fallen, than another leaped into the place, as if emulous of his companion's fate. In passive obedience, however, the Turks do not surpass the Russians. A Muscovite officer who had boasted before a company of guests that his soldiers would obey any order he might give, commanded a number of them to march directly over a lofty precipice : and they would have done so to a man had not his voice checked them at the last moment.

The Ottoman service offers but few inducements to foreigners. The Turks are slow to perceive merit, and still slower to reward it. "*To-morrow*" is constantly upon their lips, while the society of even the first officers cannot be agreeable to a cultivated person, or one who is accustomed even to the decencies of life.

We hear much of foreigners in the Ottoman service, yet but few of them acquire positions of importance. Their connection with the army is nominal, rather than actual. The gradations of rank are multiplied in a manner very convenient for amateur warriors, who are ambitious to become lions in the clubs of London and Paris by campaigning a few weeks along the Danube or in Asia. The Mussulman still looks with contempt upon the Giaour. The Turkish soldier will not be led into action by an officer who has to give his orders through an interpreter. It is generally the Mussulman *bimbashis* and *kaimakams* who head the columns.

Yet I was surprised at the number of political exiles in the Turkish service. There were rough Tartars, cut-throat Italians, and numberless adventurers who seemed to subsist upon their hatred to Russia. One day a Pole presented himself, who, although very lame, had walked a distance of two hundred miles merely for an opportunity to fight the enemies of his country. At the head quarters of Muza Pacha I met Baron Z——, a young Hungarian nobleman, whose remarkable experiences greatly interested me. His father had been so long imprisoned for political reasons and subjected to such barbarous treatment, that when released he was a drivelling, white-haired idiot. The sons swore revenge. On the breaking out of the Hungarian insurrection every one of them enlisted, and fought the Austrians as the enemies of their liberty and the murderers of their father. At the close of the war the Emperor spared the life of the young Baron in consideration of his youth, but exiled him from his country and confiscated the estates of the family. The cavalier took refuge in Bavaria, but soon after quarrelled with a government official, and was obliged to leave the kingdom. After a short stay in Switzerland, he ventured to revisit Hungary in disguise, and even spent a few days with the remnant of his family. In the beginning of the Russo-Turkish war, Servia opened a promising field for the Baron. The Prince employed him to organize a large force of cavalry, but the enterprise was speedily abandoned on account of the remonstrances of the Western Powers, who suspected Russian interference. An intrigue at Belgrade occasioned a personal affair between the Baron and the Austrian consul, and it became necessary for him to seek his fortunes elsewhere. He embarked secretly on board a small Turkish vessel for the lower Danube, but was wrecked on the way, and lost everything except his dress and well-battered sword. The Baron had walked the entire distance from Kalafat. I gave him a shirt, a luxury he had not enjoyed in many weeks, and shared my pocket-money with him: the poor fellow had almost forgotten the color of ducats.

One of my associates in Bukarest was an intelligent German surgeon, known as "The Hakeem." He also had served in the Hungarian war. Having at its close emigrated into Turkey with Kossuth, and enlisted as a surgeon, he had, for a number of years, followed the fortunes of Omer Pacha. The Hakeem was a noble fellow. I remember he used to show me a curious memento of the friends from whom he had been exiled. He had transplanted a number of hairs from their heads to his delicate arm, where they appeared to flourish as well as upon the cranial soil.

I was walking one evening in the garden of Tchis-medjiou in company with the Hakeem, when fortunately we met Iskender Bey, attended by two servants and a pipe-bearer. We were introduced, and had a long conversation relative to the war and his own remarkable life. The Bey, now a Colonel of the Turkish cavalry, is, next to Omer Pacha, the most important personage who took part in the Danubian campaign. The Russians will remember him, for he has slain his hecatombs. He is about fifty years of age, of medium size, but powerful organization, with a beard and hair of glossy blackness, and a pair of eyes capable of sending out lightning glances from beneath their overhanging brows. His uniform was splendid, if not gaudy, and as we walked along among the *élite* of Bukarest who had assembled to enjoy the music and the loveliest of evenings, people would turn round, stare at my companion as if he had been an emperor, and whisper to each other, "There goes Iskender Bey." He is of Tartar origin and a Mussulman by birth, his father having emigrated to the Crimea, where our hero was born and inherited the title of a Count, as well as an estate in Bessarabia.

Expelled from the Crimea while a mere youth for political reasons, Iskender Bey became a sworn enemy of Russia, and in the character of a chivalric soldier, has personified in his travels the Wandering Jew, having taken part in almost all the remarkable wars of the last thirty years. He was in Spain during the Carlist war, in Portugal during her revolutionary struggles, and left the Peninsula decked with no less than eleven orders. In 1836 our knight errant was at the siege of Herat in Central Asia; the Opium war called him to the Flowery Empire, and he especially distinguished himself at Canton. After the termination of the Chinese war, he found his way to Algiers, and took part in most of the engagements with Abd-el-Kader. Iskender then left the French service, and the year 1848 found him in Hungary under Bem, his patron and idol. The sorrowful events of '49 drove both of them to Turkey, with fifteen thousand others. He at once entered the Turkish service, and under Omer Pacha took part in the expeditions against the Montenegrins and Bosnians. A gallant victory terminated the last-mentioned campaign, for which he received the thanks of the Sultan and the rank of a Pacha. Austria and Russia protested, and the Bey voluntarily resigned his position. His services at Kalafat are well known. The Cossacks shudder at the mention of his name. After the affair of Silistria he hung like a consuming fiend upon their retreating squadrons, and a few days before I met him, had returned from a daring and successful reconnoissance along the Pruth. Of the Bey's gallant conduct at

Eupatoria, and his being wounded in battle by a personal enemy, the reader is doubtless well aware. He speaks French like a Parisian. Besides his wanderings in the Old World, Iskender Bey also informed me that he had travelled extensively in the United States and the West Indies. It marks a day in one's life to meet with the hero of so many battles.

At Bukarest I also found one of my countrymen, Major Burr Porter, of New Jersey, who enjoyed the confidence of Omer Pacha. He attained the rank of *bimbashi*, and at the close of the war was honored with a decoration for his services.

The Turks love the sword, but have a holy horror of the scalpel. It is a precept of the Koran that the human body shall not be opened, even though it contain a jewel. For several years after the establishment of the Medical College in Constantinople, the Sultan Mahmoud was obliged to procure Christian subjects for dissection through the Austrian Minister.

The Mussulman hakeems divide all diseases into two classes—nervous affections of the face and those of an erysipelatous character; and secondly, all maladies not included in the above. Some of the Emirs profess to cure the former by means of charms, incantations, and mysterious remedies, of which they claim the monopoly. When the cure is not effected, however, they insist that it is not from the inefficacy of the means employed, but from the fact that the disease does not belong to the class in question.

Poujulat relates an incident which came under his observation in the slave-market in Constantinople and illustrates the occasional cruelty of the Turks in the employment of remedial agents :—

A female Abyssinian was suffering from an inflammatory tumor on the right arm. Her master, supposing it to be a plague-spot, ordered molten lead to be poured upon the affected part. This heroic treatment caused the most exquisite suffering, and the poor slave besought her master, with tears and cries, to desist. Poujulat inquired, through his dragoman, if molten lead was efficacious in the treatment of the plague. "It either kills or cures at once," replied the Mussulman; "and, by Allah, that is what I want."

Comparatively few Turks practise medicine. The professors of the healing art in Turkey are mostly Greek and Italian adventurers who make the simple Moslems the dupes of their charlatanism. Even those who are employed professionally in the Seraglio, and penetrate the mysterious harems of the Turkish grandees, do not hesitate to administer preparations followed by the most fatal effects. The Imperial license to practise anywhere in the Sultan's dominions can be obtained for a few piastres. The Turks do, indeed, profess to teach medicine in the schools attached to the mosques after the doctrines of the old Arab authors, but the practice is

founded upon no definite system. Their simple remedies, however, are usually more efficacious than the
treatment dictated by the ignorance and superstition of
the Greeks. The believer in fatality does not fear death;
and this is the principal reason why in times of the
plague the Turks suffer less than the timid Christians.

Among the Slaves the practice of medicine is confined chiefly to magicians and sorcerers. Surgery, as
among the Turks, is monopolized by the knights of the
razor, that instrument being employed alike in shaving
the heads of Mussulmans and the faces of Christians,
in circumcision, bloodletting, and the removal of tumors. The mountaineers of Bosnia and Montenegro
have an efficacious method of treating the wounds received in their almost perpetual conflicts. There are
no midwives. The women frequently bring forth alone
in the woods or fields, at a distance from any habitation.
Soon after the infant is born the mother washes it in
the nearest brook, and then pastures her flock, or continues her labor as before. The child being constantly
in the open air and not impeded in movement by over-
much clothing, speedily acquires the use of its limbs,
but is generally nursed by the mother until her next
pregnancy, though five or six years intervene. Un-
weaned children are not unfrequently heard discussing
the quality of their beverage, and, as everybody smokes,
have been known to throw aside the pipe to have recourse to the maternal breast.

As among all barbarous or semi-barbarous people, the absence of favorable circumstances causes the premature death of children that are naturally feeble. Those only who possess vigorous constitutions reach maturity. A rapid increase of population is thereby prevented, but the survivors are more healthy and vigorous than the majority in civilized countries. This is especially the case in the mountainous regions, where the natural strength is increased by a temperate manner of life.

The Slaves have for ages been acquainted with hydropathy. In case of a febrile attack, the Servian at once avails himself of the exorcising prayers of his priest, and drinks largely of cold water. For inflammatory diseases he imbibes freely of an infusion of pepper or gunpowder and slivovitza—a vile brandy made from plums. The patient then covers himself warmly, so as to get rid of the malady by profuse perspiration. An infusion of hot wine and gunpowder is considered a specific for the fever and ague. Lumbago is driven away by severe frictions. For constipation, a bullet is swallowed, or a heated stone applied to the abdomen. The latter remedy is also employed to dispel rheumatic pains. Vinegar is taken to give tone to the stomach. Sugar, however, is the heroic remedy. M. Pouqueville says that they give it to persons in the agony of death in order that they may die sweetly.

CHAPTER XI.

RAMBLES IN BULGARIA.

"Danubio, rio devino
    Que por fieras naciones,
    Vas con tus claras ondas discurriendo."

LOPE DE VEGA.

'Prayer is better than sleep."

THE Turks rise early in order to invoke the Prophet. The *cawas* of Ibrahim the khan-keeper, led to my quarters by some mysterious agency, woke me at an early hour. He shouldered my carpet-bags and led the way to the khan, where, as he declared, they had been waiting an hour for my arrival.

Oh, the delusions of Oriental exaggeration! The escort to guard me against the bashi-bazouks had dwindled down to two Turkish soldiers, one of whom was sick and the other charged with a large bag of piastres for a Mussulman merchant in Stamboul. These, in default of a banking system, had to be conveyed hundreds of miles, and, in my opinion, were a capital temptation for klephts and hyduks.

The magnificent horses promised the day before, which were to rival the swift coursers of the Hafter, I found to be wretched hacks of the vilest Bulgarian blood, incomparably more wretched than anything equine to be found in the wide kingdom of Connaught. I am confident that, taken together, they did not exhibit one of the seventy good traits which, according to the best Arab judges, belong to every good horse. What magical wand could have converted the creatures of my imagination into such detestable hivans? They seemed to be formed merely of osseous tissue and the organs of respiration, packed tightly in a cutaneous integument, the solution of whose continuity revealed here and there the workings of the skeletons within. Baron Munchausen would not have entertained for a moment the thought of reaching Varna with such animals, to disturb whose stable equilibrium but a single breath of air seemed necessary.

But the arabá to which these promising steeds were harnessed—what beautiful word could express a more perfect delusion! Not a particle of iron or metal of any kind had been used in the construction of that nondescript vehicle, good for nothing but in name. Upon four wooden wheels was balanced a rude box framed of sticks of wood interwoven with pieces of bark. Bows had been bent over the top so as to support a coarse mat, in the shade of which might repose the weary traveller.

Ibrahim looked upon me with lofty contempt, as
with a single effort of the hand I produced a luxation
in almost every joint of the curious structure.

"*Bosh! bosh!*" I shouted into his ears—a Turkish
word signifying all that is worthless and contemptible
in things verbal or material. I was tired of Silistria,
and plainly saw it would be of no avail to rouse up the
fanatical in Ibrahim. The *cawas* of the dirty, yellow
turban and shuffling babouche declared that not another arabá could be found in the city. "*Pekee!
pekee!*" "good! good!" whispered the Turkish soldier
with the piastres, who, instead of drawing his cimiter
to force me into the arabá, ingeniously threw his arms
around my neck and besought me to go.

I meekly inquired of Ibrahim how long it might
take me to reach Varna in the conveyance he had supplied. His answer gave me a clearer comprehension
of the Turkish character than medicating a whole regiment of the Nizam, or poring for weeks over the ple-
thoric tomes of Von Hammer. Drawing himself up to
his full height, and seizing with one hand his magnificent beard, he shouted, "*I* am not Allah! how should
I comprehend time and distance?" and meekly added,
"There is but one God, and Mohammed is His Prophet;" a sentence that cuts the gordian-knot of all
Ottoman difficulties.

We started. The very dogs barked at us until they
lost the power of utterance; and veiled women ran out

to look upon the departing howadji. I could only wonder whether the awkward, waddling bundle of clothes
before me enveloped the blushes of sweet seventeen or
the frowns and wrinkles of seventy winters. We passed
through the southern gate of Silistria, and took the road
· which winds up the ravine between Arab Tabia and the
Medjidie.

Looking back, I bade a final adieu to old Danubius,
the one great river of Europe. It was on the Danube
that I had enjoyed some of the wildest scenery of the
Eastern world. I had there become acquainted with
all the beautiful features of German social life—there
learned to honor Hungarian virtue and patriotism.
Amid the strata of expiring civilizations I had seen
much which carried the mind back to the time when
the tramp of Roman legions was heard along the
Danube, and Roman life throbbed in the busy camps
and cities of the Ister, long ago given up to desolation
and solitude. Even in these remote regions the victorious eagles left the impress of civilization, for, as Pom-
pey said, the foot of a Roman soldier had but to touch a
foreign soil, and new institutions would spring forth
as if spontaneous.

What wonder, O reader! that the ancient Egyptians
deified Nilus! He scatters fertility like a god; and
without him there had been no Egypt. Great rivers,
like hoary temples and the everlasting mountains, have
a mute eloquence of their own. The mythology of

Greece, instinct with imagination, crowned every rock with an Oread, hid a Naiad in every fountain, and if it did not, like the Egyptian, deify rivers, it at least made them sacred to the gods, and converted their sylvan banks into retreats for the graces and the muses. Like the illustrious French traveller, who roamed over the Eastern world more as a pilgrim than a mere gatherer of facts, I have always had a passion to press my lips to the bosom of great rivers, believing it were better if man and nature were more familiar. Thus have I drunk from the Mississippi, the Thames, the Rhine, the Rhone, and the Danube; thus also from the Nile, the Jordan, the Ilissus, and that lesser stream of Asia whose murmuring waters often listened to the songs of Homer.

Rivers are the moving highways of the nations. In the earlier ages of the world they slowly accomplished what the steam-ship booming on the ocean, and thought leaping across the globe on telegraphic nerves, are now doing to solve the destiny of the human race. Their Briarean arms embrace the earth. The earlier migrations crept slowly along their banks, and much of the commerce of the world still flows in their channels.

The familiar and high-sounding names of Eastern rivers are apt, however, to give a wrong impression of their size and importance. The Danube and the Nile are indeed magnificent streams; the former receiving the waters of a hundred rivers, with many nations clustered on its banks, the latter flowing through a thousand miles of desert without a single tributary. The Jordan is worthy to be called a river only when swollen by the winter rains: the Eurotas of Sparta is a mere mountain-brook. The Simois, and that stream on the plain of Troy which the gods called Xanthus and men Scamander, are scarcely visible except to the eye of faith; the Cephissus, which waters the groves of the Academy, and once waked the swelling thoughts of Plato, would not, in this practical age, propel an ordinary saw-mill; and the Ilissus, the Ilissus of Athens, that far-famed river sacred to the muses, can be leaped across by a child, and furnishes scarcely water enough to purify the rags of a few Greek women, the unpoetical descendants of the *Musæ Ilissiadæ,* who once wandered along its banks.

Never shall I forget that inky, leaden Bulgarian sky, or the cold wind which, cradled among the icy peaks of the Balkans, swept down the ravine through which we were passing. The Wallachian plain, the minarets of Silistria, the Arab Tabia, and the Medjidié, were soon out of sight, and drawing my travelling-cloak closely around me, I stretched myself at full length on the bottom of the arabá, to meditate upon the pleasures of travel among semi-barbarians. Of romance there was none: romance belongs to civilization.

I found the arabá much better than I had expected. From its looseness of construction it yielded gently to the sudden elevations and depressions in the Bulgarian road, and swayed to-and-fro like a ship in a storm. The horses were not nimble, nor did their peculiar manner of locomotion correspond to anything I had read in the German work on the gaits of animals, but, like the arabá, excepting a few vicious tricks, they surpassed all expectations.

On reaching the elevated plateau which flanks Silistria, the winding road stretches off in a south-easterly direction towards the Euxine. As we advanced, the country became more hilly and broken. The ravines were well wooded. Many of the slopes bore a close resemblance to the oak-openings of the West; and from time to time we passed through magnificent forests that would do credit even to American scenery. The soil would be exceedingly fertile, were it not for the great scarcity of water during the months of summer and autumn. The first day's journey I saw but a single stream. The region, for many miles in the interior, had been occupied by the Russians, and presented a scene of the utmost desolation. Hordes of marauding bashi-bazouks had destroyed the little left after the forages of the Cossacks. The Bulgarian cabins were reduced to ashes, and their inmates swept away by the rude breath of war. The fountains erected here and there by Moslem piety or Moslem pride had fallen into decay, or had recently been broken and defaced by ruthless hands. The Russians plunged their dead horses into the wells, and the apparition of outstretched

12*

legs from the limpid water was not peculiarly gratifying
to a thirsty traveller.

The road was in a state of nature. Selim, a paragon
of Oriental ease, was perpetually losing his way among
the diverging routes, and the sick man patted along
behind us, on the spare Bulgarian pony. Abdallah,
my right-hand man, and withal a plump, good-natured
Turk from the camp of Achmet Pacha, mingled his
amatory chants with the sighs and groans of the arabá.
He seemed happy, just returning to Stamboul, after a
long campaign on the Danube, and sang *güzal! pek
güzal!* (my beautiful! my very beautiful!) hour
after hour, in drawling, nasal tones, that could not
have been equalled by a Scotch master of psalm-
ody.

We met a long string of arabás from the interior,
drawn by red-eyed buffaloes, and loaded with grain for
Silistria. I did not omit the Turkish salutation, *Aleikum
salaam* in answer to *Salaam aleikum!* (Peace be with
you!) to the drivers of these anomalous animals before
vehicles still more anomalous. No other quadruped,
bovine or equine, combines so perfectly all the points
of ugliness as the Bulgarian buffalo; and certainly, the
cunning hand of man cannot devise another vehicle so
ludicrous and indescribably wretched as the Turkish
arabá, whose original must have been in use among the
nomadic peuplads of Orchan and Timour. Magnificent
word, typical of that Oriental exaggeration which for

ever flatters with high-sounding names, and disgusts with the shabbiness of the reality.

We made comparatively little progress, and at nightfall reached Koutchouk-Kaïnardji, a large Bulgarian village, where the celebrated treaty of that name was signed on a drum-head, in the year 1774, by Field-Marshal Romanoff and the representative of the Grand Vizier. In that convention, since so often invoked by Turkey as well as Russia, the Porte recognised the independence of the Tartars of the Crimea, and granted to the Russians free navigation in all the seas of the Ottoman Empire, thus opening the route to Constantinople to the Muscovite fleets, and foreshadowing evils innumerable to the Turks. Catharine, by way of compensation, restored to the Ottomans Bessarabia, the Danubian Principalities, and the islands of the Archipelago, previously conquered by the Russians.

We left Koutchouk Kaïnardji long before daybreak. For some distance the road led through a deep gorge where the groans of the arabá awakened echoes resembling the gibberish screams of disembodied spirits, whom I imagined to be waiting in that Stygian chasm for a passage to the other world. Emerging at last we entered a magnificent forest with elevations interlocked here and there with silvery streams. The face of the country was far more interesting than between Silistria and Kaïnarji. To all appearance the Cossacks had not extended their forays beyond the latter place.

Our slow progress gave me ample time to study the *flora* and *fauna,* as well as for personal adventure in the wilds of Bulgaria. Indeed to have accelerated our speed beyond a walk would have been attended by the most disastrous consequences to the arabá and our cloud-pawing steeds. By degrees I became greatly interested in the latter. The sight of them carried my thoughts back to a lost antiquity, for in their manner of locomotion I discovered a striking resemblance to the one-sided gait still retained by the elephant and giraffe, and known to have been highly fashionable among the quadrupeds of the pre-Adamic world.

The heart of the Bedouin is not more effectually won by the tearful eye, the plaintive moan, and the tender feminine ways of the camel than was my own by the contemplation of those mathematical lines and points, those time-worn volumes of conic sections (bound in horse) belonging to Ibrahim, the khan-keeper of Silistria.

There was another retarding cause. Selim, Abdallah, and Zabat, simple children of nature, heard sermons in the running brooks, the murmurs of whose waters invited them to prayer. They paused by almost every stream and after the ablutions, made in the precise manner prescribed by the Prophet, bowed reverently towards Mecca. To behold these children of Islam mingling their orisons with the jubilee of awakening morn, now prostrate upon the earth, now stretching their hands toward the stars, was a scene worthy of Veronese and Claude Lorraine.

We had ridden three hours without breakfast, and I began to complain of Selim for having neglected to provide something for me to eat on the way.   At last we approached a cluster of houses, but on finding no khan, betook ourselves to the place where several Turkish farmers were threshing grain with horses.   A circular piece of ground some four rods in diameter, trodden hard and surrounded by a high fence, appeared to have been used as the common threshing-floor of the hamlet from time immemorial.   The sheaves of wheat were brought from the adjacent ricks, and eight or ten wild-looking Bulgarian horses turned in loose and kept revolving round the lazy Turk in the centre until the wheat was disengaged by the action of their nimble feet.

They were partaking of their morning repast, and hospitably invited us to be seated with them.   The fluid portion of the meal consisted of sour milk, an article of diet in great favor with the Turks, and pure cold water from a neighboring spring.   The solids were served in the shape of enormous griddle-cakes, cemented together with butter of the most dubious quality, and of bread which, notwithstanding much experience, I at first took for granite.   I sat on the ground and ate as greedily as any one in that dusty group.   While travelling in England it occurred to me that the word host is derived from the Latin *hostis*, signifying an enemy; but, generally, the Turks will receive nothing in return for hospitality like the above. In fact, my escort set about the matter as if there had been no necessity for an invitation from Baba Bashi, the farmer. Sometimes, however, the good Mussulman, who invokes the blessing of Allah upon the head of the departing howadji, does not object to having a few piastres slipped slily into his hand.

Baba Bashi learned by accident that I was a hakeem. The physician stands in high repute with the Orientals. To consult the oracle of Esculapian wisdom the cadi dismisses his court, the mollah his school, and beys spread their table with eastern hospitality. I need not here relate how many curious cases were brought forward for my examination, and how much gratitude I often evoked by a word of sympathy and advice. Baba Bashi at once requested me to see a sick child in his family and conducted me to the hamlet for that purpose. We entered the courtyard surrounding his house, and after a short pause in the *selamlik*, or male apartment, proceeded to the *harem*.

Though simply a Turkish farmer, Baba Bashi was evidently in good circumstances, and I was not a little surprised at the extent of the establishment within those unpromising mud walls. Two or three low structures had been united into a single edifice, the exterior of which had never been desecrated by paint or whitewash. The prominent architectural idea in the construction of a Turkish house is to separate the male and female apartments and make the rooms square. The apartments are generally low and well ventilated, the latter being rendered necessary by the smoking habits of the Osmanlis. The ceilings of Turkish rooms are usually ornamented, but on entering the *selamlik* of Baba Bashi my attention was at once attracted by the artistic embellishments on its walls.

Like Sterne's wig, they were both above and below criticism. Clays of various colors had evidently formed the plastic material for those curious pictures, the execution of which I could attribute only to the architects of the amorphous griddle-cakes just eaten with the Bashi.

There stood a camel and lion complacently eating fruit from the branches of the same tree, the "ship of the desert" betrayed only by his hump, the tawny king of the beasts partially lost in the dim perspective, from which he was "pawing to get free." Finless fishes sported among clouds, while animals aerial and terrene, never caged in the mental menageries of Landseer or Rosa Bonheur, floundered in waterless seas,

"Huge, unwieldy, wallowing in their gait."

The *harem* was provided on three sides with a raised divan. In one corner stood a number of slender chibouques for females. On the open side of the room was a rude wood-colored case for dishes and clothes.

On our approach there was a regular stampede among the children. I presume that they have since often been told, "Be good children now, or that beardless howadji will come back again and carry you away!" The mother remained seated upon the divan.

"Dost thou think, Hakeem Bashi, that the child will recover?" inquired Baba of me, after I had carefully examined it.

"I hope so," I replied.

"Give it medicine, O Hakeem, that it may not die," solemnly enjoined the Bashi.

Here was a professional dilemma. I had not been able to procure even a sugar-coated pill at Silistria, and my medicine case was as empty as a contribution box after a charity sermon. But remembering the purifying and tonic effect of cold water, I gravely remarked, in the best Turkish I could command, "Turn the child's face towards Mecca twice a day, and wash it with the water that Allah gave to be used by the Faithful."

There is but one sight more sad than that of deserted cities and villages: it is to behold well-filled cities of the dead in places once busy with life—to step from gravestone to gravestone in solitudes once throbbing with multitudes of human beings. This sense of loneliness in the wilds of Bulgaria often weighed upon me with a secret terror.

Here we come upon a little village, consisting of a few Turkish and Bulgarian huts, with a cemetery near

HIGH LIFE IN ROUMANIA.

p. 122

at hand, covering acres of ground, and dotted with tombstones fallen or leaning in all possible directions; and there, on the open plain, or in some shady grove, traversed "Harvest Fields of God," as the Germans beautifully call these resting-places of the departed, in the loneliest solitude.

Bulgaria is the desert of Islam—not a desert of sand, but of rich, uncultivated wastes.

Populous cities sprang up in the time of the ancient kings, some of which did not lose their importance until long after the Turks encamped in Europe. With the Moslem invasion, however, expired the Bulgarian spirit. Their ancient renown passed away before the rapid *essor* of Ottoman conquest. Many of their cities and villages were swept away, while others, left untenanted and alone, have so mouldered into dust that not a trace of them now remains.

In vain I searched for the monuments of her ancient power. Yet among the Balkans the traveller now and then meets with reminiscences of the Slavo-Bulgaric rule in the primitive customs, and traditions of the people, and the crumbling remains of a rude and ancient architecture. Nor are there wanting the memorials of cruelty and oppression in more modern times.

Far away to the northward, near the Servo-Bulgarian frontier, there is an immense conical mound formed of twenty thousand human skulls. Whitened by the snow and rain, it gleams on the plain of Nissa like a

tower of Parian marble. The winds from the mountains, sighing through the innumerable cavities of the
skeleton heads, give them doleful, doleful voices. To
a few still cling locks of hair, like mosses and lichens,
which, floating in the wind, add unspeakable horror to
this most barbarous monument. The twenty thousand
Servian and Bulgarian warriors who fell, fighting hero-
ically on the plain of Nissa, were worthy of a better
mausoleum. The Turks point proudly to this monument of their own erecting as a memorial of their
prowess. The Servians, now independent, point to it
with equal pride as a proof of the cost of liberty, and
an eloquent incentive to its preservation.

Bulgaria will likewise one day be free, and her rude
children will chant the songs of liberty, around this
monument of cruelty.

Near Missolonghi, in Greece, where Byron died,
there was also formerly a large pyramid of skulls, which
had once belonged to Greek patriots, but were thus
piled up by the Turks during the Greek revolution.
"Peace to the ashes of the patriotic dead;" but every
Anglo-Saxon, gone to sentimentalize on the battle fields
of Greece, has carried away one of the rattling craniums
as a reminiscence until the pyramid is now reduced to
half-a-dozen sorry specimens, quite unworthy of the
brains which once grew big with Platonic thought, and
throbbed with the pulses of Attic fire.

Yet there can be no fairer seat of empire than Turkey

in Europe. It is endowed with the eternal advantages of nature. Washed by the Euxine, the Ægean, and the Adriatic, and boasting of the noblest rivers and richest plains, its commercial and agricultural resources are not surpassed by any other part of the globe. The northern slope of the Balkans is covered with rich forests. A deep humus extends almost up to their summits. And southward, " while the mountaineer kindles his fire on the glaciers, the olive, the fig, and the pomegranate grow far below in valleys that know no winter." There, is a land of gentle breezes, of purple skies, of all the soft delights of the great-eyed Orient.

But under Turkish rule, which " consumeth for ever," the monuments of ancient art and power have mouldered away. The hum of business and the noise of commerce have yielded to the silence of death, and the sites of populous cities are marked only by the silent cities of the dead.

The Danube is the main geographical feature connecting European Turkey with Central Europe. It seems to invite the return of the Germanic nations toward the soil of Asia, the cradle of their race. The east of Europe lies open to the surplus population of the West. Her half-starved myriads might find a near asylum on the uncultivated plains and in the rich forests of European Turkey. Despotism has decreed otherwise, but from those weary and pent-up millions streams of emigration burst forth, like the fabled fountain of the sacred Arethusa, and forcing their way through other channels, reach the shores of the Western World—the home of a free people who love, and who have struggled, to be free.

CHAPTER XII.

TURKISH TRADITIONS.

"Ye who love a nation's legends,
  Love the ballads of a people,
  That like voices from afar off
  Call to us to pause and listen;
  Speak in tones so plain and childlike,
  Scarcely can the ear distinguish
  Whether they are sung or spoken.

 * * * * * *

  Listen to these wild traditions,
  Stay and read this rude inscription."

Towards sunset the arabá ascended a low ridge, giving me, unexpectedly, an excellent view of the old Turkish city of Bashardshik. It appeared as if sunk in a depression of the Bulgarian plain, its low dwellings enveloped in a sea of hazy, autumnal vapor, above which the minaréts and domes of the mosques rose in clear, sharp outline against the eastern sky. Slowly the arabá wound down to the deserted gate; slowly it traversed the lonely streets. Selim at last halted in front of the khan which, by special command of Mohammed, and in compliance with the spirit of Eastern hospitality, must be kept in every Moslem town for the rest of the traveller. A venerable Turk received us at the door, with many salaams, given in all the rotundity of Oriental expression.

The khan was a low, rude building, divided into two compartments—one for ourselves, and the other for the horses. A fire was kindled in one corner, for light and coffee-making. A few Turks dropped in, one after another, and curled up their legs on the mats, to see the howadji, or learn the latest news from the Danube. The Russians had just recrossed the Pruth.

"The *Moskos* are dogs of infidels, whom we can suffocate merely by spitting upon them!" exclaimed a grave Mussulman; "if each of us do but throw a stone we shall destroy them! Great is God, who doth cause the gales of victory to blow in favor of our sublime Padishah!" But they shuddered, and seized their beards in terror when I alluded to the late depredations of the bashi-bazouks. Bashardshik had formerly contained fifteen thousand inhabitants, but was then well-nigh deserted. A few weeks previous, a band of those pious robbers had scattered the peaceful inhabitants, destroyed several mosques and khans, and laid whole streets in smoking ruins.

We were silently intermingling fragrant vapors of latakieh with aromatic Mocha, when the apparition of a Turk in the low doorway of the khan, with a circular board balanced upon his head, gave us to understand that the evening meal was ready. The Mussulmans use neither tables, napkins, knives, nor forks. We squatted around the circular board, elevated a few inches above the floor by a single leg, and with left hands thrust into our pockets, or under the folds of our garments—for with the Moslems the left hand is unclean—proceeded to discuss the meal. The first dish was a species of fast-day soup, of an infinitesimal degree of fatness and solidity, and eaten with wooden spoons, which my companions were careful to turn upside down when not in use. What true Mussulman, O reader, would be guilty of sumptuary extravagance, in view of the awful declaration of the Prophet, "Verily, the fires of hell shall roar like the lowings of a camel in the bellies of such as use vessels of gold and silver!"

Then followed black Bulgarian bread, exhibiting the obvious qualities of petrifaction, and mysterious compounds of meats and vegetables, evidently not a product of that celestial *cuisine,* the secret of which the angels are said to have imparted to Abraham. The Turks boast of fifty preparations of milk, but my soul longed for a little butter devoid of capillary ingredients. The long ride and the indescribable motion of the arabá,

"Taking me here when I meant there,"

had given me an appetite, and I eat as heartily as any one in that turbaned group. But I could not help thinking of the reasonableness of an imposition formerly levied by the beys and pachas travelling in Bulgaria. The inhabitants were obliged to pay a *tooth-tax* by way of indemnity for the wear and tear of the dental organs of their masters in masticating the villanous compounds furnished them.

Captain Adams, of the Japan Expedition, once told me that the Japanese officials who were feasted on board his ship, used knives and forks for the first time with all the grace of Parisians. I cannot say as much of myself in eating *à la Turque*. I confess, however, to occasional feelings of curiosity not unlike those experienced by my companion at the Pyramids, when partaking of a royal banquet with the King of the Sandwich Islands. Assurances had been given that no dogs would be served on the occasion. The King ate of a favorite dish brought from a side-table. The Captain could think of nothing but dogs—of dogs of all the ages, colors, and flavors afforded by the *apotheoses* of Anubis. Everything he eat and drank seemed to savor of the canine. A nicely cooked dish before my friend so excited his curiosity that, turning to the King, he inquired—

" Isn't that *really* dog, your Majesty ?"

" No," replied the King; " if it were, Captain, you'd see me laying into it."

The Turks look upon dogs as unclean; but I will not answer for all their dishes.

Pilaff, the crowning glory of every Turkish repast, was brought on; but I determined to have a chicken wherewith to finish my evening meal. I could think of the Turkish word for wings and legs, but was unable to call to mind the phrase for the *tout ensemble*, roasted nicely upon coals. An idea struck me. Rising to my feet, I gave a tremendous crow, which, for once in my experience, burst the floodgates of Ottoman gravity, and probably immortalized me in the estimation of my companions. Then they smoked their pipes gravely, and exclaimed, "God is great!" After that philological triumph, the fowl was quickly forthcoming. And, hereafter, when those statuesque Moslems meet together in the khan of Bashardshik, they will, doubtless, tell of the howadji who spoke to them as they had never heard man speak before.

During the monosyllabic conversation that ensued, I had occasion to show them a Congress knife and Colt's revolver. Having examined them long and attentively, they filled their chibouques, and exclaimed, "How great is God! The giaours of America are wiser than the giaours of England and France, because they make better knives and pistols! God in his mercy hath permitted a glimmering of light to enter the corners of your eyes. May he take ten years from our lives, and add them to the years of our Sublime Padisha! Wherever the sun shines, does he not beam upon a land of Mussulmans? The ambassadors come from the East

13

and the West, and the North and the South, to feed
upon our bounty! Behold how the infidel nations are
destroying each other! Let us devoutly thank God
who, in this war, hath been pleased to bring about a
state of things for the benefit of our cause, wherein one
kind of infidel dog is fast killing off another kind, so
that we may soon expect to see the entire race of unbelievers exterminated!"

Thus spoke my companions between coffee and
tobacco. Remember, reader, they were simple Mussulmans of the old school—inhabitants of a town in a
remote province of European Turkey, still retaining a
fanatical belief in the superiority of Islam. How differently converse the Europeanized dwellers along the
Bosphorus, who have tasted the bitterness of Navarino
and Sinope, and in their humiliation lost—utterly lost—
both the enthusiasm of their once victorious faith, and
the illusion of Empire!

One or two of my turbaned friends, more inquisitive than the rest, ventured to inquire about my country.
"O Effendis," I replied, Abdallah translating what I
said into Turkish, " our Padisha dwelleth in the mansions of intelligence and understanding! One and
thirty nations obey him, and in a land that extends
from the rising to the setting sun new cities and empires are ever springing up as if by magic to lay their
golden sceptres at his feet. Each subject is equal to a
pacha; and the sun, wherever he shines, beams not

upon a land of fairer women. The mountains are chained to each other with bars of iron, and the seas linked together with bands of silver. Men fly swifter than the winds, in chariots of fire. They are transported from place to place in floating palaces; and though separated from each other a hundred days' journey, hold converse by the lightnings!" My Moslem friends smoked on in silence. Then the Effendi, who at first had "torn out his eyes in admiration" of my pocket-knife, exclaimed at long intervals, "O Hakeem Bashi, how hath the devil multiplied the cunning inventions of the unbelievers! What machines hath he not found out to disturb the pious meditations of the faithful, and bring discord into the universe! God is great!"

My companions evidently began to regard me as a wandering story-teller, come from the land of the setting sun to bask in the radiance of the Grand Seignor. A fellow-feeling arose between us.

Dramatical exhibitions, and the entertainment of printed fiction, are wanting in the East, but the imaginative Orientals find a congenial amusement in listening to the recital of marvellous stories. Throughout the lands of Islam, from Belgrade to Bassora, from the Mœtian Estuary to the unknown fountains of the Nile, you will find the roaming romancer. Sail upon the Tigris or the Nile, bury yourself in the Hedjaz, or the delicious solitudes of Arabia the Blest, traverse the deserts of Irak, or the wastes of Syria—everywhere you will meet with the wandering story-teller, ready to delight the people with his simple narrations; everywhere you will behold eager groups impatient to catch the bewitching words that fall from his lips. In the larger Turkish cities the *Medaks* (story-tellers) form corporate bodies, with a sheik at their head, called *Imeddah*. They may be seen in the caravansaries and khans. They linger lovingly in the *kahvés* of Oriental cities, prolong the pleasures of the delicious *kief*, and practise their poetical profession in barber-shops and baths. The *Medaks* always commence with an invocation to the Most High: "Praise to Allah, and to his favorite Mohammed, whose black eyes beam with sweetness! He is the only apostle of truth!" The audience, "fit, though few," responds *Amen*, and the narration begins. Some of them improvise, but for the most part they relate new and marvellous histories, or embroider the arabesques of imagination and the imbroglios of adventure upon some well known theme. Now they suddenly break off the narrative at the climax of interest, like the ingenious sultana of the Arabian Nights, and now, to prolong the story and multiply the expected paras, weave in other tissues of romance, varied by a thousand *nuances* of surprise and interest. And then again, with marvellous "skill of song-craft," they intermit, from time to time, their silvery prose with the luxury of verse. But the

object is ever to reverse the maxim of the Latin
poet :—

"Semper ad eventum festinat; et in medias res
Non suis ac notas, auditorem rapit." .

The Arabs call these social reunions *Musameril*, dis-
courses by moonlight or by the glimmer of the stars.
When the sun touches the sandy ocean the roving Bedouins bivouac for the night. And in the cool of the
purple evening they group themselves round him of
the eloquent lip and the restless eye, to listen to the
poems of Antar, or to the poetical fables of the desert,
enriched with glowing words from the chambers of his
imagery. The more varied and marvellous, the greater
the delight; for the active imagination of the Bedouin
believes as readily as it creates. Thus amid the tents
and camp-fires on the lonely desert, and under the
silent stars, they draw out the long hours of the night,
and the patient camels, crouched upon the sand, reach
their long necks over their masters' shoulders, and
gaze inquiringly with their soft eyes, as if they, too,
caught the meaning of the bewitching words.

In our rude khan of Bashardshik the want of a professional story-teller was more than supplied by my
companions. Abdallah was the first to begin. He was
a plump, good-natured Turk, who had picked up considerable English in Constantinople, having been for
some time in the service of an English gentleman.

Through his interpretation, and my own knowledge of the Turkish, I was enabled to understand my companions.

Every day Abdallah showed me in pantomime, with flashing sabre, how he had cut off the heads of the *Moskos*, and how he would cut off the heads of the bashi-bazouks, should they attempt aught of harm to the travelling hakeem. Nor could I prevent him from throwing his arms around my neck repeatedly, and hugging me like a bear. On telling him that I was a giaour, he would only laugh, and exclaim, *pekee! ben pekee!* (Good! very good!)

"Ahmed Ali," began Abdallah, "having lived his appointed time, the angel of death carried away his soul to the confines of non-existence. His friends hastened to bear him to the grave on the same day, according to the command of the Prophet. As they proceeded with the bier, they came to a place where two roads met. 'Let us go this way,' said part of them. 'No,' said the others; 'this is the way.' Then they disputed warmly, and had set down the bier from their shoulders to fall upon each other with blows, when behold! Ahmed Ali rose up, and stretching his pale arm to the right, exclaimed, 'That is the way!' and then laid himself down as before!"

"*Eli Allah!*" half-whispered my companions, hardly knowing whether to credit Abdallah or not. The uneducated Turk has indeed a facility of belief second only

to that of the Hungarian farmer, who one day went
down to Semlin on business. The inn was crowded.
He could be accommodated only on condition of sharing a small chamber with a Capuchin monk. To this
he assented, and wishing to set out for Belgrade at an
early hour the next day, charged the host to wake him
betimes in the morning. The latter did so, but the
countryman, in dressing, inadvertently slipped on the
gown of the Capuchin. Breakfast despatched, bill
paid, and much of the distance to Belgrade left behind,
he happened to bring his sleeve and nasal organ in
close proximity, when the odor of snuff betrayed the
monkish habit. ˙Not even the possibility of a mistake
on his part occurring to the Magyar, he soliloquized,
angrily, "A curse on the stupid host of the Three
Lions; he's waked up that filthy Capuchin instead of
myself!"

Many of the Turkish legends, and perhaps the most
interesting, relate to Biblical subjects, especially to the
lives of the Patriarchs. The Koran is to a great extent
modelled after the Old Testament, surcharged, however,
with Oriental exaggeration, and furnishes curious departures from Scripture history that must have floated
down the sea of tradition.

The Moslems begin their legendary cycle with the
recitals of Genesis. What the inspired historian gives
in concise terms they employ in detail, embellishing it
with the rose color of their imagination: what Genesis

does not give at all, they relate with perfect confidence.

Thus we are told that our first father was born on a Friday, in the afternoon, at the precise hour when the muezzin calls the faithful to prayer. When God had determined to complete his work by the creation of man, his four superior angels brought earth wherewith to form the body of Adam, from the four quarters of the globe, but for his head and heart they brought earth from Mecca and Medina. The body of Adam, even before being animated by the divine breath, was so beautiful that the angels stood in admiration before it, excepting Iblis, the Spirit of Evil, whose history is borrowed from that of Lucifer.

God at last summoned the soul that was to vivify the body of the first man, and had already reposed for centuries in floods of light. But, not wishing to abandon the luminous ether to enter into a terrestrial body, it refused to obey the command of the Almighty. " Thou shalt enter this body in spite of thyself," replied God ; " and to punish thy obstinacy, shalt one day be compelled to leave it in spite of thyself." He then breathed the soul into the organs of Adam, who immediately opened his eyes, and beheld the celestial throne with this inscription, " There is but one God, and Mohammed is his Prophet."

The Turkish legends affirm that Adam, while in Paradise, articulated the names of all the plants and

animals in seventy-seven different languages. God
gave him a bunch of the grapes of Paradise of which
he ate and then fell asleep. On awaking, he beheld
the woman, drawn from his side during his sleep, and
moved forward to embrace her. But the beautiful
Eve, already acquainted with Mussulman usages, said to
him, " God is my master; I cannot become thine without his consent; and, moreover, it is not proper for a
woman to marry a man without first receiving a dower."

The good Adam, unable to reply to this sage reason-
ing, invoked the assistance of the angel Gabriel, and
obtained from him these consoling words : " God gives
thee Eve for a wife. He made her for that purpose,
and commands thee to love her as thyself. Instead of
giving her the dower which she demands, pray twenty
times to Mohammed, whose soul floated before the
Eternal Throne thousands of years anterior to the creation of the world, but whose body shall be engendered
by thee."

Iblis, the Mussulman Devil, wishing to dispossess
our first parents of Paradise, addressed himself first to
the peacock, which had the vanity of a singer and the
self-conceit of a dandy, as originally, according to the
Moslem traditions, that most beautiful of birds was
endowed with an admirable voice. The vain creature
listened to the flattering words of Iblis, but being of a
timid disposition, counselled him to call to his aid the
serpent, at that time the most charming of all animals.

13*

Large as a camel, he carried upon his graceful neck long floating locks like those of a girl. Upon his skin burned the most beautiful colors. His head was like a ruby, his eyes like diamonds, while his body exhaled an odor of musk and amber. His sweet songs delighted Eve, whose faithful companion he was until led away by Iblis.

"Thou shalt grow old! thou shalt die!" said the Evil One to the serpent; "but by three magical words I can assure thee constant beauty—an eternal youth; and these three words I will reveal to thee if thou wilt introduce me into Paradise." The serpent regarding himself in the mirror of a lake, and seeing himself so beautiful and coquettish, was frightened at the idea of decrepitude, and in order to attain the fountain of youth, took Iblis in his throat and fraudulently introduced him within the precincts of Paradise. The genius of Evil there met the innocent Eve, and frightened her as he had already the serpent with the prospect of age and death, to escape which there was but one remedy—to partake of the forbidden fruit. This is said to have grown upon a tree whose bark resembled gold, the branches silver, and the leaves emeralds. Upon each of the branches grew seven heads glittering like precious stones, each containing five grains of the forbidden fruit, white as snow, sweet as honey, and odoriferous as musk.

The Moslems excuse the fault of Eve by coloring it

with all the seductive circumstances to which she, in her innocence, was exposed. "Frail men," say they, "should not be without pity for the frailty of their first mother." But Adam, it is affirmed, resisted for a period of eighty years all the solicitations of Eve to partake of the forbidden fruit, which she had found so agreeable to her taste.

Miltonic verse has not more beautifully-described the consequences of that great fall from celestial virtue. Adam was chased from Paradise by the gate of Penitence; Eve by the gate of Pity. The peacock was deprived of his melodious voice, the serpent of his primitive form, and Iblis cast down into the depths of hell.

The Eagle then said to the Whale, with whom he had lived in peace on the shores of the ocean, "At present we must separate, for man has become our enemy, and we can escape his cunning and his cruelty only by retiring; thou to the depths of the waves, and I to the clouds above."

Adam in his solitude wept so much that from the lids of his left eye, continually suffused with tears, sprang the source of the river Tigris; from the right eye that of the Euphrates. All nature wept with him, and the animals were touched with commiseration. Eve wept also; the tears which rolled down her cheeks became pearls; those which fell to the earth were transformed into rubies. Though far separated, the zephyrs bore to the ears of Adam the sighs of 1 e; the east wind bore the groans of Adam to the ears of the disconsolate Eve. At last, God, moved by such suffering, sent the angel Gabriel to the penitent Adam. "Repeat this invocation," said Gabriel: "There is but one God and Mohammed is his Prophet. Drink water, build mosques, and henceforth Satan will have no power over thee."

The history of Noah and of the Deluge are very similar to the narration given in the Bible. The Mussulmans merely add in reference to the latter that when the Ark, floating upon the waters, came near the mountain where the *Kaaba* was guarded, it made the tour around it seven times, like a pious pilgrim.

In our group sat a venerable Turk whom his companions called Kitab Effendi. They looked up to him as to a father, and it was evident that the Effendi was one of the oracles of Bashardshik. He was a Mussulman of the old school, with a beard as white as the morning, and wore the full, many-colored turban and rich flowing robes which are now being fast supplanted in European Turkey by the rectilinear Frank costume, but retain their graceful folds in Damascus and Grand Cairo. He was our "marvellous story-teller." We grouped ourselves around him on the mat, and the flickering light cast strange shadows upon the wall. Travelling as I had done from nation to nation, I could hardly realize that I was studying life in a remote and semi-barbarous province of European Turkey.

Here are some of the legends related to us by Kitab Effendi:—

"Abraham was born in Babylon in the reign of Nimrod, the heathen king. Upon the Friday night in which this glorious prophet, whose miracles a whole lifetime would not suffice to enumerate, came into the world, Nimrod saw, in a vision, all his idols overthrown and heard a voice crying, 'Wó, wo unto them who turn not to the faith of Abraham!' On the following morning he consulted his priests and magicians. They informed him that a child would be born who should deprive him of his throne and his divinity, for Nimrod had caused himself to be adored as a god. Forthwith, like Herod, he ordered all the new-born children throughout the kingdom to be murdered. But by the inspiration of Gabriel, the mother of Abraham secreted her child in a cave, where he was nourished from the five fingers of God. From one of his fingers dropped pure water, from another milk of ambrosial flavor, from the third honey, from the fourth the juice of dates, and from the fifth nectar.

"His mother came to see him, and one day found the child in profound meditation.

"'Who is my God?' inquired he of his mother.

"'Myself,' replied she.

"'And who is thy God?'

" ' Thy father.'

" ' And the God of my father ?'

" ' Nimrod.'

" ' And the God of Nimrod ?'

" His mother, unable to answer the last question, gave him a box on the ear, and remained silent. But Abraham said to himself, ' I know no other God than he who hath created the heavens and the earth.'

" Several years afterwards his father, who was a sculptor, charged him with the selling of idols. Abraham carried them in the public place, and cried, ' Who will buy a vile merchandise most prejudicial to whomsoever may keep it in his house ?' With this announcement he was sure to return home with all the images.

" On a certain day when the inhabitants of the city were gone on a pilgrimage to one of their heathen edifices, Abraham secretly entered the temple and broke into pieces seventy-two idols. Arrested and brought before Nimrod, he was condemned to be burned alive—burned solemnly upon an immense funeral pile of such enormous size that forty days were required to collect the most combustible materials. The infernal pile was lighted. Nimrod caused Abraham to be brought forward, and in sight of the whirlwinds of flame bade him declare who was his God. ' My God,' responded Abraham, ' is he who hath the power to create and the power to destroy.'

" ' Then,' cried Nimrod, ' I am God; I hold in my

LOW LIFE IN ROUMANIA.

p. 136

hands life and death,' and ordering two slaves to be brought he cut off the head of one and set the other at liberty.

"'Thou canst slay,' replied Abraham, 'but thou canst not make alive. Let them bring me four birds, and in the name of my God thou shalt see what miracle I can accomplish.'

"The four birds were brought. Abraham cut them into a thousand pieces, and then calling each bird by its proper name he bade them come to life, when forthwith they rose towards the heavens, singing as they took their flight.

"Nimrod, whose pride was only irritated by this miracle, ordered the soldiers to seize Abraham and throw him into the flames by means of a machine whose model had been furnished by Satan himself. Abraham invoked the aid of God, and instantly the flames were extinguished. In the place of the funeral pile leaped forth a fountain of perfumed water, and Abraham appeared by its side clothed in a caftan of silk brought by Gabriel from Paradise.

"Abraham was so jealous of his wives that he constructed for them a magic city—a city of iron, whose walls were so high that the light of the sun could not penetrate within. The sombre rooms of this ancient harem, in which the wives of the Patriarch were imprisoned, were lighted with garlands of pearls and crowns of diamonds. Our father Abraham was a great traveller. Sara, his

constant companion, resembled Eve, and was so celebrated for her beauty that the Patriarch took the wise
precaution of carrying her in an iron chest.

"Behold him arrested one day on the bank of the
Jordan by a custom-house officer who wished to examine
the baggage. The good Abraham, carrying no contra-
band articles, as he believed, allowed him to prosecute
the search for a time without molestation. But when
the latter came to the chest containing Sara, 'Stop,'
cried the Patriarch, 'suppose that this box is filled
with the richest silks, and I pay you ten times the
ordinary tariff?' 'No,' replied the officer, whose
suspicions were excited. 'Suppose that it is filled
with diamonds, and I pay you twenty times the legal
duty?' 'No!' shouted the ferocious officer, and opening the mysterious chest by a skilful movement of his
nimble fingers he beheld the ideal form of Sara. For
a moment he stood petrified with admiration, and then
ran away to announce the marvel he had just discovered.
The wicked king confiscated the rare importation, and
caused Sara to enter his palace. The sorrow of Abraham can be more easily imagined than described.
God, however, moved by the conjugal tenderness of
the Patriarch, caused the walls of the palace to become
transparent, and Abraham afar off was able to witness
all that took place. When the wicked king approached
his beautiful captive, and was about to embrace her,
his outstretched hand was struck with palsy.

" 'Away from me!' cried Sara, 'I am the wife of Abraham!' And the king called the Patriarch, asked pardon for his culpable intentions, and made him a present of his slave Hagar."

"God be praised for the creation of woman!" exclaimed my companions, and then smoked a few minutes in silence. We drew more closely around Kitab Effendi.

"In consequence of this a multitude of people became believers in the Prophet. Nimrod, thinking presumptuously to destroy the God of Abraham as he had attempted to overcome Abraham, ordered a large box to be made with an opening towards the earth and another towards the heavens. He then commanded them to fasten four rods to the upper corners of the box, and upon these rods to place pieces of flesh. Four vultures were then brought and tied to the four feet of the chest. Armed, and accompanied by his faithful vizier, he seated himself in the chest in order to make war upon God, whom, in his rage, he wished to annihilate. 'If I gain the victory,' said he, 'I shall be delivered from Abraham, but if I am conquered by the God of Abraham, he can reign as I have reigned over the heavens, the earth, and their creatures. As soon as the vultures were let loose, they strove to reach the pieces of flesh above them, and thereby raised the chest among the clouds. After a day and a night Nimrod said to his vizier,—

'Open the door towards the earth, and tell what thou seest.'

"'I see the earth, O Prince, and the dust,' replied the latter. They continued to wander during another day and night, and the vizier again opened the door towards the earth, and responded to Nimrod, 'What I behold, O King, resembles smoke.' He was then ordered to open the door towards the heavens, and having done so, replied, 'I behold what I saw when looking upon the earth.' After another day and night, when nothing was to be seen either in the direction of the heavens or the earth, the king drew his bow and shot aloft three arrows. The Almighty sent back by Gabriel the same arrows, after their points had been stained with blood. 'I have destroyed the God of Abraham,' cried Nimrod, and forthwith he changed their direction towards the earth, to which he returned without harm.

"Nimrod, persisting in his blindness, attempted with sacrilegious audacity to build a tower that would reach the stars. His edifice fell in ruins upon the workmen. Abraham had already gained a multitude of disciples, and scorned the power of the king. The latter collected an army in order to capture the prophet; and resolved to destroy him by the most cruel punishment.

"To overcome this proud sovereign Abraham asked of God only the aid of a fly.

" ' Let it be according to thy desire,' responded the All Powerful, ' but I will send thee an insect seventy times smaller than the one thou hast mentioned.'

" At the command of the Creator, the king of the flies collected his winged squadrons, which precipitated themselves upon the soldiers of Nimrod with such impetuosity as to put them to rout. Nimrod himself fled, and took refuge in a tower. But a fly pursued, entered with him, and harassed and stung him, without his being able to catch the insect. Now alighting upon his lips, and then upon his nose, it at last penetrated into the brain, and fed upon its substance. The insect grew and developed itself in a marvellous manner. The king could get peace from the dreadful torment only by having his head constantly beaten with heavy mallets. At the end of forty years the head of Nimrod burst open, and the fly coming out as large as a pigeon, said to the dying king—

" ' Behold how God can destroy, by one of his smallest creatures, such as refuse to believe in him.'

" After Jacob had listened to the strange dream of Joseph, he was so completely absorbed in his reflections as not to hear the voice of a beggar who was asking for alms, and allowed him to go away without receiving anything. For this momentary abstraction he was condemned to bitter suffering.

" When the four sons of Jacob, after having sold their brother, came to relate to their father that Joseph had been devoured by a wolf, 'There are no wolves in the country,' exclaimed the Patriarch, unwilling to know the extent of his misfortune.

"'Ah! thou believest there are none,' said one. of the offenders; 'we will bring thee the very one which tore our beloved Joseph to pieces.'

"In fact, they did bring in an enormous wolf. But by the justice of God the beast opened his mouth and said, 'Son of Isaac, do not believe the oaths of these criminal impostors. I am a wolf of a far off country, and have wandered about several weeks in search of one of my little ones. How could I, who am simply an animal and experience the tender anguish of animals, how could I carry away the son of a Prophet of God?'"

"When Joseph had lived for a time in the house of Potiphar, he became enamored of Zuleika, the wife of the king, who also came to love him in return. But he resisted all her tender supplications and fled. Potiphar would not believe the story invented by Zuleika for the purpose of injuring Joseph, and retained him in his service. The female friends of Zuleika were equally incredulous. To revenge herself she invited them one evening to a feast in her palace, and when they were cutting oranges with sharp knives caused Joseph to appear suddenly before them. So astonished were they at his marvellous beauty that they all cut their hands, and did not perceive what had happened until the table was covered with blood.

"'Indeed!' exclaimed Zuleika, exulting over their stupefaction. 'You blame me on account of my love for Joseph! Yes, I love this man, whose appearance has so dazzled you.'

"Potiphar, yielding at last to the instances of his wife, ordered the virtuous Joseph to be imprisoned.

"Behold the termination of this strange history! Joseph had been raised by the favor of Potiphar to a high degree of power. One day, when visiting the granaries provided by him against the years of famine, he met in the street a female, whose dress, whose pale face, and suppliant attitude indicated a pitiable state of misery. Touched by the sight of such distress, he handed her a purse of gold, when the woman said to him, 'I do not merit thy compassion.'

"It was Zuleika, who had exercised such an influence upon his destiny, but so pale and feeble that Joseph could hardly recognise in her the beautiful wife of Potiphar. Moved by pity, and doubtless by the tender sentiment of affection, he cared for her as for a sister. In this new atmosphere she revived like a faded rose to which rain and sunshine have been given, and quickly recovered her lost beauty. She was a widow, having, after the death of Potiphar, been driven from her palace, and abandoned by all the world. Joseph loved her in her misfortune; and Zuleika became in time the wife of her generous benefactor.

"The father of Moses was one of the viziers of Pha-

raoh. Before the birth of the Prophet, the heathen
king troubled, like Nimrod, by a dream, ordered all the
new-born infants of Egypt to be murdered, and the preg-
nant women to be thrown into the Nile. The bloody
decree was executed. Seven thousand infants were
slain : seven thousand women kissed the waters of the
Nile, Johabed, the wife of Amias, alone escaping.

"On the night in which Moses was born, all the idols
in the Egyptian temples were overthrown, and Pharaoh
was troubled by a dream more dreadful than the former.
New search was made. The soldiers entered the house
of Johabed, who had merely time to cast her son into
an oven before her dwelling was set on fire. When
the soldiers had left, the infant Moses cried: 'Be of
good cheer, mother! God hath saved me from the power
of the flames.'

"But Johabed, fearing greatly for the safety of her
child, resolved to entrust him to the bosom of the Nile.
On her way to the river she was met by a soldier, who
attempted to raise the lid of the box in which the
infant Moses was concealed. At that moment the
earth opened, and swallowed the soldier up to his chin,
and a voice exclaimed, 'Let this woman go in peace, or
thou diest.'

"Moses was saved by one of the daughters of Pharaoh, and brought up in the palace of the king. At the
age of five years he played with the sceptre of the monarch whose power he was one day to overthrow. He

trod the crown under his feet, and on one occasion threw
Pharaoh himself from the throne. After his return
from the land of the Midianites, he confounded by his
miracles the seventy thousand magicians of the king.

" Having delivered his people from their cruel bondage, Moses was summoned to receive the laws of God,
and the Angel Gabriel raised him so high, that he
plainly distinguished the movement of the *kalam* (the
pen) with which the secretary of the celestial host
wrote down the Ten Commandments. In the confidence inspired by such favor from Allah, he asked
that his nation might become the first people upon the
globe. But Allah responded ;

" ' Thou askest what is impossible. I have already
granted that supremacy to the followers of Mohammed,
who shall one day be masters of the universe.'

"While the Israelites were marching to the conquest
of the promised land, Moses, desirous of contemplating
the wondrous works of God, set out to travel. He
voyaged for thirty years in the east and west, in the
north and the south. After many wanderings in distant countries, the Patriarch returned to his tribe, but
instead of being received as the wisest of men and the
first of legislators, he saw his fame as a prophet and a
traveller eclipsed by the gold of a banker. During his
absence there had risen up a man among the Israelites
—a man who had never ventured near the flames of
Sinai, and had not the least admiration for the wonder-

ful works of creation, but who had spent his days in
ingenious speculations among the money-changers of
the wandering children of Israel.   This individual became so marvellously rich that forty beasts of burden
were required to carry merely the keys wherewith to
unlock his treasures.

" Despising in his pride of wealth the poor Moses,
who returned from his travels on foot, he would not
recognise him as the lawgiver of Israel.   In order to
make him contemptible in the opinion of those who still
retained some feelings of respect and gratitude for
their ancient leader, he instituted a process of law
against him, and suborned false witnesses.   But these
witnesses were stung in their consciences before the
tribunal, and proclaimed the truth.   Moses triumphed.
The people again received him for their leader, while
the earth opened and swallowed up the banker with all
his wealth.

" At the age of a hundred and eighty years Moses
saw that he was nigh unto death.   Weeping, he asked
of God what would become of his wife and children.

" ' Go thou,' replied God, ' to the rock on the sea-
shore and strike it with thy rod.'

" The rock divided asunder, and out of it came a
worm, which cried three times—

" ' Glory to God, the All-Powerful, who hath not
forgotten me in my solitude !   Praise to God who dost
nourish me !'

" Then said God unto him—

"'Behold! if I care for the worm hid in a lonely rock upon the seashore, how can I, O man, abandon thy children ?'

" *Allah akbar ! Allah kerim !*" (God is great! God is merciful !) exclaimed my companions.

" After the death of Joshua," continued Kitab Effendi, " the chiefs of Israel, who had been sorely beaten in several conflicts with Goliah, assembled to deliberate upon their sad situation. Then appeared before them a holy man, Samuel, who declared he was sent of God.

"'What must we do to escape destruction ?' asked the chiefs of Israel.

"'You must renounce the worship of idols, confess the true God, honor your parents, treat your wives with consideration, and lastly, render homage to the Prophets,' responded Samuel.

"'The Prophets! Who are they ?'

"'First, Adam, Noah, and Abraham, for whom the Lord did great miracles, then Moses and the Prophets who shall come after me—Jesus the son of Mary, and Mohammed. The testimony of each of these is complete in his time, but has been, or will be, set aside by that of the successor, except in the case of Mohammed.'

"'Jesus! Who is he ?' demanded the auditors.

"'It is he who has been announced in the Tora (a Moslem book) as the Word of God. He will be born

14

of a virgin. Before his birth he will proclaim the immaculate nature of his mother and the puissance of the Creator, then he will cure the sick, raise the dead, and from a little earth make living animals and birds. The wicked men of his time will seek to put him to death, but shall deceive themselves in crucifying a common person in his stead, while Jesus himself will enter gloriously into heaven.'

" After giving the lineage and exalted character of Mohammed, Samuel related to the conclave of Israel what would happen to the Prophet of Mecca during a single night. The angel Gabriel would wake Mohammed and conduct him to the open country, where he would be presented with the miraculous winged horse Borak, the same which Abraham made use of in travelling from Syria to Mecca. This horse has the feet of a dromedary, the wings of an eagle, a body of diamond, and the head of a young girl. Upon his breast he bears this inscription, ' There is but one God, and Mohammed is his Prophet.'

" Mounted upon this animal the Prophet was to visit Sinai, Bethlehem, and Jerusalem, to repeat his prayers at each place, and then, on stairs of emeralds and flowers, mount up to the seventh heaven, where he would be initiated into all the mysteries of the creation and the government of the universe. He would there contemplate the happy inhabitants of heaven, and look down into the depths of hell. The eternal abyss would reveal to him all the different kinds of torments there inflicted. Those who had oppressed the poor were condemned to scratch like fowls in an arid soil which yielded no nourishment. Usurers and extortioners beheld their bodies swell from moment to moment in a frightful manner, while liars, calumniators, and tale-bearers had their tongues and lips twinched every instant with red hot nippers of fire.

" 'Between heaven and hell,' continued Samuel, 'Mohammed shall see Abraham, the father of the faithful, who smiles whenever the gates of heaven are opened, and weeps when a new victim is cast into hell. He shall behold the happy inhabitants of heaven reclining on voluptuous couches under silken pavilions and eating from vessels of silver and gold the richest viands, of which the last morsel shall be as acceptable to the taste as the first. Then will be pointed out to him the Pool of Life, whose waters dispel thirst for ever, and the tree of Toba, so large that the fleetest horse cannot cross its shadow in a hundred years, whose branches are hung with the most delicious fruits and moved in dulcet harmony by the soft winds of heaven. He shall look down upon the blissful fields of Paradise, strewn with pearls and diamonds and beds of musk, where among perpetual fountains and in the cool shade, the faithful shall be served by black-eyed houris, beautiful without blemish, and subject neither to age nor death.'

" 'We believe in God and his Prophets,' replied the

chiefs of Israel. 'Pray for us, and deliver us from Goliah.'"

Solomon, however, is the great favorite of the Orientals. They invest his character with all that is marvellous in eastern fiction.

"Tell us of Solomon," said a Turkish merchant at my side, charging his long chibouque for the dozenth time, "tell us of Solomon, O Kitab Effendi!" A little flame still flickered upon the hearth, and the strange shadows on the wall became less distinct. The venerable Mussulman resumed his story—

"The night in which Solomon came into the world, the angel Gabriel cried, 'A child is born to whom Iblis and all the demons shall be subject.' He was endowed with such sagacity that when a mere youth he instructed his father in the most difficult things, and one day confounded all the doctors of the law.

"After the death of his father, eight angels with innumerable wings of all forms and colors came and bowed down three times before him.

"'Who are you?' demanded Solomon.

"'We are the angels of the eight winds of the earth,' answered they. 'To thee we do homage. Call us when thou wilt, and we will breathe the soft zephyrs or wake the tempest. Cast this stone into the air, and forthwith we shall be in thy presence.'

"The eight angels then disappeared, and four others came. 'We govern,' said they, 'all the animals in the air, on the earth, and in the waters under the earth. When thou wilt have us appear place this upon thy head,' and one of the angels gave him a talismanic stone with the inscription, 'All creatures praise the Lord.'

"Solomon directed the angels to assemble before him a pair of all the different species of animals. In the twinkling of an eye his wish was accomplished, and the beings of creation presented themselves, from the monstrous elephant down to the smallest worm. Then the great king with royal benevolence spoke with his legions of subjects, and listened to their complaints. The legislator of men, he also became the legislator of animals, condemning their evil habits and reforming the abuses of their governments.

"But Solomon took most pleasure in conversing with the birds of the air, for he understood all the varieties of their melodious language and the sage maxims of the beloved little musicians of the good God.

"'For many creatures it were better not to live,' sighed the melancholy dove.

"'To be content with one's lot is the greatest of blessings,' sang the nightingale.

"'Be just and thou shalt be recompensed,' cried the lark.

"'Death will come at last,' screamed the eagle.

"'Think of thy Creator, O vain mortal,' chanted the martial cock.

"Solomon was especially delighted with the pigeon, and invited it to make its home on the walls of the Temple, which he was about to build. A few years afterwards the pigeons had multiplied so greatly, that their extended wings formed a shady pavilion over the innumerable bands of pilgrims who came up to Jerusalem on the occasion of the great feasts.

"Still another angel appeared before Solomon, and gave him a diamond, with the inscription—'There is but one God, and Mohammed is his Prophet.'

"'By virtue of this stone,' said the angel, 'thou shalt rule over the *djinns*, who belong to the world of spirits, and are far more numerous than all the men and animals on the earth together. They were created angels of light, but having fallen, were banished from the presence of God. The world was inhabited by the *djinns* seventy thousand years before the creation of man. Some of them acknowledge the true God, while others, plunged into the errors of idolatry, worship fire, and adore the sun and the stars. The former hover perpetually around good men to protect them; the latter, on the contrary, ever seek to do them harm.'

"By the talismanic influence of this ring Solomon subdued the entire race of the *djinns*. He obliged them to build palaces and to erect a temple after the model of the *Kaaba* of Mecca. The female *djinns* wove garments of wool and silk for the poor of Jerusalem. They were also required to roast every day thirty thousand oxen and thirty thousand sheep, besides innumerable birds and fishes, all of which were placed upon tables several miles in length. The *djinns* sat down at tables of iron, the poor at tables of wood; at tables of silver were seated the chiefs of the army and the high officers of government, while the men distinguished for their piety and wisdom were served by Solomon himself at tables of pure gold.

"But with all the favors heaped upon him Solomon was not proof against pride. While regarding one day the multitudes enjoying his feasts, he exclaimed in a moment of blindness, 'Would that God would permit me to feed for a single day all the animals of the earth!'

"'What thou wouldst do is impossible,' responded God; 'but thou mayest attempt it: I will permit thee to begin to-morrow with the inhabitants of the sea.'

"Solomon ordered the *djinns* to load a hundred thousand camels and a hundred thousand mules with grain and fruits; then he went down to the seashore and cried with a loud voice—

"'Come ye, who reside in the depths of the waves, come and I will satisfy your hunger!' Then there came to the surface of the waters swarms of fishes to which they threw sacks of grain until all were satisfied. But suddenly there appeared a whale as large as a mountain. Solomon threw to him hundreds of loads of fruit and grain, and continually the insatiable monster

opened his mouth for more. At last the provision was
all gone, and the whale cried—

"'Give me, give me whereof to eat, never have I
suffered such hunger!'

"'Ah!' cried Solomon, overwhelmed with astonishment, 'are there many of thy species in the sea?'

"'Many?' replied the monster, 'there are seventy
thousand, of whom the smallest is of such a size that
thou wouldst disappear in his bowels like a grain of sand
in the desert.'

"At these words Solomon fell upon his face, and
weeping, prayed God to pardon his wicked presumption.

"Behold how the great king travelled to Mecca and
Medina. A silk carpet was woven by the *djinns* four
leagues in extent. Upon this carpet they placed the
throne of Solomon, and around it seats of gold and
silver for the multitude of persons who were to accompany him. When all the preparations had been completed, Solomon seated himself upon his throne, and
commanded the winds to do their duty. They transported the aerial caravan, and at the same time a cloud
of birds with extended wings formed a shady canopy
over the head of the king and his companions.

"While returning to Jerusalem the Patriarch perceived, from a single ray of sunshine piercing through
the winged pavilion, that a bird was wanting at his
post. He demanded of the eagle the name of the de-

linquent, and the eagle, having called over the names
of all the birds, announced the desertion of the lapwing.
An instant afterwards the lapwing appeared, trembling
and bowing down his head in the presence of the great
king.

" 'I have done wrong,' said the bird, 'and merit
punishment.'

" ' Explain thyself,' answered Solomon, who was
angry, but would not condemn the delinquent without
a hearing.

" ' At Mecca,' continued the lapwing, 'I met with a
bird of my acquaintance, who gave me such a picture
of the marvels of the kingdom of Saba (Sheba) that I
could not resist the desire of visiting that country. I
have seen the treasures of that land, which, O king,
thou shouldst conquer, and its queen Balkis, the most
beautiful woman of the universe.'

" Struck with this recital of the wandering bird,
Solomon at once wrote a letter to queen Balkis, engaging to convert her to the true faith.

" The offending lapwing was his messenger.

" The queen of Saba read the letter and then assembled her viziers for their advice. But they declared
that as no one equalled her in wisdom, no one could
venture to counsel her in so important a matter.

" ' Well!' exclaimed Balkis, ' I shall know whether
he is a prophet or not. I will send him the most magnificent presents, and if he be dazzled by them it will

14*

prove that he is not superior to other men. I will pro-
pose to him different questions, and if he be not able to
answer them surely he is a false prophet.'

"Her ambassadors set out for Jerusalem with a
thousand carpets woven with gold and silver, a crown
of fine pearls, and the precious products of Arabia the
Blest. They carried likewise a casket containing a
pearl that had not been pierced, a diamond though
which passed a tortuous hole, and a cup of crystal.
Balkis demanded that Solomon should pierce the pearl,
pass a thread through the diamond, and fill the cup
with water obtained from neither the heavens nor the
earth.

"Solomon having been informed of these things
caused the *djinns* to weave carpets that were many
miles in length, and still more magnificent, and also
build walls of gold and silver. At the sight of these
marvels the ambassadors of Balkis did not even venture
to show their presents, and could hardly be prevailed
upon to open the casket. Solomon at once pierced the
pearl by means of a powder provided by the *djinns*.
He ordered a slave to leap upon one of his fleetest
horses, and from the sweat that ran down its flanks he
filled the crystal cup with water which came neither
from the heavens nor the earth. The third problem
was the most difficult. But he passed a thread through
the sinuosities of the diamond by means of a minute
worm which drew the thread after itself, and thence-

forth, by way of recompense, was fed upon the leaves of the mulberry.

"Solomon then sent word to the queen of Saba that if she did not renounce the worship of idols and submit to his power he would overrun her country with a formidable army. Upon the return of her envoys she at once set out for Jerusalem in order to abjure idolatry and acknowledge the supremacy of Solomon. He awaited with impatience the young queen whose beauty had been praised with so much enthusiasm.

"But a singular report embarrassed the sovereign of Jerusalem. It was whispered in secret that the ideal form of the Sabean queen terminated in the ugly feet of a quadruped. How was Solomon to learn the truth without giving offence? He could not say to the queen, ' Show me thy feet, O Balkis!' In place of the floor of the hall where he was to receive her, he arranged a transparent crystal under which ran limpid water. Balkis, when stepping upon the crystal, supposed that she had to cross a stream, and graciously raised her robes ; and the king, who was watching with uneasy solicitude, perceived under the silken folds of her garments the most beautiful feet in the world. A few days afterwards Balkis became the wife of Solomon.

"Would that he had remained faithful to the commandments of God! But the great king, who had once failed through pride, was destined to fall again by the passion of love. He became enamored of the daughter of a heathen king, who introduced her idols into the palace of Solomon, where the true God alone should have been adored. A *djinn* took away his ring, his robes, and his sceptre, and having assumed the form of the king, installed himself upon the throne. Solomon, despised by his ministers and insulted by his own servants, was driven from the palace, and for forty days wandered in the desert a prey to the most bitter reflections. But as he had not taken part in the idolatry himself, the Lord had compassion upon him and restored him, greatly enlightened by his errors, to his former power.

"Solomon had thus ruled over his vast empire a great number of years when one day the angel of death appeared before him. The Great King demanded of him how the term of life is marked off for different individuals.

" ' It is hardly permitted me to stop in the work in which I am constantly engaged,' replied the angel, 'but I cannot refuse the favorite of God an explanation. Know then that I am only the messenger of another angel, whose head reaches ten thousand years' journey above the seventh heaven, and whose feet are plunged the distance of five hundred years' journey into the bowels of the earth. This angel whose name is Osrein is so strong that, if God would permit him, he could easily overthrow the globe with a single hand. He it

GIPSY ENCAMPMENT.

p. 135

is who indicates to me the place whence I have a soul to take. He has his eyes constantly fixed upon the *Sidrat-Al-Muntaha*, the tree of life, which bears as many leaves as there are human beings. When a child is born a new leaf puts forth with his name upon it; when his last hour is come the leaf withers and is plucked by Osrein.'

"'And the inferior angels,' continued Solomon, 'how are they employed?'

"'Two of them keep watch upon every mortal, one on the right hand and the other on the left. They observe every word and action; and at the end of the day are relieved by two other angels and fly up to heaven. The angel on the right side records every good action, and when the mortal commits a sin says to the angel on the left, "Forbear for seven hours to record it; peradventure he may repent, and obtain forgiveness."'

"'How dost thou collect the souls of men?' inquired Solomon, 'and what becomes of them during Buzak, the interval of time between the tribunal of the sepulchre and the resurrection?'

"'For the examination of the sepulchre,' answered the angel, 'the soul reenters the body. If the person has been just it is again drawn gently out of his mouth; otherwise it is beaten out of him with dreadful blows. The bodies of the dead remain in their graves, but their souls have a foretaste of the doom that awaits them in dreams and visions. Those of the faithful hover near their sepulchres in a state of felicity, or wrapped up in silk cloths, are placed in charge of a bird which will watch them in Paradise until the day of judgment. The spirits of the martyrs enter into the crops of green birds that feed on the fruits and drink of the streams of heaven, while the souls of those with whom God has been most pleased become as snow-white birds and nestle under his throne. The souls of the wicked are tied up in sacks of tarred cloth, and cast down to the gate of perdition, where they shall remain in misery until the resurrection.'

" 'The angels—will they also die?' inquired Solomon.

" ' All beings shall die at the blast of extermination, first men and then angels. At the second sound of the trumpet of Israfil, Michael and Gabriel shall fall by my hand, and I, Azrael, the angel of death, then perish under the eyes of the Almighty. Throughout the vast extent of creation God only will exist. He will then exclaim, " To whom belongs the earth?" and no being shall answer. But after forty years of rain and darkness the trumpet shall sound again and the dead shall awake, angels first and men afterwards.'

" ' Who among men shall awake first?' demanded Solomon.

" 'Mohammed the Prophet. Israfil, Gabriel, and the other angels will repair to Medina and cry, " Come, O most beautiful and purest of souls! reanimate thy body, which is without blemish." Then he shall come out of his tomb. Gabriel will present to him the winged Borak, and give him a standard and a crown sent for that purpose from Paradise. "Come, thou chosen of the Lord," a voice shall exclaim, "already is Eden spread with flowers, and the *houris* await thee." Then the rest of mankind will awake from their sleep of death and be conducted to the Valley of Jehosaphat for the last judgment.

" ' That will be a terrible day when each one shall think only of himself. "O God!" Adam will cry, "save me! save me! impute to me neither the iniquity of Eve nor that of Abel." "Preserve me from hell," Noah will pray, "and do unto my children what seemeth good unto thee." Abraham shall say, "I invoke thee not for Ishmael nor for Isaac, I invoke thee, O God, only for myself." In that dread hour Moses will forget his brother Aaron. Mohammed alone shall pray for all the world. The day of judgment shall be preceded by signs and portents. There will be a total eclipse of the moon, the sun shall rise out of the west, and the earth be enveloped in smoke. Men shall even envy the quiet of the grave.

" ' At the sound of the trumpet of Israfil the earth will tremble and the mountains be levelled with the plains. The moon, the sun, and the stars shall fall into the sea, and the firmament melt away. The earth will then open and the souls fly in quest of their bodies.

The dry bones of the dead will rattle, the scattered limbs be brought together, and the very hairs of their heads congregate.

" 'The duration of the day of judgment shall be an age. It shall be a day of sighs and griefs, a day of tribulation and anguish, when the cup of sorrow and misery must be drunk, even to the very dregs thereof. To the perverse and the ungodly every thing shall become as aloes and bitterness. For them there will not be one moment of repose. They shall behold nothing agreeable, hear no voice that shall delight, while their terrified imaginations will represent to them only spectres and tortures, and the howlings of demons.

" 'Then Mohammed will intercede for his people.

" 'After the final judgment, made according to good works without distinction of persons, all mankind must prepare for the inevitable passage of Sirat, the sharp-edged bridge of seven arches. This bridge is three thousand years' journey in length, narrow as the thread of a spider's web and sharp as the edge of a sword. It requires a thousand years to ascend the first side, a thousand to cross over, and a thousand more to descend. They who make the entire passage shall be admitted to the joys of paradise, but infidels and all wicked persons shall fall into perdition from the different arches. The faithful shall, however, at last all be redeemed."

"Good God!" exclaimed my companions, "how dreadful to our sight will this formidable bridge appear!

What virtue! what secret grace from the Most High shall we not need!

"'Tell me,' continued Solomon, 'when shall the resurrection come?'

"'God only knows,' replied the angel of death, and having answered Solomon, he prepared to carry away his soul.

"'Canst thou not prolong my life until the comple-.tion of the temple?'

"'No,' responded the angel, 'thy hour is come.'

"'The will of God be done, but let my death be unknown to the *djinns* until they have completed the house of God.'

"The angel removed the soul of the Great King, but his body was left seated upon the throne, clothed in royal robes and all the insignia of office. There it remained in the usual position of the monarch, the races of men and genii paying their customary homage at a respectful distance, until the staff upon which the corpse leaned had been gnawed by the worms, and gave way so that the body fell to the ground.

"Until the time of Mohammed," continued Kitab Effendi, "the angel of death appeared to mortals in a bodily form. But when he came for the soul of the Prophet, the latter said to him, 'O Azrael, thou art terrible to behold! It is not proper that thou shouldst thus show thyself to mortal men, for it can easily happen that they die from excessive fright before having

said their prayers.   I am a man of courage, but confess
that I cannot look upon thee without a shudder.'

"He then besought God that Azrael might become
a spirit, and his prayer was granted."

At a late hour we spread our mats upon the floor
and lay down to rest. The escort and one or two
Turks who tarried with us all night slept soundly with
their yataghans by their sides. My repose, however,
was disturbed by hideous phantoms which had their
origin in the abominations of the Turkish çuisine, but
borrowed the forms of the hide-bound quadrupeds in
the adjoining chamber, whose spasmodic breathing har-
monized admirably with the snoring of my prostrate
companions.

CHAPTER XIII.

LIFE IN BULGARIA.

> " By foreign hands thy dying eyes were closed,
> By foreign hands thy decent limbs composed,
> By foreign hands thy humble grave adorned,
> By strangers buried, and by strangers mourned."

WE left Bashardshik at an early hour, and the arabá
wound slowly up an elevation east of the city to reach
the table land which stretches away towards the Euxine.
It was a morning of autumnal freshness. A cool wind
crept down from the Balkans, and never did my pulses
throb with a sweeter or heartier life !

Near the city gate we passed by an old Turkish
fountain, calling to mind the palmier days of Islam. A
group of white-armed, laughing girls had assembled
there, who fled as we approached. They may have
been the naiads of the fountain. Melpomene and Thalia would not have tripped away more gracefully over
the dewy velvet.

I have frequently noticed Turkish boys as beautiful
as Astyanax. Ottoman children of both sexes are indeed remarkable for their beauty, as well as for the

sweetness and dignity of their behavior. The latter
arise from their being brought up in the harem. The
father takes little part or interest in their education,
and the young mind is left entirely to the sweet influences of maternal love, which is unusually strong in
Oriental society, from the fact that female life is confined to a narròw and exclusive sphere. Filial and
maternal affection, retained through life and touchingly
manifested on all occasions, is the result of this training.

From the strong admixture of Circassian blood, and
to a limited extent that of the Greeks, the Turkish is,
perhaps, the most perfect type of the human race.
Freedom from excitement, political or moral, exemption
from the corroding cares of business and that happy
alliance of movement and repose in the open air, which
the Turk so much loves, conduce to the development of
manly beauty, and are highly favorable to longevity.
The Moslems, among whom I moved, silent and statuesque men of the graceful beard and flowing robes of
the Orientals, combined the dignified bearing of an ancient Athenian with the majestic gravity of a Roman
Senator.

The confined and fretful life of the harem is, on the
contrary, destructive to female charms. Married at the
age of twelve or fifteen years, Turkish ladies become
ugly at twenty-five, unendurable at forty. Their mode
of dress also seems to render the beautiful less beautiful, the uncomely more uncomely. Moreover, their

unangelic way of sitting cross-armed and cross-legged after the manner of their lords, gives them distorted spinal columns and round shoulders, while the universal habit of smoking contributes to convert the rich tints of Circassian beauty into the sallow wrinkles of premature age.

The Indians believe that deformed bodies are prisons into which souls are cast for great crimes committed in a former life. Among the Turks, who contend that a base soul must inhabit a deformed body, the cultivation of physical strength and beauty is held to be the highest duty after the chief points of religion.

As we advanced I observed a large number of *tumuli* scattered over the plain, many of which were of considerable size. They resembled those found along the lower Danube and on the steppes of Russia, and belong to that class of rude but very ancient monuments existing in almost every part of the world, from the plains of Central Asia to the prairies of the far West. The Turks call these conical mounds, *Tepe*, the Bulgarians, *Hunka*, or graves of the Huns. Their resemblance to the Pelasgian tumuli and to the mounds along the Volga and the Mississippi indicates that all nations have like conceptions of art at like periods of their development. A religious idea may have suggested the erection of some of them. I have not unfrequently seen mounds of the shape, as nearly as possible, of animals known to have been worshipped in ancient times, but for the most part

they are doubtless simple monuments to mark the resting-places of the dead. Recent excavations in the
tumuli of Bessarabia have disclosed, as is supposed, the
tombs of the ancient Sarmatian kings. Ask the Bulgarian peasant who erected them, and he will answer,
" God only knows." The Turks say that they are simply elevations marking the sites of Ottoman camps on
which were formerly displayed the horse-tail sandjaks
of victorious sultans and pachas. My imagination,
however, associated these mysterious monuments with
ancient Scythian heroes and Bulgarian kings. As I
looked upon them I thought of those classic souvenirs
of the friendship of Achilles and Patroclus on the plain
of Troy—of the lofty mound believed to contain the
ashes of the son of Peleus—but now, as in days of old,
guiding to the Rhœtian port—

> " Sea-wandering barks that o'er the Ægean sail,
> With pennants streaming to the southern gale."

These silent watchmen of the Bulgarian plain may
have witnessed *adieux* as touching as those of Hector
and Andromache ; heroes as noble as Ajax and Ilus
may sleep beneath them ; but unlike Ajax Telamon
and the Trojan king, their deeds have been embalmed
in no immortal Iliad.

Now and then from an elevated point I looked down
upon the low and immense Dobrudsha stretching away
in the distance, like

"that Serbonian bog
Where armies whole have sunk."

It is intersected by Trajan's wall, built centuries ago
and extending from the point where the Danube makes
a sudden sweep towards Moldavia, to Kostendji on the
Black Sea, while far beyond, at the north, the Danube
itself flows into the Euxine. The extended plains, or
rather morasses, of the Dobrudsha are well wooded, but
want the magnolia to make them equal to the low banks
of the Mississippi and the Savannah. The soil is exceedingly fertile, the atmosphere humid and insalubri-
ous. The inhabitants, numbering some sixteen thousand
families, represent not less than sixteen nationalities, but
the majority are of Tartar origin, whose ancestors were
driven from the Crimea during the convulsions which
preceded and attended the incorporation of that peninsula into the Russian empire.

They exercise faithfully the laws of hospitality prescribed by the Koran. When a traveller enters one of
their villages, the heads of the families dispute among
themselves the honor of receiving and entertaining him
gratuitously for three days.

Among them there are not far from 10,000 Cossacks,
descended from families who fled from the Ukraine after
the fall of Mazeppa, their leader, and Charles XII.
Though fixed to the soil and become farmers like the
Bulgarians, they still exhibit traces of their ancient
nomadic life. Like their ancestors, they pray and

preach in the open air. They also cherish a profound antipathy toward the Russians. Their ancestors sought refuge in the Dobrudsha, while others of the same race wandered round the shore of the Euxine to the mouth of the Halys in Anatolia, but the fact of their having escaped did not save them as well as Mazeppa, then dead, from being excommunicated by the Russian Empress. Catharine forbade even to pronounce their name in holy Russia. It is from this region that the Tartar couriers employed in Turkey are generally selected, and both Tartars and Cossacks have been organized into light cavalry regiments for the Ottoman service by Saydik Pasha.

When the Russians last withdrew from Bulgaria several hundred Cossack and Tartar families were in part persuaded, in part compelled, to follow them to the Pruth. There, however, they were cruelly abandoned. While travelling in Wallachia I often met bands of them wandering from village to village, and begging piteously for bread.

At a great distance to the southward loomed up isolated mountain-peaks, the forerunners of the Hæmus. Morning and evening when the sun-god whirled his flaming chariot above the Euxine, or when his panting steeds traversed the fiery chambers of the west toward far-off Atlantis, they were spread with cloths of gold as if the Olympians had been assembled on their summits for royal banquets. Now the storms pierced their quivering flanks with darts of lightning and wept floods of crystal tears in a rage or in penitence, and then the clouds, the smiling daughters of old Ocean, winging their way up the sky on the soft wind threw their fleecy mantle around those frowning brows as girlish innocence will sometimes throw a veil over the face of bleeding, shame-stricken age.

The *terrain* over which I was passing had been consecrated to bloody Mars. By a strange fatality the children of the Occident and the Orient have repeatedly met on the plains of Eastern Europe to fight the decisive battles of the world. What legions have trodden her soil in the ebb and flow of conquest!

> " One sanguine tide scarce rolled away,
> Another flows in quick succession."

After the fall of Silistria and the capitulation of Varna, in 1829, the Russian General, Diebitsch, conceived the bold plan of leaving the Grand-Vizier in the intrenched camp of Shumla, and by crossing the Balkans, strike a blow at the very heart of the Ottoman Empire. This hardy achievement, which gave him the name of Zabalkanski (Crosser of the Balkans), was executed, and carried dismay among the Ottomans. The Russian General procured a favorable treaty of peace at Adrianople, although his serviceable force did not amount to more than 15,000 men, an army which

15

the Turks would have despised had they known its real strength.

Darius, in his memorable expedition against the Scythians more than twenty-three centuries ago, also crossed the Balkans, but in an opposite direction. He passed the Danube, as he had already the Thracian Bosphorus, on a bridge of boats, but his immense army soon melted away in the swamps of Moldavia, beneath clouds of Scythian arrows. Forced to retreat, the monarch overran Thrace and Macedonia—to have his hosts shivered in battle by the Greeks on the plain of Marathon. Hunyad crossed the Balkans from north to south, in the year 1443, and the Sultan Amurath fifty-three years earlier in the opposite direction.

There are many souvenirs of the poet Ovid in Eastern Europe. The Hungarian points proudly to his supposed tomb at Szombathely. The Wallachian peasant, able at this day to comprehend the language of Ovid, conducts the traveller to his so-called tower and prison at Karansebes in the valley of Temes, which, according to the tradition of the country, the Roman soldiers hastened to visit when Trajan led them into Dacia. A small lake in Bessarabia still bears the name of the poet. There is a tradition that he learned the language of the Getæ and composed poems that moved the hearts of the barbarians. The poet himself says—

"Didici getice sarmaticeque loqui."

The peasants relate that there once came to their
country, from the banks of a far-off river, a man who combined the goodness of a parent and the sweetness of a
child. He sighed continually, but when speaking to
any one honey seemed to flow from his lips. Even Von
Hammer, the prince of Orientalists, was unable to locate
with certainty Tomi, the place of the poet's exile and
death. It was probably on the Euxine, north of Varna,
near Ovidipol.

I know nothing more sad than Ovid's *Tristia*, written in this distant region and fairly perfumed with
tearful memories of his native land. A gifted son of
Italy, enriched with the best culture of classic Athens,
Ovid was the sweetest and most subtle of that tuneful
throng which Augustus assembled at his Court, nominally to enjoy the Imperial patronage, but in reality to
clothe in the most seductive coloring the despotism he
was introducing in Rome. He became frivolous and
licentious, and wishing to reduce to a system the "Art
of Love," published a poem under that title. The im-
morality of this work was the ostensible cause of his
banishment to Scythia, but as the Augustan age was not
remarkable for virtue in high places, the Roman Emperor doubtless had reasons for banishing the author of the
"Art of Love," which have never been made known
The plaintive songs of Ovid moved a world to tears, but
could soften neither the inflexible Augustus nor his
successor, Tiberius. He spent the last fifteen years of

his life on the inhospitable shores of the Pontus Euxinus, ever sighing for the soft skies of Italy, for that Rome whose glory was at the same time the subject and the inspiration of his verses. Let those who would deify tyrants by prostituting genius to their praise, and are willing to kiss the hand that has smitten them to the dust, remember the fate of Publius Ovidius.

I expected to reach Varna by night, but for the first time among the Turks was agreeably disappointed. On ascending the crest of an elevated ridge early in the afternoon I beheld all at once the Black Sea bounding the eastern horizon—Varna stretched out like a map at my feet, and its harbor filled with vessels belonging to the allied fleets. *Thalatta! thalatta!* I cried, after having traversed Europe, and was as much delighted to behold the Euxine as were the Ten Thousand under Xenophon to look upon its glad waters after their retreat from the Euphrates. The point from which I began to descend was at least 300 feet above the level of the sea. Varna appeared to be not more than a mile distant, but the arabá required two long hours to reach the city gate. At my right was the little river Devna, along which the English and French had previously encamped. Beyond this stream and the twin lakes through which it runs, was the high ridge that terminates in the promontory of Galata. The Emperor Nicholas encamped upon the latter in 1828, but it was now dotted with the white tents of a regiment of the Nizam.

There are several large swamps in the immediate vicinity of Varna, and a more fatal place could not have been selected for the rendezvous of the allied troops. That, however, was but one of the errors on the part of the Allies which marked the progress of the Eastern question through the entanglements of cabinets and the stratagems of camps.

Peace to the ashes of the brave thousands smitten down by disease along the lethean Devna! Impatient of glory, they were condemned to an inglorious death by men unfit to lead the armies in the Orient—men less accustomed to the camp and the tented field than to the more Paphian warfare of St. James and the Tuileries. Says Aristophanes: "The laws of Athens are discussed by sages and executed by fools." In reference to the Eastern war it might be said with equal truth: "Patrician fools discussed in London and Paris, and plebeian heroes executed on the bloody fields of Alma and Inkermann." And comparing the painful inefficiency of Lords and Dukes with the heroic conduct of Miss Nightingale, we may aptly use the words of Xerxes after the battle of Salamis: "In this conflict men have acted like women, and women conducted themselves like men."

Varna, the ancient Odyseum founded by Milesian colonists, is the best port of Bulgaria, but has not the strategic importance of Schumla. For that reason mainly it has not recovered from the effects of the Russian siege in 1828.

The City wall, outside of which are extensive barracks,
is mounted with some two hundred pieces of artillery.
The defences are much stronger on the sea than on the
land side, and where it is practicable the wall is surrounded by a deep *fosse*. The city has a population of
17,000 souls, and is the residence of a Greek Metropolitan.

A few English and French troops were still posted in
Varna to supply the Commissariat in the Crimea. Selim
set me down at the Turkish Khan, where I was obliged
to remain for want of better accommodations.   On my
arrival I called upon the English Consul, who agreed
with me that Americans are great travellers. The French
had done something in the way of naming the streets
and numbering the house. "*Rue Rivoli, Place Con-
corde,*" and other familiar French names reminding one
of magnificent Paris, appeared, however, rather out of
place when applied to the filthy lanes and muddy corners of detestable Varna.   I found myself among shar-
pers and adventurers of every religion, language, and
color.

While wandering one day over this chequered
mosaic of nationalities—this pandemonium of war and
crime, of filth and wretchedness—I encountered a
scene of which only Western civilization can boast,
which was Oriental only in the accident of its locality.
A few dissolute women who spoke the language of Vic-
toria, but in whose persons Venus and Bacchus had

united their worst characteristics, were engaged in a drunken brawl in the open street with a number of Scotch and Irish dragoons. The French police were attempting to abate the nuisance, and their elegant " *Écoutez, Mesdemoiselles ; venez chez nous,*" seemed wasted when addressed to these pugnacious courtesans following in the track of war. A crowd of long-bearded Mussulmans had collected to gaze on that strange embodiments of Western civilization in their midst. I shall not soon forget how these turbaned philosophers shook their heads and turned away in disgust, saying, "O Allah, the Merciful, deliver us from the faults of our friends. By the beard of the Prophet, one Mussulman maiden is worth more than seven of the most beautiful daughters of the unbelievers."

The Koran forbids the use of intoxicating drinks. The law of Islam is capable, however, of an elastic interpretation, and there are those among the faithful who contend that the interdiction is against the abuse, rather than the use of alcohol. But, withstanding modern innovations, the great majority of Moslems condemn it, even in the form of remedies applied internally or externally, believing with the Prophet that " the sin committed by drinking wine is much greater than the advantage reaped from it." Those who have made the pilgrimage to Mecca are most scrupulous on this point. Generally they will neither make nor drink wine—

neither buy nor sell it—nor the implements with which
it is made, in order to live by such traffic. Unfortunately, however, there have been many departures
from the early purity of the faith of Islam. The island
of Scio was conquered by the Grand-Vizier Kipriuli
on account of the excellence of its wines. Many of the
Turkish poets have celebrated in verse the pleasures of
the flowing bowl. Even the Dervishes, those pious
showmen and cunning Jesuits of the East, are not proof
against the temptation. Some of the Sultans have been
addicted to intemperance, and the last Padisha, Mahmoud, died of *delirium tremens*, actually—though of
tubercular consumption, officially. One of the first acts
of Abdul Medjid was to throw into the Bosphorus
several thousand bottles of wine surreptitiously introduced in the Seraglio by the Kislar Aga. It is affirmed,
however, that the Sultan has of late become addicted
to the vice of his predecessor. The soldiers of Omer
Pacha drank freely of *schnapps*, a vile liquid invented,
they declare, by the devil, long after the promulgation
of the Koran. This is the only instance of legal acumen
I have ever discovered among the Turks. I do not
remember to have seen more than half-a-dozen Moslems completely overcome by the influence of *French
water*.

Let us, reader, be grateful to the " Camel driver of
Mecca " for the good that his religious system has accomplished in the East. The Koran is a judicious code

of health, applied on a magnificent scale, and while we thank Mohammed for abolishing idolatry and destroying caste throughout the wide domain of Islam, we have also to thank that "sanitary commissioner run mad," for restraining millions from the use of intoxicating drinks, in a climate where the temptation to use them is exceedingly great and the consequences more fatal than elsewhere. Alcohol decimated again and again the English army in the Orient.

·Travellers making a hasty tour of the Continent are generally guilty of egregious error in their estimate of the extent of intemperance in Europe and its effect upon social institutions. They see comparatively few drunkards in the streets, and without caring to make a closer examination, are ready to affirm that intemperance scarcely has an existence in western Europe, that France, Italy, and the States of Germany constitute the Utopia of modern drinking.

Professor Oppolzer, a physiologist and physician of world-wide celebrity, whose cliniques I attended at Vienna, often deprecated the drinking habits of the Germans, as deleterious to health and general happiness; and in my opinion the Viennese are more unhealthy and shorter-lived than the inhabitants of New York. In the hospital, cases of *delirium tremens* were of frequent occurrence. One of the most common and obstinate forms of disease was distension of the stomach, caused by drinking immoderate quantities of wine and beer.

15*

Professor Hyrtl, of Vienna, by far the greatest
anatomist of the age, used to say that he could distinguish, in the darkest room, by a single stroke of the scalpel, the brain of an inebriate from that of a person who
had lived soberly. Now and then he would congratulate the class upon his possessing a drunkard's brain,
admirably fitted from its hardness and more complete
preservation for the purposes of demonstration. When
the anatomist wishes to preserve a human brain for any
length of time, he effects his object by keeping that
organ in a vessel of alcohol. From a soft pulpy substance, it then becomes comparatively hard. But the
inebriate, anticipating the anatomist, begins the indu-
rating process before death, begins it while the brain
remains the consecrated temple of the soul, while its
delicate and gossamer tissues still throb with the pulses
of heaven-born life. Terrible enchantment, that dries
up all the fountains of generous feeling, petrifies all
the tender humanities and sweet charities of life.

Were the Germans to dispense somewhat with
wine and beer, they would become more clear-headed,
thoughtful, and virtuous. Their ontological vagaries
would in part disappear, the despotic anti-liberal tendency of their literature would cease to exist, and
German infidelity, that muddy stream of presumption
and pedantry, would, when viewed in a clearer light,
become more repulsive and less injurious. With them
the grosser appetites are suffered to

ARGISCH—ANCIENT CAPITAL OF WALLACHIA.

p. 156

"—— drink up the liberal sap,
The vegetating vigor of philosophy,
And leave it a mere husk."

It is a common remark in Germany that to deprive the people of their wine and beer by increased taxation upon those articles, would at once cause a revolution ; in other words, wine and beer, with music and the concomitant pleasures, all furnished at a cheap rate, are acknowledged to be important means in the hands of German tyrants for keeping their subjects oppressed. Casks of lager beer, butts of wine and fiddle-bows, the props of despotism and the upholders of dynasties! This is not saying much for the gallantry and heroism of the people; nor in my opinion are they worthy of liberty who are willing to take in exchange for it the ravishments of wine and revelry. If it is melancholy to see an individual drowning his sorrows in wine, what is it to see cowardly nations dissolving their griefs and disappointments in the Lethean forgetfulness of intoxication? And this is the case not only in the Germanic States, but throughout western and central Europe, England in part excepted. In view of these facts, the evils flowing from the use of intoxicating drinks in Europe are greater than in the United States. The individual excesses may not be so great and repulsive as in our own country, where there is more activity and more complete exhaustion, but Heaven preserve us from sinking into the Dead Sea of European intemperance, involving the loss of both morality and liberty.

Before setting out for Constantinople, I spent a few days in studying the characteristics of the Bulgarians. An excursion in the interior, in the direction of Schumla, gave me a better knowledge of their customs and every-day life, than I had hitherto been able to obtain. The usual mode of travelling is on horseback, with a Tartar guide. The Bulgarian horses are fast and sure-footed, but the fatigue of sixteen hours in a Turkish saddle would have been scarcely endurable had it not been for the new scenes and incidents which my journey constantly afforded. Instead of resting at the Turkish khans, as had been my practice, I sought out the humble cottages of the Bulgarians, experiencing everywhere the hospitality which is proverbial in the East.

The Slaves of Turkey exhibit the imposing number of more than 7,000,000 souls. Covering the Balkans from the Euxine to the Adriatic they are divided into two great branches, the Servian and the Bulgarian. The latter, occupying the northern slope of the Balkans, numbers 4,500,000 souls. Besides the Principality of Servia, the Servian branch of the family embraces Montenegro, Bosnia, the Hertzegovina, and numerous districts of Albania and Epirus.

The Balkans signify *mountains of defence*, and in their fastnesses the mountaineers retain to a greater or less extent their ancient privileges. After the battle of Kossova, in the year 1389, when the victorious Turks put an end to the old Servian kingdom, the refugees betook themselves in numerous bands to the thunder-riven recesses of Montenegro, where to this day their enemies have not been able to penetrate. The Servian Slaves occupy the wildest portions of Europe, and they owe their present independence, complete in Montenegro, and virtually so in Servia, as much to the inaccessible nature of their country as to their own brave hearts and hands.

As the Greeks of European Turkey claim the sea and congregate in cities, so the Slaves prefer the mountains and the plains. Those of the Servian branch are shepherds: the Bulgarians are cultivators of the soil. The former are less civilized than the Greeks, but more consistent in their political views. Of all the races belonging to the Illyrian triangle they exhibit the best guarantees of a prosperous future, and are marching slowly but surely in the road of progress. Having more of an Oriental character than the Greeks, they regard the Ottomans with less aversion, and although sympathizing to a certain extent with their co-religionists of Russia, prefer a successor of Mohammed to a Greek Prince or a Russian Czar, on the throne of Byzantium.

Not a few of the Slaves have become fanatic converts to the Mussulman faith, and it is an instructive fact that general apostasy has taken place only in the provinces under aristocratic *regime*. Thus the Bosnians embraced the faith of the Islam for the sole purpose of preserving their wealth and privileges, while the Albanians sacrificed their religion for independence, such being their horror of servitude. The following, from Lamartine, is equally applicable to Albania, Bosnia, and parts of Epirus and Macedonia.

" The Caucasus in Asia, and Albania in Europe, both situated at the head of two great gulfs of the Mediterranean whose waters are united by the current of the Bosphorus, appear to have a geographical and moral correspondence to each other. The Albanians are the Circassians of Europe : the Circassians are the Albanians of Asia. These two groups of mountains appear to have given birth to like men, like women, and like customs. It is from these two sources, as from the snows upon their summits, that have been derived for five centuries, by the frequent combination of three distinct nationalities, the spirit, the intrepidity, the beauty and mettle of the Ottoman race. They love arms, combats, adventures, races on the sea or upon the land, the perilous feats of brigands, fields of battle in whatever cause, and military engagements in the camps of the Sultans of Egypt, Syria, and Constantinople. The regular discipline of the European armies they find too burdensome. They prefer the éclat of individual exploits, the license of the Ottoman camps, the hand-to-hand conflict upon the impetuous steeds of Arabia or Transylvania, the civilization which permits slaves to rise, at the caprice of the master, from servitude to the rank of Vizier or Pacha, and the religion that gives harems and slaves to heroes.

"Their spirit, like their customs, is poetical: their popular songs, especially those of the heroic epoch upon their compatriot Scanderbeg, call to mind the songs of Homer rather than the effeminate chants of modern Greece. Like Achilles, they mingle poetry, music, and the war dance. In the leisure of their life, by turns somnolent and feverish, they are to be seen sleeping listlessly in the sun, upon the roof or terrace of their houses, chanting their own exploits to the accompaniment of a rustic lyre, or dancing, like women.

"Each city, each province, each village acknowledged the authority of a prince, a lord, or bey, who governed despotically according to the traditions or customs. This subjection of the cities, provinces and villages to their respective lords or feudal princes, diminished in no wise the sentiment of general liberty and passion of patriotism, supreme motives with the Albanian."

The Bulgarians are more numerous than the Servians, but in many respects inferior, being for the Turks "hewers of wood and carriers of water." Though wedded to peace, they have not forgotten that their ancestors established an ancient kingdom along the

Danube; that their armies have more than once carried
terror to the rulers of Byzantium. To them belongs
the northern slope of the Balkans; but they have also
penetrated into Thrace, Epirus, and Macedonia. Too
weak to avail themselves of their numerical superiority,
too timid to fly to independence, they show a disposition to fraternize with the Greeks and the Servians.

The·mercantile and maritime character of the
Greeks, the pastoral disposition of the Servians, and
the agricultural tendency of the Bulgarians—in these
we have the elements of a great people, for the establishment of whose power nothing but union is necessary. Could the two races be amalgamated, Ottoman
authority in Europe would speedily pass away.

To impart an idea of Bulgarian life, I cannot do
better than employ the poetical description of Cy-
prian Robert:

" Nothing is more like a group of savage huts than
a *celo* or Bulgarian village. Always remote from the
high road or from the waste space to which that name
is given, and consequently invisible to most travellers,
the *celo* usually stands in a meadow along the border
of a stream which serves it for a ditch and natural
defence. These villages are very numerous, succeed-
ing each other from league to league. Each consists of
four or five groups of houses, separated from each other
by grass-grown spaces. The courts surrounded by a
thick hedge are like so many islands in a sea of ver-

dure. The huts composing one of them are usually ten
or twelve in number and are either formed of wattles,
so as to resemble great baskets, or are sunk in the ground
and covered with a conical roof of thatch or of branches
of trees. Each species of creature has its separate
abode in this ark of the wilderness. There are huts for
the poultry, for the sheep, for the pigs, for the oxen,
and for the horses; and in the midst the proprietor
occupies a cabin which serves him for cellar, granary,
kitchen and bedroom. The family sleep on skins spread
on the ground round the hearth which is a circular
hole sunk in the middle of the room. Little more than
the roof of these dark dwellings rises above the ground;
you descend into them by a short flight of steps, and
the doors are so low that you must stoop as you enter.
Nevertheless these poor huts are as clean and as
neatly arranged inside as they can be made by the
indefatigable *baba* (Bulgarian housewife), to whom employment is so necessary, that she plies her spin-
dle even whilst cooking, or carrying her goods to
market.

"The Bulgarian women are gentle, compassionate
and laborious. The motherly and sisterly care they
bestow on the stranger guest in their cabin is really
affecting. He sleeps on the same floor with the mother,
the wife and the daughters of the household. They
are, next to the Greeks, the handsomest women in
European Turkey, and are especially remarkable for

the length and luxuriance of their hair, with which
they could literally cover themselves as with a garment: it often sweeps the ground below their feet.
The young girls let their tresses flow loosely, and their
only head-dress is a wreath of flowers, or a single rose.
Those whose charms are on the wane, adorn themselves
with necklaces and bracelets of glass beads, a girdle of
copper gilt, and an ugly head-piece in the form of a
helmet, festooned with strings of piastres, paras and
ancient coins dug up in the fields.

" Like the son of the steppe, the Bulgarian is in-
separable from his horse. In the country parts every
Bulgarian has one, the very poorest not excepted, and
never goes even a few hundred yards from his cabin
except on horseback. Skulls of horses or buffaloes
are planted on stakes in front of his dwelling, as a
symbol, apparently, of a prosperous condition. The
Bulgarian and the Turk, though living in the same
country, clothe themselves quite differently. The Turk
came from the south, and wears loose garments of
linen or cotton; the Bulgarian, on the contrary, being
a son of the north, is always warmly clad even in
summer. His costume is the same as that of his
ancestors on the cold plateau of Northern Asia."

CHAPTER XIV.

" Frigidi me cohibent Euxini litora Ponti
Dictus ab antiquis Axenus ille fuit."

" We rub each other's angles down."

HAPPY was I when the hour of my departure for Constantinople arrived. In the Turkish khan, where the
faithful reposed perpendicularly by day and horizontal-
ly by night, I had smoked away precious days in the
most listless ethnographical observation—spent whole
nights in the most active entomological pursuits. The
khan-keeper was a paragon of honesty and good-nature.
He really seemed sad when I paid him for the sleep
afforded by the most unyielding of mats, the unnum-
bered cups of black coffee, and pipe-loads of fragrant
latakieh; and the slipping of a few extra piastres slily
into the hand of the good Mussulman for the excellence
of his long chibouques, gave a peculiar unction to his
parting benediction.

Happy, indescribably happy, was I to leave that
rendezvous of all the villany and wretchedness follow-

ing in the track of war, and embark on the French steamer lying at anchor in the offing. The wheels soon began to revolve. The black monster wound her way with difficulty through the fleet of transports, and then turned her prow toward the Bosphorus. The fortresses and mosques of Varna were soon shut out from view. The tent-crowned summit of the promontory of Galata gradually sank beneath the sea, but the high bluffs along the coast and the distant Balkans were in sight all the afternoon.

For the first time in my life I felt myself really on classic ground, and my thoughts were as light and buoyant as the trembling moisture of the Pontic wave. True, I had seen where the Roman triremes approached the shores of Britain, and traversed provinces dotted with Roman camps and cities, but the dimpled waves of the Euxine had yielded to the prow of the Argo, while the expedition of Cæsar and the period of Roman conquest seemed as of yesterday compared to the fabulous age of the Argonauts, or to the later time when the shores of the Euxine were studded with colonies founded by persons who had left the cities of Greece for the enjoyment of greater liberty, or in consequence of false predictions of the Oracles. Steaming down the ancient Mœsian Coast, I first found myself surrounded by the myths and solidarities of antiquity.

For several hours the Euxine was calm and smooth as a mirror. But before sundown the fleecy clouds

gathered in dark festoons, huge nebulous masses collected around the summits of the Balkans, as frowning
warriors assemble around their chiefs, and then took up
their stately, aërial march, trumpeted by thunders and
heralded by vivid lightnings. The first breath of the
tempest just ruffled the surface of the sea; the ripples
curled into waves weaving their crisped smiles as if in
scornful defiance, and in a short time we could have
justly quoted the lines of Byron—

> "There's not a sea the traveller e'er pukes in
> Throws up more dangerous breakers than the Euxine."

The night closed in with a storm, and I retired below
to study the varied characters among whom I had been
thrown.

The steamer is not only a triumph of civilization,
but is, in the East, one of its chief agents and promoters.
It will, with other causes at work, ultimately regenerate
the Orient. Had it been introduced a century ago,
before the Ottoman Empire reached the last stage of
dissolution, there would now be hope for the Osmanlis.
The steamer brings people together, keeps them together,
and compels them to learn of each other. The decks
of the *Euphrate* exhibited little mosaics of nationalities
and arabesque costumes. A simple wanderer from the
Western World, and apparently the only traveller on
board, I found clustered around me, as if by enchantment, not only the denizens of civilized Europe, but the

dusky children of Africa and the wild sons of the nomadic nations of Central Asia. Strange sight it was, and a remarkable proof that the prejudices of race and country are gradually wearing away, to see Turkish soldiers mingled with the Horse-Guards, Turcomans and Arabs jostled by Germans and Anglo-Saxons, and French ladies elbowing their way through a crowd of veiled Moslem spectres. Our ancestors may have separated from each other at the dispersion of Babel. We spoke different languages and had different sympathies, but the twenty-two hours' passage from Varna to Constantinople unavoidably gave us new impressions. In the social as in the sidereal system, bodies cannot come near each other without silently exerting a reciprocal influence.

The majority of the passengers were sick and wounded soldiers from the Crimea on their way to the hospitals of Scutari and Constantinople, or returning to their native land. They were ragged, emaciated, and downcast. Poor fellows! plebeian nothings in the Titanic conflicts of kings and races! What mockery to them "the pride and pomp of glorious war," and how cruel its bloody circumstance! They belonged to the fourth class of passengers, and most of them had to remain all night on the forward deck, exposed to the pitiless storm. The third class was made up of Turks and Armenians, who occupied half of the hurricane-deck and were protected overhead by a canvas awning.

The Turk *en voyageant* is fond of a large retinue of
servants. If his harem be in process of transportation,
he also carries an incredible quantity of baggage for
sleeping and culinary purposes. The Ottoman is independent of the steamer which transports him even for
the water he drinks and the fire that ignites his tobacco.
Except in the hurry of departure, he mingles but little
with the crowd on board. Spreading his blanket on the
square feet allotted him, he squats upon it cross-legged
and cross-armed, and remains relatively motionless
during the voyage, blow high or low, in sunshine or
in storm. The limited space on the deck of the
Euphrate rendered the carrying out of the harem
principle somewhat difficult. The female sex is much
the same the world over in the mode of maintain-
ing its rights, and judging from the hurried accen-
tuation, sea-sickness and promiscuous bedfellowship
seriously disturbed the usual equanimity of Eastern
manners.

The first and second cabins were occupied by English, French, and Turkish officers of the higher class.
The two former associated little with each other. One
would have supposed from their jealous remarks, that
the sons of England and France were fighting face to
face instead of shoulder to shoulder in that great crusade
in the East—so true is it that their boasted alliance existed not in the hearts of the two nations, but was the
offspring of circumstances liable to be changed at any

moment by the death of Napoleon or a revolution aimed at aristocratic power in England.

The Turkish officers belonged to the new school of Moslems. They had the levity of Parisians, drank *French water*, and were given to other Christian usages. There were also with us a few officers' wives who had followed their husbands to the Orient, but the weeds of mourning plainly indicated that war and pleasure do not always march together.

The Euxine of grand and severe reputation—the *axenos*, or inhospitable, of the Greeks in contrast with their soft and tranquil Ægean—is about three hundred miles in length from east to west, but much less in width, being of the shape of a Scythian bow. In it are mingled the crystal floods of the Ural and the Alps, the melted congelations of the North, and the weepings of warm showers on the Pontic slope of Anatolia. The Euxine is tideless, and notwithstanding it receives the perpetual inundations of forty rivers, is decidedly saline. Looked down upon by four mountain chains, the Carpathians, the Hæmus, the Taurus and the Caucasus, and exposed to the winds that sweep over the Steppes of Russia, we could not expect to find it pacific. But the traditional dangers attending the navigation of the Euxine have been studiously magnified by the Russians, who well know that they will to a great extent disappear after the erection of light-houses along the coasts and the completion of accurate charts.

I cannot forbear alluding in this connection to an adventure of the Emperor Nicholas on the Black Sea in the year 1828. He and the Grand Duke Michael embarked at Sevastopol on a small steamer—*l'Impératrice de la Mer*—for Varna, then besieged by the Russians. Count Nesselrode, with several persons of dipomatic reputation, took passage on the *Penteleimon* which was to bear the other steamer company. A terrific storm came on. The vessels were disabled and separated. The one which carried Nicholas and his fortunes was driven to the opening of the Bosphorus, and the commander proposed to run in and surrender as the only possible means of saving the lives of those on board. To that proposition the Emperor would not listen—preferring death to such a humiliation. After a marvellous escape they ultimately made the port of Odessa. Nesselrode and the members of the diplomatic corps with him arrived at Sevastopol after eight days of perils and gastric perturbations, glad to have escaped, but convinced that Neptune is no respecter of persons.

The poet Ovid, in one of his epistolary odes *ex Ponto*, complained of the barbarity of the people and the inhospitable nature of the climate:—

"Cumque alii causa tibi sint graviore fugati
Ulterior nulli quam mihi, terra data est
Longius hac nihil est nisi tantum frigus et hostis,
Et maris adstricto quæ coit unda gelu."

16

The climate is now milder than in the time of Ovid. Certain causes have operated in diminishing the excessive cold of eastern Europe from century to century. Vienna, on the upper Danube, occupies the site of the Roman camp of Julia Vindobona. We read that when the legions were encamped there under Marcus Aurelius, frozen wine was brought upon the tables of the officers, a luxury that is not enjoyed by the modern Viennese.

Herodotus relates that the Thracians crossed the Cimmerian Bosphorus upon the ice. Strabo speaks of an engagement by the cavalry of Mithridates on the frozen Euxine, and a naval victory afterwards gained by him near the same spot. He also repeats the story of Herodotus that in the region of the Euxine the horns were sawn from the heads of the oxen in order to prevent their being frozen off by the excessive cold of winter.

Jason, according to the poetic fables of the ancients, which ascribe heroic motives to all adventurers, traversed the Euxine to capture the golden fleece, or rather, making a considerable allowance for the fillibustering character of his expedition, to obtain the superior wool of Colchis. The great number of rivers flowing into the Euxine have from time immemorial rendered its waters as famous for fisheries as its shores have been celebrated for their wealth in cereals. And while the lofty argosies, freighted with the luxuries of

Corinth and Athens, visited the Euxine for the same object that has, within the last fifty years, directed innumerable English prows to Odessa, namely, the substantial realities of grain and tallow, fleets of hardy fishermen bent their way thither for the treasures of Neptune, less valuable indeed than those of Ceres, but still greatly sought after. The exports of grain and fish from the coasts of the Euxine to the cities of Greece, are mentioned by both Herodotus and Demosthenes.

It would be impossible to describe the horrid discomforts of my first and only night upon the Euxine. To sleep without being lashed to the berth, or packing oneself away like a choice piece of furniture in a box, was quite impossible. Every timber in the vessel seemed to have forgotten its ordinary tune, and squeaked and crackled forth a gibberish sound. The huge ship would roll from side to side, and like a tired giant, lie panting on the waves. Checked one moment in her course by a heavy sea, the pulseless arms of her engines seemed almost to stop, and then, gathering new strength from the "floods of living fire" within, she would again dart forward like an arrow—

> "The beating of her restless heart
> Still sounding through the storm."

During the sleepless watches of the night I often thought of the Argonautic adventurers who, we are told,

"Were the first that ever burst
    Into that silent sea,"

and of the rich argosies which visited the Pontus after
the enterprise of the Milesians had dotted its coasts
with famous cities and converted the *axenos* of the
Greeks into the *euxinos*, the hospitable,—a name which
it has ever since borne.

Amid the howlings of the storm there came dim
visions of the many-tongued nations on the shores of
the Euxine.

I saw on its rugged heights bands of horse-taming
Paphlagonians and Huns navigating its bays with fleets
of canoes burned from the trunks of trees. There
arose out of the chaos of these mythic and barbaresque
times the Tauri cruelly decoying mariners upon the
rocks of their Chersonese to sacrifice them afterwards
upon bloody altars, and the Getæ pursuing their
enemies across the frozen Boristhenes with poisoned
arrows. There also were the *indomiti Dahes* of the
Caucasus, defying the arms of the Romans and of the
Pontic kings as they have those of the Turks and Russians in modern times. Gentler visions came also—of
beautiful Iphigenia forced to become the sanguinary
priestess of Diana, and of Medea, whom ancient myths
surround with all the horrors of sorcery, but who, I
delight to think, possessed no other magic than that of
beauty, was guilty of no crime but that of love. I beheld joyous dances once more in the cool groves of

Angora, and bethought me of gentle Hylas drawn beneath the waves by the nymphs.   There had also lived
Mithridates, one of the idols of my boyhood readings.
The one and the only illustrious name belonging exclusively to the history of the Pontic kingdoms, it conse-
crates the very soil on which he lived.   After all, the
great and heroic man is the noblest product of the
earth; and I would travel further to see a Webster
standing by the grave of Milton or Shakespeare than to
behold the seven wonders of the world.

The past yields to the present.

The expedition fitted out from Varna, surpassing
everything of the kind in the extent and completeness
of its appointments—the siege, to which those of Vienna
and Saragossa can hardly be compared—the Euxine
swept of a powerful navy and a rich commerce—these
were the quick-coming events of a few months.   Hosts
of men speaking almost every language and exhibiting
almost every type of the human race, were brought
hither, not for the purposes of commerce in a region
fitted by nature to be the commercial centre of the
globe, but to destroy each other and gratify the ambition of monarchs.   With the Allies the late war was
nominally a struggle of civilization and liberty against
barbarous despotism, but seas swept of commerce,
sacked cities, and burning villages, were the foot-
prints of their path.   The very armies enriching with
their blood the granary of Europe were in part

provisioned from the prairies of our own great West.

Such are the anomalies of war.

I was on deck at an early hour of the morning to catch my first glance of the Bosphorus and the coast of Asia. The storm had swept past. The stars twinkled as brightly as when they guided the ancient mariner venturing out timidly upon the Inhospitable Sea. The moon was sinking behind the hills of Roumelia just visible in the distance, at whose rock-bound bases a long line of flashing breakers gleamed like the sheen of many tremulous spears. The air was deliciously soft and warm, and there was not a breath of wind to re-kindle the rage of the clanging sea, but wave pursued wave as if eager to catch the first kiss of rosy morning —to cradle and roll themselves to sleep in " the voice-less caves " of the Anatolian coast, or broken and tired with a longer march, to rest like weary Titans against the adamantine bases of the Caucasus.

A wounded French soldier from the Crimea had died during the night, and his comrades were already as-sembled on deck to commit his body to the sea. From the moment he came on board at Varna, his pitiable condition had greatly interested me. The brave young fellow was proud of being numbered among the children of glory and of France, but he had hoped to see once more the sunny hills of his beautiful native land. The rude breath of battle dries up the sweet charities and the tender humanities of life, but it is only during its hot rage that the soldier is without compassion; at other times he is a man. When, after the death of the wounded soldier, I saw his brother-in-arms lay aside with care the sword and the *chapeau* to be used no more, together with the little mementoes that bespoke a mother's love, though the actors were humble, I could not help thinking of the friendships which sprang up between the warriors before the battlements of Troy, as of Achilles and Patroclus, of Ajax and Teucer. They who were grouped around me had witnessed the carnage of Alma without a shudder, they had often stood in the presence of death; but when the waves of the Euxine closed above their companion-in-arms, and danced as if in triumph over a new victim for their dark and silent mansions, more than one officer turned away to conceal the tear he could not repress.

Next to Christianity, Islamism embodies the purest conception of the Deity. Stript of all the tissues which Asiatic sensuality has woven around the system, it has much of the naked and austere grandeur of Protestantism. The pious Moslem seems ever aware of the immediate and universal presence of Allah, reigning alone in his terrible unity far above the sensual mansions of the Mussulman's heaven. Laboring or journeying, in the caravan or in the camp, he cherishes everywhere the devotional spirit peculiar to Orientals, and making the ablutions with sand where water cannot be obtained, permits nothing short of absolute necessity to interfere with his invocations to Allah and the Prophet.

When I first came on deck I noticed several of my Moslem *compagnons du voyage* engaged in their expiatory lustrations and morning prayers. It was an impressive sight to see those simple children of Nature piously stretching their hands towards the fading stars. None could have been more earnest, none more sincere than they, " transacting in their peculiar manner the great business of salvation."

Then occurred a scene which gave me a lasting impression of the devotional character of Islam, but in the connection, appeared strangely ludicrous. Among the passengers there was a wealthy Turk from one of the Danubian cities on a pilgrimage to Hebron with his four handsome wives, half-a-dozen children, and man-servants and maid-servants I cannot say how many. The Effendi was a man of rank, and had taken evident pleasure the day previous in showing me a gold watch presented him by the Sultan. His servants had brought the ewers of fresh water, with gold-embroidered napkins, and spread the piece of Persian carpet, on which the Effendi, after having performed the ablutions and determined by the compass the direction of Mecca, bowed reverently towards the holy City. The storm had driven us a few miles from our course, and the steamer changed her direction for the highlands of the Bosphorus a moment after my Moslem friend began his

MALE DACO-ROMANS.   p. 162

devotions. The Nubian touched his matter's shoulder lightly, and informed him that he was no longer praying in the direction of Mecca. The Effendi rose at once, looked again at the compass, and rearranging the carpet, went through the prescribed prayers, as unmindful of our presence as if he had been worshipping in the solitude of Sahara. There is a sleepy, unspiritual absorption in Oriental worship, there is something pharisaical in this parade of prayer, but of one thing I am certain; the Moslem is never ashamed of the religion of the Prophet.

We are near the Bosphorus. The shore is bold and rugged, both on the European and the Asiatic side. The highest elevations, separated from each other by wooded ravines, here barren and there crowned with forests, can hardly be called mountains, but are the forerunners of the mighty Hæmus and Bithynian Olympus, frowning at each other across the Bosphorus, or shaking hands beneath its placid surface. The fortresses of Kilia and Riva, the former on the European, the latter on the Asiatic side, are the outworks guarding the entrance of the Bosphorus. Two or three villages can be seen perched like eagles' nests upon the rocky slopes of the promontories.

On the summit of a height on the European shore is situated a large, ancient round tower, which Domysias called *Turris Timœa*, but was in reality the old Pharos from which torches were held up at night to save vessels navigating the Black Sea from being ship-

16*

wrecked on the Cyanæan rocks at the entrance of the Bosphorus, or on the Thracian coast. The former were called Cyanæan or bluish, from their color, and also the Symplegades, or rocks striking together. The story of their mobility doubtless arose from the fact that, rising scarcely six feet above the surface, they appear and disappear as the waves pass over them. This, however, was a splendid point for the poet of antiquity, who represents Jason as steering out boldly upon the Euxine in accordance with the advice of King Phineas, but the treacherous Symplegades closing before his vessel had passed between them, she lost part of her stern, which—substituting nautical for poetical language—means simply that the Argo struck a rock and unshipped her rudder.

From the wildness of the coast I can readily believe that the ancient inhabitants, a barbarous and cruel people, used to light fires in the most dangerous places in order fatally to decoy the mariner.

We enter the Bosphorus and soon sweep by the ancient *Faunum* or Hieron, where once stood a temple to the Twelve Gods, and where the Ægean Phrygos, and afterwards Jason, on his return from Colchis, dedicated altars and instituted sacrifices. Nothing, however, can now be seen of the temple of Zeus and Posidon on the Asiatic side, or that of Serapis and Cybele opposite. The straits of Hieron, between one-third and one-half a mile in width, are the narrowest part of the Bosphorus.

Here, from the earliest times, were the outposts of its shores against the attacks of northern barbarians; here also it was that vessels sailing in and out of the Euxine were obliged to pay toll to the masters of the adjacent heights.

After the development of the maritime power of Athens, Byzance, with the Pontic and Hellespontic cities, became her tributary. To pay the tribute annu‑ ally demanded of them the Byzantines in turn levied toll upon all vessels passing through the Bosphorus. And to show the extent of the commerce then floating through this channel, I may state that the distant Rhodi‑ ans demanded an exemption from the payment of the "Bosphorus Dues," and finally obtained such an exemp‑ tion on the ground that they were exclusively a mari‑ time and commercial people. At a much later date Hieron became the theatre of frequent Byzantine and Venetian contests. The Genoese obtained possession of the Straits of Hieron in the fourteenth century, and the remains of their castles are still to be seen on the oppo‑ site heights. The Heruli appeared here in the year 248 A. D., with five hundred boats. At this point the Goths crossed over into Bithynia. The Russians advanced as far as Hieron the first time in 865, again in 941, and in the year 1832, 25,000 Muscovite troops landed not far below and encamped on the plain of Scutari as allies of the Turks to prevent Constantinople from falling into the hands of Mohammed Ali.

A point of land on the Asiatic side was in ancient times called the Anchor Cape, from the tradition that Jason took a stone anchor from that spot. It afterwards became a shrine, and ultimately the pious Byzantines made a saint out of the reputed anchor of the Argo. Strange how the vestiges of heathenism are mingled with the usages of the Eastern Christians, how hoary temples have been converted into churches, and the Olympian gods baptized into Greek and Latin saints! The Immaculate Virgin has usurped the place of the Artful Venus, Jupiter has laid aside his Homeric thunderbolts, Mars has put off the severe habiliments of war, and the tablets once relating the labors and loves of the gods are now inscribed with the *Pater* and the *Credo*. The same is to a certain extent true of Western Europe. An old record made in the time of King Edgar speaks of Westminster Abbey as occupying the site of an ancient temple of Apollo, while the immense number of oxen's heads once found near St. Paul's Cathedral, as well as traditions, go far to show that a temple to Diana stood upon the spot.

The Bosphorus is about sixteen miles in length, and averages half a mile in width. The seven promontories jutting far out into the stream and the seven corresponding bays make it crooked, and at certain points render the current turbulent.

It is the opinion of many *Savans* that until long after the creation of Adam, the Aral, the Caspian, and Black

Seas formed one immense body of water, occupying much of Central Asia, the steppes of Russia, and a great part of Turkey in Europe. The five successive basins through which the Danube descends to the Euxine must also have been, in pre-Adamic times, large inland seas. The geological formation of European Turkey in particular appears to warrant these suppositions. A terrestrial revolution probably opened the Bosphorus at the time of the Flood, and the Hellespont subsequently, thus forming a connection with the Mediterranean.

Hence the Greek, or rather the Pelasgic traditions respecting the two deluges of Oxyges and Deucalion have great historical interest. Merely the highlands of Greece rose above the surface, but on the breaking through of the Gibraltar—an event which probably occurred after the cultivation of the Pelasgic races to a considerable extent—the water subsided, enlarging thereby the continents of Europe and Asia, and forming the islands of the Ægean.

"The Samothracians related," says Diodorus Siculus, "that the Pontic Sea had once been a vast pool of standing water, which, swollen by the rivers flowing into it, first overflowed the country to the Cyanæan rocks, and after forcing its way through the Thracian Bosphorus, formed the Hellespont."

Plato is also cited by Strabo as having remarked that for some time after the early deluges, the remembrance of which was preserved in traditions in other places than Samothrace, only the summits of the mountains were inhabited, the water as yet extending over the level ground; that men descended first to the hills, then upon the plains, and thus by degrees reached the sea-shore; and that improvement in dispositions, customs, and modes of life accompanied these changes of situation, so that from wild rustics without laws, they became social, civilized, and well regulated.

The islands in the Mediterranean look as if they had been washed and rounded by the action of water. The shape of the islands of the Archipelago and the form and direction of the headlands of Greece and Asia Minor plainly indicate that an immense body of water once flowed down from the Euxine. Candia, it is true, lies with its long diameter in an eastern and western direction, but there the current must have been deflected towards Sicily. There is a magnificent audacity in this theory, but scientific facts appear to give it strong support.

And now begins, from the deck of the *Euphrate,* the most magnificent panorama of which the world can boast. We can neither paint lightning, nor give in words the flush of Aurora. Equally impossible is it to describe the marvels of beauty collected along the blue waves of the Bosphorus. The Orient and the Occident are here brought together, and the stately grandeur of the North softened by the gorgeous ara-

besques of the sunny South. Nature has exhausted
her resources, History lavished her choicest associations, and Art piled up her moresque and chiselled
wealth in the work of ennobling these enchanting
spots,—so enchanting that the Oriental poets sing of
their renown in heaven as celestial abodes.

Along the Bosphorus, rolling like a mighty serpent
of seven coils, between the dark Euxine and the silvery
Marmora, Creator and man have collected all that is
most beautiful in form, color, or grace. Here are rugged mountains and sylvan valleys, the melody of birds
and the music of water, the aroma of the cypress and
the breath of flowers. Its rushing waters—how often
they have mingled their perpetual dirge with the hurried tumultuous tread of barbaric hosts! Its forest-
crowned heights—how often they have echoed and
reëchoed the thunders of angry nations! Glorious
region,

> "That circling seas admire,
> The land where Power delights to dwell,
> And War his mightiest deeds can tell,
> And Poetry, to sweetest spell,
> Attunes her voice and lyre."

Buyukdere, Therapia, Bebek, and a score of other villages, inhabited by Greeks, Turks, and Armenians, are
passed in quick succession. Here is a summer palace
of the Sultan, and there the residence of a foreign

ambassador. Here are graceful kiosks and konaks, there cupolas and khans. In one place the minaret of a mosque rises out of a sylvan retreat, in another an oriental kahve is the resort of pleasure-seeking groups. Crumbling castles are not wanting nor forts bristling with cannon.

On these terraces, washed by the lapsing waves, and shaded with orange and jasmine, statuesque Moslems make the delicious *kief:* in those romantic retreats, cooled by the perpetual showers of fountains, naiad and nereid bands of Turkish beauties "do congregate" to enjoy the sweet earth and the balmy air— the choicest luxuries of the Orient. Now we glide by the palace of a pacha, who, a Sejanus at home and a Verres in the provinces, has grown wealthy by extortion in some distant part of the Empire, to live in eastern magnificence on the Bosphorus; and there, behind trellised *jalousies,* flit the pearls of lordly harems, rich in the wealth of Circassian charms and Georgian curls.

We notice the spot where Mandrocles of Samos built the bridge for the army of Darius, and where the latter sat enthroned to see his myriads cross the Straits. Here is pointed out the giant plane-tree, under which Godfrey of Bouillon is said to have encamped; and yonder reposed Rinaldo, happy alike in war and in worship—Rinaldo, ever fortunate in labor and in love. Here is the mausoleum of the brave Barbarossa, and there once stood a pillar of Simeon the Stylite. What more fitting place could the anchorite have chosen for his self-inflictions than where, with alternate homage, the hills of Asia and Europe lay their golden shadows at each other's feet on the blushing bosom of the Bosphorus!

Shooting past a headland, the Queen of eastern cities rises before us like a sphynx from the waves. As we approach the Golden Horn, that grandiose Constantinople—sleeping voluptuously on a couch of seven hills, letting her feet dip in waters of sapphire and emerald, and bathing her dome-tiared head in a roseate and purple atmosphere—becomes incomparably beautiful.

The wish of my youth is gratified, and my thoughts seem lost in the bewildering imaginings of an Oriental dream:

> "The European with the Asian shore
>   Sparkled with palaces; the ocean-stream,
>   Here and there studded with a seventy-four,
>   Sophia's cupola with golden gleam;
>   The cypress groves; Olympus high and hoar:
>   The Twelve Isles, and more than I could dream,
>   Far less describe, present the very view
>   That charmed the charming Mary Montagu."

CHAPTER XV.

STAMBOUL.

"Though all other cities have periods of government and are subject to the decays of time, Constantinople alone seems to claim to herself a kind of immortality, and will continue a city as long as the race of mankind shall live either to inhabit or build her."   GYLLIUS.

"Eastern opulence jewel thick."

THE steamer hardly cast anchor at the opening of the Golden Horn before she was surrounded by a fleet of *caïques*,—light boats of one or more sets of oars, of which not less than twenty thousand are said to ply on the waters of Constantinople. The *caïdjis*, or oarsmen, stalwart Greeks with brawny arms and picturesque costumes, were importunate to set us ashore. Their frail barks remind one of the Gondolas of Venice, but are so sharp and light that the passenger is obliged to sit immovably on the bottom to avoid being capsized. The lower part of the Bosphorus and the Golden Horn were crowded with vessels of every kind, and bearing the flag of every nation. I noticed many small boats coming in loaded with fish, especially the Xiphias, or Sword

Fish, which is here very abundant. Another species reminded me of a common saying among the Greeks, that no sane person would carry Tunny Fish to Byzance, or owls to Athens, as rarities. In the spring vast shoals of fish swim up the Bosphorus, swarming after each other in such multitudes that they can be taken out of the water with the hands.

You land at a low, filthy wharf, crowded with Greek and Turkish idlers, and if initiated into the ways of the Orientals, avoid the ordeal of the Custom House by slipping a few piastres into the hand of the officer. Your baggage, it matters little how heavy or voluminous, is piled upon the back of a *Hamal*, who can walk easily under a burden of three hundred pounds. Having traversed the muddy lanes of Galata, you begin to toil up the steep eminence of Pera. No one demands your passport; no one inquires after you: you are in fact unnoticed, save by some cunning Greek, already importunate to become your *cicerone*, and the troops of half starved dogs wandering in the streets. You behold little or none of the pomp with which governmental authority is maintained in the cities of Western Europe —witness but few military preparations for the purpose of preventing popular outbreaks or drying up individual drops of disaffection. No ponderous wheels of government are to be seen, nor is the clash of its operations to be heard. Like the stranger who lands upon our own shores, where man can restrain and rule himself, the first impression is that you are among a people without government.

Contrast is the law of the Orient. Under an absolute form of government you are surprised to find the enjoyment of almost unlimited freedom; and, where all else is unchangeable, to behold the slave of to-day a Pacha or Vizier to-morrow.

Pera is the Frank suburb of Constantinople and the urban residence of the foreign ambassadors. The principal hotels were crowded with English and French officers, and rather than take up with indifferent quarters at a fabulous price, I obtained private lodgings, with the privilege of taking my meals at an Italian restaurant near by.

At the hospitable residence of Mr. Brown, I met Mr. Smead of Cincinnati, O., a gentleman well known as the founder of a noble philanthropic institution in his native city, and one of the largest contributors to the Washington Monument. Like myself, he had reached Constantinople by way of the Danube and the Euxine. I was delighted to make the acquaintance of a gentleman of so much taste and cultivation—an acquaintance which ripened into friendship beneath the palm trees of the Nile, and gladdened many lonely hours among the mountains of Syria and Palestine.

Following the Europeanized street on the crest of the promontory upon which Pera is built, we reach the ancient tower of Galata. It is several hundred feet above the Bosphorus, and furnishes from its top the finest view to be had in Constantinople; a view, I may add, second in interest to none in the world. Let us ascend this ancient Genoese structure, now used for a fire telegraph.

We are on the Western or European side of the Bosphorus. East of us and on the opposite side is Scutari, the only Asiatic suburb. At the south, separated from us by the harbor, and seated proudly on her low hills is Stamboul, than which earth cannot afford "a mightier stronghold for a mighty conqueror." The Bosphorus, whose general course is from north to south, deflects here somewhat to the east, but just before it flows into the Marmora, a bay is given off on the European side. This bay, which forms the harbor of the Golden Horn, is about half a mile in width, where it communicates with the Bosphorus, and sweeps round some four miles into the country, to terminate near the Sweet Waters of Europe.

The Golden Horn derives the latter part of its name from its shape, while the epithet Golden is expressive of the riches wafted by every wind from the most distant countries into a harbor secure from storms, and large enough to float the combined navies of the world, though capable of being locked with a chain.

Pera crowns the summit of the promontory on which we stand, while its base is skirted by three other suburbs, Top-Hane, beginning with the northernmost,

Galata, and Kassim Pacha. Stamboul herself is of triangular shape, and built upon the tongue of land between
the Golden Horn and the Marmora, the Seraglio being
at the apex of the triangle and opposite Scutari, on the
Asiatic side.

Standing on the Tower of Galata I first understand
why Constantine abandoned Sigeum to build a city at
my feet which was long "the bulwark of the Eastern
Empire, and the benefactress of the world." Here I first
realize why Constantine prefered Byzance to Rome and
Nicomedia, and made it the Capital of his empire.
Before me are that "two-fold river and triple sea,"
immortalized by classic story and the events of modern
times. It was Constantinople that Fourier proposed
for the Capital of his harmonian Omniarchat. A few
years ago, Constantine, the brother of the present Czar
and the most ambitious aspirant for the mantle of the
Greek Emperors, visited Stamboul, and for the enjoyment of the magnificent prospect before us ascended
to the spot where we now stand. When the flattering
Greeks around him pointed out how nature had destined
Constantinople to be a centre of civilization and a seat
of Empire, he remarked: "Ah! what would it not
become were this descendant of a barbaric nomad
driven from the throne of the Cæsars, and the favored
land of your ancestors revert to its rightful owners!"

Before us are the snow-capped Olympus of Bithynia, hills softened with verdure, beautiful islands with

Greek names, looking up smilingly from the sparkling Marmora, and a great city, boasting of innumerable memories and monuments of the past. The shores of Europe and Asia, rivalling each other in beauty and losing themselves in the purple distance, the soft sky and balmy air of the Orient, the minarets and domes, the towers and crumbling walls, monuments of Grecian, Byzantine, and Tartar art rising out of groves of cypress, and, in fact, all the happy accidents that arise from a marvellous union of nature, history, and art, form a panoramic picture which I cannot describe.

Favored by Neptune and built by the direction of Apollo, Constantinople appears to be exempt from all inconveniences, and at the same time to enjoy all possible advantages. Like Alexandria she holds the keys of two Continents, and like Corinth claims sovereignty over two seas.*

Other great cities have risen along the shores of the Mediterranean. But Carthage hardly survived a single siege by the Romans; Corinth and Athens, though rebuilt by Julius Cæsar, were unknown in the middle ages; and Alexandria became a third rate city after the conquest of Omer. Even Rome, "sustained by the sanctity of St. Peter and the grandeur of the Roman name," has not kept pace with the City of Constantine.

Power and dominion have ever gravitated toward this point, while the commerce of the world has

* Gyllius.

flowed to it spontaneously. Stamboul is even more
to the Turk than London to the Briton, or Paris to the
Frenchman. Byzantium, long an object of contest
between the Athenians and Lacedemonians, took the
part of the Romans against Mithridates, and afterwards became the capital of the Eastern Empire.
From the banks of the Bosphorus the Roman legions
ruled Hungary and Illyria at the west, Asia Minor and
Syria in the east, and Greece, the Archipelago, and
Egypt at the south. From the Golden Horn sailed out
those fleets which carried troops to the most distant provinces of the Empire. The Turks exercised in turn the
same dominion, but such are the uniqueness and importance of Constantinople in a military point of view,
that she did not succumb to the barbarians until a thousand years after the fall of Rome, and the Sultans were
encamped one hundred years at Adrianople before they
were able to reduce the Capital of the Eastern Empire.

   Leaving the tower of Galata, let us pass through
the gate of the old Genoese wall—for Pera was once a
Genoese colony,—and descending to the water's edge,
cross the Golden Horn in a *caïque,* or on one of the
two floating bridges connecting Galata with Stamboul.
We enter the city near the wall of The Seraglio. The
dragoman, a wily Greek, who allows nobody to cheat
us but himself and his particular friends, procures donkeys at the gate. We mount for our first stroll in
Stamboul, but find the animals so inactive that

a propelling force is required in the rear in tne shape of Turkish boys with enormous cudgels, the power behind the throne being greater than the throne itself!

O the delusions of Oriental exaggeration!

When viewed at a distance Constantinople seemed a thing of ravishing beauty, but fairly within her walls, the hallucination vanished like a dream—all thoughts of grandeur and magnificence passed away, and I wondered how a labyrinth of indescribable streets and rows of tumble-down houses could have produced such a marvellous ocular deception. A few gorgeous structures, with a multitude of hovels, have ever been the type of the Oriental city, and remain so to this day. The pious Moslems of Stamboul, like the ancient Egyptians, reserve marble and granite for the habitations of God, and leave to mortal men mere cabins of wood and clay, no more enduring than themselves.

The narrow, crooked ways are paved with boulders, and judging from their present condition, have not been repaired since the days of Justinian. The mosques, baths, and other public edifices are in a few instances imposing, but nineteen-twentieths of the buildings in Constantinople would disgrace any Christian city. The Europeanized dwellings in Pera, the new marble palace of the Sultan near Top-Hane, the first of the kind ever erected, and the stone buildings in the Greek quarter of Phanar, are also exceptions to the general rule.

Turkish houses are usually built of wood, or as is

often the case, stone-work is carried up a few feet, and a wooden superstructure then erected. Most of them are so built as to incline over the street, and thus partially shut out the rays of the sun. At first I was afraid to venture beneath the dilapidated structures, apparently leaning towards each other for mutual support, but remembering how slowly everything moves in Turkey, entertained no further fears of being buried under a mass of rubbish. The windows are provided with filagree work, through which pretty eyes, belonging to the odalisques of a wealthy grandee, or to the wives and daughters of the humble, look down unobserved upon all that is passing below.

Many of the Turkish restrictions of former times have lost their force, but according to the Moslem law the dwellings of the faithful should be white, yellow, blue, or rose-color, and those of the Armenians and Jews, black or brown. The Greeks were formerly required to give their houses a sombre color. The Turks leave whole provinces depopulated, but almost pile dwelling upon dwelling in Stamboul, so fond are they of the social life of cities—so parsimonious are they, there, of space. The genius of decay has taken up its home among the habitations of the Turks. The tottering edifice is propped up to the last, and when it falls its ruins are scarcely removed for the ephemeral structure to be reared in its stead. But these frail tenements are the cause of innumerable evils to the

Turks. Conflagrations often sweep away thousands of houses at a time. Byzantine writers speak of a sea of fire which consumed twenty thousand dwellings in a single night, and from this fact, as well as from others, we infer that the Stamboul of to-day does not differ materially in the character of its plebeian homes from the " City of Constantine" in the days of the Emperors.

What most strikes the attention of the traveller on entering Constantinople, is the stillness that everywhere prevails, stillness that is startling and terrible amid the throbbing life of myriads of human beings. The leaden silence is unbroken save by the cries of the water-carrier, and of the itinerant trader disposing of his petty fabrics in the streets, or by the feuds of the canine population, far more cunning and sagacious in their way than the lean and learned pigs which a cele-brated novelist dwelt upon so largely in his description of New York. Or an awkward arabá, gilded without and ornamented within with lily-fingered beauties, comes rolling and thumping down some stony lane, drawn by a pair of small grey oxen, or sorry horses. The Turkish ladies are taking air and exercise; and should you wish to see them unveiled, so as to disclose the luscious tints and outlines of Eastern beauty, make a stand by one of the deep ruts, for not even the charm-concealing yasmak is proof against the badness of Constantinople roads.

As the summer day advances, the heat becomes intolerable, the silence more intense. The sun whose morning glories purpled the east while his golden locks were still bathed in the waves of the Marmora, now blazes like a burning meteor. His blistering rays, falling directly upon the city, or reflected by the sea and strait, penetrate everywhere—penetrate the slimy depths of mud, the twin sister of yesterday's choking and blinding dust—penetrate the heaps of offal left to rot and breed all manner of creeping and sickening things almost on the steps of the holy mosques—penetrate the pools of liquid corruption into which the last night's rain has washed the vilest garbage, the bones of animals that have died in the streets and had their carcasses consumed by dogs and flesh-eating birds, and all the indescribable filth that accumulates in a Turkish city.

It is hot, sweltering, melting hot! The filthy dogs lie down in the street to be trodden upon, or slink away into secret places; sheep and goats dirt-besmeared and covered with vermin, the shadows of lean kine and cast-off donkeys no longer dispute the way with men and dogs, but pant and drowse in the shade of tottering walls and houses. *Hamals* and water carriers, contented with the few paras earned in the cool of the day, repose around the fountains, or lie undisturbed on the cool marble of the mosques. Idlers and the effeminate repair to the bath. There are no customers save under the cool arches of the bazaars. Traders sleep over their pipes, or drawing a thread before the entrance to their little shops, flock to the *kahvé* for Mocha and sherbet, to enjoy there, in Oriental quietude, the "*jucunda oblivia vitæ*" of Horace.

> "Never saw I, never felt a calm so deep!
> The river glideth at its own sweet will;
> Dear God! the very houses seem asleep,
> And all that mighty heart is lying still."

One feels as if wandering in the silent city of eastern fiction, whose busy multitudes were in an instant converted by magic into fixed pulseless stone. The muzzein announces the hour of the mid-day prayer, and calls the faithful to the invocation of Allah. Multitudes still attend, but not with the zeal of former times. Then, merchant and artisan, idler and beggar, hastened to the mosque, or made the ablution at the nearest fountain. Then, all Islam inspired by one common motive, bowed towards Mecca, all Islam pronounced the names of Allah and the Prophet, and again was lost in the utter absorption of Eastern worship. Grand idea, that thus arrested and directed for a time the whole life-current of millions, exchanging, as if by magic, repose for the bustle of religious preparation, and the din of traffic for the silence of devotion!

The joy of the joyful and the sorrow of the sorrowful, the toil of the laboring and the *ennui* of the idling, the playful sport of children and the apathy of age, the curiosity of the curious, the anxious care of the statesman, the eager haste of the courier, the greedy

covetousness of the miser, and even the anguish of the
culprit led forth to execution, all these were momentarily forgotten in a warm feeling of devotion and entire
reliance upon the will of Allah.

Our desultory course brought us under the arches of
the Aqueduct of Valens, a work bearing the marks of
many centuries, but still employed for its original purpose. It is less extensive than similar works in Italy,
but suggests several points of resemblance between
the ancient capitals of the Eastern and Western Empires. The old Rome was built on seven hills along
the Tiber; the new Rome on seven hills along the Bosphorus. The City of Romulus had its Circus Maximus;
the City of Constantine its Hippodrome; Rome boasts
of her seven imperial Basilicas and the Church of St.
Peter; Constantinople of her seven imperial Mosques
and Santa Sophia. Here, save in power and perpetuity, the resemblance ends, for as the Romans multiplied
basilicas and baths, the Turks build largely in kiosks
and konaks, cupolas and khans.

The aqueducts supplying Constantinople with fresh
water, have their beginnings among the hills a few
miles distant, where cool streams are wholly or in part
diverted into them, and reach the city after many
doublings and windings. The Aqueduct of Valens is
essentially a Roman work, but I was surprised to learn
that the modern structures conveying water into Constantinople, and even some of the most ancient,

FEMALE DACO-ROMANS.   p. 163

were built not by foreign engineers, but by rude Arnauts from Epırus and Albania. These mountaineers, who can neither read nor write, and have no idea of scientific engineering, relate that their Macedonian ancestors learned the art of hydraulics from the Persians during the conquest by Alexander the Great.

By water everything lives.

We strolled leisurely through the *Bezestan* or grand bazaar. It is an immense labyrinth of narrow streets roofed overhead and lined with hundreds of little shops of the size of child play-houses. The gates are opened at sunrise and closed at sunset. You can ride through the crowds that repair there to buy and sell.

Stamboul is the great depot of Oriental merchandise. Hither, by the Euxine and the Mediterranean, by the Nile, and over vast seas of floating sand, are brought the productions of Oriental Asia, of India, of Europe, and of Africa. It is the rendezvous of merchants who deal in gold-dust, perfumes, ostrich-feathers, vestments of many-tinted radiance, and the tissues of "woven air" made to envelop Eastern beauty.

On the Asiatic shore of the Bosphorus meet the Caravans of Damascus and Bagdad importing the rich fabrics of Bombay and Calcutta; and vessels still anchor in the Golden Horn laden with troops of pouting Nubians and jetty Abyssinians to be sold for slaves.

In the *Bezestan* you may see opals, diamonds of Visapour and Golconda, pearls of Ophir, talmas, and

tarbouches heavy with golden ornaments, and all the
rich tissues embroidered by the henna-tipped fingers of
the East.   Here you can purchase gold and ivory
wrought slippers, worth ten thousand dollars, or an
humble article adapted to the most plebeian foot.   Here
you can buy a pipe, that greatest luxury of the East,
worth, with the amber mouth-piece and the rings of
precious stones, the price of a fortune.

In the place where curious weapons are exposed for
sale the traveller has before him the whole picturesque
arsenal of ancient Islam; saddles and trappings worthy
of the swift coursers of the Haftar; pieces of armor
with jewelled incrustations that may have served Saladin
or Haroun Al Raschid, with blades of Khorassan, Albanian pistols, and fierce yataghans in endless profusion,
and of almost incalculable value.

Never before did I feel like calling silver trash, and
look with contempt upon the purchasing power of gold
ducats.

The treasures of the *Bezestan* belong to wealthy Mussulmans, who sit all day like tailors, looking gravely
upon their merchandise, and careless, apparently, of the
chances of trade.   Wishing to purchase a couple
of chibouques, I reined my donkey up at one of the
stalls where pipes were sold, and directed Demetrius to
inquire the price.   The well turbaned Mussulman
twitched the muscles of his eyes, expelled the smoke
from his nostrils, and answered,

"Two hundred piastres, O howadji."

'I will give you fifty."

The man of ample trowsers throws back his head, and raises his eyes as if calling heaven to witness the injustice done him by naming so low a figure.

"I will give you fifty piastres."

Three minutes of silence; my donkey, seized by a sudden caprice, thrusts his nose in the face of the Turk, and brays in a most spasmodic and excruciating manner. Everybody laughs.

"God is great!" exclaims the merchant. "Take the pipes, O howadji, for one hundred and seventy-five piastres."

"Impossible, O Effendi! Demetrius, let us go."

We ride but a few steps when the merchant calls us back. He invites us to dismount, and be seated on the cushion. A servant brings lighted chibouques and cups of coffee from the adjacent shop. Discursive conversation in monosyllables occupies a few minutes, which has its use in a country where there are no newspapers.

"How much will the howadji give?"

"Seventy-five piastres, and count the money in gold."

The merchant nods, which means, "No, Effendi, they cost me that sum;" and the grave pipe-dealer, who, a short time before, consumed his smoke in stoical silence, now expatiates eloquently upon the value and perfection of the two chibouques.

"Here are eighty piastres for them."

"In the name of Mohammed take them for one hundred and twenty—" after three minutes of silence.

"I cannot."

"The American howadji has much gold; by my two eyes they are cheap at one hundred!"

"Here are ninety."

The Mussulman lays hold of his jetty beard. "*Kismet!* (God hath willed it;) the pipes are thine, O howadji!" and a bargain, involving the outlay of $3.50, and half an hour of parleying, is closed with the dignity of potentates trafficking in provinces and kingdoms.

The Oriental bazaar is an adjunct of the caravan, the business habits of the Turks remaining much the same as among their nomadic ancestors. Yet the bazaars of Constantinople are to the Turks what the agora was to the Greeks. The Moslems are believers in classification only when applied to slippers, sables, and similar articles exposed for sale.

Here is the resort of the Cairo merchants, there high capped Persians traffic in the rich shawls of Thibet and Cashmire, and in a long, arched way, through which one can pass when going up from the Golden Horn to St. Sophia, are sold the drugs and precious perfumes of the Orient. In one street you find nothing but copper vessels, while another is occupied by scribes who busy themselves in writing letters and copying manuscripts. They hold the paper in the hand, and write neatly with a pointed reed from right to left. A slave stands by with the inkstand, which when its long handle is thrust under the girdle, might easily be mistaken for a weapon designed to shed blood instead of ink.

With the Moslems the ink of the learned is equal in value to the blood of the martyrs.

The bazaars are the resort of the idlers of Stamboul. They often become the theatre of curious intrigues and entanglements from the fact that Turkish females enjoy more freedom there than in other public places. On a certain day not many months ago, says Rolland, a beautiful Moslem female might have been seen standing before one of the shops of the Bezestan. Her eyes, moist and expressive of agitation, and an appearance of discontent which the transparent *yasmak* did not conceal, indicated that she was not at that moment experiencing the philosophical quietude which her religion both recommends and inspires.

"See," said she to the aged female who accompanied her; "see, my mother, if my objections to this union are not well founded. A husband who is old, ugly, and infirm! Who says he is enamored of me, when he is only jealous! Who bestows ten times less care upon me than upon the chief of his wives! Who lets me languish in solitude without procuring me a single pleasure! He is rich, it is true; but he is also avaricious; and what advantage to me his wealth if I am not permitted to share it with him? See how I am clothed! What jewels does he give me? He would even forbid me to visit my parents and friends! Ah! I do not see a female pass by without sighing for her lot; and especially do I envy those Frank ladies who act as they wish, who speak as they please, and whose husbands adorn them with the choicest presents afforded by the *Bezestan*."

At the conclusion of this philippic, to which the mother listened attentively, the two Mussulman ladies entered the shop, filled with Moslem and Christian purchasers, who regarded with silent admiration the grace and beauty of the discontented Ayesha.

They were followed by a young man whose dress and figure marked him for a child of the Orient. He was a Levantine, the only son of an opulent Genoese family long established in Constantinople. Understanding Turkish perfectly, he had not lost a word of the conversation. His curiosity was excited to learn more concerning the fair Moslem of nineteen summers. The latter lavished naïf terms of admiration upon the marvels of taste and beauty exhibited by the merchant. Chagrined at not being able to make so valuable purchases as the Christian ladies, she criticised their dress with cutting raillery, and laughed outright when the poor Europeans attempted to try on the bracelets and slippers designed for the more delicate limbs of the daughters of the Orient. Then her former sadness returned, and she threw herself upon the divan, saying in a low voice, "How happy are these Christians in having husbands whom they love, and by whom they are beloved!"

The moment was favorable for a suitor. Such in fact our Levantine had already become. He approached, and in a low tone of voice addressed the fair Ayesha. While the mother was engaged in looking over the cashmires and jewels, the youth poured into the ears of the beautiful Moslem that intoxicating melody of words which always fascinates the daughters of Eve. A half hour more, and the enamored one had accepted the present of a magnificent necklace. It was, moreover, secretly arranged that she should return the next day under the pretext of paying the generous Levantine. The meeting on the morrow was followed by another and another. The mother, deceived at first, afterwards became an accomplice, and the two wooers were shortly the most passionate and happy lovers in the world.

The jealous and avaricious old husband happened to be detained in Syria by important business. As he had no eunuch, Ayesha lived under the protection of her own family and enjoyed almost unlimited freedom.

But the best things have an end.

The husband returned to Stamboul the very moment when least expected. On seeing him enter his house,

Ayesha, without calculating the consequences of such a step, fled to her lover; and the latter was under the necessity of disclosing the *bonne aventure* to his parents, declaring at the same time that he would live or die with the object of his affection. In former times they would have been bound together in a leathern sack and made to kiss the blue waves of the Bosphorus. The first care was to conceal them. The Sardinian minister was induced to intercede, but limited his good offices to the Levantine. The latter protested that if separated from Ayesha, he would deliver himself up to the Turkish authorities.

The young wife had a sister attached to the service of one of the sultanas, who offered to intercede for her. Informed that they were willing to overlook in part her offence, she responded that death was preferable to a separation from her lover. This persistent heroism in a passion so sincere interested every one acquainted with the circumstances. High dignitaries interfered, and the offending ones were enabled to take refuge on the steamer for Egypt. The Genoese merchant at last induced the Turkish husband to repudiate his wife in consideration of several thousand piastres. Difference in religion then remained the only obstacle to a union pursued through so many difficulties. Thus at present the father of the Levantine maintains that Ayesha is about to become a Christian, while the mother of Ayesha insists that the young husband is on the point

of embracing the faith of Islam. After all what matters
it? God is great! and the religion of lovers—is it
not love?

From the Bezestan Demetrius conducted us to one
of the Turkish baths in the vicinity. There are said to
be more than three hundred of these establishments in
Constantinople, some of which are built of marble, but
in general their external appearance is far from imposing. The door is curiously ornamented with arabesques, and we enter upon a mosaic pavement. The
principal rooms are circular, and dimly lighted by
means of small convex pieces of glass inserted in the
domes above.

The *tellaks*, or servants of the bath, were muscular
Turks, dressed like athletes. From long confinement
in a heated atmosphere, their tawny skins had grown
yellow and glossy like parchment. One of them assisted
me to undress in the small antechamber, twisted an
enormous turban round my head, and thrust my feet
into wooden clogs four inches high, in order to protect
the tender soles from the blistering heat of the marble
pavement. These preparations completed, I hobbled
after him into a large inner room, arched over head
and heated from below. Its atmosphere was surcharged
with a fiery and penetrating vapor, which blinded my
eyes, and took away my breath. I wished to escape
from the heated furnace, but in vain. In a moment,
however, a copious flow of perspiration burst from the

pores of my body, and I soon felt comparatively cool, though breathing steam.

They informed me that there was another room still warmer, usually preferred by Mussulmans, and especially by females, who, the reader may be aware, can both give and endure more calorific rays than males. Through the vapory atmosphere I could see the dim outlines of several human beings nearly naked and apparently engaged in extracting the life from as many prostrate victims. Could it be that I was in the strange and silent kingdom of the gnomes! Alas for the sea of pleasures I had anticipated! Mustapha, into whose leathery hands I resigned myself with the meekness of an infant, extended my body upon a marble slab, and began a succession of deluges, alternately torrid and frigid. Then, with rose-perfumed soap, and the soft fibres of the palm, he manipulated upon me with such dexterity, that in a few moments I found myself enveloped in a white and fragrant cloud of tepid saponified vapor, which, however, disappeared like magic on his immersing me in cold water.

Under these cloudy metamorphoses, delugings, soapings, and plungings, my soul and body were greatly in danger of being separated from each other. I merely remember looking up into the india-rubber face of my torturing demon, and imploring for mercy. That calendar of inflictions was at last exhausted. Wound round with curious pieces of cloth, I was con ducted from the infernal region to a large airy room, and told to extend myself upon a divan. A lighted chibouque with a glass of delicious sherbet brought back a realizing sense of my identity. Then began a course of frictions, kneadings, and other heroic operations, which must be felt in order to be appreciated. I was sprinkled with rose-water, and handled like a loaf preparatory to baking. Again were soul and body in danger of losing company. My palms and soles, made so sensitive by the bath, were rasped with pumice stones, and the parchment-skinned demon of a *tellak*, as if to disable me for life, insisted upon cracking every joint in my body, beginning with the fingers and ending with the toes.

My sufferings terminated, I lay extended I know not how long upon the divan, sipping cups of fragrant Mocha between puffs of the jewelled chibouque, and experiencing all the delicious sensations to which a Turkish bath can alone give rise. The cutaneous blissfulness produced by the Oriental barber, the dreamy elysium of *kahvé*, the placid intoxication of the *kief*, and even the seventh heaven of hasheesh, can hardly be compared with that etherial sensation of limpidity, that marvellous flexibility and oiliness of being, which I experienced before dressing, and some time afterwards. Cost for bath, coffee, and latakieh, with backsheesh to the *tellaks*, four piastres, or sixteen cents.

On certain afternoons of the week these establishments are open only to females.   Large parties of Turkish ladies usually repair to the same bath with their servants, to spend several hours in its enervating pleasures; and as one passes by these sombre buildings, he often hears the ringing laugh of merry girls, or the song of female improvisatores hired for the occasion, and can imagine what hoydenish romping, dalliance with water, and playfulness there must be within.

CHAPTER XVI.

" A chasm,
As of two mountains, in the wall of Stamboul,
And in that ghastly breach, the Islamites,
Like giants on the ruins of a world."

MORE historical than all else at Stamboul are the
walls that surround the city. They occupy nearly
the place of the old fortifications erected by order
of Theodosius II., and demolished by Septimius Severus. Although " after the Parthenon and Balbec,
they are the most magnificent ruins which attest a
seat of empire," it is too evident that Constantine the
Great built them in haste. Segments of broken columns, and pieces of sculptured marble are strangely intermingled with brick-work and rough blocks
of granite. The walls of Constantinople are twelve
miles in extent, and provided with more than five
hundred towers. Most of the twenty-eight gates have
been celebrated in history.

Constantinople has been beseiged twenty-nine times,

and eight times taken and pillaged. Old Byzance saw before her walls Athenians, Macedonians, Romans, Thracians, Bithynians, Celts, and Persians. The city of Constantine has trembled before Goths, Huns, Arabs, Persians, Saracens, Russians, Bulgarians, Hungarians, and Turks. During these various vicissitudes of fortune there have been encamped before her gates old Greek commanders and old Roman emperors, new Greek autocrats and new Roman Cæsars, Arabian caliphs and Bulgarian krals, Slavonian kings and Ottoman sultans.

On a pleasant afternoon we rounded the point of the Seraglio, and oared leisurely along the wall which skirts the Sea of Marmora, reading the inscriptions on its gates, and tracing here and there its wave-worn foundations far down in the crystal water. Arriving at the south-west angle of triangular Stamboul, we disembarked at the Chateau of Seven Towers, the *Irde-Koule* of the Turks. This Mussulman Bastile, which has witnessed the *denouement* of so many tragedies begun in the Seraglio, was founded by Zeno, finished by Alexander Comnenus, and rebuilt by Mohammed, the Conqueror. But four of the seven towers have been standing since the earthquake of 1768. They served alike as a fortress, treasury, and prison for the ambassadors of powers at war with the Turks. Hither the dethroned Sultans were dragged by an enraged populace. Here six or seven imperial heads have rolled to the earth, and these gloomy walls have often been crowned with hideous wreaths of grinning skulls.

But this ancient castle, in which the Athenians are said to have kept their treasures, is now merely a monument of the past. No stranger is admitted within its gates. Its dungeons, its whispering halls and rooms of torture are deserted. The laughing waves of the Marmora which break against its foundations,

"Conscious of their endeared retreat,"

no longer blush with human blood or mingle their melancholy dirge with battle-cries, while the jasmine and the ivy have kindly woven a green mantle over the crumbling towers, like a veil of forgetfulness.

Turning away from this tableau, grandiose alike in its majesty of ruins and in the souvenirs of history, we mount the horses provided for us, to ride along the walls which defend Stamboul on the Thracian or land side. Beginning at the Seven Towers they sweep over the steep and rugged hills to the suburb of Eyoub, on the Golden Horn, four miles distant from the Marmora. The rays of the declining sun give a golden tinge to the distant mountains of Thrace, and impart a serene and indescribable beauty to the crumbling towers and bastions. Beyond them is Stamboul, low and compact, merely the minarets and domes of the mosques rising to view above the lofty walls, while on the outside vast cemeteries occupy most of the space in the direction of

Eyoub. The barren hills gradually lose themselves in the Thracian plain on which the squadrons of the Nizam occasionally go through their evolutions. Here and there a shepherd may be seen guarding his little flock. Dreadful solitude to be experienced beneath the walls of a great city!

The very genius of decay broods over the monuments of power and military valor before us. But one can hardly conceive of nobler or more picturesque ruins than these triple lines of fortifications, wall rising above wall, and ditch sinking behind ditch. Vines have clambered far up the crumbling towers as if to sustain their tottering strength; and the thousand plants and shrubs of a luxuriant vegetation, compassionately concealing the ravages of time and war, line the silent walls, from which once looked down serried hosts, glittering with shield and spear. The moat, said to have been more than a hundred feet deep, is nearly filled with rubbish; and the soil, enriched with the blood of so many battles, bears flowers, and shrubs, and cresses.

The mouldering battlements, the unfilled breaches, the melancholy views inspire painful emotions. Behind these ramparts, which the wretched Greeks foolishly believed impregnable, crumbled away the last wreck of the great Roman empire. Beginning with a single city on the banks of the Tiber, she overspread almost the entire globe, to shrink again to the dimensions of a single city along the Bosphorus. Yet under the protection of these ruins the empire of the Cæsars survived long centuries until the formation of new societies, prolonging antiquity down to the middle ages, and forming a grand connecting link between the world of Rome and the world of the present.

As I rode by the gates, rendered memorable by great historical events, my imagination pictured the scenes enacted there centuries ago. Before the *Aurea*, or Golden Gate, now walled up like many others around Stamboul, I beheld the triumphal processions of the Emperors, which entered the city at this point from the time of Theodosius the younger. By the gate of Adrianople loomed up before me the wild hosts of the Avars repulsed by Heraclius and his brave Greeks. Still further on I paused for a moment where Alexius Comnenus entered the city to usurp the throne, and where the imagination, busy with the historical past, represented Justinian the Great making his triumphal entry, met by the prefect of the city and the entire Senate— a scene worthy of the historical painter. Before the gate of St. Romanus I conjured up the grand events of the last siege of Constantinople, the fatal assault on the 29th of May, 1453, and the death of Constantine, who, however he may have lived, died like a Cæsar.

Years had been spent by the Ottomans in making preparations for this remarkable siege. On the sixth of April Mohammed appeared before the city and en camped behind the hill which faces the gate of Caligaria.

A hundred thousand cavalry with curveting steeds and all the equestrian finery of standards and trappings in which the Turks delight, formed the confines of the camp on yonder plain. A hundred thousand active besiegers composed the right wing toward the Seven Towers, and fifty thousand the left wing, extending as far as the palace of the Blachernes, in the direction of the Golden Horn.

A monstrous cannon, cast at Adrianople by a Hungarian renegade from the service of Constantine, was dragged before the gate of St. Romanus, also called Cannon Gate, or the *Top-Kapousi*, since the siege. This piece, unquestionably the most enormous mentioned in the history of siege artillery, required for its conveyance fifty yoke of oxen. Two hundred men marched on each side of the frame of thirty waggons on which it was supported, " to maintain the equilibrium of the rolling weight." The bore is declared to have been twelve palms in diameter, and in the first trial, which veiled Adrianople with smoke and was heard the distance of several leagues, a stone ball, weighing nearly a thousand pounds, was projected a mile, and then buried itself a fathom deep in the earth. Seven hundred men were appointed to serve this enormous engine of war. A Hungarian envoy from Hunyad, then in the Ottoman camp, gave directions for its proper use, but with all their eager haste it could be discharged but seven times a day. After a few trials the brazen-mouthed monster

burst, killing the founder and many soldiers besides.
Flanking this enormous cannon were two others of
the same calibre, while in all, fourteen batteries were
opened against the wall of Constantinople on the Thracian side.

In this remarkable siege both ancient and modern
instruments of warfare were employed. Volleys of
musketry attended clouds of spears and arrows, and
parks of awkward artillery aided the slow work of balis-
tas, catapults, and movable turrets. By means of the
last the tower of St. Romanus was at last overturned.
The Turks, however, were driven from the breach and
their enormous wooden turret set on fire. The next
morning, when Mohammed saw the ditch cleared and
the tower of St. Romanus built up as strong as before,
he swore by the hundred and twenty-four thousand
prophets that he never believed the Greeks able to
accomplish so great a work in a single night.

Day followed day and effort succeeded effort, but
without success to the Ottomans. Their batteries were
frequently dismounted by the well-directed aim of the
besieged. The soldiers of Mohammed, harassed every
moment by the inextinguishable Greek fire and
floods of boiling oil, were kept constantly engaged in
replacing the wooden towers, destroyed by the artful
enemy. The deep trench, filled by the Turks during
the day, was as uniformly emptied by the persevering
Greeks during the following night.

Mohammed at last hit upon a bold project to gain possession of the Golden Horn. During a single night he caused seventy galleys and brigantines of from two to five banks of oars to be conveyed by land from Beshiktasch, on the Bosphorus, across to the termination of the harbor, the mouth of which was closed with a chain. The distance was between five and six miles, and the way led across high hills and deep valleys. The planks over which the vessels were drawn were anointed with the fat of sheep and oxen. Upon the prow of each stood the captain, and at the stern of each the pilot. The sails were spread, the trumpets sounded, the drums beat, and at the return of day the besieged saw with equal surprise and terror the seventy Turkish vessels cast anchor in the Golden Horn, and range themselves before their walls. The place where they slid into the Golden Horn is still pointed out to the traveller at the stairs of *Shah-kule*, back of the Okmeidan.

"At the sight of this spectacle they understood," says a Turkish historian, "that their ruin was about to be accomplished. Words escaped not from their mouths : the dark gloom of despair settled upon their hearts." A prediction long before spread abroad among the people, announced that Constantinople would fall when they should see *ships sailing upon the land.* Seven weeks had passed. The Greeks still mounted the ramparts and repelled every attack. Four of their towers, however, had been demolished, a large breach was open at the gate of St. Romanus, and the Ottoman army occupied the *fosse*, half filled with the ruins of the fortifications.

Mohammed, either to obey the law of the Koran, which enjoins that peace be offered to an enemy before extermination, or to learn whether the city would be able to hold out longer, sent a last message to Constantine. Arrived before the Emperor, who was surrounded by his court, Espendiar-Oghlon, the envoy of Mohammed, exhorted him to disarm the wrath of the Sultan by a prompt and entire surrender, and thereby spare the inhabitants the miseries of slavery. But in the council which the Emperor immediately convoked, the voice of honor and of courage reduced to despair was alone heard.

"If the Sultan will grant peace, and in respecting it, imitate the example of his predecessors," responded Constantine to the envoy of Mohammed, "I give thanks to God. Moreover, no one of those who have besieged Constantinople has either lived or reigned a long time. Mohammed can impose a tribute upon me, but never will I surrender the city which I have sworn to defend."

Behold to what Constantinople had already fallen! From a city with a population of a million souls when taken by the crusaders in 1204, she contained in 1453 not more than 200,000 inhabitants. The emperor ordered a census to be taken of the citizens, including also

the monks able and willing to bear arms, and the
number fell short of five thousand. The actual force
was limited to seven thousand Greeks, many of whom
were mercenaries, and two thousand Genoese soldiers,
with fourteen armed vessels. And at the very moment
when the empire was to succumb, Constantine Paleologus was the butt of the sarcasms and maledictions of
his fanatical subjects for having invoked, even in vain,
the aid of the Occident. "No!" cried the Greeks in
the public places, and under the windows of the Imperial palace; "No! we want neither the Latins nor
their aid. Away with the abominable worship of the
Azymites!" "As for me," said the Grand-duke No-
tharas, "I would a thousand times rather see in Constantinople the turban of the Turk, than the tiara of the
Pope."

Never before in Constantinople had the strife of
religious factions risen so high; never before had schis-
matic hatred burned with such fury. Greeks and
Latins fought with each other, instead of uniting for
the public defence. The churches were empty. St.
Sophia, after the semblance of a union of the schisma-
tics, and the desecration of a Latin mass, was deserted
by the Greeks, as if their temple had been changed into
a mosque or synagogue. The monks and nuns rejected
every confessor who had recognised the *henoticon*, the
decree uniting the Latins and the Greeks. Priests
refused the sacrament to the dying of the opposite

ECCLESIASTICAL COSTUME. p. 186

SHOEING AN OX.

party; and what to many was a greater scandal, a novice adopted the faith and even the costume of the Mussulmans, ate meat in Lent, and adored the Prophet.

At the sight of the fleets and armies of the son of Murad, despair seized upon the inhabitants of the city. Gloom and terror enveloped them as a shroud. Their active imagination discovered everywhere the signs of celestial anger. The prediction to which I have alluded passed from mouth to mouth. Flaming meteors, sinister prophecies, and pious revelations, troubled their trembling souls. They exhumed from the archives of the state a pretended prophecy of the Emperor Leo VI., that the empire of the East was about to pass away.

In the court-yard of the Mosque of Bajazet II., there is an ancient porphyry sarcophagus, now much broken, and unnoticed alike by Moslems and Christians. Yet it is said to have contained the ashes of Constantine the Great, and in former times was, doubtless, esteemed a valuable relic. Upon the cover of the sarcophagus, now nowhere to be found, there is declared to have been a Greek inscription, consisting only of initial letters, the meaning of which the learned sought in vain to determine.

In the fifteenth century a certain Genadius, who afterwards became Patriarch of Constantinople, interpreted the inscription as meaning that Constantinople would soon fall into the power of the Turks, but that the latter should ultimately be expelled by a "blonde

nation " coming from the North, and uniting with the
ancient inhabitants.   The golden-mouthed Chrysostom
foretold the fall of Constantinople, and a prophecy an-
nouncing the destruction of the Eastern empire was
found among the oracles attributed to the Sibyl of Ery-
threus.

It is related that Michael, the first of the Paleologi,
having inquired of a priest what would be the destiny
of the empire under his descendants, the latter exclaimed merely, "*Mamaimi!*"   But this word, without
meaning in itself, indicated, said they, by the number
of its letters, that there would be but seven emperors of
the family of the Paleologues, and that the last would
be driven from the throne.   A similar presage was extended to the family of Osman.   It likewise would give
but seven princes, and then lose the heritage of the
Seldjoukids.

A Byzantine writer reports that while Hunyad was
deploring his defeat after the battle of Kossova, an old
man came up to console him, and said; "Since the
Greeks have not been exterminated, the Christians shall
always be unfortunate: to put an end to their reverses,
Constantinople must fall into the power of the Turks."
They spoke also of the prediction of Leo the Wise,
based upon the discovery of two tablets, found in the
monastery of St. George.   These tablets were divided
into a certain number of parts, and contained, one the
series of Greek emperors, the other that of the patri-

archs from the time of Leo. But upon both of them were vacant spaces; to one tablet was wanting the name of the last emperor, and to the other that of the last patriarch.

These predictions were the lugubrious shadows of coming events, having their origin in a general belief that the empire of the Constantines was about to pass away. Thus in all times there have not been wanting similar predictions, some contradicted, and others confirmed by what has actually taken place. Nor does history despise the light which such presages cast upon the times in which they are made and believed. There are veritable prophecies, so to speak, emanating from a superior mind, skilled in penetrating the essence of things and able to judge of the future from the past. Others there are based only upon humiliating superstitions, and provoked by appearances that are purely external and accidental. The former, having their origin in a profound knowledge of the course of human affairs, do not address themselves to the superstitious instinct of the masses, and consequently exercise but little influence over them. The latter, born in passion, and propagated by ignorance, have frequently served as a lever to move the unthinking multitude.

The study of these predictions often enables us to penetrate more rapidly the spirit of an epoch, and comprehend the character of a nation, and the condition of a government more clearly, than long experience or patient investigation. Nations, like individuals, prepare themselves for good or evil fortune, according as their presages of the future have been dictated by a consciousness of power or of importance. Accidental prophecies have, indeed, sometimes decided a victory or a defeat, but those which a people continually repeat to themselves, contribute necessarily to their prosperity or decadence, and must be regarded as among the active elements of their destiny. They reveal the interior dispositions in which they had their birth, and of which they are a faithful image. Thus courage and force, which are conscious of power, prophesy victory. Feebleness and baseness, in pretending to be condemned by an irresistible fatality, seek beforehand an excuse for their defeat. These general principles find abundant application in the history of the prophecies, of both Christians and Turks, relative to the fall of Constantinople.*

The Ottomans, whose religion condemns alike superstition and incredulity, ascribe to Allah and their prophet alone the power of reading the future. Said Mohammed one day to his disciples :

" Have you not heard speak of a city, one side of which looks toward the land, and the other two sides toward the sea ?"

" Yes, envoy of God."

* Von Hammer.

"Verily, I declare unto you, the last hour of judgment shall not come until that city hath been conquered by seventy thousand sons of Ishak. Approaching tho ramparts, they shall combat neither with arms, nor with balistes and catapults, but with these words: 'There is no other God than God: God is great.' At their sound one of the walls looking toward the sea shall fall down, then the other, and finally the ramparts on the side of the land; after which the faithful shall make their victorious entry into the city."

These prophecies had so powerful an influence upon the Arabs, that seven times under the Caliphs they attempted to gain possession of Constantinople. During the longest of these sieges they cultivated the fields on the Thracian side of the city, sowing and harvesting for seven successive years.

"Mohammed the Conqueror," says Erliya Effendi, "was governor of Magnesia during the lifetime of his father Murad II. and spent his time in studying history and conversing with excellent men, from whom he acquired a perfect knowledge of the commentaries on the Koran and the sacred traditions. Having learned that the infidels from Frangistan (France) had landed at Acre, the port of Jerusalem, taken possession of Askalon, and invaded the dominions of the Sultan of Egypt, from which they carried off much plunder and many prisoners, he was so much grieved that he shed tears.

18*

"Weep not, my Emperor," said Ak-Shemsu, "for
on the day when thou shalt conquer Stamboul, thou
shalt eat of the spoils and sweetmeats taken by the
unbelievers from the castles of Acre, but remember, on
that day, to be an acceptable judge to the faithful." At
the same time taking off the shawl twisted round his
turban he placed it on Mohammed's head, and announced the glad tidings of his being the future conqueror
of Stamboul. They then read the noble traditions of
what the Prophet foretold concerning Constantinople.
Mohammed on this, covering his head with Shemsu's
turban, said, "Affairs are retrieved in their season," and
returned to his studies.

The ambitious Sultan was fond of adding to the
namaz, or midday prayer, another prediction of the
prophet: "The faithful shall certainly possess Constantinople : most fortunate of commanders will be that
commander; most fortunate of armies that army."

Such was the condition of affairs when the son of
Murad encamped before the walls of Constantinople,
with 250,000 men; when, in the lofty language of a
Turkish historian, "The luminous imperial army,
resembling a sea without limits, precipitated itself in a
thousand impetuous torrents upon the castles of darkness."

The general assault was to take place on the twenty-
ninth of May, the fatal day to Constantinople, as pre-
dicted by the astrologers in the camp of the Sultan.

On the evening of the twenty-seventh Mohammed
assembled the chiefs of the army. To them and his
soldiers, he promised the entire booty, reserving to himself only the houses, and the land upon which the city
stood. To those who should most distinguish themselves he offered *timars* and even *sandjaks*, and to the
soldier who would first scale the walls, the government
of his richest province. Seated on horseback and
holding in the right hand his golden sceptre, the Sultan
swore by the prophet of Mecca, by the soul of his
father, by his children, and by his cimiter, that the
Koran should prevail. His harangue was received
with acclamation, and shout after shout rolled along the
long lines of the soldiers of Islam. Dervishes ran
through the camp promising an eternal youth amid
the fresh rivers and streams of paradise to such as
should fall with arms in their hands.

The day preceding the assault each one was enjoined
to fast and make seven ablutions. At night-fall the
trumpet gave the signal for a general illumination.
Then all the tents along the Bosphorus and on the
heights of Galata became resplendent with light; then
the greater part of the Golden Horn and the bivouacs
extending away in long lines to the Sea of Marmora
blazed with innumerable lamps and torches. The besieged mounted the walls to behold the amazing
spectacle, and half surrounded by seas of fire, believed
at first that a terrific conflagration was sweeping away

the camps and fleets of the Ottomans. But the chants and dances of the dervishes, and the wild Moslem shouts of *Allah-illah-Allah* passing from squadron to squadron and echoing from hill to hill, soon announced to them that the Moslems were celebrating their victory in advance. Then despair settled upon the Greeks. They ran wildly in the streets and thronged the churches. Gloom and confusion and darkness reigned everywhere, and above the lamentations and prayers of the people swelled the *kyrie eleison,* mingling its solemn strains with the Bacchic frenzy of the Turks.

But at the dawn of day came

> "The sound
> As of the assault of an imperial city,
> The hiss of inextinguishable fire,
> The roar of giant cannon, the earthquaking
> Fall of bastions and precipitous towers,
> The shock of crags shot from strange engin'ry,
> The clash of wheels, and clang of armed hoofs,
> And crash of brazen mail, as of the wreck
> Of adamantine mountains, the mad blast
> Of trumpets, and the neigh of raging steeds,
> And shrieks of women, whose thrill jars the blood,
> And one sweet laugh most horrible to hear,
> As of a joyous infant waked and playing
> With its dead mother's breast; and now more loud;
> The mingled battle cry—-ha! hear I not,
> ' By This Conquer !'—A'lah-illah-Allah !' "

While the chiefs and the soldiers were dying upon the

walls, the populace awaited in the churches the fulfilment of a prediction, which, in their weakness, they
had readily accepted. It was declared, upon the faith
of an ancient prophecy, that the Turks should enter
Constantinople, and advance as far as the column of
Constantine : but at that moment an angel, descended
from heaven, would place a sword and sceptre in the
hands of a chosen king, and command him to avenge
the people of God. Then, it was assured, the Turks
would take flight, and be pursued by the conquering
Greeks even to the confines of the Ottoman empire.
But no avenging angel appeared, and the superstitious
multitude were awaked from their flattering delusion
by the shouts of the victors, the nearer tramp of the
Tartar cavalry, and the clash of battle-axes on the doors
of their sacred temples.

The walls of Constantinople remain in nearly the
same condition that they were in after the siege of Constantinople, more than four hundred years ago. But
little has been taken away and nothing added save the
ivy and the verdure. The indolent Turks have not
entirely closed the breach through which a great part
of Mohammed's army entered the city, and behind
which the last of the Constantines fell, covered with
wounds and with glory. This is the strongest portion
of the wall, and yet such was the disparity between the
Greeks and Turks, that I wonder the latter did not
sooner burst through the fortification. Near by, on the

most elevated ground inside the walls of Stamboul, is
the ruin of the palace of Belisarius, the residence of
the last Emperor; and the old palace is likewise an
inextricable labyrinth of ruins.

From the former of these, Constantine, after he had
striven in vain to save a people who would not save
themselves, and lost everything but honor, went forth
to die, though not without lingering for a time in the
solitary halls of his ancestors.   And the Conqueror
who had just stamped his ensanguined hand upon a
marble pillar of St. Sophia, touched with momentary
pity in the deserted home of the Cæsars, repeated a
verse of the Persian poet, "The spider's web is the
royal curtain in the palace of the Emperor, and the owl
is the sentinel on the watch tower of Afrasiab."   Time
avengeth the wrongs of suffering nations; and the
traveller may, ere long, repeat the same appropriate
words in the blood-stained halls of the sons of Orchan.

About midway from the Seven Towers to the Golden
Horn, the road deviates from the wall and leads to the
church of Balukli, a place much frequented by the
Greeks.   Here no Turks are to be seen, the women are
unveiled, and there is often a hurrying to-and-fro of
eager groups.   The convent-like church is surrounded
by a gloomy wall.   In the immediate vicinity is a
Greek cemetery, which, from the absence of trees, and
the careless manner in which the monuments are arranged, is by no means so interesting as the burial-

places of the Turks. Several of the Greek patriarchs have been buried in the court-yard of the church. The Greek emperors were wont to repair to Balukli in great pomp on Ascension-day, and here also important marriages were formerly celebrated.

Our dragoman conducted us down several steps to the body of the edifice, which is cleaner and prettier than the generality of Greek churches. A few priests were celebrating mass in their usual monotonous manner, and with the nasal twang peculiar to Eastern worship. "*Thos psari, effendis?* (will you see the fishes, gentlemen?)" says one of them, and he leads us down to the fountain of Nicetas, the healing virtues of whose cool and refreshing waters were sung by Nicephorus, and extolled by Philus in Greek iambics. The fountain is of crystal clearness, and in it are swimming a few streaked fishes roasted, as the legend tells us, on one side.

A monk sat here frying fishes, when Mohammed entered the city. As some one announced to him the triumph of the Turks, he exclaimed: "What! I shall believe you when I see these fishes come to life and leap from the pan in which I am cooking them." And forthwith, to the amazement of the incredulous cenobite, they leaped from the frying-pan into the fountain before us. The church built to commemorate this miracle was destroyed at the breaking out of the Greek revolution, when it is declared that the fishes were again miraculously preserved.

Descending to the Golden Horn we reach Eyoub, one of the fifteen suburbs of Constantinople. It is a delicious sylvan retreat, where no Christian is allowed to reside, and whose holy mosque, built by Mohammed II., no Christian is permitted to enter. The Moslem temple is an airy and elegant structure of white marble, in which the Turkish Sultans are inaugurated.

When the new Padisha has girded on the sword of Osman, the illustrious founder of the Ottoman dynasty, turning to one of his ministers, he exclaims: "*Keyzyl-elmada giorus chelem!*" (May we see each other in Rome!) Though now a mere formality, this ceremony shows how the haughty sultans once meditated supplanting the tiara by the turban. It carries our thoughts back to the time when the taking of Otranto in Apulia by Achmet Geduk Pacha, caused as much terror in Rome as the appearance of Attila on the Mincio—when there was trembling in the Vatican, and the Papal power almost determined again to remove its seat to Avignon.

Times change. We have seen the throne of the Osmanlis, before which the representatives of great kings once bowed the neck and held the voice subdued, threatened to be submerged by the returning waves of invasion; and the hand which formerly issued the bulletins of victorious armies and the recitals of conquest, stretched forth supplicatingly to the powers whose subjects were a few years ago termed *dogs of infidels.*

" Let him that gives aid to the Turks be excommunicated," stands written in the canons of Rome. But in the late war the Gallic defender of the Catholic faith became the firm ally of the Sultan. The *kyrie eleison* and *Allah-illah-Allah* rose together, while the followers of CHRIST and the followers of Mohammed went into combat shoulder to shoulder, bearing side by side the crescent and the cross. Yet in this crusade of Louis Napoleon, the Occident and the Orient have been brought together on a magnificent scale. Thus are made acquainted men who have hitherto met only on fields of carnage, and seen each other only through the smoke of battles. Thus also is made to fall the ancient enmity of races.

The mosque derives its name from Eyoub, the standard-bearer and companion-in-arms of Mohammed, who was killed at the siege of Constantinople by the Saracens, 668 A.D., and buried here. The spot having been revealed to Mohammed II. in a vision, he erected a mosque and mausoleum in honor of Eyoub.

There are many other mausolea of persons distinguished in the annals of Islam under these dark cypresses. The most remarkable tombs are those of old Hussein Pacha and the Sultana Valide, the glorious mother of Selim III.

I noticed many gilded monuments exhibiting great taste, and do not think there can be a sweeter resting-place for the dead than quiet, beautiful Eyoub.

Slight elevations of mason-work or stones chiselled
at the top to the shape of turbans, mark the graves of
the faithful, the size and the inscriptions also sometimes
indicating their character and profession. A flower or
some simple device is inscribed in the case of females.
The Moslems press the earth with no ponderous marble
slabs, in order that on the day of judgment the bodies
of the dead may spring up without impediment. They
scrupulously avoid burying two persons in the same
place, and have the beautiful custom of planting a cypress over the grave of a relative or friend, circumstances
which account for the size of Turkish cemeteries and
their being converted into the parks and pleasure-
grounds of Ottoman cities. The Mussulmans bury their
dead upon the day of their death, and hurry them to
the tomb, for the Prophet says: "If the departed one
be blessed, hasten with him to the place of destination:
is he accursed, get rid of him as soon as possible." The
nearest relatives assist in supporting the bier. For that
pious office the Koran promises a great blessing, and
the only time that a Turk moves swiftly is when he
is carrying a brother to the grave. They run out and
assist each other, believing that the body of the departed is uneasy until consigned to the dust whence
it sprung. The Imaum or priest interrogates the dead
upon the articles of faith contained in the Koran, and
the silence of the latter is ingeniously construed into
affirmative answers. A few handfuls of earth are

thrown into the grave, the assistants respond *amen*, and the soul is left alone with eternity. Instead of a coffin they employ two planks so placed as to leave an open space where, as they say, the examining angels can sit down and converse with the departed. For a like reason the shroud is seamless, and left open at both ends. A stone is placed at the head of the corpse for the convenience of the two angels, under the supposition that this act of civility will make them more indulgent.

When the angels visit the sepulchre in order to institute an examination, the soul of the defunct is supposed to return for a time to the body. One of them raises the dead to a sitting posture by the queue of hair, which every true Mussulman allows to grow for that purpose. This preliminary examination consists of four questions relating to the cardinal points of religion and the direction in which the dead has said his prayers. For several days in succession after the funeral the relatives and friends of the deceased repair to his grave to pray, beseeching God to deliver him from the torments inflicted by the black angel in case the examination be not satisfactory. They encourage him earnestly by name to "fear not, but answer bravely." On the Friday following the interment, refreshments of various kinds are carried to the grave, of which the passers-by may partake freely. The souls of the faithful are thought to linger around the tombs

in blissful beatitude, not unmindful of the attentions of
their surviving friends.

This mode of sepulture is not without good in a
country where the plague is common and premature
burials occasionally take place. It sometimes happens
that persons buried in this clumsy manner recover, and
are able to force the barrier separating them from the
outward world. It is related that a Turkish blacksmith,
who had been buried in the morning, returned home
during the day, enveloped in his shroud. Being somewhat taciturn, he directed his footsteps at once to his
shop, to the great terror of his assistants, and without
saying a word to any one resumed the work of the previous day.

"Such a delightful bathing-place as Eyoub," writes
a Turkish traveller, "is nowhere else to be found."

"Every Friday many people crowd to this place, where
those who like, bathe in the water. Here lovers and
the beloved mingle together without restraint, and take
delight swimming in the sea. You fancy that you
behold the angels of the sea bathing amongst the
angels of mankind dressed in blue aprons.

"Near by is an old well that goes by the name of
Yan Kayussi, the well of souls. If a person who has
lost anything perform here a prayer at two *rika'at,*
devoting the merit of it to Yussuf and asking that
great prophet to describe what he or his relatives have
done amiss, a voice is heard from the bottom of the

well, describing the place where the lost thing or person may be found. This well answers anything except about the five great secrets known only to God, as for example, if any one should inquire, "Will the child about to be born be a male or female?" the only reply is "wait a little."

Almost directly opposite Eyoub, on the Golden Horn, are Kassim Pacha and the Old Bagnio. The former contains the great naval depôt and shipyard of the Turks,

"——with its never-ending cares
Of tarring, pitching, and repairs."

Mussulmans are not good seamen. The crews of their tall ships are not even proof against seasickness. They tell the story of a Turkish commander who was directed to visit Malta on important government business. After beating about six months in the Mediterranean, he returned and reported to the Kapudan Pacha that he had not been able to find the island.

Refreshing ourselves with a cup of coffee at the kiosk, whose foundations are bathed by the limpid waves of the Golden Horn, let us take a four-oared caïque to visit the sweet waters of Europe. The picturesque caidjis handle their frail but elegant barks with admirable address. Shooting up the little river which flows into the Golden Horn, we reach in a few minutes one of the most frequented places near the Turkish capital. It is an oasis in the desert which extends down to the very walls of Stamboul, for if one ascends the hills on either side, nothing meets the eye but a wide desolate waste. This delightful retreat is named the Sweet Waters by the Franks, and Heavenly Waters by the Turks, but the crystal flood of the Cydaris is not fit to drink. Here, where

> "——in shadiest covert hid
> The tuneful bird sings darkling,"

the Sultan has a summer palace, half-Occidental in style and furniture, and Half-Oriental. Except the harem, which we were not permitted to visit, and the sumptuous marble baths, it would suffer in comparison with many of the villas along the Hudson. An artificial water-fall is near, and on the green plots feed the stately coursers of the Sultan.

On sunny afternoons and balmy evenings Turkish ladies do love to congregate on the sylvan banks of the Cydaris. Then the cool sherbet is drunk in the shady kiosk, and the Ottoman lays off that dignity which he wears in all other places, to become a playful child. Then and there only, upon European soil, do you fully appreciate the life of the soft Asiatics. The Turk loves Nature, from the fact that he is a stranger to Art, and at the Sweet Waters of Europe he enjoys her blessings without restraint. Its solitude induces the *far niente*—and the delicious *far niente*, is it not, O reader, the secret of the life Oriental?

The silvery laugh of sportive girls mingles with the music of running waters, the rustling of leaves, and the notes of the bulbul. Armenian maidens let fall the veil in the eagerness of sport, and groups of dark-eyed Greeks, as beautiful as Thalia and Melpomene, dance upon the green velvet, to music Orphean only in the graceful movements it accompanies. Here the Circassian forgets she is a slave, and the Nubian joins her mistress in the merry laugh.

On one of the hills which overlook the promenade of the Sweet Waters there is an immense kiosk, untenanted and uncared for. No one visits the fountains in the lonely gardens. Rank weeds have grown up in the shady walks, and lifeless trees show their squalid branches in the midst of luxurious vegetation. With all this solitude and decay is connected a story of spiritualized affection rare among the Turks. Mahmoud converted the kiosk into a dwelling-place for the favorite of the imperial harem. Here the Sultan was wont to repair, to forget the chagrins of the sovereign in the tendernesses of love. The beautiful Circassian died. The brave-hearted Sultan could find no solace for his grief. He ordered that no hand should desecrate the asylum of his lost happiness. In his saddest hours he would often come here to weep alone. Abdul Medjid, when he ascended the throne, respected his father's wish, and no one now approaches the solitary pavilion, still wearing the emblems of mourning.

The shades of evening gather around us. As we
glide down the Cydaris and the Golden Horn, the full-
orbed moon rises from behind the Bithynian Olympus,
and bathes in liquid etherial light the mosques and
towers of the seven-hilled City. Caïques filled with
grave Osmanlis and their silken-eyelashed treasures flit
by us on the Golden Horn, whose depths are no longer
vexed by a thousand moving keels. The dimpling and
silvery waves weave their crisped moonlit smiles around
the motionless hulls, and break against them with the
low murmur of the sea. In our flashing wake roll up
myriads of emeralds and diamonds, rivalling in momentary splendor the orbs of night, trembling in the
heavens as if in fear of God. A balmy influence seems
to descend from the turquoise sky, through an atmosphere of opaline transparency. My sensations and
perceptions become exquisite beyond description, and
the current of my thoughts flows into dreamy imaginations. The very pulses of my being throb with a new
and delicious life—a life known only in the sunny
Orient.

CHAPTER XVII.

ASIA.

" ——the place of a thousand tombs
That shine beneath, while dark above
The sod, but living cypress glooms,
And withers not, though branch and leaf
Are stamped with an eternal grief,
Like early unrequited love."

"The tinkling bells already do I hear,
Proclaim the caravan's departure near."

THERE are certain moments which we set down as the
most important of our lives, to which our thoughts have
previously converged, and from which, as a shining
centre, diverge our brightest experiences. That was
one of my "life moments," when having taken a *caïque*
at Galata and glided past the point of the Seraglio, I
stood, in a few moments, on the soil of Asia. I seemed
transported at once a thousand miles further into that
indefinite Orient. My thoughts leaped across centuries. I conjured up before me the shadows of ancient
empires, and on a soil consecrated by prophets and

19

patriarchs, felt myself surrounded by the mysteries that envelop the origin of the human race.

Scutari, celebrated for its cemeteries and vineyards, is the largest suburb of Constantinople, and, like her, reposes upon seven hills. It was built in the earliest times of the great Persian monarchy, and doubtless owed its ancient name, Chrysopolis, the golden city, to the circumstance that the Persian tribute was there collected.

Near Scutari is the old Chalcedon, now Kadi-keui, founded seven years before Byzance. A few ruins are still to be seen, but no one would judge from them that he stood upon a spot rendered famous by the oracles of the gods and the councils of men. When the Megarians inquired of the oracle 667 B.C., where they should found the new city of Byzantium, the answer was, " Opposite the Blind," alluding to the stupidity of the Chalcedonians in not having selected a point on the Golden Horn for the site of their town. Yet a person could travel over the entire globe and find but one situation more favorable for a city than that of Chalcedon.

Scutari is the great rendezvous for the caravans trading between Constantinople and the Asiatic cities; and from this point set out annually thousands of devout Moslems on the weary pilgrimage to Mecca. Here, for the first time, I saw the camel on its native soil of Asia. From the encampments in the outskirts of Scutari, where their drivers linger only for a few days as if fearful of

MONASTERY OF NIANZO.

p. 189

contact with civilized life, these patient creatures gaze
with long wondering looks from beneath their drowsy
lids upon the hills of Europe, to them "a fabled and
forbidden land."

The cemeteries of Pera and Scutari are the Hyde
Park and Champs-Elysées of imperial Stamboul. Cool
and shady retreats are they; and on sunny afternoons,
particularly during the Moslem festivals, when a greater
degree of liberty is enjoyed by the female sex, groups
of veiled women may be seen seated on the grass or the
fallen monuments, sportive and merry even in the presence of the black eunuchs who act as their attending
genii. But a few feet distant, perhaps, a lonely being
is planting flowers in the tear-moistened earth,—flowers
as sweet as those which Rousseau placed in the chamber
of his dying Heloise. Woman is ever kind, ever devotional; and where the stoical Mussulman thinks it
unmanly to shed a tear, the Circassian, bought with his
gold, finds no other solace for her grief.

These vast cemeteries are exceedingly unhealthy as
places of public resort on account of the noxious exhalations from the soil. The Ottoman, thanks to his belief
in fatality, is molested by no considerations of that kind;
he spends many of his days in pursuit of pleasure upon
the very spot where he expects his body will return to
its native dust. By night even paper lanterns flit, like
ignes fatui, among the marble monuments of the dead,
speaking with silent voices and wet with dewy tears.

Could the graveyards around Constantinople be cultivated they would produce grain enough to feed its
immense population, while the fallen and scattered
monuments would suffice to build a city. The Turks
never bury two bodies at the same place; and a slight
calculation will show what countless multitudes sleep
along the blue waves of the Bosphorus. Byzantium
was founded more than 2500 years ago, and during
much of that time its population has been greater than
that of the present Constantinople. Suppose 500,000
people to have lived there twenty centuries. Let three
generations pass away in a hundred years, and we have
the dust of 30,000,000 human beings! Constantinople,
with its throbbing life of nearly a million souls, is empty
and deserted compared with the silent cities of Pera,
Scutari, and Eyoub, as all living, moving humanity is
but dust in the balance against the countless multitudes
who have lived and died before us! The whole earth
is a sepulchre.

The Turks regard their sojourn in Europe as a temporary encampment. They love the soil of Asia, which
belongs to Islam, whence sprung the founder of the
Ottoman dynasty, and prefer sepulture, however humble, in Scutari, to a resting-place ever so beautiful in
magnificent Pera or sylvan Eyoub.

. Every hour of the day dark processions move across
the Bosphorus with muffled oar and mount the narrow
way leading up to the chosen burial-place of Islam, fitly

named the "Ladder of Death." On this spot, crowded with perennial cypress and memorial stone, we witness in strange contrast the indecent haste of Turkish burials and the dreamy pleasure-seeking of the Orientals, the most touching exhibitions of sorrow and the liveliest manifestations of joy, with littleness and greatness, poverty and splendor, pollution and purity, mingling with the dust side by side!

The gloomy surroundings are emblematical of decay; and where else can man and nature so sympathize with each other? Yet by a singular contrast one's thoughts often assume a poetical if not a romantic cast among the dew-weeping monuments of the dead, and the entanglements of leafy mound-embosoming glades invite to the sweeter entanglements of love.

At the head of each grave is a little orifice—too often enlarged by the dogs or jackals—conducting to the ear of the deceased, that he may be enabled to hear the sighs and lamentations of his relatives. By the foot of the column also there is usually a flat stone hollowed in the middle to form a small basin, in which the friends of the deceased place flowers and perfumes.

"A day comes, however, when the flowers fade, and are not renewed; for grief for the departed is not eternal, and life were intolerable without forgetfulness. Water from the clouds replaces the rose-water, and the birds of the air come to drink the tears of the heavens from the reservoir which once received the tears of affection.

The doves dip their wings in these baths of marble,
drying themselves in the sun while they coo from the
summit of the superincumbent monument; and the
dead, deceived, might suppose he heard a sigh of faithful sorrow.   Nothing could be prettier or more graceful
than this winged life, hovering and singing among the
tombs."*

After a long ramble on the Asiatic shore, Demetrius
conducted me to the *Téké* of the Howling Dervishes.
Their convent stands on the slope of the great hill of
Scutari, not far from the Bosphorus, and is reached by
a road leading through the cemetery.   The *Téké*, where
the Dervishes are supported in part by the Sultan and
in part by "their indecorous humbug," is in every respect more humble than the convent of the Whirling
Dervishes on the European side of the Bosphorus.
With singular emotions, however, does one approach it
through that dark wilderness of cypresses in whose lugubrious shade the myriads of funeral columns seem like
whited ghosts—

"In stony fetters, fixed and motionless."

A Nubian slave, after having served the company
with coffee and pipes in the courtyard of the convent,
led us up a stairway and along obscure corridors to a
low gallery, whence Frank travellers are permitted to

* T. Gautier.

witness the spectacle, while a crowd of Turks occupied part of the floor below. A second gallery was set apart for females. The large, square room had more the appearance of a cabinet of curious old weapons and musical instruments than of a place of worship. The walls were hung with poniards, lances, and other rude implements of warfare. Triangles, drums, and tamborines were intermingled with pikes and yataghans, the former of which are employed in every weekly performance to excite the enthusiasm of the actors, while the latter are not unfrequently taken down in the bloody melées on the great days of the Ramazan, when the fanatic exaltation knows no bounds.

And now the performers appear on the stage.

Some twenty men gravely enter and kneel on sheepskins with their faces toward Mecca. Alternately inclining, rising, and prostrating themselves, they address their preliminary invocation to heaven with all the sanctimonious zeal of Mussulmans. The majority of them wear the long pelisse and grey conical hat, the distinctive dress of Dervishes. Some, however, have the old Turkish costume,—the turban, caftan, and bobouche—and even two or three of the younger performers are attired in the closely fitting tunics of French civilization. The latter are not Dervishes, but persons expiating some offence that weighs heavily upon their consciences by participating, for a time, in the penible, devotional exercises of these eastern fanatics.

After the preliminary invocation, which is mental rather than oral, three of the dervishes chant a kind of litany, with a nasal twang that would do credit to a Jewish synagogue. The assistants respond "*amen*," and then begin the peculiar ceremonies of the order. The sheepskins are thrown into a pile against the balustrade, and the Scheik of the *Téké*, a venerable Mussulman, seats himself upon them. The others, coming forward one by one, kiss his hand and range themselves in a semicircle before him.. Two musicians commence a monotonous recital from the *Borda*, in praise of the Prophet, accompanied by slow and regular strokes upon a tamborine. The Dervishes slowly incline their bodies forward and backward, with a slight lateral motion, murmuring at the same time in a low tone of voice. This oscillatory movement gradually increasing, becomes animated, precipitous, violent. The savage actors are seized with a wild frenzy. From statuesque figures they speedily convert themselves into frightful mountebanks.

Simultaneously with these movements they begin to pronounce slowly the profession of faith, "*La illah illah lah*," divided into six syllables, each of which is made to correspond with a single inclination of the body. Their motions quicken; their pronunciation becomes more rapid; and as the orgies increase in violence, we distinguish only the wild cry of "*il-lah*," and finally the single sound "*lah !*" hurled forth at the top of the

voice, and interrupted now and then by an outcry of
" *hu !*"

The breasts of the actors in their hideous panto-
mimes heave like the breast of a wounded lion. Their
lips foam and vibrate incessantly with the ferocious
metallic notes of " *La hu !*" Their faces are inundated
with perspiration. They beat their humid chests and
shoulders with the long locks of hair allowed thus to
grow in imitation of the Prophet. Their bodies become
distorted by frightful muscular tension, and the blood-
shot eyes seem ready to leap from their sockets.

Now the Scheik takes part in the orgies, and soon
surpasses all the others in the violence of his contortions. Formerly the *Rufaï* of Scutari, for that is the
name of this sect of dervishes, used to take red hot iron
in their mouths, and carry balls of fire in their hands,
without any indications of pain or injury. These feats,
however, have been discontinued, in the neighborhood
of Constantinople, though they are still exhibited in
other parts of the empire.

Meanwhile the fanaticism of the Dervishes has
reached its height. Vertigo attacks them. The gur-
gling sounds grow confused; the power of utterance is
nearly lost. Some are carried away swooning, some
leap with violence and fall prostrate on the floor, their
bodies convulsed, and foaming at the mouth; others
cry " *Ya Hu !*" (Jehovah!) and others still " *Ya Me-
ded !*" (Oh Help!); while, as the exhausted voices be-

19*

come scarcely audible, we hear once more the silvery
notes of the anthem in praise of Mohammed, or of
Ahmed Rufaï (the founder of the sect). " O Mediator!"
" O Physician of souls!" " O Beloved!" which now by
contrast seems soft and beautiful. The bodies fall upon
each other, and the little arena looks like a place of
combat.

Now follows what is still more grotesque—still more
horrible. Three young children are led in, and long
pack-needles thrust through their cheeks, passing into
one and out of the other. The Scheik, after engaging
in the Thesmagorian dance of the *Rufaï*, is believed to
have the gift of healing by the imposition of his feet.
Half a dozen invalids make their appearance: they
prostrate themselves on the floor, face downward. Several mothers also come in and place their tender
infants in the same position, and the grave charlatan
steps upon each, not even omitting the children submitted to this strange therapeutical treatment.

And yet—can you believe it, O reader?—with the
exception of a few of the most fanatical, all this raving,
all this ecstasy of holy inspiration, is a mere hoax, intended to make fools of the spectators, an indecorous
humbug, kept up to please the women behind the
screens, and especially the savage children of Asia, who
throng Constantinople, and take supreme delight in
these exhibitions. The *Tékés* supply the want of other
theatrical shows. For the Moslems the performances

are gratuitous, but it is customary with Frank travellers to make the pious actors a present of a few piastres, and, if I am not greatly mistaken, the jingling of filthy lucre adds not a little *éclat* to these fine religious frenzies.

The Dervishes are the religious showmen of the East.

Unlike the ecstasies and contortions of the *Rufaï*, and yet savoring of mountebank tricks, are the performances of the Whirling Dervishes of Pera. The *Téké* of the latter, communicating with the street by a marble portico inscribed with letters of gold, is a chaste and beautiful edifice—a sacred abode well fitted for religious contemplation. The parterre is cooled by the jets of perpetual fountains, and the long vestibules are crowded on the days of the *Zirs*, or public ceremonies, with troops of Turkish females. There nothing is ascetic. The *giaour* is introduced even into the most sacred place. The Moslem female often lets fall her *yasmak*. The humbug is decorous. The enthusiasm is subdued and moderate. There are no severe contortions, exhaustions, and foamings at the mouth. Sleek gentlemen are these Whirling Dervishes. We feel that we are in the presence of the Jesuits of Islam.

The liberal Mohammedans, and especially the wild nomads of Asia, find something more stirring and congenial in the Téké of the *Rufaï*, than in the sombre mosques of Stamboul, or even among the more sedate Whirlers of Pera. Both of the *Tékés*, however, furnish a kindly, enthusiastic devotion, "which the Ulemas disdain, and to which the Imaum cannot descend :" hence their popularity.

The preliminary invocations, the chants and music of the Whirling Dervishes of Pera, do not differ greatly from those of their more savage brethren on this side of the Bosphorus. The performers, however, are better shaved and dressed, wearing conical hats, and long, white gowns. Their speciality of worship consists in whirling upon the naked feet so long, so regularly, so rapidly, so harmoniously, that it is impossible not to mistake them for whirligigs, or automatons, made to rotate by some secret mechanism. During this spiritual pirouette, the expression of the whirlers is vacant : their arms are extended in the form of a cross, the palm of the right hand turned upward, and the left downward, while the long loose shirts, confined at the waist, expand so as to resemble a wheel. To look at these persons revolving fifty times per minute gives us a sensation of dizziness, and we wonder that they do not fall to the floor. From long practice, however, they are perfectly at home in the graceful twirl, but are careful not to continue it to the point of producing cerebral conges- tion. The pretended ecstasy induced by this solo waltz does not manifest itself upon the placid faces of the per- formers.

The Whirling Dervishes are of the order of *Mulewi*, or Mystics, founded by the poet Mewlana, who is said to have whirled miraculously four days in succession, without food or refreshment of any kind, his companion, Hansa, playing all the time on a flute. Mewlana then passed into an ecstatic state, saw visions, and received from Allah wonderful revelations concerning the establishment of his order.

Islamism, though it has adopted the Dervishes, is not accountable for their idolatrous practices. Idolatrous they are, for, as the ecstatic waltz of the Mulewi is symbolic of the harmony of the spheres, and scarcely differs from the dance learned by the ancient Corybantes from the wild tribes of Asia, the cries, the perilous leaps and bloody flagellations of the *Rufaï* represent the forms of the proscribed worship of Isis and Cybele. The Indian Fakir was the prototype of the Mussulman Dervish. Dervishism is, in reality, older than the "sayings and doings" of Mohammed, and had its origin east of Mecca. It is the revival of certain pagan rites and dogmas, and represents the impression of the barbarous past upon the system of Mohammed—the old Oriental polytheism leaguing itself with the Unitarian doctrines of the "camel-driver of Mecca," just as Christianity has adopted many heathen usages. Mohammedanism, like Catholicism and Calvinism in more modern times, sought to restrict its believers to a few narrow dogmas. Hence arose the different orders of Dervishes, giving a more liberal interpretation to the Koran, and rejecting the idea that it opens the only way to Paradise. Yet these numerous orders, like the sects of Protestantism, represent not so much differences of belief in the fundamental points of religion, as the devotional manifestations of certain classes of minds.

"Let there be no monks in Islam," was a command of Mohammed. But such is the inclination of the Arabs to ascetic life—a life that seems in harmony with the lonely solitude of the desert, that this injunction of the prophet was shortly supplanted by the declaration of the Koran, "*El fakru fakhri*" (Poverty is my glory). Hence arose the class of ascetics called Dervishes, from a Persian word signifying door-ushers, corresponding to the Fakirs of India, a class leading a life of penance and mortification. They professed an exclusive devotion to the service of Allah and total absorption in his contemplation, and having no time to devote to other pursuits, were consequently dependent on the alms of the charitable. The Caliphs Abu-Bekr and Ali were founders of the first two orders. One of them professed to derive miraculous power from meditating upon the perfections of Allah; the other from pronouncing his name a thousand and one times in quick succession. Thus the former declare that when Mohammed, during the Hegira, took refuge in a cave to escape from his enemies, he was preserved, not by the miraculous spider-web, but by meditating upon the goodness of Allah.

The Dervishes, without exception, believe that every man has two souls, one the animal, and the other the movable or wandering soul. They also affirm that there are seven places in the human frame where prayer may be habitually offered.*

The orders, or paths of Dervishes, as they are termed by the Moslems, multiplied in proportion as the true faith declined, until, at the present time, they number more than thirty. The founders of the different orders left certain rules relative to the conduct of the members, and the mode of worship to be followed. Each sect, also, has some peculiar distinction of dress. I have already alluded to the *Rufaï* and *Mulewi.*

The *Sadys* are held in high repute for their wonder-working power. They handle serpents and scorpions with impunity, and even eat them, as if their founder had served an apprenticeship with the serpent-charmers of Egypt.

The *Begtaschi* are likewise worthy of notice. Their founder, Hagdi-Begtasche, also organized the corps of the Janissaries. The *Begtaschi* and Janissaries regarded each other as brothers, took the same part in civil dissensions, and as distinct organizations, perished the same day. The *Begtaschi* are, for the most part, foreigners and outcasts, living as mendicant devotees, and "affecting to pass for santos, or saints, though, to speak the truth, they are loose souls, notorious hypo-

* J. P. Brown.

crites, and, commonly, great drunkards." Most of the
Dervishes, in fact, indulge in wine and brandy, in order
to give them the degree of gaiety required by their
faith. I well remember one of the *Begtaschi*, who
served as a kind of chaplain in a company of *bashi-
bazouks* along the Danube. He had followed the
rude warriors, with whom he was associated, from the
wilds of Central Asia. With legs and feet bare, the
skin of a wild beast thrown over his shoulders, and
a rude battle-axe in his hand, he sang verses in praise
of the soldiers, as they marched, and offered up prayers
for the glory of Islam and the prosperity of the empire.

The *Sadys* and *Begtaschi* are the most expert sorcerers and jugglers among the Moslems, commanding, by
their pious tricks, the veneration and the pockets of
the populace. Their services are in special demand for
the interpretation of dreams, the recovery of lost and
stolen goods, the cure of barrenness, the arresting of the
evil eye, and untying the marriage knot; for which
purposes they employ prayers, insufflations, charms,
and exorcisms. I have no doubt that the Dervishes are
practically acquainted with Mesmerism, and the devices
of modern spiritualism.

The Sheiks, or chiefs of the Dervishes, must be
chosen from among the members of the particular
orders which they represent, and afterwards be confirmed by the grand mufti at Constantinople. To them
are ascribed miracle-working powers. A Turkish

bookseller, wishing to sell a "Life of the Turkish Saints," recommended it as follows : "Here is a full account of a Sheik at Konyah, who, whenever he wished to take a sail, had only to seat himself upon a cabbage leaf, over which he had blown, and it would convey him across the water in any direction he desired."

All of the Dervishes are allowed to marry, but with the exception of a single sect, who permit no married person to enter their *Tékés*, must spend the night preceding their *zirs* in a convent. They all suffer the beard to grow, and many allow the hair to fall over the shoulders. Members are initiated by whispering in their ears certain mystical words at stated intervals. With the *Mulewi* the novitiate perfects his spiritual training by serving a thousand and one days in the convent kitchen. The Dervishes carry rosaries of 33, 66, or 99 beads, and are required, in almost all the orders, to repeat several times daily the seven secret words, or names of Allah, pertaining to the seven heavens, seven earths, seven seas, seven plants, seven tones, seven colors, and seven metals. The most zealous undergo the severest voluntary penances, rivalling, especially on the seven holy nights, the self-mortifying devotions of the Hindoo Iogis.

Notwithstanding many of these Turkish saints practise enormities which, in other countries, would bring them to the gallows, they exercise a powerful influence in all the lands of Islam. Nearly all of the Turkish poets have been Dervishes. They personify a popular element. Dervishes have not unfrequently excited mobs and rebellions against the government. Their vagaries and frenzies appeal to that respect for asceticism which is strong in the Orient and "far older than Christianity or Mohammedanism," and, though absurd in the extreme, are too powerful to be dispensed with. Hence the power of the Dervishes over the superstitious populace; hence also the Sultan builds convents for them, and occasionally goes in person to witness their grotesque orgies.

Leaving the Téké of the Howling Dervishes, we procured horses to ascend the mountain of Bulgurlu, whose summit affords the finest view to be obtained on either bank of the Bosphorus. While passing up the principal street of Scutari, I was amused to see an Italian traveller giving his wife evidently her first lesson in riding on horseback after the manner of men, as is customary with Turkish ladies. It seemed very awkward business for both, and the lady could not but blush at her unnatural position. Let those of my fair readers who meditate a trip to the Orient forget not to carry with them a side-saddle, unless they see fit to adopt the Turkish trowsers, and become *oriented* entirely.

The street led us by the mosque of the Sultana Validé and the great hospital of Scutari. The former, like the imperial mosques of Stamboul, enjoys the privilege of being illuminated on the great nights of the

Ramazan. The latter was erected by the Sultan Mahmoud, to serve as barracks for ten thousand troops, which number it easily accommodates. A few Russian prisoners confined within showed their shaggy heads at the barred windows, and did not appear to be dissatisfied with their fate. There, as in the Crimea, the presence of that ministering angel, Florence Nightingale, assured the languishing sufferer that the still voice of humanity was not altogether hushed by the rude tumults of war. She has her reward. Her simple name is dearer to the British soldier than the whole list of England's aristocracy, blazing with wealth and titled glory, but selfish at heart, too proud to stoop even to save their common country, and too weak and incompetent to maintain the position afforded them by their rank.

Pleasant cottages were scattered here and there along the way. We often paused in the shade of the limegroves to breathe the sweet fresh air of Bulgurlu, and enjoy opening and changing vistas of incomparable beauty. Over the spring of Djambya, on the slope of the mountain, the Sultan Mohammed IV. erected a pretty dome. This spot, more than any other on Bulgurlu, is frequented by Turkish and Perote ladies. The water of the fountain, styled "heavenly" by the Turks, is the purest to be found in the vicinity of Stamboul. A number of persons were sealing the crystal fluid in bottles for the use of the sultan.

The view from the summit of the mountain, near where Tiberius and Mauritius built their hunting palaces, is grand beyond description. At the right is the sullen Euxine with its dark overhanging cliffs and crags, while far below us runs the "sapphire thread" of the Bosphorus, on whose enchanted wave-washed margin are clustered smiling villages that gleam like pearls set in green and silver. There, embraced by the sea and the Golden Horn, reposes queenly Stamboul, garlanded by her daughter cities; and as the eye sweeps along the eastern shore of the Marmora, it rests, in the azure distance, upon the stately Olympus of Bithynia, a magnificent background to a magnificent picture. Where else with a single *coup d'œil*, can you look upon so much that is beautiful and historical?

At the base of Mount Olympus lies Broussa, " the ancient capital of Bithynia, the retreat of Hannibal, and the cradle of the Ottoman empire." Broussa has declined from its glory in the fourteenth century, but the pastoral tribes which dwell upon 'the neighboring mountains do not differ greatly from the rude bands of Erthogrul, that migrated there five centuries ago from the shores of the Caspian.

At Broussa was buried Bajazet, the first of the Ottoman chiefs who styled himself Sultan. Tamerlane, issuing from the lands of Iran with twenty-seven kings at his stirrup, according to the account of an old Turkish writer, demanded submission of Bajazet. "The latter, with the spirit and courage of an emperor, refused to comply. Tamerlane thereupon advanced with an immense army, comprised chiefly of Tartar hordes. Bajazet's horse fell in battle, and the Sultan himself, not being able to rise before the enemy were upon him, was taken prisoner and carried into the presence of the Asiatic conqueror. Tamerlane rose when the Sultan was brought in, and treated him with great respect. Then they sat down together on the same carpet to eat honey and clotted cream.

" 'I thank God,' said Tamerlane, ' for having delivered thee into my hand, and enabled me to eat and discourse with thee. But if I had fallen into thy power what wouldst thou have done with me?' Bajazet, from the openness of his heart, came to the point at once. " By heaven, if thou hadst fallen into my hands I would have shut thee up in an iron cage and never taken thee out of it to the day of thy death!'

" 'What thou likest in thy heart, I like in mine,' replied Tamerlane, and ordering an iron cage to be brought, forthwith incarcerated Bajazet according to the wish he had himself expressed. The Emperor died soon after, and Tamerlane returned to Central Asia."

Whether Bajazet was imprisoned in this manner has long been a controverted point with historians. There is, however, but little doubt of its actual occurrence, for, as Sir William Jones beautifully remarks: " While the abstract sciences are all truth and the fine arts all fiction, we cannot but own that in the details of history truth and fiction are so blended as to be scarcely distinguishable."

Hannibal spent the last years of his life in exile at Broussa, and ultimately died there, a victim to the ingratitude of his country. When the Romans sent an ambassador to Prusias to demand Hannibal, the king had the baseness to abandon the illustrious African. He took poison, saying—

"Let us deliver the Romans from the fear of an old man, exiled, disarmed, and betrayed!"

Scipio, like Hannibal, was thought unworthy to die in the land he had honored. After wandering through many countries as strangers, they are said to have met in Asia, and conversed familiarly about their conquests and defeats.

Scipio inquired—

"In your opinion, Hannibal, who has been the greatest general in the world?"

"Alexander," responded the Carthagenian.

"And the second?" continued Scipio.

"Pyrrhus."

"And the third?"

"Myself."

"Then how would it have been had you conquered me?" demanded Scipio, laughing.

"I would have placed myself before Alexander."

The sun had almost touched the distant mountains

of Thrace when we descended from Bulgurlu to the
Sweet Waters of Asia. There is no place more beautiful than this on the green margins of the Bosphorus.
A few splendid Turkish villas were being slowly built
in the vicinity. As Neale remarks, workmen of every
nation and religion must of necessity be employed, and
as their sabbaths and holidays fall on different days of
the week, all the difficulties are encountered that were
experienced at the tower of Babel. The Turkish carpenters are absent on Fridays, the Jewish laborers on
Saturdays, and the Armenian masons on Sundays. The
Greek plasterer has a holiday on Monday, and the
Catholic whitewasher one on Tuesday, so that months
are consumed in erecting an ordinary dwelling.

Gorgeous old forest trees, pure sweet air, a crystal
brook singing through sylvan retreats as romantic as
Vallambrosa—these are the lovely attractions of the
Sweet Waters of Asia. Here, especially on fête days,
assemble the wealth and beauty of Stamboul. "Happy
Turks!" wrote Lamartine, "always reposing in the
place of their predilection, in the shade of the tree they
have loved, on the banks of the stream by whose murmurs they have been charmed, visited by the doves
which they cherish, and perfumed by the flowers they
have planted. If they do not possess the earth during
life, they possess it after death."

I behold my first sunset in Asia.

Yonder beneath the tufted foliage rolls the Bosphorus like a silver-crested serpent of many folds. The evening breeze creeps softly and slowly up the valley, wafting along the fragrant breathings of the flowers and the parting songs of the birds. It is as if an angel of light were hastening from the embrace of the dewy earth, and she, closing her myriad eyes of flowers, should smile, and blush, and weep at his royal departure.

We take a sharp *caïque*, and in a few moments are floating near the old Seraglio. And now, as evening advances, the muezzin ascends one of the tapering minarets of " Aya Sophia." Putting his hands to his mouth, he chants three times, " There is but one God, and Mohammed is his Prophet. Come, ye faithful, come to prayer." Reader, five times from sunrise to sunrise, during four hundred years, without the omission of a single day, that chant, so soft and musical, has floated over the city of Constantine.

What changes since the Crescent supplanted the Cross on yonder splendid dome! Islamism, with its ancient glories trailing in the dust, has fallen upon evil times, but the faith of Mohammed still exists. How perishable is man compared with systems and creeds! The old temples of the Caliphs have fallen in ruins, the worshippers therein, and they who called them to prayer, have mouldered into dust, and caravans of weary pilgrims, thirsting for the heavenly waters of Paradise,

TRAVELLING BY CARUTZA IN WALLACHIA.

p. 270

"Have folded their tents like the Arabs,
And as silently passed away."

Even now, in the manner, but without the fervor of earlier times, a few devout Mussulmans bow upon the marble pavements of the mosques. Sweeter than the chime of vesper bells floats away the chant of the muezzin on the still evening air. The turbaned sentinels take up the sound, and echo back its melody, while a soft chorus of air-voices from the three hundred mosques of Stamboul swells and sinks away, " Come, ye faithful. Come to prayer."

"Night fell, and dark and darker grew
That narrow sea, that narrow sky,
As o'er the gleaming waves we flew,
The sea-bird rustling, whirling by—
The cliffs and promontories there
Front to front, and broad and bare;
Each beyond each, with giant feet
Advancing as in haste to meet."

CHAPTER XVIII.

ISLAM.

"Verily the true religion in the sight of God is Islam!"—KORAN.

"Seat thyself by the side of the poor, and thou wilt augment the value of thy bounty."—ALI.

St. Sophia, the Cathedral of old Constantinople, and sumptuous monument of the new Greek architecture, once dedicated to the Eternal Wisdom (Sophia) but now the pride of Islam, is the shining point of attraction in Stamboul. Even the magnificent Crescent, gilded with fifty thousand gold pieces, and mounted upon the dome by the successor of the Caliphs, can be seen glittering in the sunbeams one hundred miles at sea.

I have not space for a detailed description of this ancient Christian temple, which has existed in some form or other for the last fifteen hundred years. Its foundations were laid in the twentieth year of the reign of Constantine, the same year in which the Council of Nice was opened. It was burnt in the reign of Arcadius, by the faction of St. John Chrysostom, and rebuilt eleven years after by Theodosius II. It was burnt a second time under Justinian, and restored by the same

Emperor, much enlarged, and with infinitely greater splendor. The dome has twice fallen in, the sacred cross was thrown down by an earthquake in 1371, and various other accidents have befallen "the pride of the city of Constantine."

The plan of the temple of Divine Wisdom is said to have been laid down by an angel who appeared to Justinian in a dream. All the temples of the old religions were made to contribute to its construction. One hundred chief architects, under Anthemius of Tralles and Isodorus of Miletus, directed the labors of the ten thousand workmen employed upon the present edifice. The temple of Divine Wisdom is supported upon the columns of Isis and Osiris, or the pillars of the temples of the Sun and Moon at Heliopolis and Ephesus, of those of Pallas at Athens, of Phœbus in Delos, and of Cybele at Cyzicus. Every kind of granite, marble, and porphyry was employed in its construction, as Phrygian, Laconican, and Proconessian.

While it remained a Christian temple, the sacred vessels for the twelve great feasts of the year, made of the purest gold, were almost innumerable. Of choice cloths, worked with pearls and jewels, there were forty-two thousand. There were twenty-four colossal books of the Evangelists, each of which, with its gold covering, weighed more than two thousand pounds. Upon the vine-formed candelabras for the high altar, for the gallery for females, and the vestibule, were expended 600 cwt. of the purest gold. The doors were of ivory, amber, and cedar. Three of them were said to be veneered with planks taken from Noah's Ark. The form of the holy font was that of the fountain of Samaria, and the four trumpets blown above it by angels, were declared to be those at whose blast the walls of Jericho were overthrown. The floor was to have been paved with plates of gold, but Justinian, fearing that such an expenditure would lead to its destruction by his successors, substituted one of variegated marble whose waving lines imitated the advance of the sea. At the four corners of the temple, built in the form of a Greek cross, the apparently waving marble floor rolled onward into the four vestibules, like the four rivers of Paradise. "Glory to God, who hath deemed me worthy to accomplish so great a work!" exclaimed Justinian. "O Solomon! I have surpassed thee."*

St. Sophia was converted into a Turkish Mosque the very day on which Mohammed II. took possession of Constantinople. He also built one of the four tall and elegant minarets, which give inimitable grace and beauty to a structure that would appear massive yet heavy without them.

To visit St. Sophia an imperial firman has hitherto been requisite, but a fair examination can now be made on paying some twenty piastres at the entrance.

* Von Hammer.

How gold opens the heart and unlocks the secrets of the East! thought I as I crossed the threshold, and stood upon ground sacred to Islam. We were required to take off our shoes, an indispensable preliminary to entering a mosque, both on the ground of neatness and the sacredness of a custom descended from the patriarchs. But at the gate of St. Sophia I came near getting into a serious difficulty. After we had paid the stipulated number of piastres, the keeper insultingly held out his hand for an additional gratuity. I thrust it back somewhat rudely, an act which would have cost me my life twenty years ago. The guardian raised his ponderous key, a foot in length, to strike me to the earth, but as Mussulmans are not very nimble, I easily avoided the blow. Experience had taught me how to deal with the Turks, and giving him to understand that Islam inspired no dread, I entered the Aya Sophia.

Never before did I so well appreciate the real nature and essence of beauty as when standing beneath that aërial pavilion of stone reposing gracefully on its four massive pillars, more marvellous in construction even than the larger dome of St. Peter's. Its builders were masters of living marble, for the treasures of the quarry become beautiful only when they lose somewhat of their material nature and assume lighter and more spiritual forms. I cannot describe the gigantic proportions of everything upon which the eye rests, nor trace the infi-

nitude of galleries, columns, and architectural wonders
of this great Moslem Cathedral, still bearing the traces
of Christianity.

Calvin and Luther would have retrenched nothing
from a Mussulman temple, destitute as it is of painting
and statuary, and the geometrical ornamentation of
lines, broken, crossed, and commingled. Here dwell
none of the mystic shadows and reveries peculiar to the
old Cathedrals of Europe. A tranquil river of pure and
serene light pours down through the five domes into the
body of the temple, and then floats away like an unob-
structed sea among the columns of porphyry that support
the long naves. The lines of marble pillars stand like
angels mute in prayer. Here are neither pews, nor
altars, nor statues, nor tableaux, nor simulacra, nor
saintly relics. The iconoclastic genius of Islam forbids all those embodiments of the theatrical, the idolatrous, and the sensual, which in Greek and Catholic
churches materialize the idea of God. A few mats
upon the marble pavement, a few rude candelabras and
ostrich eggs suspended from the ceiling, a few precepts
of Mohammed inscribed upon the walls and columns,
and a low tribune for the Sultan—these are the decoration of St. Sophia. All ecstasy and enthusiasm are proscribed. The thoughts of the worshipper are distracted
and menaced by no theatrical exhibition of the mysteries
of the faith ; they are restrained by no formal liturgy.
The majestic dome above us alone suggests the still

more majestic arch of heaven, beyond which dwells the invisible God.

Islamism, teaching the unity and omnipresence of Allah, basing its dogma alone upon moral culture and the goodness of God, and confining its worship to simple prayer, has torn away from between the Creator and the creature the veil suspended there by the old mythologies and the cunning priests of the Greek and Roman religions, in order to conceal behind it "their jealous, terrible, and incomprehensible divinity." But far above all emblems, and material forms, and mysteries, reigns Allah in his sublime unity. "Christianity," remarks an eloquent French writer, meaning the Christianity of the Catholics and Greeks, "more charitable to our weakness, has storied the way from earth to heaven with legions of saints and angels, reaching down their hands to those who would mount, in order to bear them to the radiant Virgin, daughter of man and mother of God, indefatigable in her intercessions and blessings. Perhaps this image of hope and consolation placed between justice that ought to chastise, and the guilty one who repents, or can repent, constitutes with its poetical surroundings the vitality of the Roman legend. Behold, how devotion to Mary dethrones insensibly in Catholic souls the severe Jehovah of the Bible, and even the good, but just martyr of Golgotha! It is not we who shall blame this quasi-deification of the misericordia, but through all these derivations of the human imagination what becomes of the idea of God ?"

A few silent worshippers are bowing in the direction of Mecca. In Greek churches the altar is on the east side, but as the holy city of the Moslems is south-east from Stamboul, the faithful, while performing their orisons in St. Sophia, look toward the corner of the mosque.

The paintings have been removed, but a few confused lines on one of the walls show us where was once a colossal figure intended to represent the Divine Wisdom. The ancient altar, made of a metal resembling Corinthian brass, has been replaced by a red marble *mihrab*, or niche of the Mussulman altar, indicating the direction of Mecca, while above hangs a piece of old carpet, almost worn to dust by the friction of pious knees, said to be one of the four upon which Mohammed was accustomed to make his prostrations. On the walls are painted in green several immense crescents inscribed with texts from the Koran. Humble and unimposing is the *Nimbar*, or pulpit of the Friday prayer, which the *kiatib* still mounts with a wooden sword in one hand and the Koran in the other, commemorative of the founding of Islam. I saw neither the sweating column, the miraculous golden ball, nor the impression of the bloody hand said to have been made upon a column of St. Sophia by the conqueror. Yet I observed here and there traces of the frescoes, mosaics, and paintings which graced its interior in the times of the Emperors. Not long ago some of the plastering was removed from the dome, revealing several beautiful pictures illustrative of Bible scenes, which, in accordance with the severe faith of the Moslems condemning all pictorial and statuesque representations of men or angels, had been concealed from sight since the dedication of Aya Sophia to Islam. The Ulemas, true to their ancient creed, advised the destruction of the frescoes thus brought to light, but the Sultan, with that delicacy of feeling which characterizes all his acts, directed that they should be carefully covered again, and added sorrowfully, "God only knows how soon the possession of this temple will pass from our hands; let it be restored to others as it came to us." St. Sophia is not perfect in point of architecture, for Greek art had degenerated in the time of Justinian. Externally the effect is injured by the great number of irregular structures clustered around the chief edifice, as well as by the walls and buttresses erected by M. Fossati for its support, without which, in fact, St. Sophia would ere this have fallen in ruins.

They relate in Constantinople that when the doors of St. Sophia were forced by the barbarous hordes of the Sultan, there was a priest at the altar engaged in saying mass. At the noise made by the hoofs of the Tartar horses upon the marble pavement and the shouts of the Moslem soldiery, the priest interrupted the holy

20*

sacrifice, took up the sacred vases, and proceeded with slow and solemn step toward one of the lateral naves. The soldiers, brandishing their cimiters, attempted to reach him, when he suddenly disappeared in the wall, that opened to receive him. They believed at first that he had escaped by a secret passage, but the masonry was solid, compact, and impenetrable. Sometimes it is said the listening ear will catch the murmur of vague psalmodies within the wall. It is the priest still living, like Barbarossa in the cavern of Kirfhausen, and muttering in his sleep the interrupted liturgy. When St. Sophia shall be restored to the Christians, the wall will open and the priest, leaving his retreat, will again appear at the altar to finish the mass, begun more than four hundred years ago.*

The superstitious Moslems anticipated the downfall of Constantinople in 1853, and many a longing Greek watched to see the priest mount with phantom tread the steps of the altar of Justinian. But though Russia attempted to react the part of Rome, and Nicholas assumed the character of destiny, the priest still murmurs his litany in the walls of the mosque.

MOSQUE OF ACHMET.

On one side of the Hippodrome, is the Mosque of Sultan Achmet with its six lofty minarets. It is these

* T. Gautier

white marble structures of marvellous height and
slenderness, often shooting out of a green forest of cypresses, like the white branchless trunks of lofty pine-
trees, that impart such elegance and airiness of form
to the many-domed mosques of Constantinople. Though
so frail that they almost seem to vibrate with the wind
they are crowned with a double or triple gallery
whence the muezzins call the faithful to prayer. As
the minarets form the peculiar glory of Mussulman
temples of worship, no mosque can have more of them
than that of Mohammed in Mecca. The latter was
formerly provided with six, and the Sultan Achmet
was compelled to add a seventh minaret to the *djami*
of the Prophet in the holy City, before completing his
great mosque in Stamboul.

The mosque of Sultan Achmet is the theatre of the
great religious ceremonies of Islam, and place of assembly for the court processions. It is there that the birth
of the Prophet is celebrated with great pomp, and there
also that the Sultan repairs in state on the two great
festivals of the Beiram. The Sultan whose name it
bears, labored upon the edifice with his own hands,
every Mussulman Sabbath during its construction, in
imitation of Mohammed at Medina, actuated doubtless
by the declaration of the Koran: "Allah will build a
palace for him in Paradise, who erects a mosque in his
honor on earth."

THE MOSQUE OF SOLYMANYEH.

From the Mosque of Achmet, we proceeded to visit
the Solymanyeh, a somewhat exaggerated description
of which I have borrowed from an old Turkish traveller.

Solyman having assembled all the thousands of perfect masters of architecture, building, stone hewing,
and marble cutting, who were found in the dominions
of the house of Osman, three whole years were employed in laying the foundations. The workmen penetrated so far into the earth that the sound of their pick-
axes was heard by the bull that bears up the world. In
three more years the foundations reached the face of
the earth, and the work was then suspended one year
that they might have time to settle, during which the
workmen were employed upon other pious undertakings. Shah Tahmas Khan, King of Persia, having
heard of this, immediately sent a great ambassador to
Solyman, with two mules laden with valuable jewels,
through friendship, as he said, for the Sultan, who,
from want of money, had not been able to complete
this pious work. The ambassador presented the Shah's
letter to the Sultan, and the latter was so incensed on
hearing its contents, that immediately, in the ambassador's presence, he distributed half of the jewels to the
Jews of Stamboul, saying: "Each Rafizi (Persian),

changed to an ass at the awful day of doom, shall bear
to the fires of perdition some Jew or other. To them
therefore I give this treasure that they may have pity
on you on that day, and be sparing in the use of whips
and spurs." Then giving another mule laden with
jewels to Sinan the architect, he said, still in the ambassador's presence—"These jewels which were sent
as being so valuable, have no worth in comparison
with the stones of my mosque, yet take them and mingle them with the rest."

It would baffle the eloquence of any tongue to describe the four great columns of real porphyry, brought
from Egypt on rafts, and the dome of azure stone which
rests upon them, like the vault of the sky. The total
number of lamps is twenty-two thousand, and there are
likewise some thousands of other ornaments suspended
from the roof. There are windows on all four sides of
the mosque, through each of which refreshing breezes
and the sweet songs of nightingales enter and revive
the congregation so that they seem to be enjoying life
in Paradise. This mosque is also, by the will of God,
constantly perfumed with an excellent odor of earthly
flowers. It is crowded day and night by thousands of
worshippers. Its *mihrab* of plain white marble resembles the *mihrab* of the mosque of Sultan Bajazet II.,
which was miraculously placed in the true position, and
by which, as is well known, all sea captains regulate
their compasses, and all the infidel astronomers of Fran-

gistan correct their watches. When it was finished, the architect Sinan said to the Sultan: "I have built for thee, O Emperor, a mosque which will remain on the face of the earth until the day of judgment, and when Hallaj Mansier shall come and rend Mount Demavund from its foundation, he will play at tennis with it and the cupola of this mosque." The humble writer of these lines himself once saw ten Frank infidels skilful in geometry and architecture, who, when the doorkeeper had changed their shoes for slippers, and introduced them into the mosque, laid their fingers on their mouths, and each bit his finger for astonishment. Afterwards on surveying the exterior, they again took off their hats and went round the mosque, and each of the ten bit his finger, that being their manner of testifying the greatest amazement.*

Demetrius conducted us into the Court of the Mosque of Bajazet to see the pigeons which are permitted to live there in great numbers, and for the feeding of which even the infidel *howadji* is expected to contribute a few paras. They were exceedingly tame, and darkened the air as they flew down to pick up the handfuls of grain I ordered for them. No one disturbs them in this sacred asylum. They are said to be descended from two birds bought by Bajazet of a poor woman, by way of charity, and given to the Mosque. The idea is beautiful, and such a one as the Turks love to cherish.

* Evlya.

Mohammed was accustomed to say, "He who is not affectionate to God's creatures and to his own children, God will not be affectionate to him. Every Moslem who clothes the naked of his faith, will be clothed by Allah in the green robes of Paradise." In one of the traditional sermons of the Prophet is given the following apologue on the subject of charity: "When God created the earth it shook and trembled, until he put mountains upon it to make it firm. Then the angels asked, 'O God, is there anything of thy creation stronger than these mountains?' And God replied, 'Iron is stronger than the mountains; for it breaks them.' 'And is there anything of thy creation stronger than iron?' 'Yes; fire is stronger than iron, for it melts it.' 'Is there anything of thy creation stronger than fire?' 'Yes; water, for it quenches fire.' 'O Lord, is there anything of thy creation stronger than water?' 'Yes; wind, for it overcomes water and puts it in motion.' 'O, Our Sustainer, is there anything of thy creation stronger than wind?' 'Yes; a good man giving alms; if he give with his right hand and conceal it from the left, he overcomes all things.'"

"O Prophet!" said one of his disciples, "my mother Omim-Sad is dead; what is the best alms I can send for the good of her soul?" "Water!" replied Mohammed, bethinking himself of the panting heat of the desert, where the thirsty Arab and Nubian place a jar of water at the head of the deceased, lest the great want of it in this world pursue them in the next. "Dig a well for her and give water to the thirsty." The man digged a well in his mother's name, and said: "This well is for my mother, that its rewards may reach her soul."

Mohammed also inculcated a spirit of kindness and forbearance toward all creatures. "Let him be a reprobate who sells a slave, injures a fruit-bearing tree, or makes lime of chiselled marble." "A man's true wealth hereafter is the good he does in this world to his fellow men. When he dies, people will ask, 'What property hath he left behind him?' But the angels who examine him in the grave will ask, 'What good deed hast thou sent before thee?'"

"His definition of charity," remarks a distinguished writer,* "embraced the wide circle of kindness. Every good act, he would say, was charity. Your smiling in your brother's face is charity; and exhortation of your fellow man to virtuous deeds is equal to almsgiving; your putting a wanderer in the right road is charity; your assisting the blind is charity; your removing stones and thorns and other obstructions from the road is charity; your giving water to the thirsty is charity."

Charity of the tongue was also earnestly enjoined upon the faithful. Abu Jaraiya, an inhabitant of Bosrah, coming to Medina and being persuaded of the apostolical office of Mohammed, entreated of him some great rule of conduct. "Speak evil of no one," answered

* Irving.

the Prophet. "From that time," says Abu Jaraiya, "I never did abuse any one, whether freeman or slave."

Equally beautiful are some of the aphorisms of Ali:

Riches are increased by the bountiful bestowal of Alms.

The silver sequin of the poor man is brighter in the eyes of God than the gold dinar of the rich.

Keep thy religion by the expenditure of thy riches,

And thou shalt gain both:

Neither expend thy religion on keeping thy riches,

For so thou shalt lose both.

The garment wherewith thou clothest another will be more enduring to thee

Than that wherein thou art thyself clothed.

He gives doubly who gives with a cheerful countenance.

As the Turks are more cruel than others in war, and especially in the intoxication of victory, so in peace, when indeed their customs must be studied in order to appreciate their virtues, they yield themselves more readily to the best impulses of our nature. The precepts of charity are especially impressed upon the minds of children. This virtue is confined to no class. The Grand Vizier and high Pachas may sometimes be seen leaning over their horses to bestow alms upon a poor mendicant. The beggar is never turned away without a gift however small, and the donor bestows "for the pleasure of Allah."

Besides the large sums given to charitable institutions and the part of every Mussulman's income which

he is enjoined to bestow in alms, instances of beneficence
are constantly occurring that would do honor to the
people of any land. Abuses naturally follow. Turkish
cities swarm with beggars, especially with mendicant
dervishes. They are to be seen everywhere, in the
streets, by the wayside fountains, in the courtyards of
the temples of worship, at the doors of the great,—everywhere except in the holy mosques.

Kindness to animals is also strongly inculcated under
the impression that they, like men, will appear in
the day of judgment. But in this respect I have seen
many painful deviations from the spirit of the Koran.
The law directs that he who maltreats an animal shall
be severely punished. Hence the antipathy of Moslems to hunting. It is regarded as highly criminal to
kill, or to deprive of liberty, animals whose flesh is not
proper for the table. Humane persons often buy such
of the hunters and let them go free. In Turkish cities
may frequently be seen cages of birds to be sold, under
the name of *azod-couchlery*, or birds to liberate on the
payment of their value.

Many of the followers of Mohammed imitate his
example in keeping in their houses a large number of
cats. Now and then a wealthy Moslem neglects wor-
thier objects of charity to bequeath his entire fortune
to the maintenance of a few favorite antiquated felines.
There is a hospital for these animals near Aleppo.

Cruel, however, is their treatment of the multitudes

of dogs to be seen in any Turkish city. The thousands
of these wolfish, filthy, cicatrized, masterless jackals in
dogs' clothing are a permanent curiosity in Constantinople. They are of a middle size and yellowish color.
More hideous, limping, teasing, yelping, starving, fighting, four-footed vagabonds cannot be found the world
over. They furnish an incredible amount of bark for
creatures that look so indescribably wretched. Besides
acting as scavengers in the streets where they live and
die, their principal occupation is to disturb the rest of
weary travellers, and a friend of mine declared they
would keep their jaws working hours after the power of
utterance had ceased. The dogs are never suffered to
enter a house for the reason that the Turks regard them as
unclean. The garment that has accidentally come in
contact with one of them must be washed in seven
waters. No one purposely feeds the curs, at least only
such as have litters of young, but now and then a pious
Mussulman gives a few paras to a water-carrier for filling the little stone troughs out of which they are permitted to drink.

Sleeping during the day in the cemeteries, deserted
houses, and even in the streets, they sally out by night,
like beasts of prey, in quest of food. Omnivora in every
sense of the word they fly at the garbage thrown into
the streets, dismember the carcases of donkeys left to
decompose in the open places, and even consume cast
off pieces of clothing. Now and then also by way of·

procuring a rare treat, they exhume a badly-buried Greek, or tear to pieces a drunkard, lodged in the gutter, unless indeed he tastes too strongly of raki or tobacco. When all other resources fail they fall upon each other, the weaker becoming food for the stronger. A strange animal is always regarded as lawful prey, and beset in the most ferocious manner.

I saw one day an Englishman walking through the streets of Pera with a huge Newfoundland dog. At the sight of the monster the Mussulmans held up their hands, exclaiming, "O terrible one! thou makest my beard tremble with fear! God is great!" Troops of dogs followed him, but were careful to keep at a respectful distance. Not so well fared the spaniel led out by a servant in Pera to take the air. The prowling curs fell upon him, and the servant could bring back to his master only a hind leg as a proof of his fidelity.

These dogs are fully as sagacious as the Turks themselves in matters pertaining to municipal regulations. Though the inveterate enemies of Franks, whose heterodox character they appear to determine by instinct, the dogs of Islam have put in practice many of the socialistic theories of the French philosophers. Aware of the advantages of association, and without abandoning the patriarchal system of government, our Oriental St. Simonists divide each city into several districts which are inhabited and policed by distinct tribes.

Alas for the sleepy traveller whose hotel happens to

stand on the middle ground of these jealous factions, and woe to the unlucky cur who ventures beyond the traditional boundaries of his tribe, be it for the prospect of a stolen bone or from an unwarrantable spirit of adventure ! The intruder is immolated at once and eaten, unless others come to the rescue, when battles and carnage ensue. It is highly amusing to see the few offal-carts of Pera pass through the different dogocracies. Troops of yelping curs follow them up to the limits of their tribe, and then give place to others. Foreign sportsmen when going to the chase are obliged to have their dogs conveyed outside the city in wagons.

In Constantinople these canine prodigies can be studied to the best advantage. The Sultan Mahmoud, among numerous other reforms, determined upon a *coup d'état* against the dogs of the imperial city. He ordered twenty-five thousand of them to be collected together, and as the Koran forbids openly putting them to death, satisfied himself with banishing them to an island in the sea of Marmora. But their plaintive cries reached Stamboul and excited the pity of the tender-hearted inhabitants. Mahmoud, who had exterminated cunning Pachas and thousands of fierce Janissaries, was obliged to yield to the demands of the populace, and the dogs were brought back after a single week of exile. Then the implacable Padisha had recourse to secret assassinations, forays, and poisonings. The dogs, however, were afterwards allowed to multiply in Scu-

tari; now they swarm as much as ever in Stamboul,
numbering, indeed, between thirty and forty thousand.

The Moslem has a genuine affection for his mosque.
It is to him what the temple was to the Greek, what
the Basilica was to the Roman. He loves to make his
ablutions at the cool fountains in its court, loves to
repose for hours under its shady colonnades, and beneath its ample dome yield himself up to the quietude
of devotion inspired by Islam. To many of the mosques
are attached hospitals, schools, baths, and kitchens for
the poor. The wayfaring and the indigent sleep under
their arcades without molestation, the guests of Allah.
The children of the poor, and often the rich, repair to
them for their entire education. With all their surroundings of time and moresque splendors, the imperial
mosques of Stamboul possess enormous revenues. To
them belongs more than half the real estate in European Turkey, together with vast possessions on the
Asiatic side of the Bosphorus. To them also falls the
wealth of persons dying without succession. The estates
of orphaned children are left in care of the mosques
until the heirs attain their majority.

At the birth of a princess in the Seraglio, it is customary to prepare presents of gold, and jewels, and
costly bridal robes, to be given her on the day of marriage. But should the rosy dreams of youth be disappointed, and death claim her as his bride, the consecrated presents are regarded as fit only for sacred use,

TOWER OF OVID.

P. 338

and are given to one of the Imperial Mosques. The amount of sterile treasure withdrawn in this manner from circulation is enormous. Since the reign of Mahmoud, the Solymanyeh alone has absorbed $6,000,000.

In one of the lower rooms of each mosque may usually be seen a number of chests and packages. When a Mussulman is about to start on a pilgrimage, or does not deem his valuables safe in his own house, he places them under the protection of heaven, for he who would steal from a mosque would add sacrilege to theft—a crime unknown among the faithful. The spider weaves her web undisturbed over gold and jewels half concealed from sight, and guarded only by the sacred character of the place. Thus the idea of religion is the prominent idea of the Mussulman mind. Thus, also, Moslem life once centring around the sandjak and the Koran, now centres around the konak and the mosque.

In the court and the Solymanyeh I observed several well-bearded Mussulmans, attentively reading the Koran, in which the faithful appear, indeed, to find a perennial source of delight. How that book hath wrought itself into the soul and life of the Orient, and shaped the destiny of its inflexible nations. Too sacred in the estimation of the Moslems to be printed, to be opened with unwashed hands, to be held below the waist, to be touched or even to be spoken of by an unbeliever, except with the idea of conversion, it is, when translated into the occidental language, heavy and wearisome

beyond measure. But when chanted in the Arabic—
for the Prophet forbade the Koran to be read—the
jingling alliteration and mellifluous flow of words are
indescribably bewitching.

The chief excellence of the Koran, in the estimation
of the Moslems, lies in its classic style and the beauty
of its language. Its pages are often clasped with gold
and jewels. Whole libraries are composed of richly
bound volumes of the sacred book. The old Moslem
warriors carried it in the left hand while they wielded
the sabre with the right. Caliphs and Sultans have
built up their political systems on its maxims. School-
boys gathered in the marble mosques of Stamboul, or
in the shady palm-groves of the Nile, take their first
and last lessons from its pages. The faithful are fond
of deriving omens from the Koran by opening it at
hazard, and reading the first verse that meets the eye.
They write its precepts upon the walls of their temples
for daily contemplation, and inscribe its mottoes upon
their banners to encourage them in battle.

Many of the Moslems are able to repeat the sacred
volume from beginning to end, and its beautiful aphorisms make up much of their daily conversation. And
when in the lands of Islam festive bands assemble, no
entertainment is more highly prized than recitations
from the Koran, given by persons whose business it is
to chant the verses of the Prophet. It is the Moslem's
companion in the caravan and the camp, in his jour-

neys and labors, ever delighting him with its beautiful thoughts, ever consoling him with its sweet words of promise.

Mohammedanism has accomplished much good in the Orient. Among the 110,000,000 Moslems who receive the Koran, it has abolished idolatry. It has taught that man can worship God without an infallible church and sin-forgiving priest. But the despotic systems of the East are as unchangeable in character as the bases of the Himalaya, and to the despotism of the Koran must be attributed the present condition of the Ottoman Empire. The idea of religion is so strongly impressed on the Ottoman mind, that without a change in faith there can be no essential change in the modes of thought and things pertaining to outward life.

The original purpose of Mohammed was to convert a few of the neighboring tribes from idolatry to the belief in one God. The idea of universal, or even of extensive dominion, was purely an after thought with the Camel-driver of Mecca, or rather with his successors. This is evident from the precepts of the Koran, and the "acts and sayings" of the Prophet. During the lunar month of Ramazan, the Turkish Lent, a rigid fast is enjoined upon the faithful. No one is allowed to eat, drink, smoke, enjoy the fragrance of a rose, or gratify any appetite whatever, from sunrise to the time when, as Mussulmans say, "a white thread can no longer be distinguished from one that is black." Trying as

21

this abstinence is under the burning sun of southern Asia, it would be still more unendurable in regions where the days are several months in length.

The ablutions also, which are so intimately connected with the worship of Islam, can be practised only in a warm climate like that of Arabia. The absolute necessity of pilgrimage, as expressed in the declaration of the Prophet, "He that does not visit Mecca once in his life is an infidel," could have had reference only to persons living at least within a few hundred miles of the holy city. Another proof is the occurrence of the month of pilgrimage in winter as well as in summer— the Moslems computing time by lunar months.

In the first war of the Russians and the Turks, the latter were obliged to raise the siege of Astrakan. They then projected an expedition into Russia, but were deterred by the Khan of the Crimea, who feared that the success of the Turks would inaugurate his own entire subjection to their authority. He represented to them that in the regions of the Don and the Volga, the winter extended over nine months, and in summer the nights were only three hours long: whereas the Prophet appointed the evening prayers two hours after sunset, and the morning orisons at the break of day. The Turks, terrified at this seeming contradiction between nature and the ordinances of religion, embarked at once for Constantinople.*

* Bancroft's Miscellanies.

The unity of God is therefore the prominent doctrine of the Koran, but there is no spirituality in that confused imitation of the Holy Scriptures. The Koran exalts God, but abases man; the Bible exalts man, and surrounds Deity with inconceivably more grandeur, in that it makes God condescend to put on the form of fallen humanity. The Koran is puerile in conception and local in application; the Bible is grand in conception and universal in application, embracing the united interests of humanity in all times and in all places. The Koran isolates, the Bible unites and expands. Islamism degrades labor, and teaches that "no mere effort of man can in any way augment the glory of God and the dominion of the faithful." Christianity ennobles labor and says, "*seek and ye shall find; knock and it shall be opened to you.*" Islamism materializes man; Christianity spiritualizes him—the former by extinguishing thought, the latter by awaking it. The one system degrades existence to an idle dream and promises a paradise of sensual gratification; the other exalts life into a heroic struggle for ourselves and our race, and promises a heaven of spiritual delight. The teachings of Mohammed leave man where they found him, while the teachings of Christ raise him to a sublime height of virtue and make him worthy of the promised reward. Hence Mohammedanism, promulgated by the sword, must be sustained by the sword, or perish for ever. "Who holds the sword holds the faith" was long the cherished motto of Islam. Yet Mohammedanism is not altogether a system of error: if so, it had long since passed away. Like other religious systems that have moulded the Oriental mind it contains some elements of truth. From these Islam has derived its vitality. Error is weakness. Truth alone imparts immortal vigor.

The superiority of the Arab race to that of Osman, enabled it to rise for a time above the despotism of the Koran. Endowed with more spirit and imagination, the Arabs became the instructors of the world in science and art; but it was only to sink to a greater depth of ignorance and darkness. After the flush of Ottoman conquest came the period of decay. When the proud descendants of Osman laid down the sword, unlike the Magyars and other conquering nomads from the east, they took up the pipe, and made of life one long delicious *kief*. From a nation of enthusiasts and conquerors, the Osmanlis became a nation of sleepers and smokers. They came into Europe with the sword in one hand and the Koran in the other: were they driven out of their encampment it would be with the Koran in one hand and the pipe in the other, crying, " *Kismet! Kismet! Allah kehrim!* (God hath willed it! God is great)!"

Yet even now there is an appearance of life in Stamboul, for as the blood leaves the extremities of the Empire, it flows to the heart. As the Paleologus promised the councils of the west to *latinize* the Eastern Empire, so Abdul Medjid attempts to regenerate the Osmanlis by reproducing French civilization along the Bosphorus. But the different types of civilization cannot be transplanted, like exotics, from country to country, and be made to flourish upon any and every soil. The elements of civilization are indeed thus transferable, but its peculiar and distinguishing type, the essential entity, must be a spontaneous development. So far as the Turks are concerned, the attempt of Abdul Medjid will prove a failure. The political institutions of the west cannot flourish under the ægis of Ottoman protection. Foreign means and foreign elements may be employed with advantage, but the plant itself must be native and not exotic.

The so called Turkish reforms are the carnival of civilization. To reduce the folds of the Turkish turban ; to diminish the amplitude of Turkish pantaloons ; to remove the veil from the face of Turkish beauty ; to substitute wine for water given by Allah ; to exchange polygamy for French prostitution—do not christianize the Turks, but they do destroy what is peculiar to Ottoman civilization, and excite the contempt of the green-turbaned hater of the Tanzimat. It is one thing to read magnificent firmans in Stamboul removing old abuses and equalizing the Christian and the Turk ; it is another thing to execute them in the distant provinces of the Empire. The Beys and Pachas, who talk pompously of reforms beside the walls of the Seraglio, become different individuals when dispensing life and death in Syria and Macedonia.

How then are the Turks to be regenerated? The Bible must be placed in their hands, and a germ of civilization be developed that shall be peculiarly Turkish, and consequently adapted to the Oriental mind. But is the Porte willing to take this initiatory step? So far from it, a converted Moslem could not live in Stamboul, were the fact of his apostacy generally known. That Arminian and Greek, Catholic and Protestant, are permitted to worship freely under Ottoman protection—results not so much from religious liberty or toleration on the part of the Turks, as from *a sovereign contempt of Christianity*, more blighting even than persecution, from that *laissez faire* policy, which has crushed the pillars of Ottoman civilization, and under which the well chiselled monuments of ancient art have insensibly mouldered away. What save Christianity can touch the leaden brain and iron heart of Islam?

Yet the Mohammedanism of to-day is far from being what it was even a quarter of a century ago. Fanaticism has in part given place to infidelity, to that absence of religious faith, which is better than error, and may be followed by a healthy Christian belief. The faithful admit that converts may be made by conviction as well as by the sword. An elastic interpretation of the Koran, inspired by the unyielding force of events and excused by the linguistic pliabilities of the

Moslems, declares that the apostate to Christianity may live although his presence is not to be endured. Already a venerable American missionary has taken up his residence in Stamboul. Already *Giaour Effendis*, no longer called " Christian dogs," are admitted within the mosque of Omer in Jerusalem ; and, reader, ere ten years have passed away, the Christian traveller shall visit Mecca and Medina without disguise. Already the Protestant Bible is sold in more than a hundred places in the Turkish Empire. The call of the muezzin to prayer is often unheeded. Instead of the ablutions, a little water is sprinkled on the hands and shoes. A few words are hastily mumbled over for prayers. Many of the Moslems drink wine, and eat the flesh of animals slain without the *bismillah* (" In the name of God "), and piously ignore the difference between mutton and pork.

The Jews had no dealings with the Samaritans. The latter, though geographically near, were in reality as remote from the proud denizens of the Holy City, as the swarthy tribes of Nubia. But when a certain man went down to Jericho and fell among thieves, in the all pervading spirit of Christian love, the good Samaritan became his brother. It is this spirit which a little band of American Missionaries is inculcating in the Orient. Though their teachings seem hushed by political convulsions and the thunders of angry powers, they are slowly breaking down the antipathy of races. They are giving examples of Christianity, of fraternity, and liberty, where true Christianity, fraternity, and liberty are unknown. And thus by the Rock of Calvary, on the Hill of Mars, and in the shadow of St. Sophia, with none of the circumstances and surroundings of great national enterprise, our humble countrymen are building up a kingdom whose foundations shall not be washed by the waves of time.

The Ramazan, or Turkish Lent, is the most important fast, followed by the most imposing festival, peculiar to Islam. During that sacred month the most Europeanized of the Turks return to the customs of their forefathers. Even the luxurious divan and the *shilteh* are not unfrequently exchanged for the sheepskin of the Turkoman's tent, while, aside from the religious character of the occasion, everything is made to recall, as far as possible, the rude life of the nomadic tribes of Orchan and Erthogrul.

The law of Islam enjoins a severe abstinence from all carnal pleasures during the Ramazan. Every Mussulman with the exception of travellers, invalids, and children, is forbidden to take food or nourishment of any kind, or even to smoke from sunrise until the dusk of evening. The most orthodox Moslems will neither smell of a rose nor caress their wives until the sacred lunar month has expired. The rich spend the day in sleep and idleness, but when the fast occurs in summer, the brawny boatman of the Golden Horn almost

faints at his oar, and the patient *hamal* beneath his
burden.

As soon, however, as the evening gun announces
the close of the daily fast, Stamboul puts on a livelier
air. The faithful betake themselves to the gratification
of such appetites as the Koran permits to be indulged,
not first to the satisfaction of hunger and thirst, as one
would suppose, but to the enjoyment of the bubbling
nargileh or the long chibouque. The night is spent in
revelry and devotion. The mosques are thrown open
to the curious and the devout, and the coffee-houses
crowded with turbaned groups listening in breathless
silence to the tales of wandering story-tellers. With
the Sultan the Ramazan closes the night before the end
of the month, one day earlier than for the rest of the
faithful. This circumstance has given rise to the Turkish saying, that on the last night of the fast the Padisha
is the only happy Moslem, or according to that Mussulman tenet which confines all true happiness to the
faithful, the only happy man in the world.

Theoretically the august Sultan is so exalted above
all other mortals, that the Moslem law permits him to
contract no matrimonial alliance with the human family.
But in order to keep up the royal succession he is presented on the last night of the Ramazan with the most
comely virgin to be found in all the provinces of the
Ottoman Empire.

The favored one, the most beautiful in a land famed

21*

for beautiful women, is selected by the Sultana Valide, the mother of the Sovereign, and by her presented to him amid all the pomp and circumstance of royalty of which Islam can boast. On that important occasion —important for the tender and beautiful being who may have lived in obscurity the day previous—the chosen one is conveyed across the Bosphorus in the imperial barge to be received by the Sultan in one of his imperial kiosks. In her train follow the high dignitaries of state—the august powers of Islam, while the resources of Oriental magnificence are exhausted to give *eclat* to a pageant so marvellous in its purpose and in its surroundings, as to appear more like a tale of Persian fiction than an actual occurrence.

On the last night of the Ramazan, let the reader transport himself in imagination to the promontory of Pera, or some other elevated point near the seven-hilled city. As darkness rolls down from the Euxine through the gorge of the Bosphorus, and descends upon the city from the region of Ida and the Bithynian Olympus, one by one the stately minarets of the Imperial Mosques become encircled with rings of fire, and seem like pharoses looming above a phosphorescent ocean, their myriad lamps mingling with the orbs of night. Queenly Stamboul appears as if bathed in an ocean of undulating light. In like manner are illuminated the fifteen suburbs of Constantinople, the ships in the Golden Horn, and the sylvan banks of the Bosphorus.

The view from the lofty tower of Galata, so incomparably beautiful by day, uniting as it does all the happiest accidents of climate and position, now becomes even more enchanting, and seems like some gorgeous Oriental dream.

At last the imperial cortège darts by the point of the seraglio. Then arises on the air the cadenced rhythm of thousands of boatmen, whose frail barks cut the sparkling waves between Pera, Scutari, and Stamboul. Then echo from suburb to suburb of the city of Constantine the acclamations of myriads whose hearts throb in sympathy for the chosen one, blooming with youth and beauty, and the envied of the beautiful, now about to be brought for the first time into the presence of her lord. Then innumerable rockets converting night into day, scatter their golden spangles among the stars, while the reverberations of artillery roll away and are lost among the hills of Thrace and Anatolia. But when, ushered into the royal presence, the chaste and mystic veil falls from the face that it has hitherto guarded from every stranger gaze, all becomes as silent as death, and night is left alone with eternity. What fortune is hidden in that first embrace? The fate of empires may hang upon the impression of a single glance, and the destiny of millions be centred in the sweetness of a single kiss! She upon whom the thoughts of an empire are thus bestowed may be forgotten to-morrow, or becoming the mother to a royal

heir, add the entanglements of policy and intrigue to
the sweeter entanglements of love, and thus influence,
directly and indirectly, the fate of millions. Strange
eventualities seem to hang upon the tissue of a
dream.

The three following days, termed the festival of the
Beiram, to distinguish it from the Courban Beiram, or
feast of the sacrifices, seventy days later, are devoted
to universal festivities and the various out-door amusements in which the Osmanlis ever delight.

Grateful, indeed, are the festivities of the Beiram
after the enervating sanctification of the Ramazan,
after a lunar month of alternate starving and feasting.
Abdul Medjid then repairs in grand procession to the
mosque of Sultan Achmet; then are exhibited the
comical farces of Kharangurez; then nothing but
joyous merry-making is to be seen from Sylvan Eyoub
to the sweet waters of Asia—from the Seven Towers
to Pera and the forest of Belgrade; and then, also,
with strange toleration and in the true spirit of Ottoman hospitality, whoever can afford spreads a banquet,
to which every one is welcome, be he rich or poor,
friend or stranger, Mussulman or Giaour.

During the festival of the Courban Beiram, it is
customary for wealthy Mussulmans to sacrifice to Allah,
and distribute among the poor as many sheep and
cattle as their fortune permits. On that great occasion
the streets of Stamboul are crowded with the bleating

folds of Ida and the Hæmus, and horned holocausts from Anatolia and the plains of the Danube. The Sultan opens the religious ceremony, in person, by giving the first blow to the first victim.

CHAPTER XIX.

MUSSULMANS AND NON-MUSSULMANS.

"Whose game was empires and whose stakes were thrones,
Whose table earth—whose dice were human bones."

In one of the wildest regions of the Alps an immense glacier, the accumulation of centuries, impends over a hamlet far below. The mountaineer whispers as he passes over it, lest the huge mass part from its icy fastenings. Men go up from year to year to measure the fissures, always widening, and ever report the avalanche as near at hand, but the Alpine glacier remains, and the villagers live on, like their ancestors before them, in a state of awful insecurity, threatened with swift destruction every moment. Such, for more than a century, has been the condition of the Ottoman Empire.

Osman, when but the leader of a nomadic band whose progenitors had wandered from the banks of the Oxus to the western confines of Asia, foresaw in a dream the future greatness of the Osmanlis. He beheld the leafy tent under which he reposed, expand until it rested on those four magnificent pillars of empire, the

Atlas, the Taurus, the Hæmus, and the Caucasus.   At
his feet rolled the Nile, the Tigris, the Euphrates, and
the Danube, covered with ships, like the sea.   In the
valleys sprang up cities crowned with pyramids and
gilded domes, while in cypress groves the prayers of the
Imaums were mingled with the songs of innumerable
birds.   Above this leafy tent, grown from the body of
Osman himself, rose the crescent, the symbol of Ottoman dominion.   Its sabre-like branches pointed to the
different cities of the earth, and especially to Constantinople, which, lying at the union of two seas and two
continents, like " a diamond between two sapphires,"
formed the clasp to a ring of empire seeming to embrace
the world.   This ring fell into the hands of Osman, and
the Turkish empire was founded, to shoot with meteor-
like brilliancy into the first rank of temporal powers.

The flood of the Ottoman invasion, following the retiring ebb of the Crusades, rolled beyond the Hellespont,
and the crescent took its way westward with such astonishing rapidity that there was consternation in Rome.
At the fall of Constantinople—an event which caused
the death of Pope Nicholas VI. and made the sceptres
of Western Europe tremble—a successor of the Caliphs
came to occupy the throne of the Constantines.   Behold
Mohammed II. terming himself the shadow and vice-
gerent of God on earth!   "Go to your master," said he
to the ambassador of Hunyad before the walls of Stamboul, " and tell him that as there is but one ruler in

heaven, so there shall be but one sovereign upon the earth !"

Nations are not immortal, and destiny loves to sport with the pretensions and pompous designations of men.

As the Teutonic tribes were drawn by a secret impulse toward the Capital, and Roman civilization sought to extend its sway westward, so the Greeks, from the time of Alexander the Great, have inclined toward the Euphrates, while the tide of Slavonic conquest has rolled in the direction of the Caucasus. Owing to the dismemberment of the Eastern Empire, the fairest seats of civilization fell an easy conquest to the Osmanlis, and the Turk sat down amidst the fallen temples of ancient cities, like Marius among the ruins of Carthage. The reminiscences of Grecian history, and the triumphs of Grecian art—what were they to the simple child of nature, trusting in Fatality and wedded to an Eastern system of government and religion as unchangeable as the mountains ? The matchless eloquence of her orators and the fine frenzy of her poets could no more touch those brains of lead than move the marble statues hewn from the quarries of Pentelicus ! As a conqueror the Turk learned nothing from the conquered ; nor would he heed the voices of civilization until the Sibyl had opened her book and read from its illumined pages the certain lesson of his destiny.

Turkey exhibits all the elements of historical interest, the circumstances attending her origin and growth yielding in magnitude only to the quick coming events that cluster round her dissolution. She was great and glorious when the nations of the West were weak and semi-barbarous. But what has she not lost? Greece and fair islands in the Ægean no longer hers; Egypt, Syria, and the land of Mecca retained only by the interference of Christian powers; the richest provinces on the Euxine incorporated into Russia; the haughty Moslems virtually excluded from Servia and Wallachia; Bosnia and Albania estranged, and Epirus and Macedonia held by the feeblest tenure—these are the humiliations of the Padisha!*

To sustain the Ottoman Empire has been the great problem of European diplomacy for the last fifty years. Careful, however, have the Christian powers been to impart no elements of strength, but to maintain the falling Colossus in weakness,

> " Ever trembling on the verge of fate."

Block after block has been ruthlessly removed from the magnificent arch of empire which once extended from Belgrade to Bassora, until the dominion of the Sultans has virtually passed away.

Islamism is an Asiatic institution, and the attempt to establish it permanently on European soil has proved a failure from the fact that there is no sympathy of

* Poujoulat

race, or religion, or otherwise, between the East and the West. Nor could that simple system by which Mohammed sought chiefly to convert a few Arabian tribes to the belief in one God expand like the tent of Arabian fiction, so as to embrace the entire regions and people of the earth.

Western Asia belongs to Islam.

Of the fifteen million Christians living under the Ottoman government more than thirteen million belong to Europe. Of the sixteen million Turks more than fourteen million live on Asiatic soil, leaving less than two millions encamped in Europe.

In view of humanity, in view of preventing an outbreak of the old Moslem fanaticism, in view of protecting the germs of Christianity springing up on Asiatic soil, the project of expelling the Turks from Europe cannot be entertained for a moment. Nor, as is generally supposed, has the Turkish Empire its centre of gravity in Asia, but in Europe. This is evident from the want of sympathy between the different Moslem races, as the Arabs and the Turks, from the advance of Mohammed Ali almost to the gates of Stamboul, and also from the events of the late war.

The Osmanli is fallen upon evil days;

> " For as he taught his sword to thirst for blood,
> So by the thirsty sword his blood is shed."

The race itself is not productive. Physiological laws

appear to check its extension as if the Turk were a monstrosity.

Notwithstanding his many noble traits, who does not detest the Turk as an incubus upon civilization? A man of distinguished incapacity, he has but two ideas—those of God and of country. Wedded to Oriental life he will neither impart to us the wisdom of the East nor turn back the streams of science and religion that flowed thence for centuries to the West. Satisfied with "the contemplation of Allah and the love of woman," his actual amount of knowledge derived from books or experience, compared with the scum of Oriental exaggeration, reminds us of Falstaff's penny's worth of bread to an intolerable amount of sack.

The Mussulman is the best of friends and the worst of enemies: a model of honesty and simplicity in private life, a paragon of intrigue and display in office. He combines hospitality with avarice, the dignity of a philosopher with the credulity of a child, and the docility of an infant with the ferocity of a demon. The Turk has a greater talent for sleeping than the foolish virgins, and would exchange a master-piece by Phidias for a pipe of tobacco. His ideas of government, of religion, and the proprieties of life, are almost the opposite of our own. In Turkey women in sombre hues ogle men dressed in flowing robes of the gayest colors; here, men in dark ogle women attired in "woven air," exhibiting all the tints of the rainbow.

But the Turk is a born ruler. He has a substratum of honesty and integrity which even his enemies must admire—a dignity and noble independence which contrast strongly with the low cunning of the Greeks, and the servility of the Bulgarians.

When Russia and Austria haughtily demanded of the Sultan the surrender of the Hungarian fugitives, Abdul Medjid replied, " What then will become of the ancient hospitality of the Ottoman Porte ? I do not ask who they are, whence they come, or what religion they profess. I take no part in their politics ; but they are unfortunate fugitives, and demand hospitality upon our soil. The laws of the Koran and the convictions of my own heart forbid me to give them up whatever may be the consequences."

The Greece of to-day is the mere shadow of a state, and the Greeks, politically speaking, would not be worthy of a moment's consideration were it not for their peculiar relation to the Turks and the other Christian races of the Ottoman Empire. They number in all about 4,000,000 souls. Of these not far from 900,000 inhabit Greece proper, independent of the Turks, but in reality ruled by France and England. More than a million are scattered through Epirus, Macedonia, and other parts of Roumelia ; while the remainder, not far from two million souls, live in Asia Minor and upon the islands of the Archipelago.

Owing to their energy and intelligence the Greeks

INTERIOR OF A TURKISH MOSQUE.   p. 462

have acquired a marked superiority over the other Christian races of the Ottoman Empire, and imparted to them something of their own national spirit and character.

Their blood is no longer the pure Hellenic. He that would look upon creatures fair as the Graces—would see the proudly curling lip, the eye melting with liquid softness or burning with Attic fire, and the classic features which served Praxiteles for models, will find them only on the sweet islands of the Ægean, or in the shady hamlets of Asia Minor. But to the Greeks have descended the name, the language, and many of the characteristics of an ancient race which gave the world patterns of heroism and virtue, and bequeathed to all coming time what was best in science and noblest in art. The waves of the Ægean, the Marmora, and the Euxine wash the strands where their ancestors erected the seats of empire.

To the Greeks belongs the *prestige* of ancient renown and qualities fitting them to play no subordinate part in the great events that cluster around the approaching phase of Ottoman history. To these must be added an innate sense of superiority to the people who have enslaved them for centuries, and the remembrance, never to be forgotten by a Greek, that the descendant of a barbaric prince occupies the throne of the Constantines. Many of the Greeks of Constantinople are opulent and powerful. From among them have been chosen, for centuries, the dragomen of the Sublime Porte. The gloomy quarter of the Phanar furnished a succession of Hospodars for the Danubian Principalities, while the reputable position of Prince Kallimaki and M. Masurus, as Turkish ambassadors at Paris and London, indicates with what success they have cultivated diplomacy.

The Greeks are, however, emphatically the traders and seamen of the Levant, and it is notorious that the majority of them prefer the condition of *rajahs* in Constantinople, with easily acquired gains, to independence in Athens, where more industry and intrigue are requisite to acquire fortune and position. So much for the patriotism of the Greeks dwelling in European Turkey!

Equally fond of mercantile and maritime life, full of spirit, naturally inclined to speculative schemes, and possessed of an unbounded love of adventurous enterprise, we would naturally expect to find them at the head of the commercial interests of the Ottoman Empire, and able, consequently, to influence for good or for evil its political destinies.

The restrictions imposed upon commerce in the Turkish Empire have, however, prevented the Greeks from developing their mercantile and maritime character to the fullest extent. Their dishonesty also causes them to be despised by the Turks and regarded with reserve and suspicion by the other Christian races. As among the Mussulmans we find rank without intelligence, so among the Greeks we find intelligence without heart.

"The ancient Greeks," says Anastasius, "worshipped a hundred gods; the modern Greeks worship as many saints. The ancient Greeks believed in oracles and prodigies, incantations and spells; the modern Greeks have faith in relics and miracles, in amulets and divinations. The ancient Greeks brought rich offerings and gifts to the shrines of their deities for the purpose of obtaining success in war and pre-eminence in peace; the modern Greeks hang up dirty rags round the sanctuaries of their saints to shake off an ague or to propitiate a mistress."

The Armenians are widely disseminated in the Ottoman Empire. They number in all about 2,000,000 souls, one-fourth of whom are established in Europe. Their parsimonious disposition and skill in financial affairs render them especially useful to the Turkish authorities. More enterprising than the Turks, and honester than the Greeks and Jews, they rank with the Ottomans as the "Pearl of Infidels," and are often termed the camels of the "Osmanlie State." They have charge of the Mint at Constantinople, and are farmers of the revenues.

• The Armenians enjoy greater religious privileges than the other Christian sects, and, politically, have no interest in ameliorating the condition of the Ottoman Empire, for individual cases of industry thrive best amidst general indolence, and superior cunning is no enemy of intrigue. They are, *par excellence*, the bankers and courtiers of the Empire, and many of them turn their attention to diplomacy, in which as well as in trade they equal the Greeks. Thousands of Armenian families, attracted by the prospect of gain, have found their way into the remote provinces of European Turkey, where they live exclusively in towns and cities.

In figure the males resemble the Greeks, and with the exception of the cap, dress not unlike the Persians. The females are not wanting in Oriental charms, but the Turkish *yasmak* and the shroud-like gowns in which Eastern women envelope themselves conceal nearly all the traits of beauty.

Of the Slaves I have already spoken.

Some philosopher has remarked that the world could not exist without the Jews. However that may be, no part of the civilized or partially civilized world is without them. They number in all less than 6,000,000 souls, yet are so widely scattered that you can visit no seaport, or place where men " do congregate " for traffic in money, in slaves, or in merchandise of any kind, without finding there representatives of this race, whose refuge is the wide earth, whose home is the narrow grave. The Jews are most numerous in Poland, whither they escaped from the States of Germany to avoid persecution. More than 300,000, mostly of Spanish descent, are settled in European Turkey, their ancestors having taken refuge there after the expulsion by Ferdinand and Isabella. Perhaps an equal number may be found in the African and Asiatic provinces of the Ottoman Empire; and so widely dispersed are they through the lands of Islam, that in the remotest cities reached by caravans you will find some turbaned, long-haired Jew ready to convert your gold into the currency of the country with a saving discount to himself. Jews are to be met with in China and on the coast of Malabar. They swarm in Bokhara and may be seen in Madagascar and on the western coast of Africa. In Cochin China there are two Jewish races, black and white. In Yemen the Jews scarcely differ in appearance from the roving Bedouins. In Circassia they are wild mountaineers, having neither the Bible nor the Talmud. In different parts of Europe they enjoy different degrees of liberty, and in the United States alone, where, indeed, the emancipation of the race began, are they entirely exempt from partial legislative restrictions.

But, sojourning everywhere, they are everywhere strangers. I have noticed that among the blonde nations of the North, the Jews have dark hair and eyes, while among the dusky nations of the South it is quite the reverse; so true is it that they everywhere form a distinct people. Differing thus physically and socially, and adopting for the most part the language and costume of those among whom they dwell, they cherish a

22

remarkable uniformity in religious belief, and think with one mind upon the destiny of the Hebrew race.

Judaism is the mother of two religions which have almost overspread the earth—Christianity and Moham- medanism—two daughters who have inflicted upon her innumerable evils, notwithstanding Our Saviour and the Apostles were all Jews; notwithstanding Abraham, Moses, and Jesus are numbered among the six great prophets of Islam. The progenitors of the Messiah, made illustrious by their supernatural origin and celes- tial guidance, the repositories of divine oracles and the chosen interpreters of the will of God,—their annals reaching to the first ages of the world and their very existence a miracle,—behold how the Children of Israel have survived the overthrow of their temple and their altars, and, dispersed among the nations, become the slaves of the human race, the sport of fortune, and the contempt of the whole earth!

A wild and terrible legend is that of the middle ages, which personified the Jewish nation by the traits of the Wandering Jew. It represents an old man, with naked feet, uncovered head, and long white beard, wandering ceaselessly over the earth. His face is pale. A mark of blood is upon his forehead. His eyes burn like sapphires beneath their oblique lids. With an eagle-like nose and blood-like eyes, squalid and harsh in features, and clad in a coarse woollen gown, he ever pursues, with staff in hand, his interminable journey.

Speaking all languages and traversing all lands, knowing not the purposes of God concerning himself, and
ever driven onward by a secret impulse, he is transported from place to place with the speed of the wind;
and as the long centuries come successively to a close
his old age renews itself with the vigor of youth, in
order that he may complete the weary round of ages.
The people wonder as he hastens past.   Once or twice
only has he paused to tell his story.   He was of the
Jewish nation; Ahasuerus by name, and a shoemaker
by trade.   Dwelling in Jerusalem he persecuted Our
Saviour, and was of those who cried " Crucify him."
The sentence of death having been pronounced, he
ran to his house, before which Jesus was to pass on
the way to Calvary.   Taking his child in his arms he
stood at the door with all his family to behold the procession.   Our Saviour, weighed down by the heavy
burden of the cross, leaned for a moment against the
wall; and the Jew to manifest his zeal cruelly struck
the innocent one, and pointing to the place of execution, bade him go on.   Then Jesus, turning to the
unfeeling child of Israel, said :—

> " Thou refusest rest to the Son of God:
> I go, for it must needs be;
> But for thee there shall be no rest
> Or repose until I return.
> Go forth on thy journey,
> Leave thine own; traverse mountains and seas,

Pausing neither in the cities nor the deserts,
Nowhere—not even in the tomb.
As an example to the Universe, and bearing
Everywhere the heavy weight of my curse;
Much shalt thou long for death, thy deliverance,
But shalt not die until the day of judgment!"

He assists at the crucifixion, and then goes forth a mysterious stranger, whose feet shall become familiar with all lands.

How age after age he longs for the sweets of death and the repose of the tomb! But in spite of death he must live on; his dust shall not mingle with that of his ancestors. He drags himself from a gloomy cavern of Mount Carmel, shaking the dust from the beard grown even to his knees. Nine grinning skulls are before him. He seizes and hurls them from the top of the mountain, and they go bounding down from rock to rock. They are the skulls of his parents, of his wife and six small children, all of whom have been able to die; but he cannot. He rushes into the flames of falling Jerusalem, and attempts to bury himself beneath the crumbling ruins of Rome; but in vain. Flying from cities and men, the wanderer seeks the solitary places of the earth. He climbs the everlasting mountains. Passing beyond the region of verdure and of dashing torrents his feet tread the seas of amethyst and opal. Above him are only peaks shrouded in mists and eternal snows. The daring eagle soars not

so high.   There are no sounds save the cracklings of
the glaciers.   The soul seems almost to touch the
heavens above.   There surely the Wandering Jew shall
rest?   No.   A pursuing angel unsheathes a sword of
flaming fire, and, lo! the wanderer beholds once more
in the heavens the drama of the Crucifixion.   The way
from earth to heaven is storied with myriads of celestial
beings radiant with light.   Before him are all the
martyrs and saints and sages who have ever lived and
died.   For a moment he gazes upon the vision; then
turns away, chased by the sword of flame and demons
of frightful form.   Again he wanders over the earth, ever
with five pieces of copper in his pocket, ever with the
mark of blood upon his forehead.   Maddened with the
agony of life, he throws himself into the crater of Ætna,
but the boiling liquid and sulphurous flames harm him
not.   The floods of lava vomit him forth, for his hour is
not yet come.   Embarking upon the sea, the wind raises
its surface into mountain waves—the vessel divides,
and all perish save the Wandering Jew.   Too light to
sink in the ocean, its waves cast him upon the hated
shore.   He plunges into a hundred bloody conflicts
without sword or shield.   All in vain.   The leaden
balls rain harmlessly upon him; battle-axes and cimiters glance from his charmed body.   Where mounted
squadrons fight with the fury of demons, he casts himself under the feet of the horsemen, and is unharmed,
so riveted are his soul and body together.   He says to

Nero, "Thou art drunk with blood." To Christian
and Mussulman, "Drunk art thou with blood." They
invent the most horrible tortures for his punishment,
yet injure him not. Leaving, in his vain pursuit of
death, the lands that throb with life and industry, the
Wandering Jew threads the solitary jungles of the
tropics. He walks in poisoned air. Fierce serpents
sport around him, but none venture to harm.

And thus he wanders,

> ————"Traversing mountains and seas,
> Pausing neither in the cities nor the deserts;
> Nowhere—not even in the tomb."

There may have been something providential in
thus bringing so many of the Jews to the confines of
the Holy Land, but it seems hardly possible that they
shall ever be restored as such to their ancient inherit-
ance. The Turks, like the Jews, refer to Abraham as
their great progenitor; like them they are strict theists,
abhor swine's flesh and practise circumcision. For
this reason they formerly regarded the Jews with more
favor than the other sects of unbelievers, styling them
Yeslir (strangers), while the Christian subjects were
called *Mousaphir* (servants). The Jews of European
Turkey are governed by a Council consisting of six
members under the direction of a Chief Rabbi, who
resides in Constantinople. Two Jews also take part in
the deliberations of the Grand Divan. Though enjoy-

ing greater privileges than are granted to their sect in any other part of Continental Europe, they are sufficiently mean and wretched. A few of them are wealthy, and serve the Porte in the capacity of bankers, but their financial operations bear no comparison with those of the Crœsuses of Western Europe, who supply nations with the sinews of war, and claim tribute from kings. The great majority, however, earn a subsistence as traders and artisans, appearing, indeed, to thrive best in the midst of universal decay and dissolution. Let the Ottoman Empire fall in pieces, and the Jews would remain *brokering* among its ruins.

Yet the Jews of the Ottoman Empire, notwithstanding their degradation, exhibit a certain intellectual tendency. They live in an ideal world, frivolous and superstitious though it be. The Jew who fills the lowest offices, who deals out *raki* all day long to drunken Greeks, who trades in old nails, and to whose sordid soul the very piastres he handles have imparted their copper haze, finds his chief delight in mental pursuits. Seated by a taper in his dingy cabin he spends the long hours of the night in poring over the Zohar, the Chaldaic book of the magic Cabala, or, with enthusiastic delight, plunges into the mystical commentaries on the Talmud, seeking to unravel their quaint traditions and sophistries, and attempting, like the astrologers and alchymists, to divine the secrets and command the powers of Nature. "The humble

dealer, who hawks some article of clothing or some old
piece of furniture about the streets; the obsequious
mass of animated filth and rags which approaches to
obtrude offers of service on the passing traveller, is
perhaps deeply versed in Talmudic lore, or aspiring, in
nightly vigils, to read into futurity, to command the
elements and acquire invisibility." Thus wisdom is
preferred to wealth; and a Rothschild would reject a
family alliance with a Christian prince to form one
with the humblest of his tribe who is learned in Hebrew lore.

The Jew has his revenge :

> "The pound of flesh which I demand of him
> Is dearly bought, is mine, and I will have it."

Furnishing the hated Gentiles with the means of
waging exterminating wars, he beholds, exultingly, in
the fields of slaughtered victims a bloody satisfaction
of his "lodged hate" and "certain loathing," more
gratifying even than the golden Four-per-cents on his
princely loans. Of like significance is the fact that in
many parts of the world the despised Jews claim as
their own the possessions of the Gentiles, among whom
they dwell. Thus the squalid *Yeslir*, living in the
Jews' quarter of Balata or Hashkeui, and even more
despised than the unbelieving dogs of Christians,
traffics secretly in the estates, the palaces and the

MUSSULMANS AND NON-MUSSULMANS.

villages of the great Beys and Pachas, who would regard his touch as pollution. What, apparently, can be more absurd? Yet these assumed possessions, far more valuable, in fact, than the best "estates in Spain," are bought and sold for money, and inherited from generation to generation.

The 8,000 Israelites now living in Jerusalem are sufficiently mean and wretched. The London Jews' Society not long ago opened a large farm in one of the valleys near the Holy City for the purpose of affording the Jewish population employment, but found that the latter preferred the corroding idleness and stinging want everywhere visible in their quarter of the city to a livelihood acquired by honest industry. One of the Missionaries of that Society informed me that it was an easy matter to make nominal converts, since many of the Palestine Jews willingly embraced Christianity in consideration of the suit of clothes given them, both as a charity and a badge of conversion. But my informant stated, in addition, that in such cases their Christianity wore out considerably in advance of the garments. I do not know, however, that the London Jews' Society ever adopted the method of ascertaining the number of their converts employed by the Russians a few years ago in one of the newly conquered provinces of Transcaucasia. An article of dress, appropriately called a *Soul-warmer*, was promised to each one who should make a profession of

22*

Christianity. *Soul-warmers* came greatly in demand, and in a short time it was found that twice as many of them had been given out as there were souls in the entire province.

The surgeon in the Jews' Hospital in the Holy City mentioned to me one of the wealthiest Jews in Palestine who, although a married man, had been power fully smitten with the charms of a Gentile maiden. To espouse the fair one he was obliged to renounce his religion. This he did, but was baffled by his quick-witted wife, who apostatized at the same time, and threw herself between the love-converted Jew and the willing Gentile. The conversions, however, were not lasting, and a short time before I visited Jerusalem, the Israelite and his wife slid back into Jewry together.

While travelling in the East I was once obliged, in consequence of illness, to spend two weeks in a Jewish family. We did not fare sumptuously every day, nor was it a matter of Eastern hospitality. There was much praying in the house in the Hebrew manner; there was no fire kindled on Saturdays; there was the covering of the face while looking toward Jerusalem in holy meditation and the observance of rites innumerable, but the sharping Israelite, after insisting upon receiving much more than I had agreed to give, prayed God and allowed me but fifty piastres to the ducat, whereas I should have had sixty. During those two weeks of tribulation I was not allowed to sit at table with the family, as they in their peculiar sanctity would not eat with a publican and sinner.

Let me not be understood as condemning the efforts made to convert the Jews in Palestine and elsewhere. Far from it. There are many faithful converts in Jerusalem. One of the most energetic Missionaries laboring in their midst is a German lady, a Jewess by birth, who has recently purchased a part of Mount Olivet for a Christian cemetery. I mention these circumstances to illustrate the degraded condition of the eight thousand Jews inhabiting the Holy City. Nowhere else are they so despised, and consequently so worthy of our Christian sympathy. It is to be hoped that the new Pacha—a liberal Moslem of the reform school—will govern them with more kindness than the Shylock of a Turk who plundered alike Mussulmans, Christians and Jews. The very boy who donkeys you all day long through the streets of the Holy City, will exhaust the calendar of Moslem saints in his imprecations upon the stubborn beast, and end with calling it a Jew. They are not suffered to desecrate with their presence the site of the Temple; nor, indeed, if permitted, would they enter the gate leading to the Mosque of Omar, from a belief that under it are buried the parchments of the Pentateuch.

A portion of the wall near the south-west corner of the "Inclosure of the Temple" bears unmistakable

marks of great antiquity. Tradition says that the
foundation was laid by David and the superstructure
completed by Solomon. The blocks of which it is
composed are of immense size, and were doubtless
brought from the immense subterranean quarries discovered two years ago by an American missionary,
Mr. Barclay, under the present City of Jerusalem.
This is the least exposed portion of the wall of the
Temple, and if indeed overthrown in any of the political convulsions which befell the city, it must have
been rebuilt with the original material. It is signifi-
cantly named "The Jews' Corner." To this spot, hal-
lowed by so many tender associations, they are permitted to repair, on the payment of a certain tribute,
to weep over the humiliation of their race and country. Hither, every evening of the week, and especially on the evening of the Jewish Sabbath, go the
sorrowing children of Israel to bathe with their tears
the foundations of their beloved Temple—with warm
tears that should melt the stony hearts of their oppres-
sors. And I have seen nothing so sad throughout the
lands of Islam as when before those tear-washed blocks
of granite they read the lamentations of Jeremiah, and
chanted with almost penitential accent—

> "Lord build, Lord build,
> Build thy house speedily!
> In haste! in haste! even in our day
> Build thy house speedily!"

The Jews of the Holy City have a house of learning called *Bice Amdrash*, where one hundred Rabbis study the law and the traditions day and night. For their support contributions are taken in all the Jewish Synagogues on the feast of the Purim. The Rabbis who are sent out from the Holy City to collect in the sums thus given, carry with them a quantity of "Jerusalem earth" to be distributed among congregations. When, in most lands, a Jew has been coffined and is about to be buried, they put upon each eye of the corpse as much of this Jerusalem earth as can be held upon a shilling. More desired by the Jew than costliest sepulture in other lands is the privilege of humble burial on the rugged slopes of Olivet, and often an aged pilgrim, bent down with years and the sorrows of his people, repairs to the City of Desolation to die there and have his dust mingle with that of his forefathers, in sight of Zion and Moriah.

Russia, whatever may have been her secret purposes in the past, whatever may be her aims in the future, has been of lasting service to European Turkey. With incalculable evils she has also brought incalculable good. The Northern Enchanter has aroused her sleeping nationalities, has reanimated her expiring strata of civilizations. More than all other powers combined, Russia has brought back to the Greek the thought of his heroic origin, and awakened in the Slave the remembrance of his ancient dominion. She has given law and organization

to the klephts of the mountains, and inspiring somewhat of her own barbaric courage in the timid Wal
lachs and Bulgarians of the plains, has taught them to
aspire to equality with their Turkish lords. Even the
rude shocks of war have tended to arouse the dormant
energies of these Christian races.

Far be it from me to apologize for Russian despotism. May the freedom of speech and liberty of action
enjoyed in Turkey never be supplanted by Cossack
violence! *Firmans* declaring all men equal before the
law, though imperfectly executed, are infinitely preferable to despotic *Ukases* asserting the divine right of
absolutism, and written, if needs be, in human blood.

The policy of Russia, like that of Austria, has ever
been first to liberate the neighboring nationalities and
afterwards enslave them to herself. Thus Russia aided
and encouraged the Græco-Slaves to break the chains
of Ottoman bondage. The normal spontaneous progress exhibited by European Turkey, slight though it
be, is mainly owing to Russian influence. By imparting to the thirteen million Christians of European
Turkey ideas of order and government, by improving
their culture, and the encouraging of industry, the
Czars have done something in the way of their rege-
neration.

Every stroke of the axe, every stroke upon the
anvil is, from the mysterious connexion of things, a
blow upon the brazen shield of tyranny. When the

last despot shall have passed away, and men learn the art of war no more, the nations can beat their swords into ploughshares: but before the dawn of that auspicious day the down-trodden millions of Europe must beat *ploughshares* into *swords*, and reach freedom through the red waves and fiery surges of revolution.

Russia, lying between the Occident and Orient, extends her arms to both. On one side she has the enlightened nations of Europe, on the other the nomadic tribes of the Asiatic plains. She has the energy and civilization of the west, but in soil, in climate, in political and national characteristics is far more closely allied to Asia than to Europe.

It is affirmed that Russia is a barrier against the irruptions of eastern barbarians. Thus far, however, she has rendered them more dangerous by imparting to them ideas of government and military organization—elements of civilization that strengthen without enervating.

Defeated in her plans of conquest it is to be hoped that Russia will enter upon the mission which Turkey should have undertaken—the blending of the East and the West. Becoming thoroughly civilized herself, she may arouse the Asiatic nations from their lethargic sleep of centuries, engraft upon them the civilization of the west, and impart to our too material conceptions something of the dreamy imagination and mystic spirit of the Orientals.

The now barren plains of Turan were once renowned throughout the world for their industry and commerce. Cities, like Samarkand, with a population of half a million of souls, became the seats of wealth and culture. The Oxus and Jaxartes, covered with ships, flowed through a land designated as an earthly paradise. It may be the destiny of Russia to restore this ancient order of things.

The enemies of Russia do not appear to realize the importance of her military position in Asia. From Achalzik, on the southern slope of the Caucasus, it is not more than four hundred and fifty miles to Aleppo. The former is an elevated point on a *plateau* from which it is comparatively easy to descend in one direction to the mouths of the Tigris and Euphrates, in another to the Mediterranean and the Bosphorus.

It is from this position that those flaxen-haired children of the north hope one day to descend to water their horses along the Hellespont and shake the rupee trees of India.

The great problems of history are solved slowly. Russia may require ages for the accomplishment of her destiny. Though beaten in a hundred battles, she will remain formidable. Her elastic power will again expand; history may repeat itself in her example.

CPSIA information can be obtained
at www.ICGtesting.com
Printed in the USA
LVHW082109100821
695013LV00012B/483

9 781377 275932